RED SCARE

BLACKLISTS, McCARTHYISM, AND
THE MAKING OF MODERN AMERICA

CLAY RISEN

SCRIBNER
New York   Amsterdam/Antwerp   London
Toronto   Sydney/Melbourne   New Delhi

Scribner
An Imprint of Simon & Schuster, LLC
1230 Avenue of the Americas
New York, NY 10020

First Scribner hardcover edition March 2025

SCRIBNER and design are trademarks of Simon & Schuster, LLC

For information about special discounts for bulk purchases, please contact Simon & Schuster Special Sales at 1-866-506-1949 or business@simonandschuster.com.

The Simon & Schuster Speakers Bureau can bring authors to your live event. For more information or to book an event, contact the Simon & Schuster Speakers Bureau at 1-866-248-3049 or visit our website at www.simonspeakers.com.

Manufactured in the United States of America

1   3   5   7   9   10   8   6   4   2

Library of Congress Cataloging-in-Publication Data is available.

ISBN 978-1-9821-4180-6
ISBN 978-1-9821-4182-0 (ebook)

For Haywood and Margaret

Man has no mean; his mirrors distort;
His greenest arcadias have ghosts too;
His utopias tempt to eternal youth
Or self-slaughter.

W. H. AUDEN, from "The Age of Anxiety," 1947

CONTENTS

PREFACE

The kernel of this book took seed in a fecund bog of my own experiences and memories. I grew up in the 1980s, when the end of the Cold War loomed but most Americans believed that the rivalry between the United States and the Soviet Union was once again dangerously close to armed conflict. Ronald Reagan set the tone with his anti-Communist rhetoric, his dramatic increases in defense spending, and the Strategic Defense Initiative, nicknamed Star Wars, which appeared in the popular imagination to be an invitation to nuclear war (few appreciated his commitment to arms control or his embrace of Mikhail Gorbachev, both of which helped usher the Cold War to the exit).

Along with Reagan's hardline stance came a revival of anti-Soviet, anti-Communist culture. *First Blood*, a thoughtful, taut thriller about a troubled Vietnam veteran released in 1982, was followed by two blunderbuss sequels, in which John Rambo is sent to various corners of the world to fight sneering Communists. He was just one of many such heroes in an era overflowing with patriotic dross: *Red Dawn, Firefox, Rocky IV, Top Gun*. We had video games like *Rush'n Attack* and *Conflict* and *NATO Commander*, and books by Tom Clancy, Harold Coyle, and Len Deighton.

It was inevitable that, in such a time, insults like "commie" and "pinko" were commonplace, and, at least in the Southern suburban world of my childhood, a suspicion of all things left-wing appeared in everyday life. I suppose I was abnormal in my childhood attention to what my teachers and parents said, but I recall, among other episodes, my fourth-grade teacher telling my class that Norman Lear was a dangerous Communist sympathizer, coming nightly through the nation's television sets. I was also aware, when I was a bit older, that all of this had a much more pernicious precedent. My grandfather was a career FBI agent, having joined

the bureau during World War II, and he recounted stories of implementing loyalty tests for the federal government in the late 1940s. The trials of
figures like Alger Hiss and the Rosenbergs were still recent memories for
many Americans, and they filtered into punch lines and story lines on TV
and in movies.

Part of the opposition to Reagan came from people who had gone
through the Red Scare and McCarthyism, and in news articles and TV
shows they warned of a new assault on civil liberties. Along the way I
picked up bits of trivia—gathered string, as a reporter would say. My high
school's nickname on the football field was the Big Red, but during the
1950s, it switched to the Big Maroon. An explanation was never given, as
far as I could find, but perhaps none was necessary. The Cincinnati Reds
did something similar, becoming the Redlegs in 1953.

All of this flowed into that bog of curiosity, out of which grew the idea
for this book. I wanted, first of all, to explain to myself what the Red Scare
was all about. I am in general fascinated by the way in which culture influences politics, and vice versa, how unspoken but widely shared ideas and
hatreds and passions drive historical change. I was also skeptical of the
conventional explanations for the Red Scare, that it was merely an American witch hunt. Around the time I graduated high school, the federal government revealed the Venona program, which had captured secret Soviet
communications and which, once decoded, offered compelling proof that
figures like Hiss and the Rosenbergs and the leadership of the American
Communist Party had, in fact, worked for the Soviet Union and against
the United States. There was substance to concerns about Soviet infiltration. But it remained clear that the response, in the form of blacklists and
congressional investigations and book bans and loyalty tests, went so far
beyond what was necessary that something else was in the mix. Explaining that "something else" became a driving force for this book.

At the same time, I had a forward-looking interest as well. This is a
work of history, and as such it is not concerned with drawing parallels
between the past and the present. I leave it up to the reader to find those
as they will; it is my hope and expectation that different people will find
different interpretations of the story I tell here, based on their own values
and biases. But I nevertheless felt that there was a throughline to be found

running from the era of the Red Scare to our current political moment. Another abiding interest of mine is the way in which culture changes, but as it does it retains elements of its previous forms, so that when we speak about some arbitrary unit like "the Sixties" or "the New Deal era" we must also look at everything that precedes it, follows it, and surrounds it. The Truman era and the Eisenhower era were not distinct and separate from each other, constituted de novo on Inauguration Day. Even the Reagan era retained influences from those bygone times. Cultural change cannot be tracked linearly or clearly; rather, it is genealogical, with traces of genetic bits passing down through the ages even as it incorporates new material, in the same way my children look and act like themselves, but also like their Scottish and Eastern European ancestors.

It is my premise, in this book, that something similar can be said about the Red Scare. That it ended for most Americans, there is no question. But it didn't end for everyone. The fact that diehard McCarthyites and other anti-Communists found themselves shut out of mainstream politics by the late 1950s only added to their conviction that a great conspiracy was afoot. That sort of passion does not go away. In his novel *The Plague*, Albert Camus writes that the "plague bacillus never dies or disappears for good; that it can lie dormant for years and years in furniture and linen chests; that it bides its time in bedrooms, cellars, trunks, and bookshelves," ready to spring to life again. Something similar happened in the 1950s, which is to say also the 1960s and '70s and, I believe, on up through today. There is a lineage to the American hard right of today, and to understand it, we need to understand its roots in the Red Scare. It did not originate then, nor is Trumpism and the MAGA movement the same as McCarthyism and the John Birch Society. But there is a line linking them. This book is not an attempt to map out that entire historical thread. I merely want to suggest, and demonstrate, that it had a particular moment in the late 1940s and in a certain political and cultural context, and that knowing where we are today requires understanding where we were then.

A note on terminology: Whenever I mentioned that I was writing a book on the Red Scare, I got one of two responses, depending on how I framed it. If I said, "I am writing a book on the Red Scare," someone would inevitably say, "Oh, which one?" And if I said, "I am writing a book on the Second Red Scare," someone would say, "Oh, there were two?" There was indeed a "first" Red Scare, in the immediate aftermath of World War I, and I discuss it in the first few chapters of this book. But it is also true that unlike, say, World War I and World War II, the later appearance of a similar event did not lead people to revise their naming conventions. No one says "the first Red Scare" and "the second Red Scare." Doing so is awkward and, I feel, a bit pedantic. In the interest of avoiding both those charges, I do not refer to the phenomenon discussed in this book as the "second Red Scare," though strictly speaking that is what it was. I hope that readers will forgive the omission, but also appreciate it.

PROLOGUE

Helen Reid Bryan—fifty-one years old, a touch above five feet tall, with dark brown hair in a tight bun and a thinning face framed by black-rimmed glasses—sat in a leather-backed chair, staring at the congressmen with contempt. She was in a hearing chamber on Capitol Hill, alone, testifying before the seven members of the House Committee on Un-American Activities, better known, with its initials slightly rearranged, as HUAC. It was the morning of January 24, 1946. Through tall windows that opened onto the U.S. Capitol, she could see gusts of winter wind kicking up wisps of snow along Independence Avenue. An FBI report had described her as "believed Jewish," though in fact she descended from Protestant ministers and Virginia gentry. Another report accused her of being a secret agent for the Soviet Union.

Bryan was appearing that morning as the executive secretary of a small, New York–based charity called the Joint Anti-Fascist Refugee Committee. It raised funds for the surviving victims of the Spanish Civil War, thousands of whom were crammed into camps on the French side of the border with Spain. The group used the money to arrange for doctors and aid to the camps, as well as passage for a small number of refugees to Mexico and Cuba, two of the only countries that would take them. HUAC had accused the group of being a Communist scam, taking money from unsuspecting donors and using it to spread radical propaganda, and even to pay off Soviet operatives. In December 1945 it had ordered Bryan to hand over her group's records. That was unnecessary: The refugee committee had long been registered with a federal board, to which Bryan dutifully submitted its records every quarter. HUAC could already see whatever it wanted. It subpoenaed her anyway, just before Christmas.

A month later, Bryan took a sleeper train from New York, along with more than two hundred supporters who gathered with her that morning outside the building. She addressed them briefly, after which they funneled into various congressional offices, hoping to find sympathetic representatives to plead her case. Neither they, nor her lawyer, were allowed inside the hearing room. Bryan entered the chamber bearing only her caracal fur coat. She carried no documents.

No one who knew her would have been surprised at Helen Bryan's defiance. She had always been her own person. She had grown up with all the trappings of white Protestant privilege: Her mother was an heiress to a Virginia cotton fortune, her father a Princeton-trained Presbyterian minister. But in college, at Wellesley, she had struck out on her own, joining protests in favor of Black civil rights and against American involvement in World War I. After graduating, and against her family's insistent wishes that she get married and settle down, she lived the Bohemian life on Waverly Place in Greenwich Village, where she mixed it up with the neighborhood's progressive set. She worked for the YMCA, which sent her to Africa to participate in a global conference on racial equality; returning home, she organized a biracial civil rights group at Swarthmore College and later helped run the pacifist American League for Peace and Democracy. She corresponded with famed Black intellectuals like W. E. B. Du Bois, worked alongside the diplomat Ralph Bunche, and became close friends with Paul Robeson, the singer and progressive activist. Helen Bryan had stood up to prejudice and bullies all her life. She was not going to back down now.

After some formalities the committee's chief counsel asked Bryan if she understood the nature of the subpoena. She nodded.

"I now call upon you to produce these papers, documents and records, in accordance with the demand made by the committee," the counsel said.

Bryan had brought a statement, and she wanted to read it. A committee staff member had told her she could. "I am informed," she said, "by—"

"Mr. Chairman," interrupted Representative John Rankin of Mississippi. "I demand to know whether or not the witness is sworn to produce these records." Rankin was Capitol Hill's most outspoken white supremacist and the puppet master behind HUAC. A powerful Southern Democrat, he had saved the committee from dissolution at the end of World

War II, then used his political might to funnel resources into it. It was Rankin who had zeroed in on Bryan's group, hoping that exposing them could lead further into what he believed was a vast conspiracy tying together Communists, liberals, and the administration of Franklin D. Roosevelt in one tidy package. "The question," he drawled, "calls for 'yes' or 'no.'"

"She is fixing to answer," replied Chairman John Wood of Georgia, officially in charge of the committee but in practice often brushed aside by Rankin.

"We don't need any speech," Rankin said. "If she is going to refuse—"

"Well," Bryan said, interrupting, "I would like to ask the chairman—"

Now Rankin was fuming. "The question is, are you going to produce those records?"

"I would like to make my statement with regard to that."

"We don't need that," Rankin spat.

And so it went, back and forth, for nearly five minutes. Finally, Wood intervened. "The committee is not concerned about your reasons," he told Bryan. "The committee is concerned about whether or not you are going to produce them or not. Are you, or are you not?"

"No," Bryan said.

"That's all, Mr. Chairman," Rankin said, not waiting for Wood to reply.

"You may be excused," Wood said.

"And I can't read my statement?" Bryan knew the answer but asked anyway.

"You can leave it," Wood said, meaning that the statement would be added to the record, but without the committee having to listen to her read it.

"No, don't let her leave it," Rankin ordered Wood.

"I have no objection to her leaving it," Wood said.

An aide showed Bryan out, so the committee could confer in private. When she was allowed back in, Rankin had won. She would not be allowed to submit her statement for the record. The committee then moved to hold her in contempt of Congress, a charge that, if approved by the entire House and picked up by the Justice Department, almost certainly meant prison. It passed, seven to zero.

Bryan's appearance and the committee's vote drew only minor notice in the newspapers, just a few column-inches on the inside pages of *The Washington Post* and *The New York Times*. But on February 5, 1946, the editorial board of the *Post* let loose. "Miss Bryan has not been in contempt of Congress; she had only been in contempt of a committee which has itself been contemptuous of its congressional mandate and of the democratic process," the board wrote. "The only sure way to curb the Un-American Activities Committee is to abolish it."

Congress did not, in fact, abolish HUAC. Instead, it became the vanguard force driving a decade-long campaign of intolerance and political oppression, the likes of which the United States had never experienced: the Red Scare. Feeding off the fever dream fear of Communist infiltration into America's schools, movie studios, libraries, military bases, and college classrooms, HUAC was the first wave in a storm of investigations, loyalty programs, book bans, and public ostracisms that destroyed thousands of careers and lives.

In a ritual that began with Bryan and would soon become numbingly common, over the next decade the committee called elementary school teachers, movie stars, longshoremen, and diplomats to its chambers to perform the same degradation ceremony. If they refused—to hand over documents, to name names, to admit membership in the Communist Party—they went to jail. If they did as they were ordered, they were punished by the public, fired from their jobs, shunned by their neighbors, and turned away by friends.

For the vast majority of the accused, no solid evidence of party membership, let alone disloyalty to America, was ever on offer from the committee. It was enough to be suspected, sometimes by simple association. Suspicion became a kind of smoke taint, easily wafting from one person to the next, so that friends who did not immediately shun an alleged Communist would themselves come under doubt. All it took was a single pointing finger to destroy a life. Thousands suffered during the Red Scare. Helen Bryan was the first.

The Red Scare was about many things, but above all it arose from the intersection of two powerful impulses coursing through American society in the immediate aftermath of World War II. One was a long-simmering conflict in which social conservatives faced off against the progressives of the New Deal. The other was the sudden, terrifying onset of the Cold War, with its prospects for a nuclear-tipped global conflict and the ensuing, all-consuming demand for loyalty. Together, these impulses unleashed an unprecedented period of political hysteria. When they finally diverged in the mid-1950s, they left behind new animosities and alignments that continued to shape—and distort—American politics for decades to follow.

The Red Scare was, first of all, a cultural war, pitting two visions for America against each other, one progressive, one conservative. The progressive vision emerged from darkness. Millions of Americans had been shocked into action by the dislocations of the Great Depression: Between 1929 and 1933 some nine thousand banks had failed, manufacturing output had dropped by 30 percent, and a quarter of all workers had been left unemployed. A massive drought turned vast patches of the Midwest into a dusty wasteland that sent countless farm families on the move, relocating to the West Coast in search of work. Shantytowns sprouted in Los Angeles, New York, Washington, and dozens of other cities.

In response, a new spirit of political engagement swept across the country. Helen Bryan was one of millions to heed the call. Labor organizers who had once struggled to rally workers found their union rolls overflowing with a rank-and-file membership eager to take on employers. Antiwar activists protested against American rearmament, while others agitated for aid to the beleaguered Spanish Republicans in their civil war against the Nazi-backed Falangists. Starting on campuses like the City College of New York, Stanford, and Swarthmore, tens of thousands of young people rallied behind the Communist-led National Student League, which led them in strikes against censorship and in support of beleaguered Kentucky miners and impoverished California farmworkers. Progressive fervor swept the land. "No man was an island," wrote the journalist Murray Kempton, who was himself swept up in the fervor as a student at Johns Hopkins. "He could not escape history. If Madrid fell, he fell with it. In his own time, he would know the night of defeat or the morning of final victory. The instruments of his salvation were his to command."

Such passion amid calamity inspired thoughts of a different, better society, much like the one reported to be emerging in the Soviet Union, where the cruelties of capitalism had supposedly been replaced by the humanism of a command economy. The capitalist West appeared to be collapsing; the Communist East, in contrast, was urbanizing, industrializing, and thriving, or so it sounded from the reports of the many journalists who reported back from Russia in the 1930s. Even those who did not aspire to live in a Soviet state admired its good works: It was, or so people believed, the only country helping Spanish Republicans, the only country abolishing gender and racial discrimination, the only country beating a path beyond capitalism to a bountiful, socialist future.

Helen Bryan never joined the Communist Party; just a few hundred thousand Americans ever did over its history. But tens of millions admired it. "A large segment of the progressive intellectual class was determined to credit the idea that in one country, Soviet Russia, a decisive step had been taken toward the establishment of just such a society," wrote the literary critic Lionel Trilling. It was not a coincidence. The Soviet leader, Joseph Stalin, had long demanded that Communist parties around the world separate themselves from the rest of the left. But by 1935 he had reversed himself: In the name of fighting fascism, he commanded them to build coalitions across the left—to join mainstream unions, endorse progressive Democrats, and check, for the moment, their insistence on ideological purity. They called it the Popular Front. The American party deemphasized its focus on revolutionary Marxism, so much so that by the end of the 1930s its rhetoric was often indistinguishable from strident New Dealism. "Communism," declared the party's leader, Earl Browder, "is 20th Century Americanism." He went even further, claiming in 1935 that the Communists were "really the only party entitled by its program and work to designate itself as 'sons and daughters of the American Revolution.'"

In big cities, especially New York and in the industrial Midwest, there were entire neighborhoods where being Communist was as normal and as admirable as being an Elk was in Indianapolis or Topeka. "You were a Communist when you went to the store to buy a bottle of milk, when you went to a movie, attended a party or a meeting, voted in the shop, sewed up the last two dresses of the day for the woman at the next machine whose kid was sick, returned a dollar to a clerk who had shortchanged himself," Vivian Gornick wrote in her memoir-slash-oral history of the party, *The Romance of American Communism*. Millions more Americans joined so-called fronts—political and cultural organizations with mainstream appeal but led or influenced by Communists. There were fronts for everything. Writers and painters joined the League of American Writers. Homemakers could join the League of Women Shoppers. Some fronts kept secret about their party affiliations, while others were open, even if they disguised how much the party controlled their agendas. The American League for Peace and Democracy, which Helen Bryan helped lead in the late 1930s, was just one of many fronts organizing the masses behind foreign policies that carried universal appeal—fight fascism! Global disarmament!—but were in fact designed to suit Moscow's interests.

The left, including many fronts, rallied to the vision of President Franklin D. Roosevelt. His domestic agenda delivered hundreds of thousands of public jobs, billions of dollars in economic support, and, above all, a "New Deal" for the American people, asserting the power of the government to create guardrails around the economy. In 1932, 49 percent of American college students supported the Republican Herbert Hoover for president; only 31 percent backed Roosevelt. Those numbers flipped, and then some, over the coming years. Hordes of young people went to work for Roosevelt's New Deal agencies—as laborers rebuilding America's national parks, as engineers designing dams, as economists plotting national recovery from the Great Depression. Even in the darkest moments of the 1930s, there was a feeling that, thanks to Roosevelt and the broad New Deal coalition, the country was being reborn. "I was in the grips of a new kind of patriotism," remembered the screenwriter Walter Bernstein, "one that transcended borders and unified people."

Roosevelt's New Deal unleashed more than an economic transformation: It catalyzed dramatic social change. It opened doors to women and African Americans. Industrial unions, newly protected by the Labor Relations Board, catalyzed an entire culture around the American worker. Even gay men and lesbians were finding occasional refuge and opportunity to be themselves amid Washington's fast-growing cosmopolitan culture. The old order was breaking down. A new America—egalitarian, diverse, tolerant—was emerging, tentatively but clearly. "Across the land, the fog began to lift," wrote the historian Arthur Schlesinger Jr. Taken together, the 1930s left was a near-seamless spectrum, running from center-of-the-road liberals to hard-core Communists, agreeing to disagree on the details but united on the big things like racial equality, labor rights, fighting fascism, and defending the New Deal.

Yet even as many Americans came together around Roosevelt and the New Deal, a backlash was brewing. Some of the complaints were about policy. Employers resented Roosevelt's pro-labor stance, as well as his fighting words attacking "economic royalists." Farmers appreciated government support but hated being told what and when to plant. Southern politicians loved the outpouring of federal aid—rural electrification, roads, dams, parks—but detested the possibility that those funds might benefit their Black neighbors. The wealthy in particular hated Roosevelt, who was, after all, a patrician himself, yet railed against them, raising their taxes and regulating their businesses. And all of them loathed the hundreds of thousands of government bureaucrats brought in to operate an alphabet soup of new federal agencies. In the mid-1930s some 36,000 people joined the American Liberty League, an organization built on opposition to the New Deal. The 1937 Conservative Manifesto, a document that elucidated a common set of principles for opponents of Roosevelt and the New Deal in both parties, included as its final demand "reliance upon the American form of government and the American system of enterprise."

The opposition was not just about policy. It was about culture. Conservatives feared the anti-capitalist rhetoric that could be heard not just along picket lines but coming from phonographs, music halls, bookshops, even Broadway. Populists like the "radio priest" Father Charles Coughlin, who had initially welcomed Roosevelt's ascendance, turned against his pluralistic, big-government agenda, filling the airwaves with conspiracy theories steeped in nativism and anti-Semitism. Isolationists worried over Roosevelt's rhetoric about defending rights and freedom around the world. And many cultural conservatives saw the changes wrought by the progressive thrust of the 1930s—the New Deal, civil rights, women in the workplace—as evidence that something sinister, something foreign, was creeping into the American bloodstream. Elizabeth Dilling, a well-to-do Chicago housewife who had made multiple trips to Germany in the 1930s, developed a massive following, particularly among Midwestern Protestants, with her claims that Communism was part of a Jewish plot to destroy Europe, and that the same thing was coming to America in the form of the New Deal. In speeches, pamphlets, and self-published books, she warned that Roosevelt's "red revolutionaries" were plotting to "snap the handcuffs on the wrists of American Constitutional liberty" through progressive taxation, public works programs, and anti-monopoly regulations.

The progressives of the 1930s claimed to stand up for the Forgotten Man, but there were many Americans who felt that the New Deal had in fact forgotten them: the small-town middle class, the religious fundamentalists, the avowed white supremacists who continued to insist that America was a country founded by and for Northern Europeans. They saw an America that was increasingly urban and cosmopolitan, industrialized and regulated, diverse and tolerant, run by what they believed was a detached elite unsympathetic to the average white American. Their sense of being dispossessed fed what the historian Richard Hofstadter called the paranoid style—the easy slide into conspiracy-mongering and disinformation that has long held a small purchase on the country's collective psyche, and which at times moves to the center of the national consciousness.

The country was changing rapidly and into something that millions of Americans could not recognize. So they lashed out. A bright thread of anti-elitism ran through the conservative populism of the 1930s, '40s, and '50s, from Congress and HUAC to the ravings of Father Coughlin. The anger's target was Roosevelt and his administration, which seemed, to the particularly fervid mind, singularly responsible for the changes. The paranoid style, from seventeenth-century witch hunts to the anti-Catholic fervor of the nineteenth century to the anti-immigrant racism of the early twentieth, had always sought a coherent, compelling, and simple explanation for rapid and disorienting alterations to American life. Now it was coming back in fashion.

Starting almost as soon as Roosevelt took office in 1933, this impression that the New Deal was being run by an East Coast elite fed into attacks on the administration as not just un-American, but as a tool of Soviet sub-version. It became commonplace for right-wing congressmen and radio demagogues to smear the New Deal as a stalking horse for Soviet-style collectivism. Later generations would call it the "deep state," the notion that underneath the layers of elected officials and public figures who sup-posedly ran the government lay the real power, a vast cadre of anony-mous bureaucrats who answered to some foreign nation or ideology. One Republican congressman from Pennsylvania said the president's National Recovery Act "Russianizes the business of America." In 1934 Hamilton Fish, who represented Roosevelt's home district in New York's Hudson Valley, said, "this administration has copied the autocratic tactics of fas-cism, Hitlerism and communism at their worst." Of course, the New Deal's critics stood for a different kind of elitism, one built on inherited wealth and white male privilege. At issue, really, were two ideas about America: one built on an expansive vision of government as the guarantor of the rights and welfare of all its citizens, the other built on a retrograde nostal-gia for an America built on privilege and exclusion.

The clash found little purchase during the 1930s, when most people were too busy trying to get work, or keep whatever job they had, to pay attention to national events. Plus, Roosevelt and his agenda were popular. They might not be perfect, but they were making strides, and at least they were doing things—while one striking aspect to the Republican Party of the 1930s was that, faced with a country in crisis and turning to the left for answers, it adamantly refused to moderate its oppositional stance. Stri-dent resistance to Roosevelt and the New Deal remained a cornerstone of the conservative agenda during the 1930s, a fact that helps explain why, even when the country entered a second major economic downturn in the late 1930s, Roosevelt and the Democrats maintained a firm hand on the nation's political levers.

The cultural conflict might have remained a skirmish had the world not finally forced itself into the nation's consciousness on December 7, 1941. Up until then, even as fighting raged across Europe and East Asia, Ameri-can leaders in both parties had hoped to avoid getting involved, while hundreds of thousands had rallied behind the banner of "America First," holding that Europe's problems were "over there" and of no concern to an America still recovering from depression. Darker versions claimed that the urge to intervene against Hitler was part of a plot by wealthy Jewish bankers.

The devastating attack by Japanese naval forces on the U.S. military installations in and around Pearl Harbor that December morning brought a swift end to such isolationist sentiment. But it also thrust the country into a new way of thinking about its own domestic security. Concerns about spies and saboteurs always arise during wartime, and not without reason: In 1916, before the United States had even entered World War I, German agents set off an enormous explosion at a munitions depot on the New Jersey side of New York Harbor that left a 375-foot-wide crater in the ground and lodged shrapnel in the nearby Statue of Liberty. But back then there was only so much that the federal government could do; there was no national investigative force, no way to coordinate with local police, no workforce to manage the sort of massive database needed to keep track of possible threats.

Things were different during World War II. Along with the rest of the federal government, the Federal Bureau of Investigation had exploded in size during the 1930s. The bureau was joined by vast intelligence agencies within each of the service branches, and a public attuned to keeping a sharp eye out for suspicious activity as part of its wartime duty on the home front, alongside planting victory gardens and collecting tin cans to recycle into B-17 bombers. More than 125,000 Japanese immigrants and Americans of Japanese descent were forced to travel hundreds of miles to live in internment camps, an undertaking only possible because by 1941 the federal government, weaned on the New Deal, had the resources and vision to contemplate it.

The war ended in American victory in August 1945, to much joy and relief at home, but there was no reason to assume that peace would mean a sudden return to the way things were. There was a comfort in total security: Clear lines were drawn between "us" and "them." The black-and-white logic of World War II convinced the men and women of the federal security apparatus that they were the good shepherds, watching over their flock and mercilessly dispatching any wolves that came along. With Germany and Italy and Japan vanquished, they went looking for new threats to counter.

Well before the United States ended the Pacific war with two atomic explosions in August 1945, even before Adolf Hitler committed suicide in his Berlin bunker three months earlier, it was clear who would be the next main enemy. The United States and the Soviet Union had been allies during the war, but mutual wariness prevailed. Though Stalin had long since given up on the idea of fomenting a world Communist revolution, he was deeply paranoid about the outside world. He held true to the age-old desire of every Russian leader for a protective buffer of neighboring countries. And he believed that his people's sacrifice during the war meant that he deserved to get what he wanted: the Baltic states, Finland, and Poland, but also Romania, Bulgaria, maybe even Hungary, Czechoslovakia, Turkey, Greece, and the Balkans. A chunk of Iran, where Soviet forces had been stationed since 1941, was not out of the question. Behind his armies advancing into Eastern Europe came political units charged with installing puppet parties, personally loyal to Stalin himself. He believed that the Americans would vacate Europe after the war, leaving large chunks of the continent to him. But he also understood that the atomic bomb, temporarily the monopoly of the United States, meant he had to play hard and fast, scooping up territory before the West realized what was happening.

The Cold War took root in the spring of 1945 on the banks of the Elbe River in Germany, where the American and Soviet armies first met. There was little cheering by the long-separated allies, mostly just confounded, icy stares. The two sides even held separate victory celebrations, on separate days—at Reims, in France, where the official German surrender took place, on May 7, and at Berlin on May 8, where the Soviets rejoiced. Roosevelt had always been willing to give Stalin some benefit of the doubt when it came to planning for postwar Europe, an attitude not shared by his other ally in the anti-Nazi triumvirate, Prime Minister Winston Churchill of Britain, nor Roosevelt's successor, Harry S. Truman.

In March 1946 Churchill, recently pushed from office by the Labour Party, traveled around the United States on a speaking tour. He chose a small academic institution in central Missouri called Westminster College to announce the arrival of a new global conflict. "From Stettin in the Baltic to Trieste in the Adriatic an iron curtain has descended across the Continent. Behind that line lie all the capitals of the ancient states of Central and Eastern Europe," he declared. He called upon the United States, as the new, undisputed leader of the West, to oppose further Soviet encroachment. Truman agreed: Just months later, when Stalin delayed in removing his forces from northern Iran, the president took up the matter at the newly founded United Nations Security Council.

This would not be another exercise in traditional great-power politics, Churchill told his audience. It would be something new: an ideological conflict on a global scale. Propaganda, fifth columns, and spies would fight battles alongside or even instead of armies. A single bullet might never be fired as the Russians push further into the West, exploiting local Communist parties and sympathizers to crack apart fragile democracies. "The Communist parties, which were very small in all these Eastern States of Europe, have been raised to pre-eminence and power far beyond their numbers and are seeking everywhere to obtain totalitarian control," Churchill said. "Police governments are prevailing in nearly every case, and so far, except in Czechoslovakia, there is no true democracy."

Though Churchill was talking about Central and Eastern Europe, observers in the United States were quick to conclude that the threat extended wherever Communism was found—even at home. Winning this new Cold War, they believed, would necessitate an unmitigated, unblinking effort to root out domestic subversion and dissent. The black-and-white logic of World War II would be extended and expanded. Spies were, obviously, a threat, but so too were those who advocated, or sympathized with, or even merely tolerated political beliefs that might offer an opening to Communism at home. The wartime security apparatus built around the FBI would have to be augmented and replicated at every level of government. Civic institutions, corporations, and every private citizen would have to be drafted into the effort. Sleepless diligence had been the watchword of the last war; it would continue to be the watchword of the new one.

In 1947 Truman instituted a loyalty program, requiring every federal employee to be screened for a possible "membership in, affiliation with or sympathetic association" with one of the more than two dozen organizations deemed "subversive" by the attorney general. "Affiliation" could mean anything: a few dollars into a collection plate at a rally, a name absentmindedly scribbled on a petition, an innocent friendship with the wrong sort of person—all was now considered in the worst possible light. Better safe than sorry. The results of the inquiries were supposed to be confidential, but enough information leaked out to give HUAC and its allies what they had been clamoring after for so long: a reason to escalate the cultural conflict.

Suddenly, the romance of Communism in the 1930s looked naïve, and not only because Stalin was revealed as a vicious totalitarian. Far-right noisemakers and anti–New Deal Republicans who had spent the last decade shouting into the void about Communist subversion suddenly had a ready audience who, if not always believing their accusations, were now unwilling to stand in their way as they charged through liberal bastions— Hollywood, Washington, schools, civil rights groups, and unions—looking for evidence to support their allegations. Such hunts easily spilled over into attacks against everything Roosevelt had built. During his 1946 Senate campaign, a small-time Wisconsin judge named Joseph McCarthy ran an ad asking, "Tired of being pushed around? Do you like to have some government bureaucrat tell you how to manage your life? . . . Who's to blame for all this? Nobody but the New Deal." He won his race handily. By 1953 the *Chicago Tribune*, the largest-circulation newspaper in the Midwest and the country's leading voice of the right, was openly railing against the "Communist-controlled New Deal."

Among their weapons was HUAC. The committee had been created in the late 1930s to go after right-wing extremists, of all things, but it had been taken over and redirected by Representative Martin Dies Jr., a reactionary Texas Democrat and the committee's showboating chairman up until the war. He tried to use his platform to expose what he insisted was a Communist plot behind the New Deal. Instead he faced relentless ridicule from the newspapers, comedians, even other members of Congress. Dies left Congress in 1945, his reputation as a laughingstock assured.

Dies was merely a man ahead of his time. Had he waited just another term, he might have found a different, more receptive national audience. Americans, victorious in a world war, should have been joyful, confident, hopeful. Instead, the late 1940s found them fearful, tired, and insecure. Millions of soldiers and sailors had seen horrific things during the war and wanted nothing more than to return home, start a family, find a job, and forget the world. Instead, they found both housing and jobs scarce. Racial violence in the South exploded as returning Black servicemen demanded the same equality at home that they had fought for abroad, only to be met by white men with bats, guns, and nooses. Labor strikes dominated the headlines—in the year following the war's end nearly five million workers walked off their jobs, often for months.

Politicians and generals were already talking about a third world war, this time with atomic weapons. Roosevelt, who had managed to hold the country together during depression and war, was dead. Public support for the new president, Harry S. Truman, was plummeting—from a high of 87 percent in the Gallup poll just after he took office, in April 1945, he was at just 50 percent a mere ten months later, on his way to the low 30s by the midterm elections of 1946. The men of HUAC, many of them Southern segregationists and right-wing Republicans who had long dreamed of undoing Roosevelt's achievements, saw their chance to strike a blow by picking up Martin Dies's old playbook: cast wide, wild charges against the White House, Democrats, and the left, and hope something sticks.

HUAC was only the beginning. Copycat committees opened in state legislatures and city councils. More than five million federal employees were investigated for potential ties to "subversive" organizations. Two thousand seven hundred were fired. More than twelve thousand quietly resigned. There was little recourse for appeal; even those who did get a hearing were unable to see the evidence against them, let alone face their accusers. The Department of Justice kept adding to its list of subversive groups, eventually numbering in the hundreds, which soon found its way into the private sector. Companies big and small, most with no possible relationship to national security, cleared their rolls of anyone with even the faintest taint—less from concern about the employees themselves, and more from fear of the many anti-Communist extremists who might call to boycott them. The Red Scare was never only about government overreach into the political lives of its citizens; it was also about the fever that it touched off within everyday American life.

Enterprising activists built and sold their own bulging lists of suspected Communists and sympathizers, often drawn from hearsay and supposition. Self-described patriotic organizations proliferated, intent on ridding their communities of Communism; one, the Minute Women, had some four hundred chapters nationwide. Parent-teacher organizations, school boards, civic clubs, and Boy Scout troops all came under scrutiny. Hundreds of books were purged from public and school libraries. The American Legion boycotted films starring actors of suspect loyalty and sent pickets to march outside theaters brave enough to show them. In 1953 the Minute Women of Houston forced the resignation of the president of the University of Houston after he allowed a pro-integration speaker on campus, on the contention that civil rights was a cover story for instilling Communist ideas in unsuspecting crowds.

Even the courts, the supposed bulwark of civil liberties, fed the frenzy. When a group of Communist Party leaders appealed their conviction for plotting the violent overthrow of the U.S. government, the renowned Judge Learned Hand, usually a reliable liberal, swatted them down. "The American Communist Party," he wrote, "is a highly articulated, well contrived, far spread organization, numbering thousands of adherents, rigidly and ruthlessly disciplined, many of whom are infused with a passionate Utopian faith that is to redeem mankind. . . . The violent capture of all existing governments is one article of the creed of that faith, which abjures the possibility of success by lawful means." In the face of such an enemy, Hand wrote, the question "is how long a government, having discovered such a conspiracy, must wait. When does the conspiracy become a 'present danger'?"

To be labeled a Communist was a social and career death sentence. Old friends stopped returning calls. Farmers and businessowners accused of Communist ties found themselves unable to get bank loans. Threatening phone calls would come late at night, and letters promising horrific violence in the afternoon mail. Tires were slashed, windows were smashed; newspapers regularly reported vigilante mobs assaulting left-wing journalists, labor leaders, and activists. Dalton Trumbo, once the highest-paid screenwriter in Hollywood who had briefly joined the Communist Party, was blacklisted in Hollywood and afterward found dead animals and bags of feces floating in his swimming pool.

The Red Scare peaked in the early 1950s. Tens of thousands of American soldiers were dying in Korea, Communists controlled China, the Soviets had detonated an atomic bomb, and millions feared another global conflagration was at hand. Fathers dug bomb shelters in their backyards. Teachers drilled their students on how to take cover under their desks in the event of a surprise Soviet attack, not just in big cities but in thousands of small towns across Middle America. Hollywood churned out movies like *I Married a Communist, I Was a Communist for the FBI*, and *Big Jim McLain*, in which John Wayne played a HUAC investigator hunting reds in Hawaii. Syndicated columnists like George Sokolsky and Westbrook Pegler, read by millions every week, made militant anti-Communism their signature story.

In a 1954 address at Barnard College, Richard Hofstadter, the historian, outlined what he called "The Pseudo-Conservative Revolt" and offered a sketch of its typical foot soldier: "He believes himself to be living in a world in which he is spied upon, plotted against, betrayed, and very likely destined for total ruin. He feels that his liberties have been arbitrarily and outrageously invaded. He is opposed to almost everything that has happened in American politics in the past twenty years. He hates the very thought of Franklin D. Roosevelt." Perhaps only a few people actually fit that description perfectly, but millions of Americans sympathized to a surprisingly large degree. A visitor from another time, or another planet, would have concluded that America was on the verge of a devastating assault from within as well as without.

Of course, there really were Communists in America, and while almost all of them were loyal Americans, a small fraction did spy for the Soviet Union. Some of them became notorious during the Red Scare, among them names like Alger Hiss and Ethel and Julius Rosenberg. But it is a great irony of the Red Scare that by the time it began, the era of Soviet espionage was almost entirely in the past. As anti-Communist fervor picked up after the war, the Soviets were in fact pulling back on their use of Americans for espionage, while the Communist Party of the United States of America was collapsing in on itself under the weight of internecine squabbles. The federal government effectively outlawed it 1949, and dozens of its leaders went to jail. But that reality meant little during the Red Scare, when it was taken as a given that Communism was an all-encompassing, all-powerful force, one that required absolute vigilance to root out, matched by a willingness to sacrifice innocents along the way. Such logic opened the door to a culture of fear—of one's neighbors, one's coworkers, one's civic institutions.

Helen Bryan's conviction on contempt of Congress charges was fore-ordained. The House of Representatives had cited people for contempt before, but usually only as a threat; rarely had it gone through with the process and referred the case to the Department of Justice for an indictment and prosecution. This time was different. Just minutes after Bryan left Capitol Hill on January 24, Chairman Wood of HUAC released a statement: "It is the purpose of our committee to determine in this case, once and for all, whether an organization such as the Joint Anti-Fascist Refugee Committee has the authority to defy the Congress of the United States, and we propose to vigorously pursue this case to its most rapid conclusion." Put in those terms, it would be hard for most congressmen, even those who opposed HUAC, to vote against the committee's prerogatives.

A few nevertheless did. Representative Helen Gahagan Douglas of California laced into HUAC for violating Bryan's civil liberties, and defended her group for helping alleviate the suffering of Spanish refugees. "The relief of suffering all over the world cannot and must not depend on the political beliefs of the sufferers," Douglas said. And after all, she added, being a Communist was no crime, at least not yet.

It didn't matter. Even liberal members could feel the political ground shifting against them. Those who might have once found the courage to stand up to a colleague like Rankin or Wood now took easy shelter behind the defense of congressional procedures, unwilling to stand in the way of HUAC. "I shall vote for the resolution today, but with extreme regret," said Clyde Doyle, a freshman Democrat from Oakland, California. "This committee is an established committee of this House. As long as it appears that the committee had acted within the law as we gave it to do, I shall feel compelled to back its lawful acts."

Rankin and Wood smiled. Of the 430 members present, 292 voted for contempt; 82 declined to vote and only 56 voted against.

A few days later, back in New York, Bryan met with her niece, also named Helen, at Ye Waverly Inn and Garden, a teahouse on Bank Street in the West Village that served a decent dinner and attracted the neighborhood's assorted intellectuals and artists. Bryan's apartment was just down the street, not far from that of her friend, the novelist Willa Cather. She was, as always, defiant. She had expected the contempt charge, she told her niece. What surprised her was how crudely the committee had gone about its business. Not a single member stood when she entered the hearing room! No one offered to help her with her coat! Decorum mattered, even at a beheading. But the fight was not over, she declared. They held her in contempt? She held them in contempt!

"Baby," she told her niece, "I hope they go to jail before I do."

PART I

1

A Blue Envelope

Dean Acheson, President Truman's prim, patrician undersecretary of state, was sitting in his office on February 21, 1947, when he received a visitor whose short message would change the course of history. Acheson's quarters, for the time being, were at the Old Executive Office Building, a cramped wedding cake of a structure next to the White House, which the State Department was in the middle of vacating for new, expansive digs in the nearby Foggy Bottom neighborhood, a more fitting home for the diplomatic arm of an emergent superpower. Half his belongings were in boxes. Crates lined the hallways.

In a profile of Acheson for England's *Manchester Guardian*, the journalist Alistair Cooke called him a "six-foot-two Velasquez grandee who has submitted, with a twinkling eye, to his present reincarnation in fine tweeds as a Connecticut Yankee." He was the East Coast elite personified. Born in 1893 in Middletown, Connecticut, he had been raised according to the exacting standards of Yankee Protestant breeding. The son of a Canadian liquor heiress and the Episcopal bishop of Connecticut, young Dean had moved easily through Groton and Yale, Phi Beta Kappa and Scroll and Key. He was considered something of a wild hare as an undergraduate, but he found his bearing at Harvard Law, where he finished fifth in his class. Along the way he fell under the tutelage of Felix Frankfurter, the school's renowned constitutional law expert. Like many brilliant climbers before and since him, Acheson went on to summit all the usual peaks: Supreme Court clerkship; partner at Covington, Burling, a top-tier law firm; high-level jobs at Treasury and State.

But even among the rarefied elite, Acheson stood out. It started with the way he dressed. Savile Row suits. Homburg hats. Cream-white shirts with starched collars that stood as stiff and straight as he did. Then there was his reddish gray guardsman's mustache, around which entire magazine profiles were written. He waxed it every morning with Pinaud's, so that its ends extended, winglike, beyond the edges of his mouth, with which it moved in careful synchronization: When he smiled, his mustache smiled; when he shouted, which was often, it seemed to yell in chorus.

For decades Acheson had come in and out of government, each time landing a little higher up the chain of diplomatic command, until he found himself, at the end of the war, in the State Department's number two position. Acheson's boss, Secretary of State George C. Marshall, was a respected military man who had overseen the war effort as Army chief of staff. He had assumed the position of secretary of state in January 1947, exactly one month earlier, and already found himself out of sync with the clubby Ivy Leaguers who populated the department's upper echelons. It was Acheson, not his boss, who best reflected the ideals and self-image of the State Department, among both supporters and critics. It was Acheson, not Marshall, who was understood to be in real control. And it was Acheson, much more than Marshall, who would come to signify the successes—and failures—of Harry Truman's foreign policy. As such, he would become a ripe target as the Red Scare unfolded.

Acheson's visitor that Friday afternoon was the private secretary of Lord Inverchapel, the British ambassador. Following the circuitous protocol of high diplomacy, the secretary asked if the ambassador might be permitted to deliver a message to Marshall, without telling Acheson what it was. But Marshall had already left on a weekend trip to Princeton for the university's bicentennial celebration. Acheson replied that unless Lord Inverchapel felt like traveling to New Jersey, he would have to wait until Monday. The visitor cleared his throat. The message was, he said, a "blue piece of paper"—diplomat-speak for a message of utmost urgency and confidentiality. He needn't say more. Acheson knew immediately what it concerned: Greece was about to fall to the Soviet-backed Communists, and the British were not going to stop them.

In the long list of foreign policy crises that Americans expected to confront after World War II, the fall of Greece likely did not rate very high.
Millions of returning GIs and their families at home had hoped their sacrifices overseas would settle the world's appetite for conflict, at least for a
while, so that they could return to some semblance of normal life. From
a high of 12 million servicemembers at the end of the war, the United
States shrank its military to just 1.7 million, with entire units deployed
in Europe seeming to vanish overnight. But the world was not going to
wait. In China, the Communist forces of Mao Zedong were making steady
advances against the Nationalists, who were foundering despite massive
amounts of U.S. support. In Central and Eastern Europe, the Soviets were
not pulling back their forces, but reinforcing them. They had made clear
that they were not going to withdraw from territory they had taken from
the Germans, and would either absorb these lands into the Soviet Union,
including the Baltics and Ukraine, or treat them as puppet states, including Poland, Eastern Germany, and Romania.

The Allies had agreed to carve up Europe during the conference of
the "Big Three"—Winston Churchill, Franklin D. Roosevelt, and Joseph
Stalin—at a summit at Yalta, on the Crimean Peninsula, in February 1945.
But now it seemed Stalin was unsatisfied with his slice of the geopolitical
pie. In 1941 he had sent forces into northern Iran, ostensibly to protect
oil fields vital to Allied war aims; he failed to withdraw them after the
fighting ended, claiming they were supporting newly declared "people's"
republics—in reality Soviet puppet governments. In response, President
Truman took the issue to the newly created Security Council at the United
Nations in January 1946.

In hindsight, the postwar era is often remembered as a time of economic growth and national confidence, of sprouting suburbs and American industrial might. It eventually became that, in the 1950s. But the
immediate years after the war were full of anxiety and insecurity. Housing
was scarce. Jobs were scarce. Those who had seen combat returned with
emotional injuries that many on the home front could not understand.
Fears of renewed inflation, or even a return to the Depression, kept Americans on edge. Labor unrest in the Great Lakes region and along the West
Coast and racial unrest in the South made it seem like the country might

come apart. And then, added to all this, was the possibility of a new armed conflict, this time with a former ally.

During the war the government and Hollywood had done their best to sell Stalin as "Uncle Joe," and the Soviets as sincere friends of the American people. Films like *Song of Russia*, released by MGM in 1944, praised everyday life in the Soviet Union, while thrillers like *The North Star, Mission to Moscow*, and *Days of Glory* valorized Russian soldiers and the U.S.-Soviet alliance. Soviet ships in the Pacific regularly made friendly visits along the West Coast. Salka Viertel, an Austrian émigré screenwriter in Hollywood, recalls a visit by a warship manned by a mostly female crew, and with a female captain. A reception for the guests took place at Los Angeles's Shrine auditorium, with Charlie Chaplin as a headliner. Lyudmila Pavilichenko, the famed "girl sniper" credited with 309 kills during the sieges of Odessa and Sevastopol, toured the United States in 1942, speaking to overflow crowds on behalf of military assistance. In 1944 the War Shipping Administration, a federal agency that managed the civilian shipping sector during the war, launched the SS *U.S.S.R. Victory*, a supply carrier, out of a Los Angeles shipyard. On hand to christen it was the wife of the Soviet vice consul for Los Angeles. And aid efforts were everywhere: Even as they scrimped change and rationed food to help the war effort, Americans gave openly and eagerly to groups like Russian War Relief, with its heart-tugging appeals about valiant Russian soldiers and their starving children.

Suddenly, after the war, Americans were being told the opposite: that Stalin was the enemy, and that the Russians could not be trusted. The Soviet leader did not do much to help counter that image. After two months of hemming and hawing over the troops in Iran, Stalin withdrew them, but immediately put pressure elsewhere. He picked a fight with Turkey over its control of the Dardanelles and the Bosporus, the two narrow waterways linking the Black Sea, and in turn southern Russia, with the Mediterranean. In mid-1946 Truman sent a naval task force to support Turkey, and eventually offered $100 million in aid to stave off Moscow-backed political and guerrilla forces. But the real crisis came next, in Turkey's neighbor to the southwest: Greece.

The Italians and Germans had occupied Greece during the war, and while they exacted untold horrors on the Greek people, the country had been lodged far in America's peripheral vision. In the logic of European imperialism, Britain had held sway in the Eastern Mediterranean, at least outside the French foothold in Lebanon. Postwar Greece was supposed to be London's concern. The United States was focused on rebuilding Western Europe. But it was also becoming clear that the Soviet problem was too big for such a divide-and-conquer approach. That point was rammed home in February 1946 by a lengthy telegram sent to Washington by a mid-level Foreign Service officer in Moscow named George Kennan.

Soviet Marxism, he wrote, was just the latest window dressing on a deep-seated "neurotic" Russian leadership class that would continue to press outward to maintain security at home. It was "a political force committed fanatically to the belief that with US there can be no permanent modus vivendi," one that disrupts "the internal harmony of our society," seeks to destroy "our traditional way of life," and breaks "international authority of our state . . . if Soviet power is to be secure." In a subsequent article in the journal *Foreign Affairs*, which Kennan wrote under the pseudonym X, he called for "a long-term, patient but firm and vigilant containment of Russian expansive tendencies." This concept, containment, soon became the basis for America's early Cold War strategy. The details would be filled in later. For now, containment meant Truman and Clement Attlee, the British prime minister who replaced Churchill in 1945, had to draw a line: The Soviet orbit could expand no further. Greece would be the first test.

For almost two years, Greek Communist guerrillas had been receiving aid and training from the Soviet Union and its allies in Albania and Bulgaria, neighbors of Greece and newly Communist themselves. It seemed just a matter of time before the country joined them. Its economy was in tatters, its people were starving, and the government in Athens was barely functioning. "Greece was in the position of a semiconscious patient on the critical list whose relatives and physicians had been discussing whether his life could be saved," Acheson wrote in his memoirs.

Britain was having a hard time itself: Aside from the damaged cities and shattered families wrought by the war, it was in the middle of a devastatingly cold winter that had wiped out personal savings and government fuel reserves. Washington had heard rumors, going back to the fall of 1946, that as a result of its economic straits, Britain might have to pull back its commitments in Greece, including the four thousand soldiers who sometimes seemed the only thing keeping the Communists from marching on Athens. And yet the blue envelope from Lord Inverchapel, an informal copy of which Acheson finally received later that Friday, was much worse than anyone in Washington had expected. The British were pulling everything out—troops, money, aid, the whole thing—by March 31, 1947, precisely one month away. On top of that, the British ambassador estimated that Greece needed between $240 million and $280 million in aid immediately, money the British would not—could not—provide.

Truman ordered Acheson to devise a response by Monday. And so, rather than retreat to his farm in the Maryland countryside north of Washington, Acheson and Charles Bohlen, one of his closest advisers, set up camp amid the packing crates and went to work. There was no question in their minds that America had to take up Britain's slack. The pivotal issue was how, and how much, and then how to sell the commitment to a Congress and a country still trying to get back to normal. "Under the circumstances there could be only one decision," Acheson wrote. "At that we drank a martini or two toward the confusion of our enemies."

The choices that were made that weekend were among the most crucial of the twentieth century. They set the stage for the Cold War, and for the establishment of the United States as the self-described "defender of the free world." And they put the country back on a war footing—not a shooting war, but one that nevertheless required all the vigilance and commitment of an actual conflict. Fortunes would be spent. The armed forces, shrinking rapidly, would be rebuilt. And the possibility of a new world conflagration, this time with atomic weapons, would loom always in the background. It was not a fight that most Americans welcomed. The Second World War had just ended. Was a third about to begin?

In the history of the anti-Communist hysteria that was to come, it is impossible to overstate just how overpowering this fear of a new world war became, and how quickly, and how it in turn distorted the debate over Communism at home. America had rapidly militarized during the war, but until then it had not been a country used to being always on the ready to fight, or to having much to do with the rest of the world at all. Its citizens had fought and sacrificed greatly during World War II. Maybe they suffered less than Great Britain and Europe, the Russians or the Chinese, but that was cold comfort to the millions of Americans who had lost sons and husbands and fathers, who had scrimped and saved and gone hungry to ensure victory. Now, suddenly, they were being told that they might once again have to sacrifice. Unsurprisingly, they looked for someone to blame.

The following Monday, after Acheson spent the weekend locked in his office, he and Secretary of State Marshall made the short trip to the White House next door to present their recommendations on Greece, and again the next day to sell the plan to congressional leaders. "I knew we were met at Armageddon," Acheson wrote. Marshall opened the presentation, but his delivery failed to impress upon the legislators the meaning of the moment. Acheson took over. "No time was left for measured appraisal," he told them. The Soviets were on the move, and would not stop unless the United States stepped in. "Like apples in a barrel infected by a rotten one, the corruption of Greece would infect Iran and all to the east. It would also carry infection to Africa through Asia Minor and Egypt, and to Europe through Italy and France." This was the domino theory, a linchpin of American foreign policy long before its application to Southeast Asia led to the war in Vietnam.

Arthur Vandenberg, a Republican senator from Michigan once known as a hidebound isolationist, was impressed. He told Truman that if he could deliver the same message to Congress, he would make sure the votes were there to make the aid package happen. But he also cautioned the president: To seal the deal, he needed to "scare the hell out of the country."

Truman did just that. On March 12, he traveled to the Capitol to deliver a message to both chambers of Congress. Acheson watched from near the front row, sitting as straight in his seat as a mourner at a funeral. He listened as Truman bemoaned the plight of Greece and Turkey. The president then asked for $400 million (or about $6.8 billion in 2023) over the coming year, along with the deployment of advisers and other resources. But in a speech that Acheson had helped write, he also swung bigger, further. This request, Truman declared, was about more than Greece. "Should we fail to aid Greece and Turkey in this fateful hour, the effect will be far reaching to the West as well as to the East," he said. "If we falter in our leadership, we may endanger the peace of the world—and we shall surely endanger the welfare of our own nation." The applause, when he finished, filled the chamber. The only member to remain seated was Vito Marcantonio, a progressive representative from New York who, though not an open member of the Communist Party, was understood to speak for it in Congress. No one paid attention: Both chambers quickly approved the president's request.

Still, not everyone in Congress, or in the public, was sold. A new strain of isolationism was emerging, as old instincts about America as an island apart from the world merged with widespread exhaustion over the war. At the crux of the matter was Truman himself: It was one thing for a giant like Roosevelt to ask for sacrifice; it was entirely another to hear it from the political unknown who seemed to have none of the dash or brilliance of his predecessor. A self-described ordinary man from Independence, Missouri, Truman was a former farmer and haberdasher without a four-year college education—the last president to lack a degree, and the first since William McKinley. Elected a county judge in 1922, he functioned mostly as a cog in the St. Louis political machine, which found him useful enough to send to the U.S. Senate in 1934. A decade later Roosevelt picked him as his running mate, more out of frustration with the moon-eyed incumbent, Henry Wallace, than out of any real affection for the Missourian.

Truman's accidental ascendence to the White House, just months after Roosevelt's fourth inauguration, struck much of Washington as a sad but inevitable turn in the history of the New Deal, the end of its heroic era, the inevitable moment when great leaders hand over the reins to little men. The left-leaning journalist I. F. Stone said that Truman brought in "the new mediocrity" of leaders valued more for loyalty and bonhomie than competence: The folksy Tom Clark replaced the renowned Francis Biddle as attorney general; Truman's crony Fred Vinson replaced the patrician Henry Morgenthau Jr. at Treasury. Acheson and Marshall, both widely regarded by the East Coast Establishment, were outliers. Everywhere else, Stone saw "big bellied, good-natured guys who knew a lot of dirty jokes."

Even those who gave Truman the benefit of the doubt believed that he was too much of an operator to be entrusted with the legacy of the New Deal, which by the end of the war had become something of a secular religion among liberals and progressives, or to navigate the foreign policy dangers of the postwar era. Because he came from a border state, Truman was assumed to be weak on civil rights. Because he came from a political machine, he was assumed to be anti-labor. Because he came from the heartland, he was assumed to have no interest in or capacity for international affairs. "A curious uneasiness seems to pervade all levels of the Government," read an editorial in *Progressive* magazine. "There is a feeling at times that there is no hand at the wheel."

One person who saw the man differently was Acheson. The New England Brahmin noticed, and valued, little details about the new president. How he kept his desk (neat). How he kept appointments (not a minute early or late). His loyalty. His decisiveness. How he read, voraciously, omnivorously—despite his lack of a college degree, Truman was better-read on history and politics than many of his Ivy League advisers. Where some saw the pigheadedness of a country simpleton, Acheson saw clarity of thought and vision. "He could, and did, outwork us all, with no need for papers predigested into one-page pellets of pablum," Acheson eulogized in his memoirs. "He would take what time was available for study and then decide." When Truman returned to Washington's Union Station from a campaign trip in support of Democrats during the 1946 midterm elections—which saw the Republicans retake Congress for the first time in fourteen years—the only person waiting for him at the terminal was Dean Acheson.

Though Truman was keen to confront Communist aggression abroad, it took him time to decide that a similarly aggressive stance was required at home. Like his predecessor Roosevelt, he had long scoffed at the notion that Soviet spies were afoot in Washington and elsewhere, dismissing those who raised the alarm as paranoid fearmongers. He was both right and wrong: Though the threat of Soviet espionage was minor, it was not an invention of the administration's enemies. Even as the president developed his strategy to confront the Soviets in Europe, evidence of Soviet espionage was mounting domestically.

As early as the late 1930s, reputable reports had circulated through Washington of suspicious pro-Soviet "study groups," drawn from the hordes of young progressive lawyers and economists who flocked to the city to stock the expanding New Deal agencies. Those groups, it was alleged, were in turn breeding grounds for spies. Some, indeed, were. The agriculture economist Harold Ware recruited about seventy bright young men—including a lawyer named Alger Hiss, a rising star in the Agriculture Department—to join his group, where they discussed the writings of Marx and Lenin and debated the likelihood of a Communist revolution in the United States. Ware made sure they were all official, if secret, members of the Communist Party, and they all paid dues. For most members of Ware's group, that was all they did. But he would occasionally ask some of the more ardent, reliable men to do more, to keep their eyes and ears open for information that might be helpful to the Soviet cause; later, he asked them to copy and pass along documents. Ware died after a car accident in 1935, but he was only one of several espionage entrepreneurs in New Deal and wartime Washington. Victor Perlo, a Columbia-trained mathematician, ran his operation out of the War Production Board. Nathan Silvermaster was an economist who recruited acolytes from the Treasury Department, among other offices. All of them fed information and documents to couriers, oftentimes Americans themselves, who brought them to their Soviet handlers in New York.

News about such groups eventually found its way to the FBI. Perhaps the most incendiary report came in 1939, when the journalist Whittaker Chambers traveled to the D.C. home of Adolf Berle, an assistant secretary of state. Chambers had been a courier for the Soviet spy machine, based in New York, but had later turned apostate. Over after-dinner cocktails on Berle's veranda, he unloaded everything he knew about Washington's espionage networks. As Berle furiously scribbled notes, Chambers named some of the New Deal's best and brightest among its members, including Hiss, the economist Laurence Duggan, the labor lawyer Lee Pressman, and the White House economist Lauchlin Currie. Berle took

Chambers seriously, but not enough to pass his notes to the FBI until four years later.

Meanwhile, Chambers had repeated his story to the historian Arthur Schlesinger Jr., who interviewed him for an article he was writing about Communism. Schlesinger was never much for keeping a secret, and soon he was relating Chambers's revelations every chance he had. He told Phil Graham, the publisher of *The Washington Post*, who told Acheson. "Everyone knew the name of Chambers," Acheson recalled. "Arthur Schlesinger was mentioning it at every cocktail party in Washington." With so much chatter, it was inevitable that word got back to Hiss, Duggan, and the rest—indeed within a few months of Chambers's meeting with Berle, someone tipped off Duggan, and suggested that he look for a new job. In other cases, rather than confront the men fingered by Chambers, senior government officials simply boxed them out of confidential conversations, or moved them to less sensitive positions. Counterintelligence against a wartime ally was simply not a high priority.

The FBI first learned of the Chambers-Berle meeting in 1943, but without corroborating evidence or any real sense of urgency from the White House, the FBI's director, J. Edgar Hoover, decided to bide his time and gather string. He did the same with the case of Arthur Adams, a Soviet agent who worked undercover for a radar manufacturer. His real mission was recruiting spies among the country's vast military-technology industry, and in particular among the various laboratories researching atomic energy, with the goal of building a nuclear weapon. In 1943 the FBI observed him approaching atomic scientists at the University of Chicago. Agents broke into his house, where they found notes on atomic research and sophisticated camera equipment. They continued to trail Adams for two years, but in 1945 he fled to the Soviet Union.

At the end of 1944 Hoover had a summary compiled of what the bureau had learned about Soviet espionage networks in Washington; it ran to six hundred pages. The report resulted in no action, neither on the part of the FBI nor the White House. It would be another few years before Hoover could piece together a complete picture of the Soviet networks in Washington and elsewhere. Still, three events in 1945 provided him a compelling glimpse.

In January, an intelligence analyst was reading an obscure journal on Far East politics called *Amerasia* when he came across an article that was virtually identical to a confidential report he had written a year before. His tip led to an FBI raid on *Amerasia*'s office, which netted hundreds of classified documents. Six people were arrested. The FBI concluded that a State Department official had regularly passed the documents to the journal, and suspected that the journal was some sort of Communist front. But there was no evidence for the suspicion, let alone that *Amerasia* had connections to Soviet agents. And efforts to indict the staff ran into legal obstacles, including the fact that the FBI had illegally bugged the home of one of the suspects. The charges were dropped and the story largely forgotten. But Hoover remembered.

Then, in September 1945, Canadian authorities informed Hoover that Igor Gouzenko, a twenty-six-year-old clerk at the Soviet embassy in Ottawa, had defected, and brought with him a briefcase full of Soviet code books and other documents. The material, more than one hundred pages in all, provided extensive evidence of at least two Soviet spy rings operating in Canada. More important to Hoover was what Gouzenko told FBI agents: Similar networks existed all over Washington, he said.

Even more significant revelations came from a former member of the Communist Party named Elizabeth Bentley. A Vassar graduate who had turned to the left during a brief period studying in Florence, Italy, she had returned to New York and promptly fallen in with a circle of Communists closely connected with Jacob Golos, the leader of the Soviet espionage effort in the United States. Bentley and Golos became lovers, and she became a courier for him, ferrying documents from Washington to New York. Golos died of a heart attack in 1943, and she was soon running his networks, making her one of the linchpins in the Soviet espionage program in America. But she was also scared. Golos had told her about the capricious, remorseless ways that Moscow liquidated agents it deemed unsatisfactory. And so, after much deliberating, in mid-1945 she decided to leave, and seek protection from the federal government.

At first, the bureau thought it was a Soviet trap. But then Gouzenko defected, and her story started to sound more plausible. In November 1945, agents called her back, and for more than eight hours she told everything: about Golos, about the party, about her various Soviet contacts. She mentioned someone named "Hiss" in the State Department, though she thought his first name was Eugene. She told them about another contact, whom she knew only as Julius, who ran a group of spies specializing in advanced military technologies. She named eighty-three people in all.

Hoover immediately wrote up a top secret report for Truman. Citing "a highly confidential source," he listed thirteen top government figures active in "furnishing data and information to persons outside the Federal government, who are in turn transmitting this information to espionage agents of the Soviet government." Hoover unleashed an army of agents on the case. At one point in late 1945 he had two hundred men running down leads. They tapped phones, including that of Alger Hiss.

Hoover had been waiting for this moment for most of his adult life. He was a rare native of Washington who stuck around into adulthood, having been born on New Year's Day 1895 in a neighborhood on the eastern side of Capitol Hill. His father oversaw production of maps for the Coast and Geodetic Survey, an agency dedicated to charting the country's shorelines. Yet his father was also often sick and weak of body, a fact that seemed to shame young Hoover and drive him to compensate. He admired Theodore Roosevelt, who had overcome his own sickly, near-sighted body (and the psychological weight of a chronically ill father) through vigorous exercise, hard work, and absolute control over his mind and body. In the early twentieth century, such choices were not just personal, but political as well. The white, Anglo-Saxon male was said to be in peril from three sides: the rise of women's rights, the loosening of Victorian-era morality, and the influx of immigrants bringing dangerous, radical ideas.

In his embrace of Rooseveltian ideas about self-care, Hoover also embraced Roosevelt's ideas about American culture and race—namely, Americanism, the belief that every citizen should adhere to an identity forged by the country's white male founders, and in doing so vehemently reject ideas and politics that might undermine it. In the 1900s and 1910s, when Hoover was still a boy, that meant defeating socialism and anarchism; later, it would mean stamping out Communism and its progressive allies. Hoover graduated at the top of his high school class, then excelled as a law student at George Washington University, where he pledged Kappa Alpha, a fraternity steeped in the white supremacist nostalgia of the Old South.

Hoover joined the Department of Justice in 1917, right out of law school. He almost immediately assumed control of the Alien Enemy Bureau, charged with tracking and arresting "disloyal" noncitizens, a category that included German sympathizers and possible saboteurs but also encompassed pacifists and antiwar activists. Hoover proved a capable, ambitious bureaucrat, who understood early on that the government's power to control dissent would rest not so much on its capacity for violence as on the ubiquity of its surveillance capacity. While in college he had clerked at the Library of Congress, and he came away impressed at its vast filing system. He built something similar at the Department of Justice, only this time for people, not books. Drawing on a wide network of informers, he planted the seeds of what would grow into the FBI's system of files on millions of Americans, most of them innocent of any federal crime. As Hoover's biographer Beverly Gage has written, "World War I marked a turning point in the history of civil liberties, the moment that the federal government began to watch its citizens and residents on a mass scale." A new surveillance state was emerging. Hoover was its chief architect.

Though he claimed to be ever vigilant against all manner of radicalism, left or right, Hoover had an abiding obsession with Communism. On July 1, 1919, he took over the Radical Division, a branch of the Justice Department's Bureau of Investigation ("federal" had not yet been appended to its name). It was good timing, for him: A wave of mail bombings in the spring, as well as an incendiary device tossed at the Washington home of the attorney general, A. Mitchell Palmer, set off an unprecedented response from the federal government, with Hoover as both a cheerleader and a quarterback. He built out his surveillance network, employing dozens of clerks and field agents to track suspects, open mail, and interview associates. The campaign culminated that fall in raids on immigrant halls and meetinghouses, with hundreds arrested in just a few hours. It was the beginning of a new phase: the deportation of "disloyal" immigrants, mostly from Eastern and Southern Europe. On December 20, nearly 250 of them were shipped out from New York Harbor aboard the SS *Buford*.

Hoover insisted that the Communist revolutions that had swept through

Russia and, less successfully, Germany would soon be replicated on American shores. He read Marx and Lenin, then built a plan for mass deportations, casting a net much wider than before to catch any noncitizens who did not adhere to his notion of Americanism. He was reflecting the times: After decades of open doors to immigrants, the country was rapidly shutting them, erecting racist exclusion policies against anyone not of Northern European or English heritage. The arrests that followed in the new year, in Philadelphia, New York, Chicago, and elsewhere, are remembered as the Palmer Raids, but as Gage points out, Hoover was their mastermind.

This time, though, he and Palmer went too far. As 1920 progressed, their shrill warnings about imminent revolution failed to play out, while civil liberties activists, as well as the acting secretary of labor, Louis Post, pushed back against their use of warrantless searches and questionable interrogation methods. People were quietly released, and no one else was deported. The first Red Scare fizzled out. But it left important artifacts in its wake. Hoover may have been publicly chastened, but inside the Department of Justice, he was a new power center. In 1924 he became the head of the Bureau of Investigation, a job he would hold for nearly fifty years. As he constructed his fiefdom, he never stopped resenting the "liberals" who constrained him, in 1920 and later. He took pride in the professionalism of his bureau, and in public, at least, talked endlessly about the limits he willingly accepted—his job, he said, was simply to investigate, not to analyze or prosecute. Few people stopped to ask what investigate meant, or whether it had any limits.

Hoover had lost a bid, in 1924 under Attorney General Harlan Fiske Stone, to expand the bureau's capacity for domestic surveillance. He decided to bide his time. Presidents and attorneys general would come and go; he would remain. In 1936 President Roosevelt, worried about another war in Europe and the possibility of renewed subversive activity at home, finally gave Hoover the permission he was looking for. During the war the bureau more than tripled in size, not just in the number of agents, from 898 in 1940 to 4,886 in 1945, but in the number of clerks, thousands of them, all to manage the FBI's ever-growing collection of files and fingerprints—up to 24 million by 1941—and a network of well over 100,000 informants. Even before the war, Roosevelt had given Hoover wide latitude to surveil potential subversives, including some of the president's political enemies—along with $150,000, drawn from an anonymous discretionary fund, to bulk up the bureau's counterespionage efforts. During the war Hoover established a liaison program with the American Legion, the leading veterans organization and a bastion of Americanism—the first of his many efforts to turn sympathetic elements in private society into unofficial arms of his surveillance state. Every lead, no matter how evanescent, was pursued; if an apartment-dweller called the bureau with a tip that his next-door neighbor might be a Communist, agents were dispatched to interview everyone in the building and then file an extensive report—all of which got added to the database.

Like America itself, Hoover and the FBI greeted the end of the war much more powerful than when it began, but also unsure of what might come next. The entire federal government had grown, and along with it came new power centers, including those, like the Central Intelligence Agency, that might soon impinge on the bureau's turf. And there was no love lost between Hoover and the new president, Truman. Like the Republicans for whom Hoover had always felt a close affinity, he considered Truman a hayseed and accidental occupant of the Oval Office who would soon be swept aside. Truman, in private, called Hoover's FBI "the Gestapo." He thought Hoover's worries about Communist infiltration were just fearmongering. The United States, Truman wrote in a letter to one political ally, was "perfectly safe so far as Communism is concerned—we have far too many sane people." Hoover disagreed. To him, the new logic of the Cold War meant that a chance to fulfill his career-long goal of taking on the American left had finally arrived. Truman, committed to selling his foreign policy of aggressive containment against the Soviet Union abroad, had no choice but to apply the same rationale at home.

Truman's initial reticence to act didn't keep Hoover from carpet-bombing the president with memos. Though he rarely spoke without evidence, he pushed his material to the limit with alarmist rhetoric, painting a picture of a vast Soviet espionage network that was poised to blow America apart. On February 1, 1946, Hoover had sent a twenty-eight-page report to Truman outlining his evidence against Harry Dexter White, an economist

whom the president had nominated to be the first U.S. executive director of the International Monetary Fund (IMF) just a week earlier. Hoover
called White "a valuable adjunct to an underground Soviet espionage organization operating in Washington D.C.," though he also conceded that
proving White was a spy was "practically impossible."

Truman tried to ignore Hoover's warning about White. But after the
disastrous midterm elections of November 1946, the president decided he
could not keep Hoover and his congressional allies at bay. He conceded
that the evidence of Soviet espionage was compelling. Plus, a strong stance
on the threat of domestic Communism, his aides argued, could be a big
help in selling his expensive foreign policy agenda. On November 25,
1946, Truman created a commission to study the problem of loyalty within
federal ranks and devise a solution.

The resulting employee loyalty program, which the president announced in an executive order on March 21, 1947—right in the middle
of the Greek aid crisis—was intended to purge the government of disloyal
employees while claiming to respect their rights. It was a gargantuan undertaking. Starting October 1, 1947, the Civil Service Commission would
screen the background of every current and new federal employee, well
over a million people, to look for any evidence of "disloyalty," a term that
was left ominously undefined. The screening would draw on files from
across the government—FBI, military, HUAC—as well as police departments, former employers, even college transcripts. Truman also instructed his attorney general, Tom Clark, to devise a list of "subversive"
organizations; current or former membership in just one would constitute
a bright red flag.

If something suspicious came up in the initial screen, even the smallest
doubt, the FBI would conduct a full field investigation, interviewing
family, friends, and acquaintances, digging into every corner of a person's life. Any derogatory information went into a file. It was then up to
the department or agency involved to decide what to do with the employee. In theory, it might mean discipline or reassignment, though in
practice, given the tenor of the time, most people who reached that point
lost their job.

Truman, it seemed, hoped that the loyalty program was a paper tiger, that it would impress many but affect few. He wanted a sop to Hoover and the right wing, and to clear a political path for his foreign policy agenda. But he also seemed to understand that the program could unleash a monster. In his executive order establishing the board, he clarified that its purpose was as much to protect innocent employees from being smeared as it was to protect the government from disloyal ones.

The flaws were apparent to anyone who took the time to read the order itself. A quartet of Harvard Law School professors attacked the order in a long letter to *The New York Times* on April 13, 1947. They pointed out that there was no provision guaranteeing the accused the right to confront their accuser, see the evidence against them, or even know the specifics of the charge. The standard for judging someone disloyal was "impalpable"—merely that a panel needed only to "reasonably believe" that an employee might be disloyal to fire them. The members of the boards would be drawn from rank-and-file federal employees, who would likely feel pressure to be tough on suspected Communists, lest they later be accused themselves of being soft. The attorney general had sole discretion over which groups went on his list (starting with eleven, it grew rapidly, to about two hundred by 1955). And the consequences for being found "disloyal" were severe, a scarlet "D" to be carried in a person's personnel file for the rest of their life. These flaws and more, the professors wrote, might be overcome by exceptionally wise and experienced implementation. Realistically, given the heightened fears of the moment, they worried the program would "miss genuine culprits, victimize innocent persons, discourage entry into the public service and leave both the government and the American people with a hangover sense of futility and indignity."

And that is more or less what happened. Its first director, Seth Richardson, seemed to consider the program's safeguards as a dispensable inconvenience and insisted that "the government is entitled to discharge any employee for reasons which seem sufficient to the government and without extending to such employee any hearing whatsoever." A few months after the program went into effect, investigators took up the case of James Kutcher, a file clerk in the Veterans Administration. During World War II, Kutcher had been sent to fight in Italy, where a German mortar shell blew off both his legs during the Battle of San Pietro. Through years of physical therapy he learned to walk with artificial limbs, supported by canes. Kutcher received the Purple Heart and was by every measure a patriot. But before the war he had also been a member of the Socialist Workers Party, an anti-Stalinist organization that Attorney General Clark had nevertheless added to his subversives list. Kutcher was fired, and spent the next nine years fighting to get his job back.

Even more worrisome was a message to Truman from Walter White, the head of the NAACP, on November 26, 1948. White wrote that he was "greatly concerned about an increasing tendency on the part of government agencies to associate activity on interracial matters with disloyalty." Black federal employees were being subjected to harassing, invasive investigations because, outside of work, they were involved in civil rights organizations. Letters arrived from labor leaders, citing similar concerns. Less than a year after signing his executive order, Truman was already coming dangerously close to equating dissent with disloyalty, whether he intended to or not.

During its five and a half years in operation, Truman's loyalty program involved 4.76 million background checks, including two million current employees and 500,000 new hires each year, at a cost of $25 million a year (about $325 million in 2023). The screens resulted in 26,236 FBI field investigations. Most were eventually cleared, but 6,828 people resigned or withdrew their applications, and 560 were fired. Not a single spy was ever discovered by the program. Its defenders argued that it succeeded by deterring potential subversives. But it also likely deterred many bright, talented people from applying because they had joined a front in college, or signed a petition supporting a labor strike. The same went for current federal employees: The order put a premium on submission and raised the price for individual expression.

In his memoirs, Truman defended the rationale behind the program but admitted that it was deeply flawed in practice. For him, its biggest sin was that, even if a person was cleared of disloyalty, the charge would remain in their file, following them the rest of their career, guaranteeing that with each new job, they would be forced to go through the same humiliating probe into their personal lives. "This is not in the tradition of

American fair play and justice," he wrote. He called the program the best he could do "under the climate of opinion that then existed," but to friends he admitted, "Yes, it was terrible."

Within a few weeks in early 1947, President Truman had enacted two of the defining programs of the Cold War. One, to aid Greece and Turkey, declared that the United States would go toe-to-toe with the Soviet Union whenever and wherever it stepped outside the Iron Curtain. The other, the loyalty program, might not have seemed as momentous at the time. But by conceding that the federal government was already infiltrated with subversives and then establishing a program to remove them that was ripe for abuse, Truman set the stage for the anti-Communist hysteria that was to come.

2

Swimming-Pool Communists

The Republican midterm landslide of November 1946 brought new leadership to Congress, impatient after so many long years under the thumb of Roosevelt and the New Deal. But there was only so much they could accomplish with a Democratic president, even one as unpopular as Harry Truman. Among the few areas where they could score points against the White House were high-profile investigations—and under the incoming chairman of HUAC, J. Parnell Thomas, that's what they got.

A red-faced pug of a man, Thomas was born John Parnell Feeney Jr. in Jersey City, New Jersey, the descendant of working-class, Irish Catholic immigrants. He changed his name to the more Anglo-Saxon-sounding J. Parnell Thomas and converted to Episcopalianism, at the time both assets in his climb up New Jersey's political ladder. He made sure he checked all the right boxes along the way: an education at the University of Pennsylvania and a long stint on Wall Street, followed by success in local offices culminating in the mayoralty of Allendale, a leafy north Jersey suburb of New York, before entering the House of Representatives in 1936.

Once there Thomas proved to be reliably extremist in his anti–New Deal politics. He joined HUAC, and despite coming from the other party he supported its chairman, Martin Dies, in his often quixotic crusade to prove that Roosevelt's agenda was a Communist ruse. When Dies held public hearings into allegedly subversive activity within the Federal Theatre Project, Thomas melodramatically amplified the charge, declaring that "practically every play presented under the auspices of the Project is sheer propaganda for Communism or the New Deal." He was considered second only to Dies on the committee in his desire for the spotlight, and often outdid the chairman in his ability to look like a fool. (He wasn't alone in that regard: During the 1938 Federal Theatre Project hearings, another member, Joe Starnes of Alabama, interrupted the project's director as she spoke about staging Christopher Marlowe's sixteenth-century play *Dr. Faustus.* "You are quoting from this Marlowe," Starnes said. "Is he a Communist?") When control of HUAC passed to the Republicans in 1946, Thomas made sure he was at the front of the line for the chairmanship.

Thomas was among the first to realize that the incipient Cold War presented culture warriors like himself with a new chance to take on the left—not just the New Deal, but progressivism itself. In a flurry of letters to President Truman in early 1947, he lacerated the White House for not taking Communism seriously. "It is a menace that is so serious, that unless it is dealt with by the law enforcement agencies of the Federal Government, the time may well arrive when the very security of our country will be impaired by this fifth column within our midst," he wrote on March 31. "It is for this reason that I address you as the President of the United States, to directly inform you of the apprehension which exists among many members of Congress, over the failure of the Department of Justice to prosecute the many serious violations of the Federal Statues by these conspirators." It was not enough, Thomas went on, to tighten up security within the government. Communism—as a party, as an idea— had to be ripped out of American society root and branch. He and his allies had been saying this for a decade or more. Now, suddenly, with U.S.-Soviet tensions rising, people were willing to listen.

During five days of hearings at the end of March 1947, just weeks after the president issued his executive order establishing a loyalty program, Thomas called forth witness after witness to describe the mounting threat posed by the Communist Party—and, by implication, to show that the president's efforts came up short. The hearings were to consider a pair of bills: one would forbid Communist candidates from running for office and forbid the teaching of Communism or expressing "the impression of sympathy" with it in the classroom; the other would outlaw the party completely. Some of the witnesses supported the legislation, while others worried that it would just drive the party underground. But all of them scrambled over each other to warn HUAC of the growing danger posed by left-wing radicalism. John Thomas Taylor of the American Legion said that "Communism is making bigger strides in this country than it has ever made before." May Talmadge, president general of the Daughters of the American Revolution (DAR) and a supporter of both bills, declared that "it is time to clean house" of "traitors."

But such histrionics could not upstage the witness who followed them. J. Edgar Hoover made a point of rarely appearing before Congress, save for his annual appeals for more funding for the FBI. So when he entered the hearing room on the afternoon of March 26, 1947, the press was there in full to greet him. He had been invited to speak on the proposed legislation, but Hoover likely had a different, ulterior motive in mind when he agreed. The fall midterms had reshuffled the deck on Capitol Hill, giving him a new, much more sympathetic audience than the Democrats who came before. The elections also signaled something deeper, a first crack in the New Deal coalition that had dominated Washington for well over a decade. And while Hoover had always managed to work with the Democrats, neither Roosevelt nor Truman had given him the power and room to maneuver that he wanted. Truman wasn't going anywhere, not for another two years at least. For now, Hoover knew he should build a bridge with HUAC.

The FBI and HUAC, he began, were a lot alike. Both were committed to "the protection of the internal security of this nation." But they differed in methods: The FBI investigated, Hoover said, while Thomas and his colleagues used their high profile to expose "the forces that menace America." The committee, Hoover went on, performed "a distinct service when it publicly reveals the diabolic machinations of sinister figures engaged in un-American activities." Once finished with his fawning over Chairman Thomas, Hoover proceeded to explain all the ways that the Communist Party was digging itself into American society—propaganda, the film industry, taking over unions—with a single end in mind: the violent overthrow of democratic government. "The Communist, once he is fully trained and indoctrinated, realizes that he can create his order in the United States only by bloody revolution." Like the committee members, Hoover pronounced Communist with a slight drawl: "COHmonist."

Hoover conceded that the party was small in number, just over sixty thousand. But he said that for each member there were ten people underground and in front organizations ready to do the party's bidding, and who therefore also needed to be investigated and monitored. And, he added, the per capita number of Communists in America was greater than that of Russia in 1917, on the eve of the Russian Revolution. America might not be on the verge of its own revolution, but in Hoover's mind it would come soon enough unless HUAC, the FBI, and everyday Americans stood up to the Communists. "They know that today it is a fight to the finish," Hoover told HUAC, "and that soon their backs will be to the wall."

Thomas agreed. He had already chosen his first target, some 2,700 miles to the west.

Hollywood had long been a bugbear of conservative politicians, an imagined den of liberal iniquity, even though the film industry was more divided, and more conservative, than the rest of the country understood. Martin Dies held hearings into its possible Communist ties in 1940. J. Edgar Hoover had opened his own investigation into film industry subversives in 1942. John Rankin had undertaken a one-man investigation in 1945, coming back with a nice tan but not much else to show for his weeks in the Southern California sun. Rankin, who at the time was temporarily in charge of HUAC while Wood was on leave, was particularly interested in proving that the film industry was controlled by Jews— which, in his mind, was tantamount to being run by Moscow. The rest of the committee humored him. "We don't know what information he had," said one congressman, "but the motion was agreed to on the theory that we ought to find out whether our acting chairman is having nightmares or whether there really is something that ought to be investigated." None of those accusations and reconnaissance efforts had proven anything, and had in fact added to the impression that HUAC was the last refuge of congressional cranks. But the onset of the Cold War, and the Republican takeover of Congress, gave new life to the idea that in Hollywood lay the evidence to prove the vast left-wing conspiracy that many conservatives had long promised to find.

Hollywood was indeed a hotbed of the progressive left of the 1930s and '40s. Nowhere outside the reddest districts of New York City did the Communist Party find such welcome and fertile ground. Many of the personnel who populated the early film industry, from stagehands to actors, were drawn from the reliably progressive theater world around Manhattan. And, perhaps, the "dream factory," as Hollywood was called, found it especially easy to idealize the Communist Party as a North Star: After all, during the 1930s, the Communists were often engaged in the heroic stuff of which movies are made, marching on the front lines of union organizing, rallying against racist violence in the South, and raising volunteers to go fight in Spain. The Hollywood elite ate it up. In her memoir *The Kindness of Strangers*, the Austrian screenwriter Salka Viertel recalled throwing a party at her home for the French novelist André Malraux. An ardent Communist, Malraux had recently been to see the fighting in Spain, and he was now in Hollywood to gin up donations. "Standing in front of the fireplace, Malraux urgently and passionately asked for help for the heroic struggle of the Loyalists and told about the great support Franco was getting from Hitler and Mussolini," Viertel wrote. "At the end Malraux thanked the cheering crowd, raising his fist in the communist salute. I turned around to see the effect and to my amazement saw ladies in mink rising and clenching their bejeweled hands."

The party was particularly attractive to screenwriters, who tended to be college-educated and better informed about world events than others in the industry. "The communists had led the antifascist fight. They had led the fight against racism and colonialism. They have dared and sacrificed the most," wrote the screenwriter Walter Bernstein, who joined the party in 1944 after getting out of the army. Inspired by the party, the screenwriters also saw themselves as uniquely positioned to change the tenor of Hollywood's output, which up until the 1930s tended to lean into hackneyed stereotypes about women, the underprivileged, and people of color. It was not usually the case, as HUAC and others later charged, that Communist-friendly screenwriters incorporated Soviet propaganda into their scripts. What they did do, though, was create dignified Black characters, independent female characters, and working-class characters whose ambitions and struggles took primacy over those of bankers, celebrities, and abusive shift managers.

The Communists, in turn, understood the value of Hollywood to the party, and treated its film industry members with care. In most cases around the country, local party branches were buried under blankets of bureaucracy: At the top sat the Political Committee, a group of seven who ran its day-to-day operations, and a National Committee of thirty-five functionaries from around the country. Reporting to them were the state-level organizations, within which were county- and city-level units. And within those, at the very base, were branches, often grouped around a neighborhood or an industry. The hierarchy was strict, the rules ironclad—except for Hollywood. Every other branch, among the restive workers of Detroit and the combative longshoremen of San Francisco, had to interact with the party's leadership through city- and state-level inter-mediaries. Only Hollywood had direct access to the Political Committee in New York.

Most Communists had to put in time selling copies of *The Daily Worker* on street corners; the Hollywood members were largely exempt from such drudge work. "Swimming-pool Communists," they were called. The party never imagined that movie stars would someday lead a revolution, or even join one. Instead, it saw Hollywood as a source of funds, especially during the Great Depression, when the film industry was about the only one in America making any money. Hollywood also helped whitewash the image of the party, when the majority of Americans considered it something foreign and at least vaguely threatening. After all, the party had declared that Communism was twentieth-century Americanism—and what else was more American than the movies?

The party never gained much from its efforts to penetrate the ranks of Hollywood. Many in the film industry admired Communism, but very few joined. There was always something more exciting to do in Los Angeles than sit through an hours-long lecture on Marx's theory of excess labor. "I knew that the Communist Party was no menace," Walter Bernstein said. "The charge that we wanted to overthrow the government by force and violence was ludicrous. . . . Our meetings might have been less boring if they had." Most screenwriters were never going to accept the strict ideological limits that party leaders demanded in their work, and most actors were never going to submit their egos to party discipline for very long. It was fun if it seemed like a game, a reason to have parties, or a boost to one's moral self-esteem. As soon as it presented obligations or required ethical acrobatics to stick with the Stalinist line, people left.

And, truth be told, Hollywood was never as uniformly left-wing as its fans and critics believed. The film industry attracts all kinds, and if the progressives seemed like the majority it was only because they were often the loudest. Many of its biggest stars were conservatives, names remembered today, like Gary Cooper and John Wayne, and others long forgotten, like Adolphe Menjou. There were also those much further to the right: There was a Los Angeles branch of the Ku Klux Klan, which even got one of its members, John Clinton Porter, elected mayor in 1929. In 1935, reportedly with funding from the press baron William Randolph Hearst, the writer Arthur Guy Empey founded the Hollywood Hussars, a uniformed paramilitary cavalry unit that, he said, was "armed to the teeth and ready to gallop on horseback within an hour to cope with any emergency menacing the safety of the community, fights or strikes, floods or earthquakes, wars, Japanese 'invasions,' communistic 'revolutions,' or whatnot."

But the real forces of conservatism in Hollywood were the all-powerful studio heads, who ruled over the industry like bickering princes. They had come from poverty, or close to it, many of them as children of immigrants from Eastern Europe by way of East Coast slums. Jack Warner and his brothers grew up among the mobsters and brothel owners of Youngstown, Ohio, before finding their way into vaudeville and from there to theaters and, eventually, Hollywood. Warner was a close affiliate of Franklin Roosevelt and so supportive of his agenda that Warner Brothers became known as the "New Deal studio." But he detested Communists within the industry. Other heads had hardened in their dislike for Roosevelt and his attacks on "economic royalists." In 1934 Louis B. Mayer, the head of MGM, forced his employees to contribute to the defeat of the socialist writer Upton Sinclair in his run for California governor on a platform to end poverty in the state. Up until America's entry into World War II, the studios regularly gave Georg Gyssling, a German diplomat in Los Angeles, a de facto veto over anti-Nazi material in their films (Warner Brothers being a vocal exception).

The studio heads did not spend too much time thinking about the Hollywood Communists themselves; they understood that the party was insular, ineffective, and ultimately self-defeating. Their worry was the emergence of labor militancy on their backlots. They still held on to the idea that Hollywood was a world apart from the rest of the country, a craftsman's town, not an industry—an idea that, not coincidentally, concealed the fact that Hollywood was in fact an industry, with tens of thousands of manual laborers, who built and painted and electrified and cleaned. And just as labor activism swept the rest of the country, it swept through Hollywood as well. It came later than elsewhere, not until the 1940s, but when it did, it was violent and divisive, cleaving the town and setting the stage, so to speak, for the anti-Communist witch hunts to come.

The studio heads hardened their feelings about the left during a series of unionization fights during and right after World War II. Since the 1920s, the studios had either fought back efforts to create unions in Hollywood or forced their employees into unions they themselves created, organizations which rarely took a position against the companies' wishes. But the social and cultural changes of the 1930s brought a new, more aggressive, more progressive generation of union activists to the fore, people willing to take on the studios even if it meant bringing Hollywood to a halt.

In April 1933, the screenwriter John Howard Lawson, an outspoken Communist, gathered nine other writers at the Hollywood Knickerbocker Hotel to create the Screen Writers Guild. The effort got Lawson fired from his MGM contract, but he persevered. Within a year they had 173 members, who pushed aggressively against the long hours and low pay that most writers endured. The Conference of Studio Unions (CSU) was similarly strident; organized by an ex-boxer named Herbert Sorrell, it was an umbrella group that in the early 1940s set about trying to peel off trade-specific unions—carpenters, electricians, set designers—from the more studio-friendly International Alliance of Theatrical Stage Employees, another umbrella group. In early 1945 the alliance tried to block a group of set designers from bolting to Sorrell's union; after a weak attempt at mediation by both sides, Sorrell called a strike. On March 12, all ten thousand of his members walked off the job. Some 60 percent of Hollywood shut down.

Negotiations dragged on, and after six months, tensions boiled over. On October 5, 1945, some one thousand striking workers massed outside the entrance to Warner Brothers, whose liberal politics gave them hope for a sympathetic audience. They were mistaken: As Jack Warner watched from the roof of a nearby building, fighting broke out between Sorrell's strikers and several dozen strikebreakers. A car was overturned. Chains and bats came out. After four hours, dozens were arrested and more than forty people hospitalized. They called it Hollywood Bloody Friday.

Eventually the studios arranged a settlement. Both sides claimed victory, but the studios were the real winners. During the strike, they smeared Sorrell as a dangerous left-winger—studio lackeys plastered the town in anti-CSU leaflets, accusing him of being a power-hungry radical who, if not officially a Communist, was still "sympathetic and definitely interested in the communist idea." (Sorrell was not a Communist, but he joked that he would take the party's money anyway.) The strike forced all of Hollywood to take sides, not on the ultimately minor question of which union best represented the industry's workers, but increasingly on whether one was for or against Communism. The ensuing fight would tear Hollywood apart.

The Red Scare in Hollywood began in mid-July 1946, just three months after Winston Churchill announced the onset of the Cold War during his speech in Missouri. In Los Angeles, a man named Billy Wilkerson entered the confessional at the Blessed Sacrament Catholic Church on Sunset Boulevard. "Father, I'm launching a campaign, and it's gonna cause a lot of hurt," he told the attendant priest. "But they are, you know, antipathetic to my faith. They are my natural enemies. And I just need to know what to do."

Wilkerson was the publisher of *The Hollywood Reporter*, and he wasn't really looking for advice. He had long since made up his mind. He had spent his career in theaters and movies, first along the East Coast and then in Los Angeles, where he flamed out as an aspiring studio tycoon but found his niche in magazines. He became Los Angeles's leading conservative. His flagship *Hollywood Reporter* was a must-read in the industry, and he anchored it with his own column, "Trade Views"—views which, more often than not, centered on the alleged takeover of Hollywood by Communists. For years he had gone after progressive groups like the Screen Writers Guild, but his charges had been vague, his warnings unsupported by evidence. No one listened. But after the strike, and with the forced solidarity of World War II giving way to the frightening realities of the Cold War, he had decided to go all in. He was going to name names. All he wanted was permission.

"Get those bastards, Billy," the priest said.

Wilkerson's column appeared on July 29, 1946. He identified eleven men by name, mostly screenwriters, as Communists and sympathizers, and indicated that they were only a representative sample. "This is not an issue that concerns merely a few hundred writers," Wilkerson wrote. "It concerns millions of readers who must depend upon the free trade of ideas." He spoke directly to Hollywood, as an industry insider who demanded the attention of studio heads. And now, he demanded a ban on anyone who had ever associated with the Communists. In other words, a blacklist.

Others soon joined Wilkerson in battle. The actor Ronald Reagan, an increasingly influential member of the Screen Actors Guild, had started his career as, in his words, a "a near-hopeless hemophilic liberal." But he had grown wary of men like John Howard Lawson, the screenwriter and Communist, and groups like the Joint Anti-Fascist Refugee Committee, which often raised money in Hollywood. "Most of us called them liberals, and, being liberal ourselves, bedded down with them with no thought for the safety of our wallets," Reagan wrote in his 1965 memoir. As his suspicions grew, he went looking for fights. At a meeting of the Hollywood Independent Citizens Committee of the Arts, Sciences, and Professions (HICCASP)—a Communist front whose acronym, he joked, was "pronounced like the cough of a dying man"—Reagan watched as members savaged Jimmy Roosevelt, Franklin's son, for proposing a resolution denouncing Communism. When Reagan stepped in to defend him, he reported that Lawson got in his face, calling him a "fascist," a "red-baiter," and "capitalist scum." The experience seared the future president. Soon he was in touch with the FBI, funneling names of suspected party members to J. Edgar Hoover.

Reagan found an abundance of like-minded liberal apostates, along with many who had never been liberal to begin with. They even had their own organization, the Motion Picture Alliance for the Preservation of American Ideals, founded in 1944 to, in the words of one conservative screenwriter, "turn off the faucets which dripped red water into film scripts." Even before Wilkerson's declaration of war in *The Hollywood Reporter*, the alliance had built strong ties with HUAC in Washington and with California state representative Jack Tenney, a former lounge singer (best known for "Mexicali Rose") who ran his own mini-HUAC in Sacramento. They established a particularly strong relationship with the American Legion. The Legion's local base, Post No. 43, was located on North Highland Avenue, a few blocks up the hill from Hollywood Boulevard, and the alliance met once a month in its capacious auditorium to hear like-minded speakers— among them John Wayne—attack Communists in the film industry.

Another leading member of the alliance was the screenwriter and novelist Ayn Rand. Born in St. Petersburg, Russia, in 1905, she had come to the United States in 1926 and settled in Los Angeles. After getting a bit part in Cecil. B. De Mille's 1927 film *King of Kings*, she had some success as a screenwriter before turning to fiction and essay writing. Her 1943 novel *The Fountainhead*, about an architect battling the forces of cultural collectivism, sold millions of copies during her lifetime. It was optioned for a film, and she returned to Hollywood to write the screenplay. For the Motion Picture Alliance, Rand wrote a pamphlet, the *Screen Guide for Americans*, a list of do's and don'ts for screenwriters and producers that doubled as a checklist for moviegoers. "The influence of Communists in Hollywood is due, not to their own power, but to the unthinking carelessness of those who profess to oppose them," she wrote. The list included headings like "don't smear the free enterprise system" (adding, "don't pretend that Americanism and the free enterprise system are two different things"), "don't deify the common man," and "don't smear industrialists," under which she wrote, "It is the moral (no, not just political but moral) duty of every decent man in the motion picture industry to throw into the ashcan, where it belongs, every story that smears industrialists as such." Class-conscious story lines and characters were common in 1930s screenplays. Now Rand was redefining them as cardinal sins.

The pamphlet quickly became a blueprint for Hollywood conservatives, and a guide to what the film industry would become under the Red
Scare. "This is the raw iron from which a new curtain around Hollywood
will be fashioned," one old Hollywood hand told Lillian Ross of *The New
Yorker*. "This is the first step—not to fire people, not to get publicity, not
to clean Communism out of motion pictures but to rigidly control all
the contents of all pictures for Right Wing political purposes." The firing
would come soon enough.

By late 1946 the Motion Picture Alliance for the Preservation of American Ideals was in close contact with Representative Thomas, the incoming
chairman of HUAC, practically begging him to investigate Hollywood.
He didn't need much convincing, and in May 1947, he went to see Hollywood for himself. He and a few other HUAC members set up a makeshift
hearing room in a suite at the Biltmore Hotel, in downtown Los Angeles.
The whole trip was allegedly confidential, but the committee's chief counsel, Robert Stripling, knew how to manipulate the media. He kept newspapers abreast of their work, meeting with a few sympathetic reporters for
a drink and a debriefing at the end of each day.

Thomas's not-so-secret fishing trip risked repeating John Rankin's own
embarrassing foray to California in 1944. But this time, the ground had
shifted, with the anti-union studio heads and Hollywood conservatives
ready to engage with HUAC. Over several days, Thomas received a retinue of friendly witnesses, mostly drawn from the ranks of the Motion
Picture Alliance: The actors Robert Taylor, Adolphe Menjou, and Richard
Arlen all attested to a vast Communist plot to take over Hollywood. Each
provided lists of Communists and sympathizers, names that the committee added to its own list, drawn from a bulging file provided by the FBI.

Not all the studio executives welcomed HUAC's intrusion into their
West Coast fiefdom. Louis B. Mayer, in an outburst typical of many executives' response, shouted, "Nobody can tell me how to run my studio!" But
Jack Warner was a surprising exception. The supposedly liberal producer
had a keen sense for the winds of public attitude, and he could tell, by May
1947, that things were turning to the right, that the zeal of the New Deal
era was beginning to sour and that the progressive moment was giving

way to a backlash. Being liberal was becoming bad for business. So Warner named names. He also confirmed a rumor that in 1943, the White House had wheedled him into producing a pro-Soviet film based on the memoir *Mission to Moscow* by American ambassador Joseph Davies. The president had worried that Stalin, facing terrible losses on the Eastern Front, would once again sign a peace pact with Hitler, and he wanted to show American popular support for the war.

Warner's confession was exactly what Thomas was looking for. It seemed to confirm a conspiracy theory spread by the Hollywood right—that the alleged Communist conspiracy linking the film industry to Moscow ran straight through the Oval Office. By the late summer of 1947 he had heard everything he needed to, and began to make plans for a blockbuster set of hearings on Communist infiltration in Hollywood.

3

We'll All Go to Jail

The screenwriter Dalton Trumbo received his subpoena to appear before HUAC on September 21, 1947. The piece of paper traveled a long way to reach him. He and his family were spending a few weeks at his Lazy T Ranch, a few hours northwest of Los Angeles in the Tehachapi Mountains, dozens of miles from the nearest town. His children saw the process servers' car approaching from far down in the valley, kicking up dust along the way. Not knowing who they were, they opened the gates for the vehicle to enter.

Trumbo was short and stocky, with a stylishly pencil-thin mustache that would grow walrus-bushy with age. He had a drooping left eyelid that he learned to conceal by keeping his eyebrow constantly arched, giving his face a skeptical, knowing look. He wrote effortlessly and fluidly, churning out stories, novels, essays, letters, and screenplays at a prolific rate; not satisfied with his output on the page, he was an effusive conversationalist, an Olympic-level ear-chewer who loved nothing more than regaling, nattering, and, above all, arguing. He preferred writing in the bathtub, with a plank spanning edge to edge on which he placed his typewriter.

He was born in 1905 in a modest apartment above the public library in tiny Montrose, Colorado, on the western front of the Rocky Mountains, and grew up in the larger town of Grand Junction, a few hours to the northwest. He was, in the words of one admirer, "a resolute indoorsman who avoided bears as well as harsh climates," but he took with him to Hollywood a rural Westerner's sense of maverick independence, a willingness, even eagerness, to buck convention. Trumbo attributed his stubborn streak to his mother, a Christian Scientist who remained devout—and kept her children out of the doctor's office—in the face of constant pressure from her neighbors to conform. He'd always been a writer, first as a high school stringer for the Grand Junction newspaper, then as a reporter for the college paper at the University of Colorado. His family had moved to Southern California before he could graduate, and to support them he went too. He took a few classes at UCLA, but after his father died, he gave up on college to find a job.

While pecking away at his typewriter as a novice novelist, Trumbo spent eight long years working the night shift at a commercial bakery. He came to hate his bosses, who cut pay and demanded unpaid overtime; his first experience with progressive politics was helping to organize a union among his fellow bakers. During that time he wrote reams of short stories and six novels, and every single one of them was rejected. He dabbled in bootlegging and check kiting. Finally he landed a few freelance articles for *Vanity Fair*, *McCall's*, and *The Saturday Evening Post*, and his ball began to roll. He found a job reading script submissions at Warner Brothers, which soon turned into a job writing his own scripts for B-pictures, and eventually for A-pictures. He didn't want to be a screenwriter; like many writers in Hollywood, it started as a way to make money and keep busy until his real passion, writing novels, took off. He did manage to publish two well-received books, *Eclipse* and *Johnny Got His Gun*. The latter won a National Book Award, more than enough reason to quit screenwriting. But Hollywood was too lucrative. In 1941 his adapted screenplay for *Kitty Foyle* was nominated for an Academy Award. By then he was earning some $80,000 a year, or about $1.7 million in today's money, making him one of the highest-paid screenwriters in the business, at a time when the median screenwriter salary was just $6,240.

As Trumbo grew richer, his politics became more radical. He had always been a man of the left, though in an emotional rather than an ideological sense. He had a reflexive sympathy for the little guy and a deep-seated hatred of capitalists. He believed in unions and civil rights, and made his opinions clear in the pages of *The Screen Writer*, the in-house magazine of the Screen Writers Guild, which he edited. He used his column to go after studio heads and Hollywood conservatives. He joined the hordes of

Hollywood stars raising money for the Spanish Loyalists in the late 1930s, and in 1940 he wrote an impassioned pamphlet in favor of Harry Bridges, a radical, Australia-born union leader in Oakland the federal government was trying to deport. In 1943 he joined the Communist Party. "To me it was an essential part of being alive, and at a very significant period of this century," he told his biographer, Bruce Cook.

Trumbo made close friends and bitter enemies in equal measure. He could not resist picking a fight. He threw himself into the Hollywood labor wars of 1945, giving a fiery speech that October at the Olympic Auditorium in which he lashed into the company unions, conservative actors, and studio heads. In 1946 he campaigned hard for Will Rogers Jr., the son of the famed humorist, who had returned from World War II to run for a Senate seat as a liberal Democrat. Trumbo urged the candidate to go after HUAC, and in particular Representative John Rankin of Mississippi, telling Rogers's campaign manager "Rankin is one of the most unpopular men in America, and an attack upon his committee can also be tied in with . . . a whole host of liberal issues." But it was a bad year for Democrats, and Rogers lost handily to William Knowland, a conservative who had made Communist-hunting a signal part of his platform. During the campaign, Wilkerson, the publisher of *The Hollywood Reporter*, had singled out Trumbo as the leader of the Hollywood Communists, calling him the "Red Commissar" (even though, by 1946, Trumbo had more or less quit the party). No one, including Trumbo, was surprised when the subpoena to appear before HUAC arrived at the Lazy T Ranch the next fall.

Forty-two others received similar notifications. Process servers tracked down actors, writers, directors, and producers at home, on film lots, or in one of the many bars that lined the streets outside studios. Twenty-four of the witnesses were considered "friendly," including Jack Warner of Warner Brothers and Ronald Reagan of the Screen Actors Guild. The remaining nineteen, including Trumbo, all progressives, were called "unfriendly" by the press and HUAC.

To be served with a subpoena was at first considered something of an honor. HUAC's investigation seemed to validate long-running fears about incipient fascism among conservative forces in the nation's capital, and here, now, was their chance to speak truth to power. Some were even disappointed not to be called. Guy Endore, a screenwriter, said, "I feel I failed to make the grade as a human being if I am not known as subversive to everything the committee stands for." The rest of the Hollywood left rallied behind those who did get called. Attorneys were chosen for the nineteen, and defense funds were established. One left-leaning director, Lewis Milestone, offered his sprawling mansion as a meeting place. A dozen or so actors and writers gathered one evening at Lucey's, a restaurant across the street from the RKO and Paramount studios, to form the Committee for the First Amendment. Eventually some five hundred people joined, including luminaries like Humphrey Bogart, Katharine Hepburn, John Huston, and Lauren Bacall.

The meetings at Milestone's mansion were lively, often fractious. The nineteen subpoenaed witnesses—which soon became just eleven; the other eight were told by HUAC to wait—were mostly strangers to one another, or at least as much as possible within the cosseted world of Hollywood. There was something that seemed contrived about the hodgepodge group, like a World War II platoon or a perilously hung jury, the sort of ensemble cast one of them might write into their films. Each seemed typecast to fill a role. Three of them—John Howard Lawson, Alvah Bessie, and Albert Maltz— were committed Communists. Trumbo was the group's nonconformist, less ideological than the others but just as eager to confront the men of HUAC. Another writer, Ring Lardner Jr., was a cool, well-heeled intellectual, the dashing son of a famed short story writer, educated at Phillips Academy and Princeton. The director Edward Dmytryk and the producer Adrian Scott were the group's doubting Thomases, already out of the party but unwilling, on principle, to break ranks. The others—Herbert Biberman, Lester Cole, and Samuel Ornitz—were in supporting roles, better known for their activism than their screenwriting chops, though Biberman was also known as the husband of the A-list actress Gale Sondergaard. "Only two of them have talent," sniffed the director Billy Wilder about the men. "The rest are just unfriendly." (The eleventh witness, the German émigré playwright Bertolt Brecht, never attended the meetings, despite living in nearby Santa Monica.)

The meetings often devolved into clashes over ideological purity. The fighting began the first night, right after Milestone's wife served the men tea and coffee and cookies. The writer and director Robert Rossen, a party member and one of the original nineteen, found himself under attack from Lawson for his work on *All the King's Men*, then in production. Lawson derided it as decadent and counterrevolutionary, criticism that felt especially out of place in a group trying to defend their right to freethinking. Rossen finally stormed out, leaving a trail of choice insults. He yelled "I quit"—meaning the party—as he slammed the door.

The attorneys for the group, also at the meetings, held mock hearings in which one of the lawyers, playing a spittle-flecked Chairman Thomas, hurled invectives masked as questions. The men had spent enough time around actors to know how to perform under pressure; the problem was what to say. Some of them wanted to proclaim their membership in the party—which, after all, was still a legal enterprise. But the majority decided to parry, refusing to answer while insisting on their right to make a statement denouncing the entire proceeding as unconstitutional. They would turn the hearings to their advantage by creating a First Amendment test case. The Supreme Court at the time leaned to the left, and they expected that civil liberties stalwarts like Hugo Black, Frank Murphy, and Wiley Rutledge would rule in their favor.

A few days before the witnesses were set to appear in Washington, Alvah Bessie, one of the screenwriters, and his wife, Helen, spent a few days visiting Trumbo at his ranch. When they arrived he greeted them at the door, took their bags, and stirred them a few stiff drinks. Helen was convinced they were in deep trouble. "Don't worry about the subpoenas," Trumbo told her. "We'll lick them to a frazzle."

They drank their drinks, then took a walk as a fiery sun set over the Tehachapi Mountains. That night over dinner, Helen asked Trumbo, "Do you really think we'll lick them to a frazzle?"

Trumbo put down his fork and looked her in the eye. "Of course not," he said. "We'll all go to jail."

The HUAC hearings on Hollywood were among the biggest media events of 1947, a year already packed with news. In April Jackie Robinson took to Ebbets Field in his first game for the Brooklyn Dodgers, breaking baseball's color line. In October, Chuck Yeager broke the sound barrier. Those were big, thrilling events, announcing new heroes into the American pantheon. The HUAC hearings were different, the literal merging of news and entertainment, starring politicians and celebrities eager to get their time in the limelight.

The hearings were scheduled for the House Caucus Room, the only venue on Capitol Hill large enough to accommodate them. A full third of the space was given over to film equipment, including rows of control panels and dozens of spotlights. Scores of reporters would sit beside them. After making space for the committee, its staff, and the witnesses, the room could hold a mere 391 onlookers—much more than a typical hearing, but only a fraction of the crowds expected to be waiting each morning to get in, eager to get a glimpse of Hollywood.

Two days before the hearings began, Thomas staged a photo op with just the staff and committee members present, along with a half dozen photographers and reporters. He strode into the room, lights flashing, arms swinging like diligent pendulums. But when he sat in the chairman's seat, the reporters below could barely see him. A quick-thinking aide brought out a few copies of the D.C. phone book and a red silk pillow to give him a little extra height. Thomas left the room, then marched in again for another round of photos, as if nothing had happened.

In Los Angeles, twenty-one members of the Committee for the First Amendment, including Lucille Ball, Humphrey Bogart, and Gene Kelly, appeared before seven thousand people at the Shrine Auditorium. Kelly, his leg in a cast, was the first to speak: "I'm here because of the Constitution of the United States and the Bill of Rights—both of which I believe in and which I believe are being subverted by something called the House Committee on Un-American Activities." More shrieks. Then they boarded a chartered Constellation passenger plane for Washington. Along the way they stopped occasionally to refuel and give short, impassioned speeches against HUAC. "Who do you think they're after?" said Fredric March, who a few months earlier had won an Oscar for his role in *The Best Years of Our Lives*. "They're after you."

Trumbo and the ten other "unfriendly" witnesses flew on their own chartered plane, arriving a few days before the hearings. Most of them holed up at the Washington Sheraton, later known as the Marriott Wardman Park, just off Connecticut Avenue. They found the city hostile, suspicious. Maybe they were being paranoid, but several noted the looks they got from passersby and the strange clicking sound on the telephones in their hotel rooms. They conversed in their bathrooms, with the taps running, or else while snapping their fingers to interfere with the FBI bugs they believed were everywhere. They preferred taking meals at Harvey's, a seafood restaurant on Connecticut Avenue near the Mayflower Hotel. Coincidentally it was a favorite of J. Edgar Hoover's, and more than once the men found themselves dining a few tables away from the FBI director.

They filled their days with preparation, press interviews, and endless meetings. They tried to push their case to sympathetic congressmen, to little avail. One of them, the director Edward Dmytryk, recalled a conversation with Representative Emanuel Celler of New York, who was known as a critic of HUAC but wanted nothing to do with them now. HUAC was growing too powerful. "I think you're absolutely right," Celler told him. "But it's a political matter. I wouldn't touch it with a ten-foot pole."

The night before the hearing, the group's lawyers met with Eric Johnston, the powerful head of the Motion Picture Association of America, Hollywood's top trade group, in a suite at the Washington Shoreham Hotel, across the street from the Sheraton. They had heard rumors, one of the lawyers told Johnston, about the Hollywood executives: The executives might go along with a plan by Chairman Thomas to create a list of people who, by virtue of their affiliations with the Communist Party or its various fronts, would be barred from working in the film industry—a blacklist. They had been told that Johnston himself had endorsed one. "We are maintaining that the Thomas committee aims at censorship of the screen by intimidation," the lawyer said. "This accusation is not merely rumor. There is ample reason for this in the public statements of its chairman."

Johnston insisted that was not the case—and if it was, he and the producers would never stand for it. They were, he told them, all on the same side. "We share your feelings, gentlemen, and we support your position," he said. "As long as I live I will never be a party to anything as un-American as a blacklist."

The room relaxed. The lawyers looked at each other and smiled. "Tell the boys not to worry," Johnston assured them. "There will never be a blacklist. We're not going to go totalitarian to please the committee."

Chairman Thomas gaveled the first day's hearing to order shortly after 10 a.m. on October 21, 1947. Six newsreel cameras turned their attention to the chairman, who squinted under the glare of a dozen spotlights. The crystal chandeliers that hung above them refracted hundreds of camera flashes, triggered by twenty-five photographers. The Caucus Room measured 3,200 square feet, and it seemed like every one of those square feet had a person in it. Aside from the 125 reporters scrawling notes, a dozen staffers flitted behind the four congressmen, all Republicans, seated behind the curved dais. Soon the acrid odor of cigarette smoke permeated the room, mixing with perfume and sweat to create a malodorous cloud that hung over the proceeding. A detachment of Capitol Police stood ready at the doors to usher celebrity witnesses past the expectant throng—or, as Chairman Thomas had warned them, to manhandle out the door those who might prove disruptive.

If the whole thing sounds like a staged production, it was a similarity not lost on observers. The *Los Angeles Times* noted a "studio-like atmosphere." The Caucus Room was frequently described as being S.R.O.—standing room only, a bit of lingo borrowed from the theater world. The *New York Times* wrote of the "ineffable touch of showmanship which the naïve Easterner associates with a Hollywood premiere, lacking only in orchids, evening dresses and spotlights criss-crossing the evening sky." To get front-page coverage early, Thomas front-loaded the witness list with big names, all considered friendly to the committee.

The witnesses played into Thomas's hands, one-upping each other with hyperbolic claims about their utter contempt for Communism and its adherents. Jack Warner, the first, offered to "subscribe generously to a pest-removal fund. We are willing to establish such a fund to ship to Russia the people who don't like our American system of government and prefer the communistic system to ours." Like others to come, he endorsed a bill, then making its way through Congress, to outlaw the Communist Party. Contrary to his earlier insistence that he wouldn't let anyone tell him how to run his studio, Louis B. Mayer asked HUAC to "perform a public service" through legislation barring Communists not just from government jobs, but the private sector. Sam Wood, a director who had once worked with the Marx Brothers and later served as the first president of the Motion Picture Alliance for the Preservation of American Ideals, identified Hollywood writers as the wellspring of industry radicalism. The actor Adolphe Menjou explained how writers like Trumbo sneaked propaganda past even vigilant anti-Communist producers. "Under certain circumstances a communistic director, a communistic writer, or a communistic actor, even if he were under orders from the head of the studio not to inject communism or un-American or subversion into pictures, could easily subvert that order, under the proper circumstances, by a look, by an inflection, by a change in the voice," he said.

Several witnesses that first day described how conservatives in Hollywood were persecuted—"cancelled," to use an anachronistic but accurate term. "If you mention you are opposed to the Communist Party, then you are antilabor, anti-Semitic, or anti-Negro, and you will end up being called a Fascist," Sam Wood said. The actor Gary Cooper, who said he didn't like Communism because it wasn't "on the level," told the committee that a pall had fallen over Hollywood: "It has become unpopular and a little risky to say too much. You notice the difference. People who were quite easy to express their thoughts before begin to clam up more than they used to."

One discordant note came on the first day, during the testimony of Jack Moffitt, film critic for *Esquire* and a "friendly" witness. As he was speaking, Charles Katz, a lawyer for the eleven "unfriendly" witnesses, came barreling down the aisle. "I represent a number of writers," he shouted. Panting, he demanded the right to cross-examine Moffitt. Thomas banged his gavel. "Put this man out of this room," he told the expectant cops. Four officers dragged him to an elevator, then out the door, depositing him roughly on Independence Avenue. "I thought this was supposed to be a fair trial!" Katz told the handful of reporters who had followed the entourage.

■ ■ ■ ■

The committee spent days digging into the stories behind wartime pro-Soviet movies, hoping to strike a vein of evidence proving a link between the White House and the Hollywood Communist Party. They found little. Warner even denied his testimony from May, in Los Angeles, that Roosevelt had talked him into making *Mission to Moscow*. That did not stop Thomas from letting Ayn Rand deliver an hour-long disquisition on the deployment of propaganda in one such film, *Song of Russia*, and its depiction of happy, stalwart villagers and townspeople.

"You paint a very dismal picture of Russia," John McDowell, a Pennsylvania Republican, said to her at one point. "Doesn't anybody smile in Russia anymore?"

"Well, if you ask me literally, pretty much no."

"They don't smile?"

"Not quite that way; no. If they do, it is privately and accidentally. Certainly, it is not social. They don't smile in approval of their system."

It was the actor Robert Taylor who sounded the shrillest alarm. Mostly forgotten by later generations, at the time he was Hollywood's reigning heartthrob and one of its reliable leading men. The audience on the morning of October 22, when he testified, was largely made up of female admirers, the lucky few hundred let into the room out of the thousand or more who had lined up before dawn outside. Screams and cheers greeted him as he walked in, surrounded by Capitol Police.

Taylor's statement was a barbed, twenty-five-minute jeremiad, a greatest-hits of Hollywood doom-mongering. The Communist Party was on the rise, he said; in fact it was poised to take over. Only emergency measures would stop it. "If outlawing the Communist Party would solve the Communist threat in this country then I am thoroughly in approval and accord with it being outlawed," he said, to such raucous applause that Thomas had to bang his gavel for nearly a minute. When Taylor finished, the police formed a flying wedge around him and pushed through the crowd. A woman in a red hat shouted "hurray for Robert Taylor." He paused just once, to autograph a comic book held out to him by a three-year-old admirer.

Among the few to sound a moderate tone was Ronald Reagan, who had taken over as president of the Screen Actors Guild a few months before the hearing. He wore glasses, intentionally or not lending him a serious air that helped people forget his appearances in regrettable films like *Code of the Secret Service.* He hated Communists too, he said. But he didn't fear them taking over the country or see a need for a blacklist or a government ban. Rather, he insisted, "I think within the bounds of our democratic rights, and never once stepping over the rights given us by democracy, we have done a pretty good job in our business of keeping those people's activities curtailed."

Dalton Trumbo finally reached the witness stand on the morning of October 28. He had been sitting, every day, in the audience next to his wife, Cleo. That morning he wore a black double-breasted suit with wide lapels, his mustache trimmed and waxed, his hair slicked back, a pair of thick horn-rimmed glasses on his face. Cleo wore a white broad-brimmed hat and smoked incessantly. He wasn't the first of the so-called unfriendlies; John Howard Lawson had appeared the day before and so enraged Chairman Thomas that he had called the Capitol Police officers to remove him. Just before they reached Lawson, the witness stood, buttoned his jacket, brushed back his hair, and returned to the gallery.

Trumbo took his seat at the witness table. In front of him sat three chunky microphones, one for each major broadcaster. The photographers were given a few minutes to capture the scene, then Trumbo was sworn in. Just as Lawson had done, he demanded he be allowed to read a statement. Thomas insisted on reading a copy; he glanced at it cursorily, enough to recognize it as a guns-blazing rant against the committee, and put it down. It was, he said, "not pertinent," and Trumbo would not be allowed to read it.

Why, Trumbo interjected, was he being denied a privilege that the committee regularly granted to witnesses? Even the avowed white supremacist Gerald L. K. Smith, who had recently testified in a separate hearing, had been allowed to read a statement. "I would like to know," Trumbo asked, "what it is that is in my statement that this committee fears be read to the American people?"

The committee ignored him. Robert Stripling, the chief investigator for HUAC, led the questions, insisting that Trumbo answer simply yes or no.

"I understand, Mr. Stripling," Trumbo said. "However, your job is to ask questions, and mine is to answer them. I shall answer 'yes' or 'no' if I please to answer. I shall answer in my own words."

Stripling asked if he had ever been a member of the Screen Writers Guild.

"Mr. Stripling," Trumbo replied, slowly, releasing each word like a bullet, "the rights of American labor to inviolably secret membership have been won in this country by a great cost of blood and a great cost in terms of hunger. These rights lave become an American tradition."

Chairman Thomas flushed with anger. "Are you answering the question or are you making another speech?"

Stripling repeated the question.

"Mr. Chairman, this question is designed to a specific purpose," Trumbo said. "First—"

Thomas pounded his gavel.

"—first, to identify me with the Screen Writers Guild; secondly, to seek to identify me with the Communist Party and thereby destroy the Guild—"

Pound pound pound.

Thomas moved to eject him, but Stripling interjected. He had another question. "Are you now, or have you ever been, a member of the Communist Party?"

A few days before, a copy of a party ID card allegedly belonging to Trumbo had leaked to the press. "I believe I have the right to be confronted with any evidence which supports this question," Trumbo said. "I should like to see what you have."

"Oh. Well, you would, Mr. Trumbo," Thomas sneered.

"Yes."

"Well, you will, pretty soon." The gallery laughed. "The witness is excused," Thomas said, and, banging his gavel once more, looked down to examine some papers, grumbled, "Impossible."

Trumbo wasn't done. He stood. "This is the beginning of an American concentration camp!" he shouted as photographers swooped around him.

Thomas pounded his gavel, louder and louder, in an attempt to drown out Trumbo.

"This is typical Communist tactics," Trumbo yelled, as officers approached from each side. "This is typical Communist tactics!"

Surrounded, Trumbo finally relented. The crowd applauded wildly, some for Trumbo, many for Thomas. The chairman continued to hammer his gavel until it broke. (The next day, he brought two, just in case.) Bogart and Bacall, sitting a few rows behind the witnesses, looked at each other worriedly.

Over the next few days, the rest of the witnesses took their turn at the stand, every appearance a repeat of Trumbo's, albeit with fewer fireworks. It became routine, with Stripling asking "Are you now, or have you ever been, a member of the Communist Party?"—and when they refused to answer, Thomas swiftly dismissed them.

There was one exception, and he came last. The cerebral German playwright Bertolt Brecht was best known in America for the biting social satire *The Threepenny Opera*, which he wrote with the composer Kurt Weill; Brecht provided the words for the hit song "The Ballad of Mack the Knife." Like many German intellectuals, he had fled the Nazis, and he eventually settled in Santa Monica, living not far from another political refugee, the novelist Thomas Mann (longtime enemies, they did not socialize together). Brecht filled his work with Marxist themes and collaborated with well-known Communist artists, but he never joined the party: He was too idiosyncratic to be comfortable in such a hierarchical organization.

With his short-cropped Caesar haircut, his rounded glasses, and his thick German accent, Brecht presented an exotic figure at the witness table. And yet he was surprisingly candid, if often perplexing, in his answers. When Stripling asked if he had ever written revolutionary plays, Brecht replied, "I have written a number of poems and songs and plays in the fight against Hitler and, of course, they can be considered, therefore, as revolutionary because I, of course, was for the overthrow of that government." When confronted with a line of his poetry calling for the people to "take over," he laughed and said it had been mistranslated. The people should merely "lead," he said, his eyes wide and mouth close to the microphone, giving every impression that he just wanted to help. Another poem ended, "All the world will be our own." Stripling asked if he wrote that line.

"No," Brecht said.

Stripling's head perked up.

"I wrote a German poem," Brecht said, "but that is very different from this." The crowd erupted in laughter.

Chairman Thomas, perhaps realizing that Brecht was too clever to pin down, dismissed him. Brecht smiled. The next day, Halloween, he left for Europe, and never returned. He settled in East Germany, where he became a favored artist under the country's Communist regime.

The remaining ten witnesses returned to a very different Los Angeles from the one they had left. There were no banners, no rousing speeches. Only a smattering of supporters greeted them at the airport. Around the studios and on the streets, passersby avoided them. A rally a few days later, staged by the celebrities from the Committee for the First Amendment, managed to pull in seven thousand people, but they might have come just to get close to Bogart and Bacall.

Thomas had abruptly ended the hearings after Brecht's testimony, promising a big announcement and a quick return to the show. "We're not through with the film industry," he swore. But in the days and weeks that followed, new subpoenas failed to appear. Instead, Thomas forced a vote of contempt for the ten uncooperative witnesses. On November 24, 346 House members voted in favor and just 17 opposed. Representative Emanuel Celler had been right when he told Edward Dmytryk that the tide had turned. The concerns over domestic Communism that had obsessed conservatives for a decade or more had, with the onset of the Cold War, become a major force in American politics. No one wanted to be seen as soft on Communism, regardless of how wrong the charges. Less than two weeks later, a federal grand jury indicted all ten.

The real shock arrived on November 25, the day after the House vote, when fifty of Hollywood's top producers gathered at the Waldorf Astoria hotel in Manhattan. They came not just from the eight major studios but many of the smaller independents too. Whatever they thought about government meddling in their business, they were quickly realizing that the mounting hysteria over Communism in Hollywood was bad for their bottom line. Over the previous weeks, ever since HUAC had wrapped up, Hollywood had become a whipping boy for the American right, with groups like the American Legion calling for boycotts against its films and staging picket lines in front of its theaters. Eric Johnston, the film industry's chief lobbyist, reported that a crowd in Chapel Hill, North Carolina, pelted a theater with rocks for showing a film featuring Katharine Hepburn, merely for the offense of joining the Committee for the First Amendment. "Our ticket buyers are being influenced against us in a cause that's growing like a typhoon," wrote Billy Wilkerson in *The Hollywood Reporter*. "That influence might well curtail everything that has made our industry one of the greats in the world."

Now, the producers shuffled into one of New York's toniest hotels for their come-to-Jesus moment, with Johnston as their high priest. As the head of the Motion Picture Association of America, he was indisputably the most powerful man in the industry. And, as a former head of the U.S. Chamber of Commerce, he offered a direct line to the bankers and investors who over the last decade had taken hold of the studios, filling their coffers with tens of millions of dollars and expecting not only high margins but calm waters in return. Now both profit and peace were at risk. It was up to Johnston to see everyone through the storm. And that meant bending the knee to HUAC. There must be a blacklist against Communists and their associates.

There was some dissent, and some executives (Samuel Goldwyn, Darryl Zanuck, and Dore Schary—"probably the most civilized and certainly the most literate man ever to achieve executive leadership of a major motion picture producing company," Trumbo wrote) were adamantly opposed. But they were overruled, and on the afternoon of November 25, Johnston released what came to be known as the Waldorf Statement. The actions of the "ten Hollywood men" had done "a disservice to their employers and have impaired their usefulness to the industry," the statement read. All of them were to be summarily fired, "without compensation," until each "purged himself of contempt and declares under oath that he is not a communist." The statement went further: "We will not knowingly employ a Communist or a member of any party or group which advocates the overthrow of the Government of the United States by force or by any illegal or unconstitutional grounds." Though the statement promised not to be "swayed by hysteria or intimidation," that is precisely what was happening. The night before the HUAC hearings began in October, Johnston had sat in a Washington hotel suite and promised there would be no blacklist. Now, a month later, he was announcing exactly that.

"It should be fully realized," wrote *The New York Times*'s film critic, Bosley Crowther, "that this action was engineered by the major New York executives, the industry's overlords, and not by the 'Hollywood producers,' a . . . subordinate group." Not that it was any consolation to the ten. One by one they fell. Dmytryk and Scott were fired together from their contracts with RKO. Zanuck couldn't stomach having to fire Lardner, so he had his assistant do it. The writers at least had the benefit of being writers; they could work through intermediaries, who would pass off their work as their own, or under pseudonyms. But Dmytryk and Scott, director and producer—what were they to do? And what of the eight who had been subpoenaed but didn't testify? They too were marked, and over time, they too would be added to the blacklist.

The ten and their supporters tried to rally the rest of Hollywood, and at first, many people were willing to look past their divisive performance in Washington. After all, the principle of free speech still applied. But Lawson, who once more asserted his self-proclaimed role as speaker for the ten, decided to make their fight the Communist Party's fight. Instead of building a broad coalition of sympathetic progressives and liberals, he subsumed the case of the Hollywood Ten to the quixotic needs of the party. At rallies and fundraisers, he and his dwindling band claimed that HUAC's behavior was clear evidence of the corruption of the capitalist system, and he bundled their plight with those of other, less savory characters, including common criminals whom Lawson called "freedom fighters." It was all just more evidence that the Hollywood Ten were toxic. Bogart called the trip to Washington a mistake. Eventually even stalwarts like John Huston, who stuck by the ten longer than most, drifted away in disgust. "You felt your skin crawl and your stomach turn," Huston said. "I disapproved of what was being done to the Ten, but I also disapproved of their response. They had lost a chance to defend a most important principle."

The ten faced one final mortification. In early December, the producers Schary, Walter Wanger, and Eddie Mannix, who doubled as MGM's unofficial fixer, telegrammed members of the Screen Writers Guild, inviting them to a meeting "to acquaint you with the intent of the producers' statement . . . and to disavow any intent of a witch hunt." They gathered on December 3 in a Hollywood auditorium, with the three producers onstage. Trumbo sat in the front row, by an aisle. It was left to Schary to do the talking. They weren't asking for the writers to endorse the blacklist, he said, but to accept it as fact. They were also asking the writers to work with them on a campaign to polish Hollywood's image. "Movies Are Better than Ever," it was called. The crowd mumbled in disgruntled consent. When they finished, the three men stepped down from the stage. As they passed Trumbo, each put a hand on his shoulder, silently, then left the hall. After a raucous debate, including a fierce attack on the producers from Trumbo, the guild voted. They too fell in line. They would not help the ten.

4

A Civil War on the Left

Harry Truman's loyalty program was about more than scaring Congress into passing aid to Europe and getting J. Edgar Hoover off his back. He needed wins wherever he could find them, because by mid-1947, it was widely assumed that he was going to lose the next year's election. The Republicans had swamped the Democrats in the House and Senate in 1946, and were still coming on strong in polls, while Truman's approval numbers floated around the mid-30s, at best. New York governor Thomas E. Dewey, the Republicans' candidate against Roosevelt in 1944, was back again. He was young but accomplished. As a dashing, energetic prosecutor in the 1930s and '40s, he had taken down mob bosses, prostitution rings, and corrupt politicians, posing victoriously for photographers outside the Manhattan federal courthouse at Foley Square, free publicity that assured him a rocket-speed trip up the Republican political ranks. He was a moderate, and at odds with his party's conservative, Midwestern wing, which strongly preferred its own standard-bearer, Senator Robert Taft of Ohio. But even Taft conceded that Dewey's moderation would be an asset in winning over liberals disaffected with Truman's performance in office.

Truman figured he knew how to handle Dewey; he'd been fighting Republicans all his life, at home in Missouri and then in the Senate, and he usually won. The threat that truly worried him came from a political force new to the national scene: a progressive coalition that refused to join the Democratic Party. Until then, the rebellious left had been a political blip; the Communists had mounted candidates, as had the Socialists, but even combined they had never posed real competition to the

Democratic candidate for progressive votes. While Franklin Roosevelt was alive, most progressives stayed in the Democratic tent. But things were changing. Under Roosevelt, the party had slowly pushed aside the conservative Southerners who had once been its base, and instead embraced labor, urban voters, immigrants, and African Americans. It was a zero-sum choice; the South would not remain for long in a coalition with people like that. The South's inevitable departure from the Democratic Party meant that Truman had to keep the rest of his constituency intact, especially the party's left wing. And as the 1948 race started to take shape, that began to look like an impossibility. An insurgent, third-party challenge was brewing, one that would bring the incipient Red Scare within the Democratic Party itself.

The challenge from the left came in the form of a curious cornstalk of a man from Iowa named Henry Agard Wallace. He was born on a farm in 1888, the son of Henry C. Wallace, the U.S. secretary of agriculture for much of the 1920s. Young Henry was a wizard of the land and all its bounty. He studied agriculture at Iowa State University, then went to work for his family's publication, *Wallaces' Farmer*. He became known around the Midwest for his uncanny ability to meld science and economics, business and old-school farming smarts into new insights that helped him grow wealthy—as it did many of his readers, who followed his prescriptions religiously. On the side he founded a seed business, the Hi-Bred Corn Company, producing highly efficient hybrid crops. He held on to it through his decades in politics; at the end of his life, in 1965, it was estimated to be worth tens of millions of dollars.

For a farmer, he had an odd detachment from everyday life. He once gave his friend, the playwright Lillian Hellman, a city dweller who had rarely set foot on an agricultural property, a fifty-pound bag of manure as a gift. His rangy height, tussled hair, and steel-gray eyes gave him an otherworldly air. "You feel that he would not tell you the time of day without first searching his soul to see if it agreed with the clock," read a profile in *The New York Times*.

Wallace was a Republican early in his career, but he switched parties just in time to catch Roosevelt's rising star. He grew close to the candidate by stumping for him across the heartland during the 1932 presidential campaign. In return Roosevelt named him secretary of agriculture. Wallace did the same thing for the department as he did for his readers in Iowa and his hybrid-seed business, championing novel ways to lift up the American farmer through economic and legal means. He staffed the department with brilliant economists and an army of Harvard Law graduates. Arthur Schlesinger Jr., who was no fan of Wallace, nevertheless considered him the greatest secretary of agriculture in history.

Wallace was at his best in the 1930s, as the immediate tasks involved in salvaging the economy gave him a way to harness his moralizing dreaminess. He fought Southern congressmen to expand agriculture assistance to Black sharecroppers. The New Deal was the apotheosis of the common man, and Wallace came to believe he was its avatar. Roosevelt chose him as vice president in 1940. But four years later, perhaps with an eye to his own mortality and a desire to choose someone more dependable as his heir, the president replaced Wallace on the ticket with Truman. As a consolation prize, he made him commerce secretary.

But Wallace would not be kept quiet. He went rogue. On the stump at home and on official trips abroad, he called for a return to the founding ethos of the New Deal. He spoke for millions who, with the end of the war, were thrilled at victory but afraid of what would come next. Eventually, he went too far. In September 1946 he gave a speech on foreign policy before tens of thousands of progressives gathered at Manhattan's Madison Square Garden. He took a few jabs at the Soviet Union, but reserved his harshest words for the administration, saying that its "current policies may eventually lead to war." Declaring himself "neither anti-Russian nor pro-Russian," he said that a "get tough with Russia" policy would fail. The only solution, he said, was to cede global security to the United Nations, including the network of U.S. and British air bases strung across the world—in essence, disarmament. "Under friendly, peaceful competition the Russian world and the American world will gradually become more alike," he said from the podium.

Wallace never named Truman or his secretary of state, James Byrnes, in the speech. But Byrnes was apoplectic, and gave the president an ultimatum: Wallace or him. Truman picked Byrnes. In his diary, the president wrote that Wallace was not "as fundamentally sound intellectually as I had thought." More ominously, in the same entry, he detected a connection emerging between New Deal purists and the far left: "The Reds, phonies and the 'parlor pinks' seem to be banded together and are becoming a national danger."

Out of office, Wallace went on a nationwide speaking tour, becoming more vocal in his attacks on the administration. In January 1947, a few months before the Greek crisis, Wallace went on *Meet the Press* to denounce the president's emerging Cold War foreign policy. The United States and Britain, he warned, "would use the atomic bomb against Russia in an aggressive way under certain conditions." His dual message of peace abroad and a renewed New Deal agenda at home resonated with voters. In March 1947 more than nineteen thousand people came to see him give another speech at Madison Square Garden; thousands more were turned away at the door. Congress, he told the roaring crowd, "is asked to rush through a momentous decision as if great armies were already on the march. I hear no armies marching. I hear a world crying out for peace." In the speech, Wallace claimed to remain a loyal Democrat. But a month later, in April 1947, he said he was changing his position. Upon landing at Washington's National Airport after the European leg of a speaking tour, he told the gaggle of reporters waiting for him that Truman's aid to Greece and his loyalty program had put the country "on the road to ruthless imperialism." A civil war was breaking out on the American left.

Truman and his supporters alleged throughout the 1947–1948 campaign that Wallace was surrounded by Communists. And they were not wrong. After several years of hemorrhaging members, the Communist Party had decided to jump into the campaign. Its leaders had no illusion that he could win. But they figured Wallace could siphon off enough liberal votes to guarantee a Republican victory. The Communists believed that doing so would show their power—and, the true diehards hoped, put the country one step closer to the apocalyptic crisis of capitalism in which they still fervently believed.

The Communists did not openly court Wallace. Instead, they flooded into the Progressive Citizens of America, a newly formed umbrella group for left-leaning voters grown frustrated with the Democrats, especially over the party's hardening stance against the Soviet Union. The new members never announced themselves as Communists, knowing that even many dedicated progressives had learned to be wary of them. The PCA welcomed them as passionate, effective workers, and as their influence grew, they poked the organization in the direction of a Wallace candidacy. They sent long retinues of callers to the offices of *The New Republic*, where Wallace was now editor, urging him to run. They filled rallies along his speaking tours and even covertly sponsored their own in his name.

Reporters and liberal politicians saw what was happening, but the Communists' ruse managed to fool the one person who mattered, namely Wallace himself. Not that he minded Communist support. In the haze of his high-minded ecumenism, he welcomed all kinds to what he came to call his "Gideon's Army" of peace-loving Americans. His friends tried to warn him. Bruce Bliven, who had preceded him as editor of *The New Republic*, took his successor aside and told him that most of the people coming through his door were sent straight from the Communist Party. Wallace said that was impossible; after all, only one person had identified himself as a Communist, and that was a reporter for *The Daily Worker*. And why would they lie? "Wallace had rather too high a tolerance for persons ablaze with intentions, or expressions of intentions, which struck him as vital to the needs of a sick world," another friend said. Michael Straight, *The New Republic*'s publisher—who, it was later revealed, had been a part of the infamous Cambridge Soviet spy ring while a student at the British university in the 1930s—said that "I knew from my own experience that collaboration with the Communist party would destroy Wallace, but I could not share my experience with him."

Wallace announced his campaign for president on December 29, 1947. A few days later the Progressive Citizens of America reconstituted itself as the Progressive Party, with the intention of serving as Wallace's electoral vehicle. At the time, he was expected to draw five to ten million votes, almost all from Truman, who in a tight race against Governor Dewey could ill afford to lose them. To Truman and the Democrats, Wallace was merely a symptom of a much bigger problem. The Communists needed to be destroyed.

■   ■   ■   ■

From the beginning of the 1948 campaign season, Truman drew a bead on Wallace's involvement with the Communist Party. His adviser Clark Clifford, in a lengthy memo laying out his vision for the race, wrote that "every effort must be made now and at one and the same time—although, of course, by different groups—to dissuade him and also to identify him in the public mind with the Communists." Truman ran with it. At a speech on St. Patrick's Day, he declared, "I do not want and I will not accept the political support of Henry Wallace and his Communists." Speaking at Gilmore Stadium in Los Angeles, he warned left-leaning liberals that Wallace was a Communist puppet. "To these liberals," he intoned, "I would say in all sincerity, think again."

The Wallace campaign was never just a Communist plot. Millions of Americans were open to his message of peaceful coexistence abroad and expanded government at home—a return, in effect, to the best parts of the 1930s, this time without the fear and insecurity wrought by the Depression. But the Communists were always part of his core, his most active supporters, his most effective organizers, and his loudest cheerleaders. "Communists perform the most complete valet service in the world," quipped Walter Reuther, the anti-Communist leader of the United Auto Workers. "They write your speeches, they do your thinking for you, they provide you with applause and they inflate your ego as often as necessary. . . . I am afraid that's the trouble with Henry Wallace."

The Communist Party itself played coy about its support for Wallace. After the party's board decided to back him in 1947, it ordered that anyone who disagreed be kicked out of the organization. At a rally in Manhattan in January 1948 marking the twenty-fourth anniversary of Vladimir Lenin's death, William Z. Foster, the Communists' general secretary, praised the Wallace campaign as "the one movement that has the possibility to put a halt to this drive toward a new war," while denying that his party had any role with it. In April 1948 its national committee announced that it would begin a recruiting drive among the non-Communist progressives still attached to the campaign, with the goal of adding fifteen thousand new members a month—or about ten times what it had been adding before then. A month later, the committee openly claimed credit for Wallace's success thus far. "Its traditional fight for a new people's party directed against the two-party system of the monopolies has once more been placed by events as an immediate, practical question before the American people," the party declared.

How much did Wallace know about the Communists' role in his campaign? He knew something—in rare moments of self-awareness, he bemoaned their self-destructive boasts on his behalf. At a press conference in Vermont, he conceded, "If the Communists would run a ticket of their own, the New Party"—an early name for the Progressives—"would lose 100,000 votes but gain four million." In July he conceded, "There is no question that this sort of thing is a liability." But he also agreed with much of what was handed to him, especially on foreign policy. When a *New York Times* correspondent asked how he squared his belief in Stalin as a peace-loving leader with the Soviet Union's rampaging takeover of Eastern Europe, he said that it was only natural for them to want a cordon of allied states around their border. "She has a right to that protection," he said. "We have to recapture the spirit of trust and cooperation that existed between Roosevelt and Stalin in 1945." Wallace might have been right that people were tired of war. But Truman had done an able job of rallying them around a new moral cause, while a new Soviet blockade of Berlin, begun in June of 1948, convinced much of the world that the Russians were on the wrong side of history. So too, it increasingly seemed to voters, was Wallace. The historian William Leuchtenburg, at the time a young Democratic organizer in Colorado, said in a memo to Washington that Wallace's campaign was "being blown to pieces by the stupidity of the Communists."

There had been divisions between the centrist liberals of the Democratic Party and its left wing throughout the New Deal era, but they were papered over by Stalin's insistence that Communists everywhere build a common resistance against fascism—the Popular Front. Communists went to work for the New Deal; they joined mainstream labor unions and centrist civil rights organizations. The Popular Front collapsed with Stalin's nonaggression treaty with Hitler in 1939, after which the Communists and their allies on the left turned on their liberal allies, who continued to demand American support for Hitler's enemies. To the liberals, the Communists' sudden hostility felt like both a betrayal and a validation of their belief that the far left could not be trusted.

The exigencies of the war, and America's alliance with the Soviets during it, put the incipient fight between liberals and the left on hold. With the end of the war, the fight was back on. In January 1947, weeks after the establishment of the Progressive Citizens of America, some 130 prominent liberals gathered in Washington to announce the creation of Americans for Democratic Action, a political clearinghouse for the left that specifically excluded Communists. The ADA was strongly in favor of Truman's aggressive foreign policy, but also supported a renewed expansion of the New Deal state at home. Its opposition to Communists and fellow travelers was both philosophical and strategic: Their presence on the left was an enormous negative for most American voters, who would be the ultimate arbiters over whether the country picked up the mantle of Roosevelt or not.

That, at least, was the idea. But some in the ADA's orbit, like Walter Reuther, took things further, endorsing efforts to rid the country of Communists entirely. Oftentimes they had personal, bad experiences: Senator Hubert Humphrey had all manner of memories of his time as a rising politician in Minnesota, where Communists had fought a scorched-earth campaign for control of the state's Democratic-Farm Labor Party. Reuther had clashed with Communists in the labor movement, who to him seemed more interested in fomenting an impossible revolution than doing the hard work of building effective democratic unions. Many of the ADA's founders from the academic world, like Arthur Schlesinger Jr., had firsthand experience of Communist activism on campus. Now, with their support for Wallace, the Communists seemed openly willing to help a Republican get elected to further their own sectarian fantasies.

Some members of the ADA, whether on their own or as part of the organization, went on to support many of the worst parts of the Red Scare: federal prosecutions against Communist leaders, loyalty oaths in primary schools and colleges, and congressional investigations; some even endorsed Joseph McCarthy, though they were careful to qualify their support, saying he at times went too far. The ADA opposed Truman's loyalty program, but endorsed a congressional effort to expand it in 1950.

Thomas Dewey may not have wanted to make Communism an issue in the 1948 campaign, but many centrist Democrats did—and in doing so helped poison the well of public sentiment against the party and the left generally.

Not everyone in the ADA was dogmatic in their anti-Communism, and several leaders worried that things were getting out of hand. In September 1948 Leon Henderson, the organization's chairman, warned Truman that his campaign against Wallace was creating a hysterical anti-Communist atmosphere that would last long after the election was over. Worse, he feared that Truman's loyalty program was being used to political ends, cracking down on innocent people as a way of demonstrating the administration's anti-Communist bona fides. "We urge you meanwhile to make clear to administration officials that political considerations must have no part in the grave business of determining a man's 'loyalty to his country,'" Henderson wrote.

Even before the influx of Communists, the Progressive Citizens of America had become a public lightning rod. When the group's Philadelphia chapter gathered in Independence Square for a protest against the Hollywood HUAC hearings, in November 1947, some 1,500 counterprotesters pushed and shoved their way through the crowd, spinning off fistfights as they went. When Wallace, during the campaign, showed up for a rally in the Red Hook section of Brooklyn, six hundred angry, fruit-flinging Truman and Dewey supporters were there to greet him. Over the coming years, a person's support for Wallace in 1948, let alone membership in the PCA, would become a mark of suspicion for anti-Communists. *The Pittsburgh Press*, a conservative afternoon daily, printed the names of local signatories to a Wallace petition—a list that would pop up in the files of many red hunters.

Wallace may have been a tool of the Communists, but his race drew support from far beyond the party. He spoke for a legitimate, widespread, discombobulating fear that Truman was driving America into another war. It was lost on no one that the war had ended thanks to the deployment of a weapon powerful enough to destroy an entire city. Veterans returned wounded in body and mind to find that life at home had in many cases moved on and did not necessarily have a place for them. Housing was scarce and prices were high. Wallace thought he understood that fear, and admirably, he tried to assuage it. But the reality of the postwar era—the rise of the Soviet Union, the fall of China, the incontestable dominance of the United States—meant there was no going back, and that Wallace's message was met with fury from both Democrats and Republicans.

Truman understood that, like it or not, the United States had no choice but to fulfill its new role in the world, to go once more into the breach. But in doing so, in steeling the country to stand up to the Soviet challenge, he chose not to dispel the accompanying fear—and, during his 1948 run for the presidency, he did much to exacerbate it. Alone, Truman's attacks on Wallace did not cause the Red Scare. But by lending it a bipartisan cover, he made it easier for tens of millions of Americans to join the hysteria.

5

Un-American Activities

Everywhere it seemed the Communists were on the offensive, and winning. In February 1948, Czechoslovakian Communists took control of the country in a Soviet-backed coup. The speed of the overthrow, and the suspicious death, in March, of Jan Masaryk, the country's anti-Communist foreign minister, shocked the world. In June 1948, the Soviets closed off access to West Berlin, which was still controlled by the Americans, British, and French; the Western allies enacted their own blockade against the Soviet sector of eastern Germany, then mounted a massive airlift effort to resupply the city. The Soviets circled the city with troops. Badly outnumbered in Europe, the United States made clear that if fighting broke out, it would use atomic weapons. In East Asia, the pro-Western Nationalists in China were steadily losing ground in their civil war against the Communists under Mao Zedong, despite heavy amounts of U.S. aid. Though the Communists would not claim victory for another year, by mid-1948 all but the most fervent anti-Communists in Washington assumed Mao was going to win, and that a rapprochement was in order. A rebellion in Indonesia, which was still in the process of establishing itself as an independent country, threatened to turn the island nation Communist, handing control of vital shipping lanes to the Soviet bloc.

The global news, full of portents of a new world war, was matched by a summer of high drama domestically. A year before, federal prosecutors had empaneled a grand jury to investigate the allegations of Soviet espionage by Elizabeth Bentley, the woman who had worked as a courier for the Russians before turning herself over to the FBI. She enthralled the jurors with her stories of spy cameras, stolen documents, and furtive meetings in Washington—but she had no evidence, and no one to corroborate her stories. Soon after she began cooperating with the government, the entire Soviet spy network had gone to ground, likely tipped off by the infamous British double agent Kim Philby, who at the time was serving in Washington as Britain's top intelligence liaison to the United States. Bentley also confirmed what the government already knew through intercepted Soviet cables: Moscow held tight control over the American Communist Party, keeping it afloat with cash and demanding fealty to Stalin's whims in return. But Hoover and others refused to reveal the intercept program to the public, leaving Bentley's testimony unsupported. Without solid evidence, T. Vincent Quinn, one of the assistant attorneys general handing the case, reported to Hoover that the jury was "aroused and incensed" and that it "wanted to do something about it but that there was [sic] no adequate laws to warrant the bringing of an indictment."

The grand jury's deliberations were secret, but its existence was widely known, and as 1948 unfolded, public criticism mounted over its inaction. "We would like to know why busy men are kept at such a task without reaching a conclusion about data which began to become available sometime in 1941," wrote the editorial board of the *New York Daily Mirror* on May 14. Conservative writers decided that a cover-up was afoot. "Although more than 100 New Dealers, many former or present high officials in such key agencies as the State Department, have been named as members of Soviet espionage network [sic], no action has been taken," wrote the right-wing columnist Howard Rushmore, himself a former Communist, in the *New York Journal-American*. "In Washington political circles, the rumor is that [Attorney General Tom] Clark, acting on administration orders, will keep the jury sitting until November." HUAC ordered Clark to sit for hours as its members grilled him with accusations and innuendo. The attorney general had hoped that the grand jury investigation would fizzle out, without anyone noticing. Now he returned to his office, called his assistants, and demanded a new approach, one that would make it easier for the government to prosecute Communists, regardless of their connections to Moscow.

The solution came from Quinn and another assistant attorney general,

Thomas J. Donegan. The government's goal, they figured, was to shut down the Communist Party. But the current investigation, even if it did end in individual prosecutions of former spies named by Bentley, would not get them much closer to that end. There was nothing connecting the Communist Party leadership with espionage networks. But, Quinn and Donegan said, there was another way to get at them: an obscure piece of legislation called the Smith Act. Over the next five years it would become the government's favorite weapon in prosecuting the Red Scare, responsible for sending scores of people to prison for nothing more than their political beliefs.

Named for its chief sponsor, Howard Smith, a powerful, pro-segregation representative from Virginia, the 1940 act was part of a brace of legislation passed with an eye toward the looming war in Europe. The idea, Smith argued, was to avoid allowing another wave of radical aliens to operate in the country, like the one he believed had threatened the American war effort in the 1910s. The act barred from entering the country any foreigners who were or had been members of violent revolutionary movements, and it required the registration of all current and incoming noncitizens. Tucked into the bill was yet another provision that would outlaw any effort to advocate or teach "the duty, necessity, desirability, or propriety of overthrowing or destroying any government in the United States by force or violence," or to organize or join "any society, group, or assembly of people" to achieve the same end. The provision passed almost unnoticed; critics focused instead on the immigration portions, unaware that this last part would become the legal backbone of the federal government's anti-Communist campaign.

Donegan and Quinn, the Justice Department prosecutors, had no illusions about how difficult it would be to win a conviction under the Smith Act. Espionage was one thing, but finding evidence that the party had tried to foment violent revolution was another. As scary as "Communism" was in general, the actual Communist Party of the United States of America was rapidly shrinking in numbers and resources. And the Supreme Court had already ruled in two other cases involving the Smith Act that simply being a member of the Communist Party was not enough to violate the law. But that was before the onset of the Cold War, and the widespread conviction that Communism was a mortal threat to America, one that had to be rooted out wherever it was found.

The two prosecutors set out to amass evidence against the party's inner circle, using the same grand jury. Bentley proved particularly unhelpful: When Donegan and Quinn pressed her to tell the grand jury that the party took the revolutionary writings of Marx, Lenin, and Stalin seriously, she told them the opposite—that hardly anyone read the party's canonical texts, which she derided as "dry as dust." She told them that the party, for all its big talk about forcefully overthrowing the capitalist system, had never taken a single step to make that possible. The party, it seemed, wanted to be taken seriously, but not literally. Now, the government was doing both.

Hoover disagreed with using the Smith Act. "I told Mr. Quinn that I was just as adverse to presenting the Communist Party brief as I was to the presentation of the Gregory case"—the shorthand name for the investigation into Bentley's allegations—"at least until the brief has been thoroughly reviewed and digested by not one, but by several real lawyers," he wrote in a memo to his top aides on April 1. Hoover was thinking politically, hoping that a delay past the 1948 elections would allow him to work with a Republican administration. But he also had a point. The Smith Act strategy was incredibly weak. The party was mostly just talk. What "advocacy" of revolution they performed was secondhand and theoretical, through their rote recitation of Marx's and Lenin's texts. There was no evidence of actual planning for a revolution in the United States. Hoover wasn't alone in that concern: Even John F. X. McGohey, the U.S. attorney whom Quinn chose to prosecute the case, initially expressed skepticism whether the evidence was enough to win a conviction.

From the beginning, the Smith Act trial was wrapped up in the politics of the 1948 election. In late June, U.S. Attorney McGohey traveled to Washington to brief Attorney General Clark. The case was ready to go, McGohey told him. At his word, indictments against the Communist Party leadership could be ready within days. But Clark's mind was elsewhere. He worried that news of the indictments would swamp the pro-Truman coverage leading up to the Democratic National Convention in mid-July. Apparently Truman was concerned as well, as he had won a promise from Clark to delay the indictments until after the convention. McGohey, a staunch professional, was offended by Clark's direction, and told him the case needed to proceed immediately. Clark then asked for the files, ostensibly for the solicitor general to review, in effect stalling the indictments for three weeks.

Finally, on July 20, the grand jury gathered in Manhattan's Foley Square courthouse to submit its indictments against twelve top officials in the Communist Party, including its chairman, William Z. Foster; its general secretary, Eugene Dennis; and Ben Davis, the chair of the Communists' legislative committee, a member of the New York City Council, and the highest-ranking Black man in the party. The indictments were unsealed around noon, and that evening FBI agents raided the Communist Party headquarters, a former garment factory in Greenwich Village. Five of the defendants, including Foster and Dennis, were there waiting for them. Davis was arrested around the same time at his home. The rest were rounded up in the coming days.

Before the men could even be arraigned, the party's national press office released a statement denouncing the charges as political, a "Truman effort to win the election by hook or by crook" and to undermine the Progressives and Henry Wallace, whose own convention was set to begin the following week. But the denunciation did not stop there; the party warned that the arrests were the opening steps in the fascist takeover and the war with the Soviet Union they had long predicted. They were an "American version of the Reichstag fire . . . the domestic counterpart of the criminal bipartisan attempts to turn the war in Berlin from cold to hot."

The defendants each pleaded not guilty, then repaired to the courthouse press room, where they took reporters' questions. Foster was visibly ailing—he was sixty-seven and had recently suffered a series of strokes—but he nevertheless joined his comrades at a table to denounce the charges and insist that "the Communist Party never has, and does not advocate, the forceful overthrow of the United States Government."

A grand jury that had originally formed to investigate straightforward allegations of espionage by Elizabeth Bentley had now, instead, set the stage for a trial based on a much thornier and politically charged question.

Was the Communist Party indeed an organization bent on the violent overthrow of the United States government? And if it was, how seriously should it be taken as a threat? Did it present a "clear and present danger," the litmus test first enunciated by Supreme Court Justice Oliver Wendell Holmes Jr. to identify the acceptable limits placed on free speech? And again if so, how far down the ladder of leadership did the charges apply? Were rank-and-file Communists also at risk of prosecution? What about former party members? These questions had no easy answers, certainly none rooted in the traditions of American jurisprudence. Instead, they would be articulated by the moment—the course of the trial, the attitude of the judge, and, above all, the mood of the country as it began to realize the enormity of the looming Cold War.

McGohey and the Department of Justice had another consideration in mind as they planned when to roll out their indictments. Elizabeth Bentley was not sitting still. She was no longer worried about her safety from the Soviet espionage network. Now she was thinking about her legacy. How would she be remembered? If, as she suspected, she became famous for her revelations, would she be valorized or vilified? She knew one thing, and that was that she could not trust the government to keep her best interests in mind.

She had already been speaking with Nelson Frank, one of the many reporters trying to get a handle on the government's machinations. He was likewise a former party member, who had used his inside knowledge of Communism to get a job with the conservative *New York World-Telegram*. At first, Bentley offered him background information about the Soviet underground in New York. But in April, she suggested she would be willing to tell it all. Frank and his colleague (and fellow ex-Communist) Frederick Woltman interviewed her for hours. She gave them everything, in the hopes that they would write her version of the story. Frank and Woltman contacted the Justice Department for comment, and agreed not to publish anything until the grand jury was finished. Whether and for how long the department could trust them to keep a secret was anyone's guess.

The newspaper complied with their promise, just barely. The morning after the indictments were handed down at Foley Square—and still hours before they were unsealed at the arraignment that evening—the *World-Telegram* appeared at newsstands across New York with the blaring head-line "RED RING BARED BY BLOND QUEEN." Frank had decided to tell a somewhat different story than the one Bentley had intended. This one was amped up with sex and intrigue, turning Bentley into a pinup beauty and the humdrum flow of stolen information that she had ferried out of Washington into a fire hose of secrets fatal to the health of the republic. It was wild exaggeration, but it sold papers, and made Bentley a summer-time celebrity.

Despite the press attention, with the grand jury headed off in a different direction, Bentley's story might have ended there. But there was someone else interested in hearing from her. Ever since the end of the Hollywood hearings in November 1947, J. Parnell Thomas, chairman of HUAC, had been casting about for a new way to get himself and his committee back in the spotlight.

He had found one possible target, a government scientist named Ed-ward Condon, the director of the National Bureau of Standards, a branch of the Department of Commerce. Condon was among the country's leading technical minds—he needed just three years to finish his under-graduate degree and two years to write his doctoral dissertation in phys-ics, both at Berkeley—and its foremost expert in the emerging field of quantum mechanics. His position at the Bureau of Standards gave him a prominent voice in shaping the future of research and technological progress during the early days of the Cold War. Among other things, Con-don very publicly opposed military control over atomic research, a stance that earned him enemies at the Pentagon and among its many allies in Congress.

Chairman Thomas was among them. In March 1948 he released a lengthy report that drew on standard FBI loyalty investigations to accuse Condon of "knowingly or unknowingly" maintaining ties to Soviet agents. He was "one of the weakest links in our security," Thomas's report said, and demanded that Averell Harriman, Henry Wallace's successor as secre-tary of commerce, either fire Condon or appear before the committee to defend him—an outcome that the publicity-addicted Thomas likely preferred. Report in hand, Thomas then demanded Condon's loyalty and FBI files—a demand that Truman firmly denied.

The Condon affair was quickly swamped by other events in that fast-paced year, but it illustrated the lengths to which Thomas and his allies were willing to go in their hunt for Communists within the federal government. Condon was the archetype of the New Deal intellectual, the sort of bureaucratic elite that men like Martin Dies and J. Parnell Thomas had long smeared as the vanguard un-American of a vast Communist conspiracy—charges that took on a new dimension with the onset of the Cold War. Thomas had selectively quoted from FBI reports about Condon and ignored their exculpatory conclusions. He claimed that the embassy of Poland, now a Communist state, had acquired 270 copies of a government science report by Condon, implying that Condon had facilitated Communist access to government secrets—even though the report was publicly available for anyone to purchase.

Journalists were quick to pounce: Marquis Childs called it the "shabbiest, meanest" attack by HUAC yet, "as un-American as anything could be." Thomas Mattingly, a D.C.-area doctor, wrote in a letter to the editor that "all that is left is for the political party in power to identify undesirables with whom association is considered subversive. Today it is a Communist. Tomorrow it can be a Negro, a Jew or a Catholic. Imagine Representative Rankin having the power to define who is un-American." Condon got off the best line, saying that if he was, indeed, the weakest link, then "the country can feel absolutely safe."

Thomas had dug himself into a deep hole, and it was left to Robert Stripling, his adept chief counsel, to dig him out. As soon as he read the newspaper reports about Bentley with her dozens of spies rooted deep inside Washington, Stripling realized he had found a way. Bentley, he insisted, "does have considerable information about some of Condon's associations which they thought was germane to the matter." Journalists had not revealed Bentley's identity in their reporting, but it didn't take Stripling and his team of investigators long to put together the clues. He issued a subpoena for her to appear before the committee on July 31, 1948.

■   ■   ■   ■

Bentley's story, as important as it was to the launch of the Smith Act trials and with them the onset of the Red Scare, was just a warm-up act for the first great media frenzy of the anti-Communist era: the Hiss–Chambers case.

Whittaker Chambers was, like Bentley, a former courier for the Soviet espionage network who had grown disillusioned with the cause. He had fallen in with the Communist Party while in college, at Columbia, where he developed a reputation as a brilliant but troubled writer. He penned poetry and criticism for campus literary journals and occasionally for left-wing publications around New York. He had a special capacity for languages, and in 1928 he translated *Bambi, A Life in the Woods*, the Austrian children's novel that became the basis for the 1942 Disney animated feature. But Chambers was also an off-putting, furtive character; he mumbled and shuffled his way across the Morningside Heights campus. In conversation, he kept his eyes on the floor. No one who met him could help commenting on his dental hygiene. The literary critic Lionel Trilling, who encountered Chambers when they were both Columbia undergraduates, wrote: "When the mouth opened, it never failed to shock by reason of the dental ruin it disclosed, a devastation of empty sockets and blackened stumps." Trilling was never close to Chambers, but he followed his career as a Communist and later as a journalist, convinced that he "virtually demanded to be coopted as a fictive character." Trilling did just that, making him the basis for Gifford Maxim, a Communist apostate, in his only novel, *The Middle of the Journey*, which appeared in 1947.

Chambers had joined the party in 1925. He was, for a time, a true believer in the promise of Communism as a delivery from the want and misery of capitalism. "Chambers exulted in his new identity," his biographer, Sam Tanenhaus, wrote. "He had abdicated his place in the 'dying world' and had discovered a meaningful niche in the world waiting to be born." But like many people who dabbled with the party in the 1930s, he gradually came to believe the opposite, that behind its utopian façade Communism offered only oppression and death. And he became convinced that democratic capitalism, though hardly perfect, at least offered the chance to achieve that which Chambers, a former atheist turned devout Christian, increasingly believed was the only thing that mattered: fealty to God.

"Faith is the central problem of this age," he wrote in his memoir, *Witness*. "The Western world does not know it, but it already possesses the answer to this problem—but only provided that its faith in God and the freedom He enjoins is as great as Communism's faith in man."

Chambers had other, more immediate concerns than the fate of his soul. Soviet agents were starting to go missing, or turn up dead. Many were victims of Stalin's campaign to consolidate power and eliminate all traces of dissent, the Great Terror that led to the murder of some 1.2 million people (or significantly more; estimates vary). One such figure, Ignatz Reiss, had refused orders to return to Moscow, knowing what awaited him; he ended up shot dead on a Swiss mountain road. Juliet Poyntz, a member of the American underground, had broken with the party and, not long after, disappeared from the streets of Midtown Manhattan, likely kidnapped and murdered by the NKVD. Those deaths and others shook Chambers, revealing the rotten core of the Communist promise. He spent months planning his defection, and finally broke with the party in 1938. He kept a cache of documents and microfilm, items he was supposed to hand over to the Soviets, as an insurance policy, and had a friend store them in a dumbwaiter at his parents' home in New York.

Chambers and his family spent time in hiding, living at twenty-one different addresses over a two-year period, and only gradually returned to the world. In 1939 he paid his visit to Adolf Berle of the State Department, naming dozens of spies working within the U.S. government. But when nothing came of it, Chambers settled into his post-Communist life. He was baptized Episcopalian at the Cathedral Church of St. John the Divine, adjacent to his alma mater of Columbia, and later converted to Quakerism. He got a job writing book reviews for *Time*, where he became a favorite of its publisher, Henry Luce. In that position and later, as the head of the magazine's world news desk, he made a name for himself as a strident anti-Communist, ringing his tocsin against what he believed was a Soviet campaign to take over vast swaths of Central and Western Europe after the war.

But his zeal eventually waned. His health suffered from his weekly commute from Pipe Creek, his farm northwest of Baltimore, to *Time's* offices in Manhattan. He made enemies at the magazine, and not only because of his politics—others simply didn't like his rock-hard convictions, which led him to write with an air of absolute authority about parts of the world he knew nothing of. Eventually he was moved to the Special Projects desk, with a workload more amenable to his health, and with the added benefit of editing his old friend, the film critic James Agee, the only *Time* employee who could match him as a writer. Meanwhile he had two small children at home, and some three hundred acres of fields to tend. He owned cows, and was never happier than when he rose early to milk them. One day he might be shoveling manure and wringing chicken necks, and the next editing copy for the country's leading newsmagazine. He would come to work smelling vaguely of farm funk, but he did not care.

The FBI interviewed Chambers five times in 1946 and 1947. He told them what he told Berle, and though it synced in large part with Bentley's information, the agents concluded that it did not amount to much. The Foley Square grand jury had not even bothered to call him. He reasonably assumed that, whatever else happened in the drama of American Communism, he had already performed his role.

He was shocked, then, in July 1948 to find an oblique but telling reference to himself in a profile of Bentley published in the New York *Sun*. He was sitting in his office at *Time*, in Manhattan, as he scanned the page. His face lost all color. His friend and colleague John Chamberlain, sitting beside him, asked if he was okay. Chambers was constantly ill of health—overweight, overworked, overstressed, with a history of heart trouble and panic attacks. Chambers showed him the article, which mentioned the FBI's interest in an unnamed New York editor who had also been a Communist. It was him, and now, he told Chamberlain, the government was going to force him to speak publicly.

"What are you worried about, Whit?" Chamberlain asked. "All you have to do is go down to Washington and tell what you know."

Chambers looked across the office, indicating the editors who, he suspected, had a conspicuously left-wing bent to their politics. "They don't like informers around here."

At first, HUAC's focus remained on Bentley. Before she could appear before the committee, she was called before a Senate subcommittee investigating the case of a young government economist named William

Remington. A son of extreme wealth, he had traveled freely among the radical left during his student days at Dartmouth and Columbia, but had seemingly buckled down by 1940, when at twenty-three he went to work for the National Resources Planning Board. By 1947 he had a plum job at the Council of Economic Advisers. But rumors about his past had followed him, and he was repeatedly subjected to loyalty investigations. The pace had quickened after Bentley included his name in her conversations with the FBI, and both the bureau and the grand jury interviewed him. He confessed to having met with Bentley. But he insisted that he never gave her classified information. To help his case, he even handed over the names of some fifty people he suspected of being Communists.

Bentley gave the committee more than enough ammunition on Remington. She told them she met with him ten to twenty times, during which he would hand her small scraps of paper scratched with notes and numbers and even whole sentences, detailing arms shipments to Russia, aircraft production statistics, and, occasionally, an odd item like the formula for making synthetic rubber from garbage. He was suspended from his job, pending an investigation. So far, Bentley was proving useful. (Remington was eventually convicted of perjury on charges stemming from Bentley's accusations.)

The House Un-American Activities Committee had its turn with her the next day, July 31, 1948. When Stripling, as chief counsel, asked if she had ever been a Communist, she replied yes, and proceeded to detail the people, places, and operations she had encountered during her nearly ten years in the party. Name after name spilled out. But the whole thing, spread over five hours and coming after so much press coverage, seemed like a letdown. Most of what Bentley said about Soviet espionage had already come out in the papers. It was shocking to hear it from the source, but not revealing. And there were many holes in her testimony. She puffed up her story, claiming that her spy network "knew D-Day long before D-Day happened," and that thanks to her the Soviets knew "practically all the inside policies that were going on inside the Air Corps." Neither statement was true. She claimed to have "quite a lot of information about General Hilldring's activities," but when Stripling asked her to specify who, exactly, Hilldring was, she admitted, "I am not quite sure myself what his status was." (John Hilldring had been Army chief of staff, then head of the 84th Infantry Division.) Notably, Bentley did not even touch on the person she had been brought there to discuss in the first place: Edward Condon. Her testimony over, the press and even the men of HUAC concluded that maybe the Bentley story was a dead end. All that remained was to hear from one more witness, Chambers, to offer some corroborating evidence.

As Chambers had feared, HUAC called him to testify in the Bentley hearings on August 3. Stripling had first heard about him while looking into the Condon case—a reporter told him that a former Communist who now worked for *Time* and lived on a Maryland farm might have information for him. Two HUAC investigators interviewed Chambers at the *Time* offices in New York in the spring of 1948 and came up with nothing. Stripling forgot about him. But after Bentley's disappointing testimony, and the criticism that she and the committee received in the press, he realized that he needed someone who could back up her story.

Like Bentley, Chambers was scared, perhaps even more than she had been. He had known too well what happened to people like him, who crossed the party, people like Ignatz Reiss, who were murdered, or people like Juliet Poyntz, who simply disappeared. But for the moment, he was second fiddle, the supporting act. Bentley had corroborated much of what he had told the government repeatedly over the years. But in the eye of the public, it was Chambers's role to corroborate her.

Chambers traveled to Washington on August 2, 1948, the night before his scheduled appearance. Upon arriving at Washington's Union Station he took a cab directly to the home of Frank McNaughton, a friend and *Time*'s Capitol Hill correspondent. The two men barely slept that night— Chambers because he was afraid of being killed, McNaughton to keep watch. McNaughton told him about the makeup of the HUAC panelists. "There is one man on the committee who asks shrewd questions," he said. "Richard Nixon of California."

Nobody besides his family much liked Richard Nixon, not then, not before, not ever. He had been born and raised with the small-town comer's resentment of the better off. He carried a chip large enough for everyone to see, and despite his claim that his lack of an Ivy League law degree kept him out of the white-shoe firms in Manhattan, it's just as likely that the hiring partners understood all too well the thirsty, dangerous ambition that a man like Nixon brings to his career.

How does one explain this man, then, who achieved almost everything a political aspirant could want in America—and who would use his role in the Red Scare to vault into the top ranks of politics? Nixon had, for one, a work ethic to put Abraham Lincoln to shame. He grew up on the rim of genteel poverty. He climbed his way to the top of a tiny college in the orange groves outside Los Angeles, to the top of Duke Law School, to the attention of the Southern California Republican establishment, and on to Capitol Hill. He was a grind, often a humorless one, but he always read the briefings, always did his homework, always knew more than anyone else in the room, even if he was far from the smartest.

But there are lots of grinds in Washington. The city then, as always, stood on the backs of a thousand class presidents, debate champions, straight-A students, and summas cum laude. What Nixon also had, the thing that made voters and colleagues and fundraisers swarm to him, was his unerring feel for the moment. He knew when to strike, when to hold off, when to tie himself to a cause and when to cut loose. He might not always be able to read a person—he was never that good with close-in conversation or combat—but he could read a room, and a country. Like an ace stock picker, he bought low and sold high, knowing that was the best way to win.

Nixon's decision to join HUAC shows that skill in all its Machiavellian frill. He had signed on to the committee at its low point, after two years in which John Rankin played Edgar Bergen to Committee Chairman John Wood's Charlie McCarthy. As a victorious first-time candidate in 1946, Nixon had seen how eagerly voters reacted to "Had Enough?," his party's rhetorical-question-as-slogan, declaring it time for America to get back to business and tough on Communism. He was careful not to go full-on against the New Deal, and he was careful not to get over his skis against Communism in Washington. Other candidates did, successful ones, and he was fine with that. Let them play the outrage card and make him look moderate in contrast.

True, HUAC under Chairman Thomas did not promise to be much better than it was under Wood. And Rankin was still there, fulminating in his race hatred. So at first, Nixon lay low. He sat out many of the Hollywood hearings, and when he did make an appearance, he threw himself behind Ronald Reagan's warning against witch hunts and blacklists. But Nixon also made sure to show his anti-Communist bona fides early. His first speech on the floor of the House, on February 17, 1947, was about a citation for contempt against Gerhart Eisler, a Soviet official charged with contempt of Congress for refusing to appear before HUAC. Nixon accused Eisler of being one of Moscow's top agents in America, and demanded that he talk or go to prison. But he also aired a note of caution. "It is essential as members of this House that we defend vigilantly the fundamental rights of freedom of speech and freedom of the press," Nixon told his colleagues. "But we must bear in mind that the rights of free speech and free press do not carry with them the right to advocate the destruction of the very government which protects the freedom of an individual to express his views."

Meanwhile he and his fellow HUAC member and future Senate colleague, Karl Mundt, created one of the few pieces of legislation ever to emerge from the committee, the so-called Mundt-Nixon bill. It would require all Communists to register with the government and for the party to declare the sources of funding for any printed or broadcast material published by a Communist front. Nixon became its floor manager. It passed the House, 319 to 58, but died in the Senate.

Nixon did not think much, at first, of the rumpled man who sat before the committee on the morning of August 3, 1948. They were in executive session, out of the public eye, to determine if Whittaker Chambers was ready for prime time. Reporters and photographers waited outside to see what came of it. Nixon, for one, doubted that anything would. "I could hardly believe this man was our witness," he wrote in his memoirs. "Whittaker Chambers was one of the most disheveled-looking persons I had ever seen. Everything about him seemed wrinkled and unpressed."

Chairman Thomas was not there that day, and so Mundt, as the ranking Republican, ran the hearing. He asked Chambers to step outside the chamber for photos. The two of them stood side by side as the photographers angled for shots, calling for different poses. "Let 'em read something!" "Make out he's showing you something, Congressman!" "Just one more!"

Back inside McNaughton, taking a seat beside his friend, said Chambers had a statement for them to read. That's when things changed. "It was three pages of pure dynamite, composed in the man's careful prose," Stripling recalled. Not only did it outline a life spent in the Communist underground, but it confirmed most of what Elizabeth Bentley had told the committee, including names and places. Most explosive, though, was its mention of Alger Hiss.

At just forty-three but with a boyish face that made him seem even younger, Hiss was already among the most powerful men in the Washington foreign policy establishment. He looked like a junior version of Dean Acheson, one of his many mentors: tall, slightly hollow-cheeked, perfectly coiffed hair, perfectly tailored suits. He had grown up in Baltimore, in what Murray Kempton called "shabby gentility," after his father, a once successful businessman, slit his own throat when an investment soured. Alger was just two. His mother raised him and his four siblings on a small inheritance. It was enough to give him the education he deserved, and from an early age it was clear he was bound for great things. He graduated Phi Beta Kappa from Johns Hopkins and soared at Harvard Law School. There he sufficiently impressed Professor Felix Frankfurter, who put him into the Boston-Washington pipeline of legal elites. He clerked for Justice Oliver Wendell Holmes Jr., worked for a spell in a top-rung Boston firm, then returned to Washington to join Henry Wallace's brain trust at the Department of Agriculture.

In 1936 he moved to the State Department, where he served in a series of increasingly prestigious positions. By the end of the war his star was glowing: He served as executive secretary for the Dumbarton Oaks conference, where the United Nations was designed; he attended the Big Three conference at Yalta, where postwar geopolitics were planned; and he served as the general secretary of the charter convention of the United Nations, in 1945 in San Francisco. A year later, with support from both Acheson and the Republican foreign policy doyen John Foster Dulles, he assumed the presidency of the Carnegie Endowment for International Peace. All this, and he was just forty-one.

Hiss's name was not new to Nixon, even though he said otherwise in his 1962 memoir, *Six Crises*. Soon after arriving in Washington, Nixon had met with John Cronin, a Jesuit priest and a leading figure in Catholic anti-Communism. The FBI had been selectively leaking documents to Cronin for years, including what it knew about Hiss. Cronin duly passed along the details to Nixon. They were just supposition, unsupported claims, possibly little better than rumor. But here, with Chambers, was something new: a man who claimed not just to have heard that Hiss was a Communist, but to know it for a fact.

Stripling knew exactly what to do with that dynamite. He had already reserved the largest room on the House side of Capitol Hill, the Ways and Means Committee chamber, in the event that a high-profile witness should come along. The Bentley hearing was held there. He suggested the committee move, and invite the press and public to join. The Ways and Means room was in the New House Office Building (later renamed the Longworth Building), across the street, and Chambers and the committee members quickly made their way there through Washington's muggy morning air, followed by a phalanx of journalists, "a buzzing surge," as Chambers recalled, who shouted to passing journalists and legislative aides "open session! Open session!" as they hustled along.

The Ways and Means room was truly grand, with capacious rows of seating split by a central aisle leading up to an angled, tiered dais, capable of seating forty-three members, when the full committee was in session. Its chairman was always one of the most powerful figures in Congress. The members of HUAC could only occupy a small portion of those seats, though the rest of the room soon filled with press and onlookers. Even as the committee and its witness took their places, technicians were installing lights, microphones, cameras and all the mechanical paraphernalia needed to bring the hearing at once to the world. Chambers understood that his moment had come, that whatever place in history he was to occupy would be defined by what happened in the next few hours. "I wondered how, with my low-pitched voice, I could even make myself heard," he wrote. The room was hot, and Chambers was operating on just a few hours of sleep.

Seated in the same chair Bentley had occupied a few days before, Chambers read his statement. He explained how he had broken with the party and warned the Roosevelt administration, but with little result. He spoke quietly, haltingly, grandiosely, comparing himself to a soldier. "I regarded my action in going to the government as a simple act of war, like the shooting of an armed enemy in combat," he said. "At that moment in history, I was one of the few men on this side of the battle who could perform this service."

He then went back in time, to describe his connections to the underground circle of Communists around Harold Ware, the economist posted to the Department of Agriculture, and to name its core members: Ware himself, plus the lawyers John Abt, Lee Pressman, and Alger Hiss. "The purpose of this group at that time was not primarily espionage," Chambers was careful to note. "Its original purpose was the Communist infiltration of the American government."

His statement was short, just three pages, but it took what seemed an eternity to finish it, especially his peroration, in which he declared ominously, with just a hint of pomposity, that Communism was "a secret, sinister, and enormously powerful force whose tireless purpose is their enslavement."

Before the committee could start its questions, the room emptied of reporters, who had rushed out to the building's phone banks to call in their stories.

Under questioning from Stripling, Chambers explained how the Communist underground worked, how the members of the Ware Group met regularly at the home of one of its members, Henry Collins, on St. Matthews Court, southeast of Dupont Circle. How J. Peters, the head of the entire Communist underground in America, would occasionally join them to deliver, among other things, fake passports. How when he quit the party, the only people he tried to bring with him were Alger Hiss and Harry Dexter White.

One night Chambers had gone to the Hiss home, "at what I considered considerable risk to myself," to find Mrs. Hiss alone. She was also a party member, and at one point excused herself to make a phone call, "which I can only presume was to other Communists." When Chambers walked in on her, she immediately hung up. Alger came home soon after, and Chambers tried, unsuccessfully, to persuade him to come along.

When he left, Chambers said, Hiss was in tears.

"He cried?" asked Representative McDowell, somewhat incredulously.

"Yes, he did," Chambers replied. "I was very fond of Mr. Hiss."

"He must have given you some reason why he did not want to sever the relationship," Mundt interjected.

"His reasons were simply the party line."

The hearing went on, but Chambers's main points were clear. When he got up to leave, only one reporter had a question for him, a spelling check. "It took me some time to realize that a part of the press, the fact gatherers, was to play a role of active hostility to me," he wrote. Chambers stayed another night in the capital, with a friend in Olney, a Maryland suburb, then returned to his farm.

The next day the papers were filled with front-page coverage of Chambers's testimony and, alongside it, denials and condemnations from the men he named. "The Thomas committee has once again disinterred an old and particularly malodorous red herring," said John Abt, who had long since left government to work for the Congress of Industrial Organizations, the labor group. He had a point, albeit a narrow one. These were charges covering activity over a decade ago, and while Chambers might characterize the Ware Group as an attempt to influence federal policy, he couldn't demonstrate it. Nor did he once even hint at espionage.

Hiss was different. The others had been foot soldiers in the 1930s New Deal, then steadily peeled off. Lee Pressman had also gone off to the Congress of Industrial Organizations. Nathan Witt, another prominent member of the Ware Group, was in private practice. But Hiss had stayed in the government, and steadily climbed. He had been a close adviser of Franklin Roosevelt at Yalta, where, conservatives alleged, the United States gave Stalin carte blanche to turn China Communist. Hiss had helped found the United Nations. He now ran the most important foreign policy think tank in the world. It was fair to assume that he might one day return to government, maybe even as secretary of state.

If he was indeed a Communist intent on directing foreign policy, he had ample opportunities to do it.

He was the very future of the East Coast Establishment, the chosen successor to a long list of mentors: Acheson, Frankfurter, Holmes, Dulles. If he was a Communist, then every dark imagining of every red-baiter would, it seemed, be proven true. If Hiss was a Communist, then perhaps the State Department really was ridden with spies, they would say. The establishment really had sold out America. There really was, they would claim, behind the $400 suits and mirror-polished patent-leather shoes, a conspiracy to turn the country over to Moscow.

When confronted by reporters, Hiss immediately denied everything, and more vociferously than the rest. "So far as I know, I have never laid eyes on Mr. Chambers," Hiss told a reporter from *The New York Times*. "There is no basis whatever for the statements he had made about me to the Thomas Committee." To prove it, he added, he had sent a telegram to the committee demanding that it give him a chance to deny the charges under oath.

PART II

6

One of You Is Lying

For most Americans, the story of the Red Scare began during that muggy August of 1948, with the Hiss–Chambers affair. Much had already happened: the Hollywood HUAC hearings, the Condon case, Elizabeth Bentley's testimony, the indictments against the Communist Party leadership. But like a pot slowly heating up, it was not until Chambers made his bombshell allegation that the country realized the water was near boiling. And suddenly, talk of subversion was everywhere, centered on the question of whether one of America's most esteemed diplomats was, in fact, a Communist. At a time of growing tensions with the Soviet Union and fears of another global war, the Hiss–Chambers story split the country. Depending on which side you were on, the performance that unfolded over the next sixteen months was a tragedy, a thriller, a Christian morality play, even a dark comedy. It is part of the postwar founding myth, the big bang at the beginning of an era, announcing who were to be the good guys and who were to be the bad.

The actors chosen to play those roles differed depending on the viewer. If one believed Chambers and not Hiss, then everything became clear: the righteousness of the anti-Communist cause, the venality of the left, the ingrained bias of the media and the political establishment. But if one believed Hiss and not Chambers, then the opposite became equally clear: that the right was fixated on destroying the left at all costs, that the forces of reaction in America were always ready to claw it back from progress, that the goodness of a man meant nothing in the face of such insidiousness. There was little room for middle ground, little consideration that both charges might be true: that Hiss was guilty, and that many on the right were using his guilt to their own ends. In some ways the actual truth at the heart of the case, whether Chambers or Hiss was lying—and one of them surely was—mattered much less than what it came to represent, the era of hysteria it did so much to catalyze and, for decades to come, the seemingly stark but in fact quite complicated conflict between left and right in America.

The symbolic distinction between the two men became glaringly apparent the moment Alger Hiss entered the House Caucus Room on the morning of August 5, 1948. It was just two days after Chambers's testimony, but Hiss insisted he was ready and eager to clear his name. It was wise of him to move fast, as this he said/he said story had already taken over the news, usually snail-paced in the August doldrums. Even the presidential campaign season had slowed to a crawl. Capitol Hill was in session, but just barely, seemingly intent on proving Truman's accusation that, under the Republicans, it was a "do-nothing Congress." But things were astir abroad. The Berlin Blockade, and America's massive airlift in response, was further sharpening the tensions of the incipient Cold War, as were daily reports of Communist advances in China. Every day, it seemed, the threat of Communism grew larger, and closer. Now it had come to the Capitol.

Hiss that morning was everything Chambers had not been: trim, confident, dressed neatly in a gray summer-weight suit with a black silk tie and white pocket square. His hair was cut tight to his head and parted on the far left. Chambers had seemed to wither under the flashbulbs of the press; Hiss appeared to blossom like a hothouse flower. He was not yet a household name, but he was liked and respected around Washington. "I remember Alger Hiss best of all for a kind of distinction that had to be seen to be believed," his friend, the lawyer Lee Pressman, later told Murray Kempton. "If we were standing at the bar with the British ambassador and you were told to give a package to the ambassador's valet, you would give it to the ambassador before you gave it to Alger." If Chambers was a rumpled old suit, Hiss was a Savile Row tuxedo.

"I am not and never have been a member of the Communist Party," Hiss began, slowly, intently. He spoke what was then called the Transatlantic Accent, a practiced set of vocal mannerisms popular among the

East Coast elite and certain Hollywood stars in the mid-twentieth century as a way of sounding more polished, vaguely British, even slightly aristocratic. He categorically denied everything Chambers had told the committee. "I do not and never have adhered to the tenets of the Communist Party. I am not and never have been a member of any Communist-front organization. I have never followed the Communist Party line, directly or indirectly. To the best of my knowledge, none of my friends is a Communist." He repeated his blanket denial of ever having met Chambers, or even heard his name until 1947, when FBI agents came to New York to query him. At Robert Stripling's request, he ran through his academic and professional career, reinforcing once more the formidability of the man seated before the committee.

Almost immediately Hiss tussled with Representative Nixon. Hiss said that multiple government officials had invited him to come to Washington in 1933 to work as assistant general counsel to the Agricultural Adjustment Administration. But he named just one, Jerome Frank, the general counsel. Nixon asked the names of the rest.

"There were some others," Hiss replied. "Is it necessary? There are so many witnesses who use names rather loosely before your committee, and I would rather limit myself."

"You made the statement," Nixon said.

"The statement is correct."

Hiss maneuvered with ease, and no small amount of condescension, among the committee's questions, tweaking and correcting their statements with lawyerly, arrogant precision. When Karl Mundt, who was sitting that day as HUAC chairman, called Whittaker Chambers a man "whom you say you have never seen," Hiss interjected, "As far as I know, I have never seen him."

He could also be disarmingly funny. When Stripling showed him a picture of Chambers, Hiss took a good look and said, "If this is a picture of Mr. Chambers, he is not particularly unusual looking. He looks like a lot of people. I might even mistake him for the chairman of this committee."

The crowd laughed, and so did the portly Mundt, who indeed bore a slight resemblance to Chambers. "I hope you are wrong in that," the chairman chuckled.

But Hiss's charisma was lost on Nixon, who sat quietly, calculating. Hiss may not have realized it at the time, but their brief exchange had made him an enemy of Richard Nixon, a man who over a long career to come would become infamous for keeping lists of those who crossed him. Hiss was Harvard, privilege, and elite condescension, the fuel that fired Nixon's resentment and ambition. From then on, Stripling remembered, "it was a personal thing."

Nixon, sitting on the dais, saw not just an enemy but an opportunity. Both Hiss and Chambers had made sworn statements, and one of them was lying. Later in the session, Nixon suggested that Chambers and Hiss be brought together, "so that any possibility of a mistake in identity may be cleared up." It was something Hiss had already requested, though it's unclear if he thought the committee would go for it. To Nixon, it was a chance to lay a trap.

Why did Nixon bet on Chambers, when the smart money seemed to be against him? For one, Nixon, with his unerring political sense, thought he smelled something not quite right about Hiss. It was not just his condescension, or his impudence. It was the lawyerly way that he crafted his statements, and tweaked those made by the committee members. And as much as Nixon disdained Chambers, he increasingly found him to be "a man of extraordinary intellectual gifts" who had "inner strength and depth." Like so many other fervent anti-Communists, Nixon saw the era's players arrayed in opposing black-and-white ranks, with every Communist a nefarious, unreliable, unmanly operator and everyone opposed to them a noble, forthright American. In that easy calculation, all Nixon had to do was decide which man was which and proceed from there.

Perhaps there was nothing to it. But Nixon was shrewd enough to know that when the herd rallies in one direction, the real money is made going the other way.

Hiss ended his testimony at 12:35 p.m. Virtually everyone in the room—the members of the committee, the press, the few onlookers who had managed to snag a seat—agreed that he had won the day. John Rankin, stepping down from the dais, shook his hand. He "absolutely took over that hearing," Stripling said, "took it over immediately." Hiss's performance, Nixon later wrote, "was as brilliant as Chambers's had been lackluster." *The Wash-ington Post* and others rushed to Hiss's side, claiming he was "innocent," having been "spattered with mud." Even Republicans were skeptical. "I don't want to prejudge the case," Christian Herter, a representative from Massachusetts, told Nixon, "but I'm afraid the Committee has been taken in by Chambers."

A few hours later, at a press conference, a reporter asked President Truman if he thought the whole search for Communists within the government had been a "red herring." Riding high off the news of Hiss's stellar performance that morning, the president heartily agreed. The grand jury, he went on, had not "revealed anything that everybody hasn't known all along, or hasn't been presented to the grand jury. That is where it has to be taken, in the first place, if you are going to do anything about it. They are slandering a lot of people that don't deserve it." Truman wanted things both ways: He used anti-Communist scare tactics when they served his foreign policy interests, and he had little concern about using loyalty tests to shore up his domestic political position. But he showed a different side in his press comments and private conversations. Like most liberals, he believed that Communism was mostly an international issue, and that domestic Communism was doomed to fail because of the strength of the American economic system and the democratic sensibility of the American public. To him, the inhospitability of the country's political soil to the hard left was self-evident and, like many liberals in the late 1940s, he assumed that the public would tire of red-baiting as soon as it failed to bring in a substantive catch. Hiss's performance on August 5 seemed proof that Truman was right.

The members of the Un-American Activities Committee retired to their chambers, in executive session away from the public and press, licking their wounds "in a state of virtual shock," Nixon remembered. Chambers, most concluded, was a fraud, and they'd been had. "We're ruined," said one. "Let's wash our hands of the whole thing," said another, by handing over the case to the Department of Justice.

But Nixon's preternatural political senses put him well ahead of the rest. He already understood that Hiss had made an unforced, potentially fatal error. All Hiss had to do was deny that he had ever been a Communist. But he had gone further, to deny that he had ever seen or known Chambers. And had used those lawyerly phrases—"as far as I know," "by the name of Whittaker Chambers"—leaving room for lapses in memory, to be claimed later if necessary. Hiss was clever, Nixon decided, but in this instance he had been too clever. Nixon bet that he could find evidence that the two men had in fact known each other, and from there, possible evidence that Hiss had indeed been a member of the Communist Party.

Nixon persuaded Mundt to appoint him as head of a special subcommittee to pursue the case, starting with a new interview with Chambers. From here on, the Hiss–Chambers affair would be Nixon's, just as he wanted. "I was opposing the President of the United States and the majority of the press corps opinion, which is so important to the career of anyone in elective office," Nixon wrote years later, with no small sense of self-satisfaction. "Yet I could not go against my own conscience and my conscience told me that, in this case, the rather unsavory-looking Chambers was telling the truth, and the honest-looking Hiss was lying."

Nixon moved quickly. Just two days after Hiss's testimony, he called Chambers back, this time for an executive session at the Foley Square courthouse, in lower Manhattan. They met in a wood-paneled courtroom on the first floor. Chambers had already replied to Hiss's denial, saying he stood by what he had told HUAC. Nixon poked and prodded at that testimony, looking for weaknesses. Had Chambers ever used an alias? (Yes, he had gone by the name Carl in the Communist underground.) How did he know Hiss was a Communist? (J. Peters, the head of the party's underground, had told him.) How well did he know Hiss, really? (Chambers unloaded a wealth of details, describing the various Hiss homes, their parsimonious furnishings and eating habits, their dilapidated Ford Roadster whose windshield wipers had to be operated by hand.)

One of the committee's aides, Ben Mandel, asked, "Did Mr. Hiss have any hobbies?"

"Yes, he did," Chambers replied. Both Hiss and his wife, Priscilla, were amateur ornithologists. "They used to get up early in the morning and go to Glen Echo, out the canal, to observe birds. I recall once they saw, to their great excitement, a prothonotary warbler."

"A very rare specimen," said Representative McDowell, a birder himself.

"I never saw one," Chambers replied. "I am also fond of birds."

Nixon returned to Washington believing that Chambers was telling the truth, but also full of nagging doubts. Chambers's memory seemed too clear, too perfect. He assigned Stripling to track down the details Chambers had supplied. He called up a friendly reporter, Bert Andrews of the *New York Herald Tribune*, for his thoughts on the testimony; he did the same with William P. Rogers, an aide to the Senate Subcommittee on Investigations, and John Foster Dulles, one of Hiss's mentors. He even went out to visit Chambers at Pipe Creek Farm, his retreat in Maryland, "not so much to get more information from him as to gain a more intimate impression of what kind of man he really was."

Nixon and Chambers were both Quakers; so was Priscilla Hiss. This is, of course, pure coincidence. But it mattered in one respect. During their conversation that evening on the farm, Nixon idly mentioned that he was a member of the denomination, after which Chambers immediately snapped his fingers. "That reminds me of something," he said. "Priscilla often used the plain speech"—thee and thou, hast and art—"talking to Alger at home." It was, Nixon realized at once, the sort of detail that only an intimate friend would know. It wasn't hard evidence, he conceded, "but the way he blurted it out convinced me that he was telling the truth."

Nixon went yet again to Chambers's farm, this time with Andrews and Stripling. Andrews was a fierce critic of Truman's loyalty program and a Pulitzer Prize winner, for a piece about the administration's Kafkaesque treatment of government employees. He grilled Chambers for three hours. The reporter came away convinced Chambers was telling the truth. On the drive back to Washington, Stripling announced that he was sure as well. But, he added, "I don't think Chambers has yet told us the whole story. He is holding something back. He is trying to protect somebody."

Hiss had become Nixon's primary focus, but the full HUAC continued to plow through Elizabeth Bentley's original charges. J. Parnell Thomas, now back in the chairman's seat, was pushing for a separate grand jury to sit in Washington, because he didn't trust the Department of Justice and the

New York jury to move quickly enough. He called a string of witnesses, all of whom declined to answer questions on the grounds that it might incriminate them, a deployment of the Fifth Amendment that would become a regular feature in HUAC hearings to come. On August 13, the committee called Harry Dexter White, the president of the International Monetary Fund and a former New Deal economist, to the witness table. He too forcefully denied being a Communist. "The principles in which I believed, and by which I live, make it impossible for me to ever do a disloyal act or anything against the interests of my country," White testified.

An avuncular intellectual with a bushy mustache and scholarly spectacles, White had initially asked Thomas if, in light of a chronic heart condition, he might take a break every hour. Thomas decided to make a joke of it. After White admitted to knowing a few of the people named by Bentley through pickup games of softball and table tennis, Thomas read White's request aloud, for the record, then laughed. "For a person who had a severe heart condition, you certainly can play a lot of sports."

White explained that he hadn't played since his heart condition set in. But Thomas just guffawed. Three days later, White died of a heart attack at his farm in New Hampshire.

In an instant, any shred of credibility the committee had left among the press vanished. HUAC was no longer merely the destroyer of careers; it was guilty of manslaughter. "I certainly knew Harry White better than the inquisitorial bigots who put the final unbearable strain on his ailing heart," wrote the journalist I. F. Stone in his weekly newsletter. "And I do not think Harry White was a Communist, if the word is to be used correctly and without quotation marks." Michael Straight, writing in *The New Republic* that week, was even harsher: "The committee has already, and illegally, assumed the role of prosecutor, jury, judge and firing squad. And after its work of character assassination, shooting seems almost superfluous."

Hiss returned to the committee on August 16, 1948, to sit in executive session. He had been told through some back channel the gist of what Chambers had told Nixon in New York, and he shifted his strategy accordingly. No longer was he so adamant about his innocence. He was reserved and cagey. Once again, Nixon took control of the questions.

Chambers, he told Hiss, had gone by the name Carl in the Communist underground. Did that ring a bell?

"I do not recall anyone by the name of Carl that could remotely be connected with the kind of testimony Mr. Chambers has given," Hiss replied.

Nixon showed him photos of Chambers. How about now?

"The face has a certain familiarity," he said. "I am not prepared to say that I have never seen the man whose pictures are now shown me. I said that when I was on the stand." That was true, in one interpretation, but Hiss was widening the loophole. He insisted he couldn't be sure unless he saw him up close, heard him speak, observed his mannerisms.

But all that, he said, was beside the point. "The issue is not whether this man knew me and I don't remember him," he insisted. "The issue is whether he had a particular conversation that he has said he had with me and which I have denied and whether I am a member of the Communist Party or ever was." Perhaps Hiss had discovered the trap he had walked into.

He and Nixon went back and forth like that, for hours. At one point Representative Edward Hébert, a Democrat from Louisiana, said, "Whichever one of you is lying is the greatest actor that America has ever produced."

Finally, suddenly, Hiss said that, in fact, he did remember a man who looked like Chambers. But he didn't know him by that name, or by Carl. He knew him as George Crosley. He had approached Hiss in the 1930s as a journalist from out of town working on an article of congressional oversight of the munitions industry. They met a few times. Crosley had asked if he knew of a place he could stay. Hiss, who had been in the process of moving, had allowed him to sublet his old apartment for a few days. He had even let him use his old car, the Ford Roadster with the hand-cranked wipers. As a gift, Crosley had given Hiss a rug. But Crosley never paid his rent, and the two fell out of touch after he vacated the apartment. He did, Hiss recalled, have very bad teeth.

Nixon pressed on, unsure of Hiss's game but sure that he was trying to give himself new ways out of the congressman's trap. He and Stripling pressed Hiss on details that Chambers had provided. Nicknames. Pets. Hobbies. "Tennis and amateur ornithology," Hiss said.

"Did you ever see a prothonotary warbler?" Representative McDowell asked, barely able to suppress his excitement.

"I have, right here on the Potomac," Hiss said. "Do you know that place?"

"I saw one in Arlington," McDowell said.

Chambers had gotten some details wrong. But by and large, Hiss unwittingly confirmed the bulk of what his accuser had told the committee. The next step, Nixon decided, was to bring the two men together.

The very next day, Nixon, Stripling, and a small contingent of HUAC members set up a pop-up hearing in a suite at the two-thousand-room Commodore Hotel in Midtown Manhattan. It was a secret operation: Chambers was first brought to Washington, then quietly back up to New York, and finally ushered through a back door into the hotel. There they held him in an anteroom while McDowell called Hiss on the phone. The two had a previously arranged appointment at the Carnegie Endowment, but McDowell said that now he couldn't make it. Could Hiss meet him at the hotel instead? Hiss arrived in Suite 1400 soon after to find Nixon, McDowell, HUAC staffers, and a stenographer waiting.

He had wanted a confrontation, but not an unexpected one. Hiss immediately threw out excuses for whatever mistakes he might be about to make—"edgy, delaying, belligerent, fighting every inch of the way," Nixon recalled. Hiss was angry for having to cancel a dinner appointment. He had just heard about Harry Dexter White's death. And, he had read in the paper that morning, the committee apparently wanted him to take a lie detector test.

Then Chambers was brought in. He stood silently as Hiss approached him, peering at his face. Hiss asked Nixon to have Chambers open his mouth, and to say a few words, to hear his voice. At one point Nixon asked that Chambers be sworn in.

"That is a good idea," Hiss said.

Nixon wouldn't have it. "Mr. Hiss, may I say something?" he asked sternly. "I suggested that he be sworn, and when I say something like that I want no interruptions from you."

"Mr. Nixon," Hiss replied, "I think there is no occasion for you to use that tone of voice in speaking to me, and I hope the record will show what I have just said."

Hiss proceeded to examine Chambers, physically and verbally. He got up close, peering into his mouth and ears, all but prodding him with a stick. Was this the man he remembered as Crosley, Nixon asked? Hiss said he couldn't be sure, at one point suggesting that he needed to speak with Chambers's dentist to discuss work he might have had done since their last encounter. Finally, he relented. "I don't need to ask Mr. Whittaker Chambers any more questions," Hiss said. "I am now perfectly prepared to identify this man as George Crosley. . . . If he had lost both eyes and taken his nose off I would be sure."

But when Chambers said that he too could positively identify Hiss as the man he had known in the 1930s, Hiss lost his cool. He shot from his chair, shaking his fist at Chambers. "May I say for the record at this point that I would like to invite Mr. Whittaker Chambers to make those same statements out of the presence of this committee, without their being privileged for suit for libel. I challenge you to do it, and I hope you will do it damned quickly."

McDowell brought the hearing to an end. "That is all," he said. "Thank you very much."

"I don't reciprocate," Hiss shot back. He grabbed his coat and hat and charged out of the room.

Years later, Nixon wrote that after the confrontation at the Commodore that evening, he had felt a certain sadness over seeing a man of Hiss's esteem act so cravenly. But at the time, he took every advantage that his coup offered. The story of the Commodore Hotel meeting was immediately leaked—by Nixon himself—and was all over the papers by the time he returned to Washington the next day. He had removed some of the stain on the committee after White's death. Called for on-the-record comments by dozens of reporters, Nixon zinged the FBI. "It is quite significant that in eight years of investigating this case the FBI has been unable to establish the fact that these two men knew each other," he told reporters. And he lit a fire under Stripling and his investigators to dig deeper into Hiss's past to find evidence to corroborate Chambers's many details.

At the Commodore Hotel, the committee told Chambers and Hiss that they would be called to a single, public hearing before HUAC on August 25, one week hence, and Stripling wrote out subpoenas for both. And it wouldn't be just any hearing, but the first congressional hearing to be broadcast live on television. Though only about 350,000 households had televisions at the time, it was a given that every living room with a set would be crammed full of friends, relatives, neighbors, and coworkers, because it was also a given that no one would be getting much work done on what the newspapers were billing as "Confrontation Day."

It was hot that day in Washington, 92 degrees, the sort of sticky, lethargy-inducing sweatbox that the District of Columbia is famous for, made worse by the lack of sufficient air-conditioning and the restrictive clothing required in any formal setting at the time. The men crammed into the Caucus Room that morning did their best to stay cool in their summer-weight suits; the women did little better in their light dresses over nylons. More than 1,200 spectators were on hand, along with scores of reporters, cameramen, and technicians.

Chairman Thomas opened the hearing with the declaration that, as a result of what was said that day, "one of these witnesses will be tried for perjury." He was right, but only in a narrow sense. In fact what the day did was to turn a complicated political mystery into a conflict rendered in stark black-and-white terms with immediate ramifications far beyond these two men, even beyond the issue of 1930s Soviet espionage. A person believed Hiss, or they believed Chambers. And while one could certainly be a liberal who believed Hiss was lying, or a conservative who doubted Chambers, such nuance was lost in the rush to draw sides. In a pattern that has long since become a part of the American cultural psychosis, each side became a caricature of itself; each side seemingly eager to prove the other's worst impressions. What became, a few years later, known as McCarthyism, the baseless smearing of one's opponents with charges of Communist sympathies or merely insufficient anti-Communist antipathies, had its parallel in Hissism, the insistence that anyone thus accused was innocent, no matter how powerful the evidence, because in an acrobatic display of circular reasoning, the accusers were obviously McCarthyites.

With the full committee seated, Stripling took the lead on questions. At one point he asked both men to stand so they could identify each other. Most of the questions that morning, though, were for Hiss, who refused to identify Chambers as anyone other than Crosley, or as Crosley-Chambers. When Stripling insisted that his name was Chambers, Hiss retorted, "I first knew him as Crosley. What his name is today I am not prepared to testify to." He was at his lawyerly best: According to a count by a *Time* reporter, he uttered the phrase "to the best of my recollection" exactly 198 times.

The committee plowed through the details of Hiss's life in 1930s Washington, piece by piece erecting the case that Hiss had known Chambers—not briefly as Crosley, and not simply as a journalist, but in a relationship far more extensive and far more nefarious than he let on. Hiss, for his part, stuck close to his story, how he had known Crosley only briefly, constructing his own elaborate explanations to fit the committee's details. He presented a list of thirty-four people, all political and legal eminences, who would testify to his good name, while he denounced Chambers as "a self-confessed liar, spy, and traitor."

Chambers took the stand that evening, eight hours after the hearing began. Speaking in his usual slow, portentous voice, he described Hiss as "a rather romantic Communist" and, he said with a note of sadness, "the closest friend I ever had" in the party. The committee asked what happened to the Ford Roadster. Chambers said Hiss had sold it to raise funds for the party—generosity he explained as common "procedure" among Communists.

Nixon, anticipating further attacks on Chambers's character, then lobbed him a softball question, asking what motive he could have for lying about Hiss. Chambers seemed to choke back tears before uttering the words that, more than any other single utterance during the hearings past and trials to come, would establish the terms of the whole affair's significance.

"The story has spread that in testifying against Mr. Hiss I am working out of some old grudge, or motives of revenge or hatred," he said, slowly. "I do not hate Mr. Hiss. We were close friends. But we are caught in a tragedy of history. Mr. Hiss represents the concealed enemy against which we are all fighting, and I am fighting. I have testified against him with remorse and pity, but in a moment of historic jeopardy in which this nation now stands, so help me God, I could not do otherwise." After a pause, Hébert suggested that not all saints are perfect. "I am not a saint, indeed," Chambers said. But by the soliloquy he had just delivered, he had already elevated himself into the heaven of the anti-Communists.

The committee could not agree on its bounty. The members were certain they had caught Hiss. The Democrats wanted to turn over their findings to the Department of Justice for prosecution. But the Republicans, led by Nixon, wanted to keep going. There was much more to be learned, they argued, though their real motive was political—the longer they kept Hiss on the ropes, the worse it looked for Truman during a neck-and-neck race for the presidency.

From there things proceeded quickly. A reporter in Baltimore had discovered that Hiss and Chambers had both been interested in the same Maryland farm property, until Hiss pulled out and Chambers bought it. Chambers then went on *Meet the Press* and repeated his charges against Hiss, this time outside the protections of a congressional hearing, opening himself up to legal action. More witnesses were interviewed. Nixon pressed for the Foley Square grand jury to reconvene, this time to consider perjury charges against Hiss, or Chambers, or both. Finally, on August 27, 1948, Hiss sued Chambers for slander, asking $50,000 in damages, about $625,000 in today's dollars.

By now both men's careers were in tatters. John Foster Dulles had told Hiss to step aside, temporarily, from the presidency of the Carnegie Endowment, and while he managed to delay such a move for a few months, there was no question about the imminence of his departure, and that it would not be temporary. Meanwhile, despite assurances from Henry Luce, the owner of *Time*, that Chambers could remain at the magazine, it was clear that his newfound, divisive celebrity had foreclosed his future on staff.

Hiss also fueled a smear campaign against Chambers. Soon after the hearing, he demanded that someone investigate this "self-confessed liar, spy and traitor," and for good measure accused him of suffering from mental illness and being "somewhat queer." "No American," he said, "is safe from the imagination of such a man, so long as" HUAC "uses the great powers and prestige of the United States Congress to help sworn traitors to besmirch any American they may pick upon."

Chambers drew further inward, growing more paranoid. In his mind, he had been a reluctant, at times unwilling witness. And while in his August 25 testimony he spoke grandly of the "tragedy of history," he seemed to feel much more the intimate side of the equation, the rift between two old friends. And now, with Hiss lining up heavy-hitter lawyers to pursue him in court, he had to do what he could to save himself. Even his lawyers, including Harold Medina Jr., whose father would soon sit as judge in the upcoming trial against the Communist Party leadership, doubted whether he could win over a jury based on what was, in the end, simply his word, and only his word. And so, one day, sitting alone with Medina in his office atop a downtown Baltimore skyscraper, Chambers blurted out, "You feel, don't you, that there is something missing?"

Yes, Medina replied.

"There is something missing," Chambers said. "I am shielding Hiss."

Ther lawyer stared at him over his half-glasses.

"Espionage."

Foley Square

For a moment, later that fall of 1948, it looked like the Hiss–Chambers affair might fizzle out, with both men badly damaged but no resolution to the mystery at its heart. President Truman won reelection in November, and despite the doubts and struggles along the way, it wasn't even close. He captured 303 electoral college votes to Thomas Dewey's 189. He won the popular vote by 4.4 percentage points. In third place: Strom Thurmond's pro-segregation States' Rights Party, which had splintered from the Democrats over its civil rights platform. Henry Wallace, the Progressive candidate, had kept driving hard against the president throughout the fall, saying in late October that Truman "has done more than any man since Hitler to promote dictatorship in this world." He insisted that there was a "hidden vote" among the American populace, and that only a great conspiracy was keeping him out of the White House. Early on the morning of Election Day, November 2, he and his wife, Ilo, rose at their home outside South Salem, New York, and drove to their polling place in the public library. It opened at eight; they were first in line. Finished, they returned home. Wallace changed into his work clothes and spent hours gardening, ignoring the day's historic events. In the end he failed to win a single state in the Electoral College, which no one expected him to. Worse, he only received 1.1 million votes. About 400,000 of those came from New York City, which means that much of the country had simply ignored him.

Truman had overcome immense odds, beating back not only an energetic Republican Party but two third parties as well. He had proven a better

campaigner than anyone had expected. His deep well of personal discipline, which his naysayers had overlooked but Dean Acheson had noticed
early on, kept him on message and on the offensive, tagging Republicans
as ineffectual and Dewey as an empty suit, bereft of vision or ideas. And he
was lucky that Dewey had refused pressure within the Republican Party to
run on Communism as a domestic issue. "You can't shoot an idea with a
gun," Dewey liked to say. "He thought it degrading to suspect Truman personally of being soft on Communism," said Representative Hugh Scott of
Pennsylvania, the Republican National Committee chairman. "He wasn't
going around looking under beds." It was a mistake that many Republicans
would learn from, and not make again.

Not only did Truman win a full term in the White House, but the Democrats took back full control of Congress, meaning that J. Parnell Thomas,
Richard Nixon, and the rest of the Republicans on HUAC would lose control of the committee—and, presumably, the momentum behind the Hiss
investigation would slow to a halt. Rumors swirled that HUAC itself might
even be shut down. Other rumors got around Washington that the Department of Justice was preparing to close its perjury investigation. Nixon,
dejected, prepared to go on a much delayed Caribbean vacation with his
wife.

But then, once more, things started to move quickly. Stripling heard
that Chambers had dropped a "bombshell" during the closed deposition
for Hiss's slander suit against him. He and Nixon immediately went to see
him at his farm. It's true, Chambers told them, resting between chores.
There was more evidence, and something big that he had not revealed to
HUAC. He wouldn't tell them what it was, though, not there. But he did
ask for a "good photographic expert."

"I don't think he's got a thing," Nixon huffed as they drove back to Washington, and put his mind toward tropical climes. He gave Stripling orders
to subpoena Chambers. He would deal with his intransigence when he
returned. Nixon needed to rest, and to rethink his future as a young Republican on the move in a Democratic-controlled Washington.

Up until then, Chambers had never said Hiss was a spy, though the accusation was certainly assumed by the public and the press. After all, at the

August 25 hearing, Chambers himself had said that "every Communist in the United States is a potential spy or saboteur and a permanent enemy of this system of government." But after revealing to his lawyer that there was indeed espionage involved in the Hiss story, he had to prove it. First, he traveled to New York, where he retrieved the cache of documents and microfilm he had hidden in the dumbwaiter at the home of his friend's parents. He presented some of the material in another confidential deposition a few days later, claiming that Hiss himself had delivered it to him. Some were photostats of originals, while others had been typed, Chambers claimed, by Mrs. Hiss.

Why did Chambers hide the evidence in the first place? The simple answer, the one Chambers himself gave, says much about the era he was ushering in and the emergent DNA of the conservative movement he was helping to create. In 1939, when he had first secreted it away, he had been afraid of Soviet assassins—a reasonable fear, because so many people he knew, who had done much less than he had done to offend the party and Moscow, had recently been murdered. But over time, his justification for withholding the material transformed into something much more paranoid. He came to see the Communist Party and its allies, including those he imagined to be high up in the administration, as something like a host of demons, intent on destroying the slightest voice of opposition. In his mind, every year seemed to prove him right, if only in the utter silence he was met with when he tried to warn the government.

He had told Adolf Berle, the assistant secretary of state, about Hiss and the rest in 1939, to no obvious effect. He had spoken to the FBI on multiple occasions, and again, heard nothing in response. And now that he was going head-to-head with Hiss, he was met not just with disbelief, but vicious rumors, lies, and character assassination. He was, according to reporters and gossips, a drunk, mentally unstable, a closet homosexual (all of which were, in fact, true). He had poked the bear, and now it was coming for him. "The simple fact is that when I took up my little sling and aimed at Communism, I also hit something else," he wrote. "What I hit was the forces of the great socialist revolution, which, in the name of liberalism, spasmodically, incompletely, somewhat formlessly, but always in the same direction, had been inching its ice cap over the nation for two decades." Believing he had nowhere to turn and no one to trust, why wouldn't he keep some of his secrets, his only asset, in his back pocket?

Now, in late 1948, Chambers realized he had to play his last card, or else the newspapers and Nixon and HUAC might move on from him. In the early evening of December 2, he met up with two HUAC investigators in Washington and took them back to his farm. He flipped on a string of lights in his garden and proceeded to a pumpkin patch. Bending over one particular, seemingly innocuous gourd, he removed the top as if it were a jack-o-lantern and from it produced a set of five metal tins, wrapped in wax paper. He had hidden them there the day before, convinced that someone—HUAC, a reporter, the FBI, maybe Soviet military intelligence—would toss his house trying to find them. "Here's what you're looking for," he told the investigators.

The men took the material back to Washington. They had the film developed. Some of it had been damaged beyond repair. But the rest was, as Stripling had probably grown tired of saying, "pure dynamite." He contacted Nixon, who in a dash of élan speedboated and seaplaned his way from Acklins Island, in the Bahamas, to Miami, then on to Washington. There, cleanly shaven, he and Stripling posed for photos, hunched over the documents with a tiny plastic magnifying glass, perusing what everyone immediately took to calling the Pumpkin Papers.

Suddenly, it was a race between Nixon and the Justice Department. Nixon wanted credit for uncovering hard evidence of Soviet espionage—and at the hands of a New Deal princeling, to boot. But after almost closing its grand jury investigation, the Justice Department moved fast too, calling Chambers to New York on December 6, 1948, and demanding that Nixon and HUAC hand over the microfilm. Nixon refused, claiming to have lost confidence in the department, which was both a fair conclusion, given its recently stated desire to shut down the whole investigation, and a politically convenient high horse to mount. And the department had equal reasons to wonder what would become of HUAC, with the Democrats coming back to power and Truman promising to shutter the committee entirely. It in turn refused to let HUAC speak with Chambers, who was under its subpoena. Stalemate.

Instead of handing over the microfilms, Nixon showcased them to the public. In a flurry of hearings in December, just weeks before Democrats were set to take control of HUAC, he called forth current and former State Department officials to attest to the documents' value and the potential damage their theft could have caused, had Chambers handed them over to the Soviets instead of hiding them in a house. Truth be told, the documents themselves were not all that interesting—low-level, procedural correspondence. But they were also the sort of items that only someone relatively high up in government would have access to. That person had then passed them on to an avowed Communist agent, Chambers. And a compelling case had already been made that the person in question was Alger Hiss.

After a heated argument in a suite back at the Commodore Hotel in New York, Nixon and lawyers from the Department of Justice reached a deal: prints of the microfilmed documents in exchange for access to Chambers. And over a three-hour interview with Nixon at the hotel, Chambers revealed all: how Hiss had brought documents home in his briefcase, to be given to Chambers to have photographed overnight, or to Priscilla, who would type them out. Either way, they went back in his briefcase and back to the State Department the next morning. And it was no coincidence that Chambers had evidence on Hiss; he had gathered material on all the major figures in his network, just in case they might become useful after he left the party.

Hiss's defenders threw out counterarguments—for example, that the typeface on the copied documents did not match the Hiss family typewriter, which had in the meantime somehow vanished. But after an expert matched the typeface on other letters written by Priscilla Hiss with the typeface on documents in the Chambers collection, the grand jury decided it had heard enough. On December 15, its last day in session, it indicted Alger Hiss for two counts of perjury: that he had lied when he said he had not seen Chambers after January 1, 1937, and that he had lied when he said he had not unlawfully given documents to Chambers. Because the statute of limitations for espionage had lapsed, it was the closest the government could get to charging Hiss with being a Soviet spy.

The news rocked Washington. After Truman's victory in November, it had appeared as if the president and the Democrats had managed to contain the Communists-in-government issue, at least as a political threat. For a moment, it had seemed like Truman was right—that the whole thing had been a red herring. Now, suddenly, it appeared the opposite was true: Not only had there been a homegrown spy in Washington, but he had been cultivated by the East Coast Establishment and given positions of increasing authority within the Roosevelt administration. Even the most paranoid versions of the conservative attack on the New Deal—that it was part of a Soviet plot to take over America—now seemed plausible.

It was Nixon's star turn, and should have been a high point for HUAC as well. But the committee always found a way to sully itself during its brief moments of glory. In 1946, following a long career in government, a man named Laurence Duggan became the president of the Institute of International Education, which facilitated student exchange programs. But like Hiss, he was dogged by rumors of espionage. The FBI interviewed him at his home in Scarsdale, a New York suburb. By December 1948, the whispers had grown louder, and it became likely that he too would soon be called to Washington to testify. On December 20, Duggan fell to his death from his office on the sixteenth floor of a Midtown Manhattan office building. The New York Police Department's report was inconclusive, ruling that he had either jumped or accidentally slipped while on a window ledge. But everyone assumed he had been driven to suicide by HUAC. Representative Mundt, when asked for his reaction by reporters, said, "We will give out the other" names "as they jump out of windows."

Coming so soon after the death of Harry Dexter White, Duggan's apparent suicide, and Mundt's crass response to it, turbocharged a new round of public recrimination. Duggan, like White, was well liked among the Washington–New York–Cambridge intelligentsia. The journalist Edward R. Murrow called on HUAC to "consult their actions and their consciences" in shame. Archibald MacLeish wrote a poem, "The Black Day," which ran in the *New York Herald Tribune* and read, in part, "God help that country where the liar's shame / Outshouts the decent silence to defame / The dead man's honor and defile his name."

Chambers insisted he never said Duggan was a spy, just a Communist. Over forty years later, the government finally declassified transcripts of intercepted Soviet transmissions. They showed what Chambers was unwilling to say: Duggan was, in fact, a spy, and an active and eager one, sending Moscow intelligence about U.S. plans for the invasion of Italy during World War II. Mundt may have been crude, but on this, at least, he was not wrong. Duggan's suicide, and the divided response to it, helped deepen the animosities of the Red Scare: The hunt for Communists was either an imperfect, messy, and absolutely necessary campaign—or it was a violent violation of civil liberties on an unprecedented scale.

Alger Hiss and Laurence Duggan were not the only alleged spies to make news as the calendar turned over to 1949. We remember Hiss's name in particular because of his prominence, and the drama of his clash with Chambers. But there was someone else, largely forgotten, who also occupied the news at the time: a twenty-seven-year-old Justice Department clerk named Judith Coplon.

J. Edgar Hoover took great pride in never having a Soviet mole discovered in the ranks of the FBI. The Coplon case was his closest call. Judith Coplon was one of tens of thousands of young, highly educated women who came to Washington during World War II to staff the rapidly expanding security state. After graduating from Barnard, she worked first for the Economic Warfare section of the War Department, and then, starting in late 1944, as an analyst in the Foreign Agents Registration section of the Department of Justice. The latter position put her in close contact with a constant flow of sensitive information about the intelligence activity of officials from dozens of countries, not just the Soviet Union but allies like Britain and Canada too.

Coplon was by all accounts a smart, serious, driven woman, and her superiors regularly promoted her, entrusting her with more and more sensitive material. She began taking graduate courses at American University. She rose steadily, even though from the beginning the Justice Department knew about her Communist leanings—an initial background check revealed that she had joined the Young Communist League in college, and she wrote pro-Soviet opinion pieces for the Barnard student newspaper. But she soon found that the government was shockingly lax about following through on such disclosures, either because there weren't enough people to do so or because the administration didn't make it a priority in the first place. The Foreign Agents Registration section where Coplon worked was located at Arlington Hall, a cluster of old buildings about two miles west of the Pentagon, in Northern Virginia. It had once been a girls school and also held part of the Army's signal intelligence operation. It was a great place to be a spy.

Coplon was not recruited by Moscow. She sought out a role in the Soviet espionage apparatus herself, and within a year she was funneling out documents and information. She was "a serious person who is politically well developed and there is no doubt of her sincere desire to help us," wrote Vladimir Pravdin, a KGB agent who posed as a reporter for TASS, the Soviet state news agency, and helped vet her as a mole. "She had no doubts about whom she is working for." She appeared, under the code name Sima, in messages intercepted as early as July 1944, though the transmissions were not deciphered until 1946. It took another two years for the bureau to conclude that "Sima is without doubt identical with Judith Coplon," Hoover wrote in a memo to the special agent in charge of the bureau's Washington field office.

As was the case with most spies, the material Coplon passed along was in and of itself inconsequential and mundane: comments on Soviet visa applications, personnel changes, granular reports about consular activities. But to the receiver, every item of information is a puzzle piece, whose shape may seem random and insignificant in itself but when added to others helps provide a full picture of a government's collective way of thinking.

By the end of 1948, the FBI, relying on intercepted Soviet communications, was sure that Coplon was a spy. But arresting her would have meant revealing the existence of the government's top secret intercept program, code-named Venona. Begun in 1943, the program was unknown even to many high-ranking White House officials, and remained that way until 1995, fifteen years after it ended. The American intelligence community, including the FBI, considered Venona so valuable that it passed over repeated opportunities to arrest Soviet spies for fear that doing so would reveal the program's existence, and perforce bring its worth to an end. Such was the case with Coplon. Instead, the bureau decided to watch her—tap her phones, track her movements, and try to learn something about the Soviets' methods. It didn't take long. The bureau told the director of the Foreign Agents Registration section about what it had found, and created a task force to run a surveillance project with Coplon at its center. In mid-January 1949 agents trailed Coplon on a trip to New York to visit her parents. Instead of heading from Penn Station to their home in Brooklyn, she went to Washington Heights, near the northern end of Manhattan. There they watched her meet with Valentine Gubitchev, a member of the Soviet delegation at the U.N. and, the bureau already suspected, an espionage agent.

Back in Washington, the FBI devised a ruse—a decoy document, filled with apparently sensitive information, that agents made sure passed through Coplon's hands. It took the agents two attempts, but on March 4 they saw her and Gubitchev in what appeared to be a handoff in Manhattan, under the Third Avenue Elevated line near 14th Street. As dozens of bystanders gawked, plainclothed agents poured onto the street, seemingly from nowhere, surrounding the couple and placing them in handcuffs.

Gubitchev had an envelope of small bills on him. In Coplon's black purse was the bureau's decoy, folded into a tiny, cellophane-taped square, along with thirty-four "slips," a type of index card that contained references to FBI surveillance reports, though not the material in the reports themselves. She also had several biographical sketches of other government employees that, the government asserted, were meant to be used for recruiting.

The Department of Justice pressed two sets of charges—one, to be tried in Washington, against Coplon alone, for espionage, and the other against her and Gubitschev, for conspiracy, to take place in New York City. The Coplon trials have long since faded from memory, overshadowed by the Hiss trial, happening at the same time. But the proceedings were widely covered, both in the national newspapers and the East Coast tabloids. As they had done with Elizabeth Bentley, reporters one-upped each other in their efforts to sexualize the defendant. They described what she wore to court, taking special note of her quasi-Bohemian look—black berets, tweed skirts—and magnified her every word spoken above a whisper to make her out to be emotional, unserious, and immature.

Coplon's gender, and her career success, were significant beyond prurient stabs at sex appeal. In her late twenties but still single, working in a professional capacity once reserved for men, her very existence exemplified the dramatic gains that women had made during the Great Depression and the war, and stood as a challenge to anyone who wanted to reverse them, now that the war was over. "She seemed the model postwar 'government girl,' fetchingly clad in snug sweaters and New Look skirts," wrote Sam Tanenhaus after her death in 2011. More than one commentator concluded that fighting the Cold War was best left to men.

Like the Hiss–Chambers affair, the Coplon case highlighted the emerging tensions between HUAC and Truman's Department of Justice. Representative Nixon was only the loudest to capitalize on the Coplon case as evidence of a failure by the department to take the Communist threat seriously, a claim that bolstered HUAC's own standing in comparison. "In my opinion," he told reporters on March 5, "this case shows why the department may be unfit to carry out the responsibility of protecting the national security against Communist infiltration."

The government wasted no time. The first trial, in Washington, opened on April 25, 1949. Coplon's defense team had a surprising strategy: Her lawyer demanded that not only the FBI slips but the underlying, highly classified files associated with them be entered as evidence. He was, in effect, daring the Department of Justice to drop the case, figuring that Hoover and Clark would rather let his client walk free than expose such sensitive material. But his ploy failed. Prosecutors fought the motion, but when the judge sided with the defense and ordered the files to be submitted, Hoover and Attorney General Clark concluded that the material wasn't sensitive enough to keep secret, and that they would rather see Coplon convicted.

The jury took twenty-seven hours to deliberate, and on June 30, 1949, it returned a guilty verdict. Right away, Coplon's lawyer loudly demanded that the judge delay sentencing until after the results of the second trial, with Gubitchev in New York, and to let her free on her own recognizance until then. The judge rejected Coplon's pleas for a delay, but the next day released her on $20,000 bail, after sentencing her to three to ten years in prison.

Coplon's next trial took place in New York's Foley Square courthouse—the same place where Alger Hiss and the Communist Party leaders indicted under the Smith Act would also be tried, at almost the same time, in the summer and fall of 1949.

If there was a main stage for this first act of the Red Scare, a single location where so many of its pivotal events played out, it was Foley Square. Built on a swamp and former slum, the thirty-seven-story building was designed in 1932 by Cass Gilbert, architect of the nearby Woolworth Building and, in Washington, the Supreme Court building. He had struggled to fill the awkwardly polygonal site with district and appellate courts, a law library, and offices for dozens of judges and clerks. He hid all these various functions behind an overpowering façade: a wide staircase climbs to ten Corinthian columns, the centerpiece of a six-story base above which rises a thirty-story tower topped by a terra-cotta pyramid. Practically every surface is detailed with symbols of law and order: owls, sheaves of wheat, busts of Plato and Moses. The overwhelming impression is one of justice, fairness, and equality before the law. The theme continues inside, with a twenty-nine-foot-high main lobby covered in polished marble—green-veined on the floor, creamy on the walls—and, beyond it, fifteen two-story courtrooms resplendent in oak and even more marble. Gilbert intended it to be a classical temple to the rule of law; in its thoughtful luxury, it is a reminder of a time when cities spared no expense when it came to the symbols of civic life.

But not everyone was impressed. When the courthouse opened in 1937, the architecture critic Lewis Mumford derided its "bad design and fake grandeur." To him it embodied in marble and bronze the tension between the legitimate hunt for those who would undermine the commonweal and the often unscrupulous means with which the hunt was undertaken, between the justice that the American legal and political system was supposed to provide and the often sordid injustice that it handed down.

Already, Foley Square had hosted the grand jury looking into Elizabeth Bentley's charges, as well as Nixon's occasional forays to Manhattan during the early days of the Hiss–Chambers affair. But it was in 1949 that the courthouse would become synonymous with anti-Communism and the Red Scare. The "three-ring circus," many called it, for the three cases tried simultaneously within it—those of Judith Coplon, Alger Hiss, and the eleven leaders of the American Communist Party.

The Smith Act trial against the Communist Party leadership began first, in January 1949, presided over by a mustachioed judge named Harold Medina. He was the son of a Mexican immigrant who got rich importing Central American coffee. A brilliant student in Manhattan's elite private schools, he recalled being taunted for his Hispanic surname during the Spanish-American War. He attended Princeton, then Columbia for his law degree. He opened his own law practice, but made his wealth off a bar-exam tutoring company that generated some $100,000 a year for him, money he used to buy a forty-six-foot yacht and a fifty-five-acre compound in Westhampton, Long Island. He stocked its library with leather-bound law books, including a handsome collection of transcripts from his trials, as both a lawyer and as a judge.

Truman appointed Medina to the Southern District in 1947, and the Smith Act case was his first major trial. The party leaders had long since decided that they would not receive a fair hearing in a capitalist courtroom, and so they intended to turn their trial into a platform for speeches and acts of defiance that, in their logic, would demonstrate the oppressive nature inherent in the American justice system. They could not have asked for a better foil behind the bench: Not only was Medina a wealthy product of the East Coast Establishment, but he prided himself as a no-nonsense, law-and-order judge who had no compunction about declaring his biases against the Communist Party. He had fully absorbed the Cold War anti-Communist logic—when the defendants asked for a delay, he quickly rejected it, saying that time was of the essence, with the threat of Communism looming ever larger. "I think the case is important to these defendants, but I think the interests of the government and the people are a little more important"—meaning that, before either side had said anything about the substance of the charges, the judge had declared that the party leaders presented a clear, dangerous, and pressing threat to the country. When the Communists and their lawyers tried to win another delay based on William Z. Foster's ill health, Medina simply sequestered the ailing party leader into his own case, allowing the remaining ten defendants to proceed.

The trial began on January 17, 1949, and would not finish until that fall, making it one of the longest federal criminal proceedings in American history. The Communist leaders got some of what they wanted when they decided to turn the proceedings into a spectacle. Outside that morning, thousands gathered in protest, checked by some four hundred police officers, with eleven more on horseback and an indeterminant number milling among the crowd, undercover. It was unseasonably warm, in the 50s, but cloudy. As 8 a.m. passed, the defendants began to arrive, alone or in pairs. Small cheers erupted as they approached. They entered the courthouse without comment.

Courtroom 110 sat on the first floor of Foley Square. Medina presided from a high-backed, red-leather swivel chair, behind which hung a red-velvet tapestry boasting a gold emblem in the shape of an eagle. Like the building's other first-floor courtrooms, Room 110's double-height walls were marble along the lower half and rich walnut paneling above, punctuated by narrow windows. The usual seating arrangement had to be altered to accommodate the defendants and their seven lawyers. Instead of sitting at adjacent desks facing the judge, the two opposing sides sat at long tables arranged in rows, prosecution first, then the defense. What little room was left at the back was set aside for the press. There was not enough space for the public, who were left to gather outside for tidbits of news, or wait to read about it in the papers.

John McGohey, the lead prosecutor, may have been reluctant to take on the case, but once he did, he built his argument relentlessly. Standing tall and straight as a flagpole, his thinning hair Brylcreemed and iron-gray, McGohey focused his opening statement on the party's re-formation in 1945, under orders from Moscow, away from the cooperative Popular Front stance of the 1930s and the war years, when its leaders insisted on the fundamental patriotism of the American Communist cause. After 1945 Stalin had demanded a renewed militancy, and according to McGohey, its leaders, including the defendants, delivered. "It was planned that there would be taught and advocated the Marxist-Leninist principles of the duty and necessity of overthrowing and destroying the Government of the United States by force and violence," the prosecutor told the jury. In fact, as McGohey must surely have read in the newspapers, the party was rapidly shrinking in members and funding, making it ever less a threat, and the year before it had thrown almost all its resources and energy into the Wallace presidential campaign, hardly the stuff of violent revolution.

McGohey drilled into the foundation of Communism, mining the movement's canonical texts for incendiary passages. "The revolutionary doctrines of Marx, Lenin, and Stalin are constantly repeated in the lectures and in the discussions, and the thinking of both the teachers and the students is constantly checked against these revolutionary writers," he told the jury. "Marxism, they are taught, is not merely dogma, it is a guide to action." Finally, he dismissed those elements of the party's new constitution, issued in 1945, that committed it to supporting American democracy as being for "legal purposes only," "mere talk" and "empty phrases." Violent revolution remained the goal, McGohey said. Judge Medina, sitting high on his bench, nodded along.

To prove his case, McGohey brought in a parade of ex-Communists to speak to the party's violent goals. The most prominent was Louis Budenz, the former managing editor of *The Daily Worker* who had renounced his Communist beliefs, joined the Catholic Church and the faculty at Fordham University, then gone on a nationwide speaking tour. But he made most of his money as a professional expert witness, paid by the prosecution, in trials such as this one. Under oath, Budenz told McGohey that party leaders often used twisted, what he called "Aesopian" language to mask the meaning of one thing by saying its opposite—advocating peace really meant advocating violence, supporting democracy meant supporting dictatorship. It wasn't true; Lenin and others had advocated using misleading phrases to get around czarist agents, but never as the key to an entire coded vocabulary, as Budenz alleged. Still, the "Aesopian" accusation proved useful, not just for McGohey but for ant-Communists everywhere, since it created a logic trap for the party's defense: The more they insisted on their peaceful intentions, the more they were secretly calling for violence.

Another witness and former Communist, Herbert Philbrick, had become a nationwide sensation after he revealed that he had spent a decade in the party as a mole for the FBI. He had little of use to tell the jury, but the exposure got him a book deal, a syndicated column, and, along with Budenz, a regular spot as an expert witness in congressional hearings and

criminal trials to come; Philbrick would soon become one of the most famous anti-Communists of the Red Scare. Other FBI informants followed,
with equally little impact, but in such volume that it made more than one
reporter wonder how many actual members the party even had.

McGohey was walking a thin line, on the verge of calling on the court
to punish the defendants for their beliefs, which were protected under
the First Amendment. Luckily for him, the defense pursued a disastrously
unconventional strategy. Rather than accept the trial as legitimate, they
attacked the entire process as a farce. "Our comrades will make the trial
court a mighty tribunal of the people so that the accused become the accusers and the enemies of the people find themselves on trial before the
huge court of public opinion in America—and the world," declared Elizabeth Gurley Flynn, a party leader who would herself be indicted under
the Smith Act a few years later. Some of the defendants even spoke of the
trial as a recruiting tool.

The defendants decided to draw out the trial with objections and time-
consuming procedural motions that they believed would expose the corruption inherent in the system. One of their lawyers demanded a ninety-day
delay so that the police officers deployed in and around the building could
be removed, claiming they were there "solely for the purpose of creating a
Hitler lie that there is some danger in the conduct of this trial." The lawyers argued during jury selection that the process favored the white middle
and upper class, who could afford to spend months attending a trial. Their
argument fell flat when it turned out that most of the jurors came from
working-class backgrounds, including the foreperson, a Black woman who
worked as a seamstress.

The defense even took shots at Medina himself, sometimes aiming for
his wealth and standing, at other times accusing him of bias. "Your honor
will certainly permit me to call your honor's attention at least to the facts
that I want to complain about, even though I am told that your honor is
not going to do anything about it," said one of the defense lawyers during yet another objection. Medina tried to keep himself in check, but he
could not always contain his anger. "I'm through with being fooled with
this case," he once lashed out. "And if you don't like it you can lump it. I've
heard so much of this I'm sick of it."

■ ■ ■ ■

Sometimes, Medina would have to pause the proceedings to compose himself. Starting May 31, 1949, he had a temporary distraction: The Hiss perjury trial had begun, just two floors above Room 110. On more than one occasion, reporters noticed the mustachioed jurist slip into the back row, for just a few minutes, before returning to his own trial.

Medina was not the only well-known face in the audience. The Hiss proceedings were a magnet for celebrities and curious onlookers. Most of the 150 spaces available on the courtroom's long wooden benches were reserved for the press, guests, and VIPs. Alistair Cooke, the famous U.S. correspondent for *The Manchester Guardian*, set up a residency in the courtroom. Renowned journalists like Edward R. Murrow were regulars.

Presiding over the trial was Samuel Kaufman, like Medina a recent Truman appointee. Medina likely took solace in knowing that he was not the only judge in the building who had to deal with overbearing defendants. Hiss was, as usual, his supercilious self, tweaking the grammar of lead prosecutor Thomas Murphy and chiding his slips in logic. "You would have ran after him for that," Murphy said at one point. "I would have *run* after him," Hiss corrected him.

Hiss may have been the smartest person in the room, but he did not seem to realize that he was no longer operating among the diplomatic elite. His sole task was to impress the twelve everyday Americans who made up the jury, and for once in his life, Alger Hiss failed. His defense team leaned on his long retinue of boldfaced names who could speak to his character, including Supreme Court Justices Felix Frankfurter and Stanley Reed, as well as Dean Acheson, who had become secretary of state in January 1949. Lloyd Stryker, Hiss's lawyer, put on a good show, with an hour-long opening statement so histrionic that Kaufman came down from the bench to the witness chair to get a closer view. Hiss, Stryker intoned, "was good enough for Oliver Wendell Holmes, and . . . I shall summon, with all due reverence, the shade of that greatest member of the Supreme Court of the United States." Hiss had done so much good for the world, only to now find his honor in doubt. "Yea," Stryker said, "though I walk through the valley of death I shall not fear, for I am with Alger Hiss."

At the same time, Stryker tried to undermine Chambers's reputation.

He had to: If Hiss was telling the truth, that meant Chambers was lying. But why, and why take it this far? Stryker offered a theory. Chambers had grown obsessed with Hiss after meeting him in the mid-1930s, and when Hiss pulled away, he had decided to destroy him. Stryker's approach had all the allure of a film noir plot, especially in its clear implication that Chambers was a gay sociopath. "In the tropics, in a place like Algiers, when a leper walks in the street, the cry is heard before him, 'Unclean! Unclean!'" Stryker said. "I say to you, 'Unclean!' at the approach of this moral leper." Even if Chambers was not pathologically obsessed with Hiss, Stryker said, could the jury trust a confessed liar and traitor? Core to Chambers's story was his double life in the Communist underground. He had pretended to be other people in order to undermine his own country. How more unreliable could one get? The lack of candor had continued, he said, even after Chambers named Hiss before HUAC, a question Stryker pressed on him on the witness stand.

"It is a fact, is it not," Stryker asked, "that you were asked by the grand jury whether there was any espionage and you said you had no recollection? Was that answer true or false?"

"It was false," Chambers replied, starring impassively at the back wall of the courtroom.

"Then you admit now that you committed perjury . . . in this building!"

"That is right."

Stryker spun on his feet and sat down triumphantly.

The jury had to weigh Stryker's character assassination against an overwhelming amount of hard evidence: the typewriter, the papers, a $400 loan that Chambers said he had received in 1937 from Hiss, matched with a $400 bank withdrawal Hiss made around the same time. The trial ended on July 8 in a hung jury, after fifteen hours of deliberation. It was a win of sorts for Hiss, though he said afterward that he did not understand how anyone could believe him guilty.

It was a temporary victory. A new trial was almost immediately set for the fall, to begin around the same time as Judith Coplon's second trial. The three-ring circus would continue.

8

Peekskill USA

Of the three trials underway in New York, it was the Smith Act case that most motivated the American left. Coplon's case seemed cut-and-dry, her guilt a foregone conclusion. Alger Hiss captivated the elite and the intellectuals, but his case was too complicated, and his personality too forbidding, for many people to rally to his side. The Smith Act defendants, in contrast, were more sympathetic. Most of them had not gone to college and came with strong working-class credentials. William Z. Foster was sick. Two of them were Black men with stories of finding solace from endemic racism in the arms of the party. And the charges themselves seemed patently, obviously intolerable. How could they go to jail for their beliefs? To countless on the left, these men were not just victims; they were martyrs.

There had been rallies in support of the Smith Act defendants staged around Manhattan and Brooklyn since the trial began. In mid-August 1949, a group of progressive musicians planned the biggest one yet: a concert just outside Peekskill, a Hudson River town a few hours north of New York City. It was a politically conservative community, but the rural area to its immediate northeast, just past the city limits, was a popular summer destination for union members, mostly in the needle trades, who brought their families up for a day, or a few, away from the city heat. Their progressive colony was racially integrated, and largely left alone by the Peekskill townspeople. The concert was to be a special installment of what was usually an annual event, organized by a group called People's Artists, Inc. and featuring folk musicians like Pete Seeger, who lived in nearby Beacon.

Its proceeds usually went to the Civil Rights Congress, a left-wing group that the attorney general had labeled subversive. This time, though, the congress was to use the money to benefit the Foley Square defendants. The organizers plastered the Peekskill area with posters announcing the concert, just as they had done in the past. But that was before the Soviets blockaded Berlin. The Cold War was heating up. Sides had to be chosen, even in bucolic Westchester County.

For the headliner, the organizers invited Paul Robeson, a Black bass-baritone who had been entertaining crowds worldwide for more than twenty-five years. He loomed tall with broad, strong features, from his sculpted face that grew softer and rounded as he aged, to his catcher's mitt hands, to his blindingly white teeth. But it was his eyes that drew in his hordes of admirers: Dark and full of searching expression, they were all the singer and political activist needed to grab hold of a crowd, on the stage or on the stump.

Even more than Seeger, Robeson was the most popular entertainer-activist on the left during the 1940s and 1950s. He had been a star football player at Rutgers—Walter Camp, the famed college coach, called him "a veritable superman"—then a talented law student at Columbia, before beginning a stage career that soon had him performing lead roles in New York and London. Robeson took up singing too, and sold 55,000 copies of his first album, a collection of spirituals. But lurking in the background, always, was his race. "He is the most remarkable boy I have ever taught, a perfect prince," a teacher said of him. "Still, I can't forget that he is a negro." He quit a clerkship at a Manhattan law firm after a secretary insulted him with a racial epithet.

Robeson's political convictions, at first quite conventional, began to shift left as he spent more time socializing with actors, musicians, and artists in New York's Greenwich Village, where he got to know prominent Communists like Emma Goldman and Ben Davis, the New York councilman who would later go on trial as a leading figure in the party. His new friends introduced him to the Communist movement and its promise to bring racial equality to Black America. In 1937 he helped found the International Committee for African Affairs, an organization closely aligned with the Communist Party. He was soon in near-constant demand by progressive groups, and he usually obliged: If there was a major fundraiser for a progressive organization, Robeson was the headliner, or an organizer, or often both. By the end of World War II he had established himself as a leading voice among the progressive left, and one of its most outspoken. He stumped for Henry Wallace in 1948, lashing out at what he said was America's imperialist warmongering.

As Robeson rose in prominence on the left, places that had once welcomed him as a singer shut him out as a speaker. In April 1947, the city council in Peoria, Illinois, blocked a reception in his honor, following the cancellation of an appearance at the local Shriners Mosque. A month later, after the New York State Assembly tried to block Robeson from appearing for a concert on public grounds in Albany, the state Supreme Court ruled that he could—but only if he sang and didn't speak. Robeson refused to compromise. "There is no such thing as a nonpolitical artist," he liked to say. "I want to use my singing for direct political action against fascism in America," he told a reporter after the Peoria incident. Liberals tried to ostracize him too: Americans for Democratic Action disassociated its chapter at Brown University after students brought him to campus.

HUAC called Robeson to testify in 1948; the hearings were, ostensibly, meant to look into Communist infiltration of the movement. It was not hard to read in them a subtext, an attempt to link Communism and the civil rights movement and thereby tarnish them both. With the singer sitting before them, the committee denounced him repeatedly as a crypto-Communist, and his utterings were dissected by witness after witness. Even the NAACP, which had given Robeson its highest award in 1944, joined in the attacks. After he seemed to say, during an April 1949 speech in Paris, that Black Americans should not fight for their country, an NAACP board member denounced him as "degenerate."

Still, if Robeson was persona non grata in parts of New York City, he was a reliable draw for the Peekskill concert. And a lightning rod: As the concert approached, it was becoming clear that things would not go as calmly as organizers had hoped, in large part because of Robeson's presence. Howard Fast, the writer and Communist Party member, was spending the summer in nearby Croton-on-Hudson, and he planned to attend the concert with his two young children. But a neighbor of his, a Black woman, warned him against bringing them. Why? he asked. There will be trouble, she said. When Fast asked how she could be so sure, she replied, "Maybe because I'm a Negro and you're white."

It was bad enough, Fast gathered, that there would be a protest rally in favor of the Smith Act defendants. But Robeson's presence touched off something more insidious. For millions of white Americans, race and Communism seemed inextricably tied. Tropes about conspiracies by Black radicals had permeated Southern white society since the 1600s. The fears went beyond runaway slaves and individual instances of violence. Uprisings, or even rumors of them, reminded white slaveowners that enslaved people wanted a very different world from the one they found themselves trapped within, and would fight, kill, and even die to achieve it. At the same time, there was a persistent myth that outside agitators were behind the rebellions, a corollary to the assumption that enslaved Black people were otherwise content with their servitude. Under slavery, it was abolitionists; a century later, under Jim Crow, it was Communists. Representative John Rankin of Mississippi was, as usual, among the most visceral and vocal, insisting from his perch on HUAC that every one of the "racial disturbances that you have seen in the South have been inspired by the tentacles of this great octopus, Communism, which is out to destroy everything."

Such racism was not limited to the South. The mere possibility that Black Americans might find Communism attractive seemed enough to rip down the thin veil of decency worn by bigots far beyond the Mason-Dixon line. "If someone insists that there is discrimination against Negroes in this country, or that there is inequality of wealth, there is every reason to believe that person is a Communist," said Albert Canwell, the chairman of the Washington State Fact-Finding Committee on Un-American Activities, one of the dozens of "mini-HUACs" that sprang up around the country in the late 1940s.

Now, it seemed, that same ugliness was emerging in Peekskill. A group of organizers had already warned the local district attorney about "inflammatory statements" directed at them from a coalition of local veterans groups, including the Veterans of Foreign Wars and the American Legion, who were planning a demonstration parade outside the concert. The march, they said, could easily "inspire illegal action and violence against a peacefully conducted concert." But the district attorney ignored them.

Fast left his children behind. He set out a bit after 6 p.m. on August 27, driving through the green backroads of Westchester County. "It was such a soft and gentle evening as one finds on the canvas of George Inness," he later wrote, evoking the idyllic upstate scenery of the noted Hudson River School painter. As he neared the entrance to the picnic grounds, he saw long lines of cars parked on each side of the road, with pockets of white men and teenage boys strung out among them. They glared at him as he passed. He walked down the park's long gravel road, much of it a causeway sided by steep embankments down to a pond on either side. In a hollow he found the concert amphitheater, with volunteers setting up lights, speakers, and two thousand wooden folding chairs. About three hundred people, including scores of women and children, were milling about, waiting for the show to start. The vast majority were Black, and most of them had come up from Harlem.

A boy came running to Fast. The men from the entrance had formed a mob. They were threatening to rush the concert site. Fast took a detachment of about forty men and boys back with him. "As we appeared, they poured onto us from the road, at least a hundred of them with billies and brass knuckles and rocks and clenched fists, and American Legion caps, and suddenly my disbelief was washed away in a wild melee," Fast wrote. Three deputy sheriffs, the only law enforcement on the scene, stepped in at one point, and it seemed like things had cooled off. But then a truck drove up from the concert, and the mob started throwing rocks. One man was hit in the temple and went down with a thud. Fast and his crew retreated, back to the amphitheater.

The mob hesitated, then followed. Night was falling. The spotlights went on, but then someone cut them off. The men in the mob started trashing the chairs, then built them into a pile and set them on fire. They grabbed a stack of songbooks and threw them into the flames. Then, on a rise overlooking the site, someone set fire to three crosses—the symbol of the Ku Klux Klan. Fast and the men formed a rough cordon around the audience goers and prepared to fight. He sent a boy off with a handful of nickels to call the newspapers.

Many in the mob were drinking from pocket flasks, and they shouted racist and anti-Semitic epithets as they massed, heaving and hot. "Lynch Robeson!" they yelled. "We're Hitler's boys! We'll finish his job!" A flare shot into the sky, briefly casting a red glow over the battlefield. Knuckles cracked. Bats slapped into hands.

The authorities arrived. First a trio of FBI agents in a car, who had been monitoring the scene at a distance and now offered to drive off the most wounded. Then an ambulance. Then, right after, dozens of Peekskill police and state troopers. The mob began to fade back into the darkness. The troopers surrounded the audience, still about three hundred strong, and would not let them leave. A member of the mob, Fast learned, had been stabbed, and rushed to the hospital. If he died, the mob would likely come at them again, this time for vengeance. It was unclear if the authorities were there to protect the concertgoers, or to keep them from fleeing for safety. Finally word came back—the man was fine. In fact, it would turn out, he had been stabbed by a fellow combatant, who had gone wild in the frenzy. The audience was allowed to leave, in the dark.

The next day some 350 people gathered at the estate of a local doctor, in nearby Katonah, for the first meeting of the Westchester Committee of Law and Order, formed in response to the violence by some of the county's leading liberals. The doctor had been one of Westchester's most vocal partisans behind the Wallace ticket, and now he was rallying his neighbors to call on Governor Dewey to investigate the riot and clean out the district attorney's office. Dozens of state troopers stood on the road outside his home, and as attendees turned onto his driveway the troopers jotted down their license plate numbers.

The organizers of the mob were defiant. They said their actions had been peaceful; whatever violence took place had come at the hands of teenage hoodlums. And, they added, the concertgoers had started it. The march, they said, had been a success. "Our objective was to prevent the Paul Robeson concert and I think our objective was reached," the commander of a Peekskill American Legion post told reporters. "Anything that happened after the organized demonstration was dispersed was entirely up to the individual citizens and should not be blamed on the patriotic organizations." Another Legionnaire, who had driven down from Plattsburgh, near the Canadian border, to represent the Veterans of Foreign Wars, concurred, and offered to buy Robeson a one-way ticket to Russia.

Robeson had never made it to the show. An official with the Civil Rights Congress had intercepted him as he prepared to leave New York and told him it was not safe in Peekskill. The next day the singer held a press conference, where he also demanded that Governor Dewey investigate. "These boys were told to do it," he said. Councilmember Ben Davis, who had taken advantage of a lull in his Foley Square trial to join Robeson, linked the riot to the country's mounting illiberalism and warned that more was to come, calling it "an invitation to violence against Negroes, progressives, Communists and trade unionists." A reporter asked Robeson about the offer of a free trip to the Soviet Union. Robeson replied that he had more of a right to stay in America than any white man did. One of Robeson's ancestors had baked bread for George Washington's troops, he said, and his father's people had been "slaves upon whose backs the wealth of this country was built."

The next day three thousand people came to hear Robeson at a rally in the Golden Gate Ballroom, at Lenox Avenue and 142nd Street in Harlem. Two thousand more people stood outside, unable to fit in. The riot in Peekskill had been a turning point, Robeson told the audience. White people in wealthy Westchester County had turned out in droves to assault peaceful Black Americans, something that was only supposed to happen in the Jim Crow South. Black people could not rely on the kindness of their white neighbors or the promises of protection from the authorities. Force must now be met with force. "We understand now that the surest way to get police protection is to be prepared to protect ourselves," he said.

The riot demonstrated what had already become clear to many on the left: that some of their most aggressive and determined opponents would come from the country's veterans organizations. It was little consolation to hear the heads of the American Legion or the Veterans of Foreign Wars promise that their focus was on Communists alone, not progressives in general; too often, their chapters and their rank and file had shown little interest in that distinction. The only such organization not to join the fray in Peekskill was the Jewish War Veterans. Its state commander declared the riot to be part of "the lynch spirit" and promised to punish any of his members who were found to have participated.

Robeson held yet another rally in the city on the evening of September 1, 1949. Just before midnight, he announced that in three days he would hold a concert near Peekskill. He predicted twenty thousand people would come out to hear him, and this time, he announced, the organizers would be ready. In fact the show was already in the works. A new site, at an abandoned golf course a few miles north of Peekskill, had already been rented. So had dozens of buses. And hundreds of men from the Furriers Union and other left-leaning trade outfits had signed up as bodyguards; many of them had seen combat in World War II. The Westchester veterans immediately announced their own rally nearby, predicting that thirty thousand men from across the state of New York would answer their call.

Concertgoers began arriving at 10 a.m., entering the golf course through a gantlet of jeering protesters—men, women, even children shouting "Go back to Russia!" The countermarch was already underway, looking for all the world like a small-town parade, with flags and bunting and even an American Legion honor guard. Despite the harassment, about fifteen thousand people passed through the hecklers to the show, this time not just Black workers from Harlem but leatherworkers from Midtown and teachers from Brooklyn, members of dozens of unions drawn from the largely white labor groups. Nine hundred cops were on hand. Three thousand guards drawn from the union workers stood in the calf-high grass, ringing a grove of trees, inside of which organizers had converted the back of a flatbed truck into a stage. Organized into platoons, they wore tan caps and brought baseball bats, though the police soon confiscated them. The cops also removed the breach bolts from the carbines carried by the Legion honor guard, just in case.

Robeson went on at 2:30. A ring of security surrounded him tightly, after hearing reports of snipers with high-powered rifles spotted on a nearby hill. Protesters, far away, tried to drown him out with drums and backfiring motorcycles, but they were no match for the concert's amplifiers. Robeson sang all his hits: "Let My People Go," "No! John No!," the final aria from *Boris Godunov*, and "Ol' Man River." The screenwriter Walter Bernstein, standing in the audience, was in awe. "His voice was not what it had been, but no one cared," he recalled. A collection plate went around. Then fifteen thousand relieved, exhausted people shuffled back to the buses, eager to get back to the city.

As the first buses made their way down the main drive of the golf course, bricks and rocks began raining down on them, thrown from the low rises that buttressed the path. Windows shattered. Mothers pushed their children to the floor and covered them with their bodies. The drivers of the last ten buses, seeing this, refused to get behind the wheel, and eventually fled on foot, leaving six hundred people stranded. Those who had come by car tried to scoot out but got stuck in a mile-long traffic jam, leaving them wide open to hand-thrown missiles. Other assailants tried to throw sand into open car windows to blind drivers. By some reports, the police were standing in the road, forcing the cars to crawl along, brandishing their weapons when panicked drivers shouted at them to move. "There was no safety anywhere. We were not even free to fight back. Neither was anyone else in the long line of cars," Bernstein wrote. "The cops were there to protect the attackers, not us." Even if they escaped the course, more pockets of assailants waited for them along the roads and backways headed out of the area. A bus carrying a group of partygoers from the Bronx fell under attack and, despite their loud protestations of confused innocence, did not escape until they wrapped an American flag around the front of their vehicle.

As soon as the organizers saw trouble brewing, they stuck Robeson in the back of a car, lying down and covered in a blanket. The next day he held yet another press conference. The room was packed with reporters, and there was no air-conditioning. Mopping sweat off his forehead with a white handkerchief, Robeson introduced a baker's dozen of witnesses, primarily Black, who testified to the day's violence, in particular against the six hundred people marooned by the bus drivers.

The witnesses told how state troopers had corralled them in the field and forced them to keep their hands in the air for almost an hour. Some were reportedly singled out for a "working over" with billy clubs. The troopers doused them in racist epithets. Eventually, after volunteers were found to drive the buses, they were allowed to leave. About 145 people were injured, four seriously, including a woman whose left index finger was severed. Irving Potash, a defendant in the Foley Square case, was hit in the eye. Rioters overturned more than a dozen cars.

The protesting veterans were, as before, proud of their accomplishments, and promised more. "We will continue to demonstrate against Mr. Robeson's pseudo-concerts or any other subversive meetings," said the chair of the veterans' coordinating committee. "We do not want Communists in this area, under any title or pretense."

The Westchester district attorney tried to write off the riot as merely the excess of teenage hoodlums. And Governor Dewey blamed the concertgoers for their violence, saying they had acted "deliberately to create an incident or breach of the peace." There was enough public pressure to force some action, and the government brought charges against eleven people, including the twenty-five-year-old son of the Peekskill sheriff.

The white people who came to hear Robeson at Peekskill were shocked by what they experienced. The threat of anti-left violence had long been implied but never carried out, and the threats that progressives and Communists faced had so far been limited mostly to the legal and professional realms. But something new was afoot in America, a paranoid viciousness born of the fears instigated by the Cold War and melded to longstanding prejudices. Not only had men—and women, and children—acting under the banner of the nation assaulted a peaceful assembly, but they had done so with law enforcement watching close by. Nor had most of them faced any consequences. Was this, then, the new normal?

Robeson and the thousands of Black concertgoers saw things differently. Certainly, as Robeson said after the first riot, this was a historic moment. But not because the violence was unprecedented. "What happened in Peekskill yesterday happens to the Negro people every day in the South," Robeson told the press conference. This time was different because it was so brazen, so open, against a mixed-race crowd. It was covered by newspapers around the country and across the world. The violence baked into the system, Robeson said, had finally shown itself. Howard Fast agreed. He titled his report on the violence *Peekskill USA.*

Helen Reid Bryan in an undated photo. (Alison Carlson)

Dean Acheson, speaking here in 1947, when he was still deputy secretary of state, became an architect of the Cold War and a target of anti-Communist conspiracy theories. (Harris & Ewing, Harry S. Truman Library and Museum)

Dalton Trumbo and his wife, Cleo, listen closely to the proceedings of the House Committee on Un-American Activities investigation into Communism in Hollywood. Bertolt Brecht sits behind them, smoking a cigar. The day after his testimony, Brecht fled to East Germany. (The Associated Press)

Elizabeth Bentley's visit to an FBI office in New Haven, Connecticut, set in motion a wave of scandals, including the Hiss–Chambers affair and the trial of the Communist Party leadership. (New York World-Telegram & Sun Newspaper Photograph Collection, Library of Congress)

HUAC's reputation for witch-hunting became a frequent subject for the nation's editorial cartoonists. (Herbert L. Block Collection, Library of Congress)

After boating and seaplaning his way back to Washington to examine the so-called Pumpkin Papers, Representative Richard Nixon posed for photographers with HUAC counsel Robert Stripling, a strip of microfilm, and a tiny magnifying glass. (The Associated Press)

Alger Hiss (*center*), once a rising star in the Democratic foreign policy establishment, walks arm in arm with his wife, Priscilla, to his sentencing hearing in January 1950. He was convicted of perjury, but the public knew the real crime was espionage. (The Associated Press)

Robert Thompson and Ben Davis, two of the Communist Party leaders tried under the Smith Act, are greeted by supporters outside the Foley Square courthouse in Manhattan. (New York World-Telegram and the Sun Newspaper Photograph Collection, Library of Congress)

Judith Coplon arrives for another day at court in June 1949. (Harris & Ewing, Harry S. Truman Library and Museum)

After the first attempt at a fundraising concert in Peekskill, New York, for the Foley Square defendants ended in an assault by local veterans, a second show was put on, this time with a cordon of defenders drawn largely from New York City unions. (The Associated Press)

Carmel Offie (*right*) in an undated photograph with his boss, Ambassador William C. Bullitt. (The Associated Press)

Harry Bridges, the pugnacious leader of the International Longshore and Warehouse Union, in 1939, during one of his many appearances before Congress. (Harris & Ewing Photograph Collection, Library of Congress)

The day Communists captured the Heartland: On May 1, 1950, the town of Mosinee, Wisconsin, staged a mock invasion by Soviet forces, played by members of Veterans of Foreign Wars; they even "arrested" Mosinee's police chief, Carl Gewess. (The Associated Press)

Over the winter of 1952–53, posters by the French artist Louis Mittelberg began appearing around the streets of Paris, showing a monstrous caricature of Dwight D. Eisenhower, with electric chairs for teeth. The text reads "They electrocuted two innocents, Ethel and Julius Rosenberg. May the murderers be cursed forever." (Louis Mittelberg)

Joseph N. Welch, lawyer for the Army, speaking with Senator Joseph McCarthy during the Army–McCarthy hearings of 1954. Their increasingly heated conversations culminated in a withering, televised attack by Welch on the senator's "sense of decency," a harangue that made Welch famous and helped doom McCarthy. (The Associated Press)

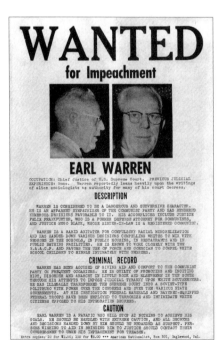

Long after the fear of Communist subversion loosened its grip on the American public, elements on the far right insisted that sinister forces had captured the levers of government. Chief Justice Earl Warren was a popular target, as demonstrated by this "Wanted" poster. (Rare Book & Manuscript Library, Columbia University)

9

A Clear and Present Danger

As summer faded into fall, the world seemed to be on the edge of apocalypse. The shocking violence in Peekskill and the high drama of the trials at Foley Square were matched by dizzying developments overseas. The spring of 1949 had seen the formation of the North Atlantic Treaty Organization, the end of the Berlin Blockade, and the establishment of the West German Republic, all reassuring signs for the Western alliance. But then, on April 23, the Chinese Communists captured the Nationalist capital of Nanjing. The inevitable declaration of victory by Mao Zedong came on October 1, adding, in a single sweep, a quarter of the world's population to the Communist bloc. The Nationalist leader, Chiang Kai-shek, fled to the island of Formosa (today Taiwan), promising to continue to wage war from there. Mao immediately swore allegiance to Stalin and the Soviet Union, and would meet with the Russian leader at the end of the year.

The greatest shock, the one that changed the world and supercharged the Red Scare, came at exactly 7 a.m. on August 29, 1949. As the hour turned over, a narrow jet of dark gray ash and dust rocketed up from the barren steppes of northeastern Kazakhstan. In less than a minute the cloud plumed out into an enormous billow, miles across. In the West they called such formations mushroom clouds, though this one, at least, looked more like a thundercloud plum tree. The explosion was generated by a device that its Soviet engineers called First Lightning. The Americans, who detected it a few days later via a high-altitude weather plane flying over the Western Pacific, called it Joe-1. President Truman waited three weeks before announcing to the world that the Soviet Union had become the second nation to detonate an atomic bomb. America was stunned. It had unexpectedly lost its nuclear monopoly, and with it, people believed, the last check against an all-out war with the Russians. When J. Robert Oppenheimer, the director of the Manhattan Project that developed America's own nuclear program, testified that fall before Congress, Senator Arthur Vandenberg of Michigan asked him, "Doctor, what shall we do now?"

Oppenheimer had no plan. "Stay strong and hold onto our friends," was all he could say.

For years now, the American public had heard worrying news about the global march of Communism, but it had often seemed tentative, marginal, easily ignored. Now, suddenly, with Communists in control of both an atomic bomb and the world's most populated country, the threat was all too immediate, and impossible to ignore. The country, *The New York Times* announced, had a case of "the jitters."

If Alger Hiss, Judith Coplon, or the Smith Act defendants had any hopes of winning their trials, world events likely put an end to them. While the Smith Act case continued, Coplon's second trial began on November 14, 1949. Her lawyer pushed aggressively to have the case dismissed because the FBI had not secured an arrest warrant. But the judge swatted away such concerns; civil liberties, it was becoming clear, had little purchase under Cold War justice. The defense team did win a motion forcing the FBI to admit that it had tapped Coplon's phone illegally, and even listened in on privileged conversations between her and her lawyer. Still the judge allowed the trial to go on, even after the FBI claimed, under order to produce the tapes, that they had been accidentally, and conveniently, destroyed. Finally the judge tipped his hand in the government's favor, announcing that it was "immaterial" where the FBI's original tip came from, and that therefore the issue of illegal wiretapping was moot. The case went to the jury in March 1950, and it took just seven hours to deliver a guilty verdict. Coplon was sentenced to twenty years in prison. Gubitchev, her Soviet accomplice, was allowed to leave the country, never to return.

Coplon's actions seemed, at first glance, proof that the Soviets had restarted their espionage efforts. But in hindsight it seems clear that she was a lone wolf, an eager accomplice who volunteered her services, rather than the tip of some subversive iceberg. It seems more likely than not that the postwar Soviet network was thinner and more ineffective than J. Edgar Hoover and the red-baiters would have the country believe. What the case did reveal was the extent and questionable nature of the FBI's surveillance practices. Hoover insisted that the raw intelligence revealed during Coplon's first trial was just that—unprocessed gossip and hearsay not meant for use by agents or prosecutors. He promised there were safeguards in place. But he never explained them. Nor did he defend the use of such questionable material to justify wiretaps and break-ins, both increasingly common tactics by the bureau.

Coplon did manage to win her case on appeal, based on her claim that the FBI did not have reasonable cause to arrest her or search her purse. It was a rare victory for civil liberties during the Red Scare, one that the lead appellate judge in the case, Learned Hand, saw fit to apologize for to the bureau. When he met afterward with the head of the FBI's New York field office, he took pains to show that he didn't have a particular problem with wiretaps, and regretted having to rule against the bureau. He had nothing but praise for it. "I think it is the greatest secret police in the world," he said, adding hurriedly, "I don't mean that in an invidious sense like the Gestapo."

Alger Hiss's second trial was likewise a perfunctory exercise, and something of a foregone conclusion. By now the tide of anti-Communism had turned so decisively that the best he could hope for was that his lawyer could poke enough small holes in Whittaker Chambers that the case collapsed in on itself. And he tried, questioning the contents of the so-called Pumpkin Papers and calling a psychiatrist to testify about Chambers's mental state.

Hiss, for his part, seemed more withdrawn during the second trial; he had lost weight, and his knife-edged wit had dulled. He came to court with his wife, Priscilla, every morning, *Time* reported, "carrying a rolled-up umbrella, wearing rubbers if there is a hint of rain." They ate together every day at the same nearby restaurant, where the owner had given them a standing reservation. Hiss must have known that his best hope was another hung jury—and also that the likelihood of such an outcome, this time, was much slimmer than the last.

On January 21, 1950, the jury found Hiss guilty on both counts, and the judge sentenced him to five years in prison. Hiss was unbowed. "I am confident that in the future the full facts showing how Whittaker Chambers was able to carry out forgery by typewriter will be developed," he said after the verdict. There were appeals, reaching the Supreme Court, which refused to hear the case. Hiss entered the federal penitentiary in Lewisburg, Pennsylvania, on March 22, 1951, and was released on November 27, 1954. He spent the rest of his life insisting on his innocence.

Dean Acheson, the secretary of state, held a press conference on the afternoon of Hiss's conviction. It had been previously scheduled, to cover a variety of topics of moderate interest. But the news from Foley Square was the only thing anyone wanted to hear about. The press conference had been on background, no direct quotes allowed. A reporter for the *New York Herald Tribune* asked if Acheson could make an exception. "As you choose." Did he have any thoughts about Hiss? another reporter asked. "Whatever the outcome of any appeal which Mr. Hiss or his lawyer may take," Acheson said, "I do not intend to turn my back on Alger Hiss."

Within hours everyone in Washington was quoting the secretary, with almost uniform contempt. Republicans in Congress rushed to condemn him. Senator Homer Capehart said he was "prouder than ever" that he voted against Acheson's confirmation. Richard Nixon, who called the statement "disgusting," accused Acheson of covering up for Hiss. Democrats jumped in as well: James Davis, a representative from Georgia, asked, "How long can Americans be expected to show respect for Acheson when he hugs to his bosom those who have betrayed their country?" That afternoon Acheson went to the White House and offered to resign. Truman wouldn't have it. Though they were worlds apart in terms of upbringing and education, the president and his secretary of state were alike in all the ways that mattered—hardworking, pragmatic, and loyal. Truman would not turn his back on Dean Acheson.

Nor did Acheson have anything to be ashamed of. Few people repeated what he had said next, after vowing not to turn his back on Hiss. Everyone who knew the man "has upon his conscience the very serious task of deciding what his attitude is and what his conduct should be," Acheson said. "That must be done by each person in the light of his own standards and his own principles. For me there is very little doubt about those standards or those principles. I think they were stated for us very long ago. They were stated on the Mount of Olives and if you are interested in seeing them you will find them in the 25th Chapter of the Gospel according to St Matthew beginning with Verse 34. Have you any other questions?" A State Department aide stood at the back of the room with a Bible, in case any reporter wanted to check the secretary's reference. (Had they checked, they would have found that it read, in the voice of Jesus Christ, "Naked and ye clothed me; I was sick and ye visited; I was in prison and ye came unto me.")

The significance of the Hiss–Chambers affair has little to do with Hiss's guilt or innocence. It typified, and did much to shape, the hardening polarization between left and right, the belief on each side that the other was not just beholden to a different political philosophy, but made of something far more sinister and inimical to the country as a whole. On the left, Hiss became a cause célèbre, a hero done wrong by vicious reactionaries. To them, liberalism was at war with a sort of proto-fascism, and Hiss was among its most prominent victims. On the right, the case was not just proof that spies really did operate among us, but that they were able to do so by taking advantage of the arrogant naïveté of the left elite, if not its willing collaboration. Alistair Cooke, the British journalist who covered the Hiss case for *The Manchester Guardian*, called his book on the proceedings *A Generation on Trial*. It was, he concluded, not just about one man's guilt or innocence; it was, fundamentally, about the progressive idealism of the 1930s being called to account on new terms effected by the Cold War, on a logic of absolute security and loyalty that declared any deviance, no matter how long ago, to be equivalent to subversion, if not treason.

Even as the Coplon and Hiss trials dominated the public's attention, the Smith Act trial droned on in the background. Judge Medina, tired of delay tactics from the defense team, cited its lawyers for contempt. And he dismissed outright their arguments that the party did not present a clear and present danger to national security. Such a requirement, Medina replied, meant "you couldn't punish anybody until the overthrow of the government was about to take place . . . it seems a little bit absurd to me."

Medina had reasons to be angry. Communists and their allies began to send him death threats in the mail, poking at his well-publicized fear of heights—a foible he had once mentioned to a reporter, thinking it was innocuous and maybe even endearing. Prank phone calls and anonymous letters carried the same message, with some effect. "It got so I just didn't dare go near a window," Medina told *Time* in 1952. "You laugh now. You think it's funny, but by golly, it nearly worked." He was melodramatically public about his change of routine during the Foley Square trials. He was up at 6 a.m., and traveled down through Manhattan with a bodyguard at the wheel. He ate a lunch of lamb and spinach every day in his chambers. After the trial ended for the day he went to a private club for a massage, then home to two martinis and bed by 9:30. He complained that he had become "a vegetable," and that he even had to give up translating Latin, his favorite hobby. Perhaps he thought that such revelations would win him sympathy with the public. Instead they only heightened the ridiculousness of the entire proceedings.

There was the occasional poignant moment, such as when Ben Davis, the Black City Council member, explained on the stand why he had become a Communist. Born and raised in Dawson, Georgia, the son of a Black newspaper editor and grandson of a slave, he had escaped to Amherst and Harvard Law. He had chosen to return home to Atlanta to practice, despite the racism that focused all the more intently on Black men of achievement. His breaking point came after he joined the defense team for Angelo Herndon, a Black labor activist on trial for insurrection in 1932. The judge, Davis told the Foley Square courtroom, had refused to refer to him as "Mr. Davis," and littered his speech with racist epithets. "I could see before me the whole treatment of the negro people in the South," Davis said. Convinced that Black people would never achieve equity in a capitalist society, he moved to New York and joined the party.

Otherwise the trial went on, day by day, stretching into fall. For weeks at a time it fell off the front pages, pushed aside by the Hiss and Coplon trials. By the time the jury retired for deliberations on October 13, they had heard from fifty witnesses and reviewed 758 exhibits. They had sat through 158 trial days. The transcript ran to five million words, collected in 21,157 pages. And yet for all that, nothing much had developed. The prosecution witnesses failed to present hard evidence that the party presented a "clear and present danger," except, perhaps, in its leaders' own minds. The government refused to reveal what it knew from its secret interception of Soviet transmissions, including recent evidence of financial and espionage connections between Moscow and the American Communist Party leadership. Despite all the insults and shenanigans from the defendants and their lawyers, their central claim seemed unassailable: They were being prosecuted for their beliefs, not their actions.

Medina made sure in his charge to the jury that there was no question how they should decide. "Words may be the instruments by which crimes are committed," he intoned on October 13, "and it has always been recognized that the protection of other interests of society may justify reasonable restrictions upon speech in furtherance of the general welfare."

It took the jury a mere seven hours, spread over two days, to find the defendants guilty. After the foreperson read the verdict, Medina ordered the men remanded to custody before sentencing. Then, turning to the defense lawyers—including Eugene Dennis, the Communist Party general secretary who had acted as his own attorney—he charged them with forty acts of contempt, and sentenced them to prison terms ranging from thirty days to six months. A week later Medina returned for sentencing the defendants, waiting until federal marshals and bomb-sniffing dogs had swept Room 110 for explosives. Ten of them got five years in prison; Medina gave the eleventh, a World War II veteran, just three years, because of his service to his country.

The defendants immediately appealed, and the following August the case, now known as *Dennis v. United States*, went before a three-judge panel of the Second Circuit Court of Appeals, led by Learned Hand, the same judge who had overseen Judith Coplon's appeal. Little known to the general public, Hand was perhaps the most esteemed jurist of the twentieth century never to reach the Supreme Court. He struggled to balance his aversion to Communism with his commitment to civil liberties and his fear that "witch hunters," he said in 1947, were being given "rein to set up a sort of Inquisition, detecting heresy wherever non-conformity appears." Yet when it came time to rule in *Dennis*, in August 1950, he wrote a forceful decision upholding the convictions. Like Medina, he argued that the "clear and present danger" test, which normally would have protected even speech as unpopular as the Communists', now had to be' understood differently, in light of the Cold War.

"The American Communist Party," Hand wrote, "is a highly articulated, well contrived, far spread organization, numbering thousands of adherents, rigidly and ruthlessly disciplined, many of whom are infused with a passionate Utopian faith that is to redeem mankind. . . . The violent capture of all existing governments is one article of the creed of that faith, which abjures the possibility of success by lawful means." In the face of such an enemy, he wrote, the question "is how long a government, having discovered such a conspiracy, must wait. When does the conspiracy become a 'present danger'?"

In other words, Hand argued, it's not always enough to wait until someone yells fire in a crowded theater. If someone announces their intent to do so, and actively recruits others to join them, then that speech can't possibly be protected under the Constitution. But that's only true if there is a reasonable expectation that an action will follow from that speech. And by 1950, there was no evidence that the party had ever taken steps to act on its words. Even if it had, what were the chances that such a tiny sect could set off a nationwide revolution? Only in the moment when the great fear of Communism was at its height could a jurist as sagacious as Learned Hand believe the Communists had any chance at all.

The Smith Act trial marked an end to the party's safe harbor within the country's political system. Hand's decision gave license to even staunch liberals to rally against Communists and their sympathizers. Summing up the changing attitudes, *The New York Times* editorial board wrote that "the nation can no longer treat with good humor groups of individuals whose admitted aim is to defeat the national purpose and aid the national enemies." The verdict opened the way for federal prosecutors to go after lower and lower ranks of party leadership, forcing even members of the rank-and-file underground. And Medina's contempt citations of the Smith Act lawyers made it unlikely that any sane attorney would sign up to defend them.

10

The Ballad of Harry Bridges

The rift that Communism caused between liberal Democrats and progressives had burst wide open during the 1948 presidential campaign,
but the intra-left tension was not limited to the political realm. It divided
academics, intellectuals, lawyers, and civil liberties activists; virtually any
domain where the left held sway became a battlefield over the meaning
and challenge of American Communism.

Among the prime landscapes of ideological combat during the final
years of the 1940s was the labor movement, with a rough-and-tumble former stevedore named Harry Bridges at the center of the action. Bridges
was tall and thin, with a hawklike face; born and raised in Australia, he
never lost his nasally accent. He had a barely controlled, manic energy, and
a dry wit and infectious charisma that won him legions of followers among
the West Coast working classes, in particular the dockworkers whose
union he led for decades. He had always been a man firmly ensconced
in the left, and had made no secret about his close ties to the Communist
labor movement. He admired them, and generally agreed with them, and
cooperated with them. By 1949, that alliance made him the central figure
in the Red Scare within the labor movement.

As a boy growing up in the Melbourne suburbs, Bridges fell in love with
the books of Jack London, and he carefully patterned his life after them.
When he was fifteen he quit school to join the Royal Navy; the recruiters
told him to wait a few years. His father, hoping to dissuade him from a
life on the high seas, got young Harry a job sailing cargo ketches between
Melbourne and Tasmania, to show him how miserable it could be. Bridges

loved it, and he soon signed up for longer voyages, as far as India. When in early 1917 a German warship appeared while Bridges's ship was in port at Bombay (today Mumbai), his captain set sail in fear while he was still ashore. Stuck, he found work as a colonial police officer. He later said it was his first encounter with the naked power of European imperialism, feeling the invulnerability that came with his crisp white uniform. He left as soon as he had enough money to get home.

Bridges was there just long enough to see more than 100,000 stevedores, railway workers, and coal miners go on strike across the country. His father, a Tory, despised the strikers, but their passionate solidarity won over young Harry. He considered joining, and later, as an exercise in self-mythologizing, said he did. But the sea was a more powerful draw, and he was soon back on ship. He passed through London, where he saw workers living in abject poverty of a sort that he'd believed impossible in the wealthiest empire the world had ever seen. And he spent time in New Orleans, where he first encountered, and quickly joined, the Industrial Workers of the World, better known as the Wobblies, a radical labor organization in the early twentieth century.

He walked off a gangplank in San Francisco in 1921 and never went back to the ocean. He found work as a stevedore doing breakbulk work along the piers of San Francisco Bay. He participated in a Wobblies strike that same year, then quit the organization when it became clear that the federal government, still feeling the afterglow of the first Red Scare, was eager to deport foreign-born leftists. He grew thin, wiry, strong; he played the mandolin, frequented jazz clubs, and danced the rhumba until early morning.

Bridges was living it up, but he was hardly oblivious to the difficulties around him. The dockworkers were at the mercy of cruel, often corrupt bosses and indifferent shipowners, and with the Wobblies struggling by the late 1920s, there was no strong representation to turn to—certainly not the company-supported unions that forced the workers to walk a narrow line toward meager rewards. After his stepson accidentally stabbed himself and Bridges's union was unable to help pay the hospital bills, he turned to radical thoughts. With his infant daughter sleeping beside him, he spent long hours in the San Francisco public library, reading his way through not just Marx but *Fortune* and *The Wall Street Journal*. He talked up the idea of a new, more militant union for the bay's dockworkers, indeed for the entire West Coast. He was just one man, but when Harry Bridges spoke, people couldn't help but listen, and follow. The writer Louis Adamic attended a Bridges rally in 1936 and came away amazed. "I have never heard a better organized, more effective, more intelligent or more sincere speech than Bridges delivered," Adamic wrote in *The Nation*.

His breakout moment came in 1934, when he helped organize a strike by the West Coast longshoremen, one of the biggest labor actions of the 1930s. Every major port along the West Coast shut down for months. The government pushed back, placing tanks and machine gun nests along the Embarcadero. Workers clashed with the police twice; both times the police shot into the crowds, both times killing two and injuring more. After the second clash—on July 5, celebrated by longshoremen for generations after as Bloody Thursday—Bridges led a mass funeral along Market Street, riding in the front car. He called for a general strike, and a few days later 150,000 workers across the region walked off their jobs. But a general strike was a step too far for the more moderate members of the labor leadership, and they sued for peace with the employers and federal mediators.

On paper, it looked like a victory for the employers. The strikers got a fraction of their demands. And both the employers and the government had succeeded in casting the strike leaders as dangerous, Communist subversives, which they used to then justify raids on strike organizers. But it was also a victory for Bridges. The strike solidified his claim as leader of the Bay Area dockworkers, and his aspiration to become their voice along the entire West Coast. He reveled in the employers' hatred—the more they attacked him, the bigger he looked in the eyes of his men. In 1937 he created the International Longshoremen's and Warehousemen's Union (soon renamed, minus the "men," to recognize its many female members), and that same year joined the upstart Congress of Industrial Organizations, an umbrella group uniting unions in industrial sectors like cars, steel, and electrical appliances. Recognizing his power, the CIO even made him its director for the entire Western Region, placing him among the organization's inner circle. A few weeks later, *Time* magazine put him on its cover, in a candid photo of him bending over a washbasin, dressed in a sleeveless undershirt. By the late 1930s Bridges was the undisputed leader of organized labor on the West Coast, and one of the most powerful union leaders in America.

Bridges had worked openly with Bay Area Communists during the 1934 strike, and rumor had it that he was secretly a party member. But the CIO welcomed men like him—indeed, even admitted Communists—into its fold. The CIO was founded just as the Popular Front was beginning, with Stalin's order that Communists join up with the rest of the left to support Europe's coming war with fascism. That meant leaving behind the party's earlier efforts to create its own, ideologically pure unions and joining—some would say burrowing into—the CIO and its member organizations. Though small in number, the Communists proved their worth to the CIO in their zeal for organizing, planning, and striking. They would go into the hottest fields of California's Central Valley to organize farmworkers, then stand on the front lines against club-wielding cops. The CIO and its founder, John L. Lewis, was happy to have them. When David Dubinsky, the head of the International Ladies Garment Workers Union, warned him against relying too heavily on the Communists, Lewis is said to have replied, "Who gets the bird? The hunter or the dog?"

By signing up hundreds of thousands of workers into his new industrial unions, Lewis threatened action on an almost unprecedented scale. During a wave of auto industry strikes in 1936 and '37, some 136,000 workers walked off the lines (or in many cases sat down on them, essentially taking over the factories) at General Motors factories in Michigan and Ohio. In January 1937 workers and police traded blows outside the site of one of the largest strikes, the Fisher Body Plant in Flint, Michigan. Lewis's militancy, and his pragmatic reliance on Communists to do his dirty work, proved a winning combination. By the end of 1937 the CIO had some four million members. Entire industries sat down to negotiate. Roosevelt and his administration, seeing political shifts at work, extended helping hands.

But even as the government engaged with the CIO, it went after its most militant members—above all Harry Bridges. To the White House, unionized labor was a good thing only to the point that it served the administration's goals, and was willing to cooperate with Roosevelt's agenda. Those who pushed further were branded enemies and dangerous radicals, even before the beginning of the Red Scare. The Justice Department tried to deport Bridges four times, at first for being a Communist, then for allegedly lying about being a Communist. By November 1940 the FBI had a file on him four thousand pages long. "Our report confirms the belief that Bridges is a Communist and that the Communist party advocates overthrow of the United States government," J. Edgar Hoover said, despite having nothing of the kind.

The file was full of allegations by unreliable witnesses, but nothing in the form of hard evidence. Frustrated, the FBI illegally tapped his phones and bugged his hotel rooms. During a stay at New York's Hotel Edison, Bridges suspected that agents had a surveillance post in the room next to his. To prove it, he and some friends went to the hotel across the street, rented a room directly across from his, and watched the agents in action. The bureau had been following him for so long, he told a reporter for *The New Yorker*, that he knew its tactics by heart and many of its agents by sight: "I've seen so many FBI men these past years that there are likely to be one or two that I have seen before in the lobby of practically any hotel I am staying at." When a red-faced Hoover reported the episode to Roosevelt, the president laughed and said, "By God, Edgar, that's the first time you've been caught with your pants down!"

One case against Bridges went to the Supreme Court, which ruled in his favor on June 18, 1945. Justice William O. Douglas wrote the 5–3 majority decision, but the strongest statement came in a concurring opinion from Justice Frank Murphy, a pro-union liberal and former governor of Michigan. Even before getting to the legal facts of the matter, Murphy outlined a decade-long conspiracy by "industrial and farming organizations, veterans' groups, city police departments, and private undercover agents" to have Bridges tossed from the country. "The record in this case will stand forever as a monument to man's intolerance of man," the justice wrote. "Seldom if ever in the history of this nation has there been such a concentrated and relentless crusade to deport an individual because he dared to exercise the freedom that belongs to him as a human being and that is guaranteed to him by the Constitution."

Five days after the decision, Bridges filed his final paperwork to become an American citizen. When the examiner asked, pro forma, if he had any "desire to change government processes except by peaceful and legal means," he replied, "that question has been pretty well litigated."

The government's campaign catapulted Bridges even higher into the ranks of left-wing heroes. The Citizens Committee for Harry Bridges gathered celebrities like Orson Welles and Lillian Hellman to raise funds for his defense. Dalton Trumbo wrote his twenty-eight-page pamphlet for distribution at one of the many pro-Bridges rallies held along the West Coast. Pete Seeger collaborated on a single with the Almanac Singers (with Woody Guthrie in the chorus) called "The Ballad of Harry Bridges," which began, "Let me tell you of a sailor, Harry Bridges is his name / an honest union leader who the bosses tried to frame." Here again was a figure from the 1930s left coming under sustained attack as the country's political culture turned to the right in the 1940s.

Bridges got very little support from the CIO. By the early 1940s, its leadership had begun to sour on its Communist membership, and not without reason. The Communists claimed to stand for worker democracy, but after taking control of a local or a union, in several cases they ran it as a clique, excluding the rank and file from decision making. They rigged elections, found ways to bar non-Communist candidates from running, played loose with finances, and forced unnecessary work stoppages because, as through a glass darkly, they thought that's what Stalin wanted. This, at least, was the broad-brush caricature with which their enemies portrayed every Communist in the CIO, even though many Communists remained loyal union members. But the fight was on. "To Communists the yardstick of a union leader's 'progressivism' is not the soundness of his labor policies but his readiness to approve Kremlin policy," wrote David Dubinsky, the anti-Communist president of the International Ladies Garment Workers Union. Joe Curran, a former Communist who ran the National Maritime Union, called their tactics "no different than those practiced by the Nazis when they destroyed the trade union movement of Germany." Everyone knew that a fiery clash between the center and left of the labor movement was coming; all it needed was a match.

By the end of World War II, American labor and the number of Communists within the movement were both at an all-time high. Nearly 13 million people, more than a third of the total workforce not employed on farms, were in unions. The Communists and their allies controlled a third of the forty-two CIO unions, including many of the largest, above all the United Electrical Workers, with its more than 600,000 members. After years of accepting no-strike pledges and wage limits to advance the war effort, the unions were ready to fight. Nearly 400,000 workers struck in 1945, including the 10,500 who walked off their Hollywood lots in March. Some 4.6 million workers struck the next year.

If labor was eager to pick up where it had left off—pushing for better benefits and conditions, along with a broader platform of civil and workplace rights—the rest of the country was not. Of course, men returning to the workforce were happy to have someone fighting to get them fatter paychecks. But broad majorities of the public opposed striking, and many blamed the Communists for the disruptive work stoppages. A Gallup poll in July 1946 found that 57 percent of Americans thought the party had at least a substantial influence in union decision making.

The business sector leaped at the opportunity—not just to roll back Communists, but to roll back many of the gains made by labor under Roosevelt. Business groups teamed with the American Legion and other patriotic organizations to argue that behind seemingly moderate union leaders like Walter Reuther of the United Auto Workers and Philip Murray, the new head of the CIO, lurked Communist puppet masters. "Reuther decides whether or not we can have automobiles," lamented the head of the National Association of Manufacturers. "Murray decides when we can have steel to build automobiles or refrigerators or homes." In September 1946, just ahead of the midterms, the U.S. Chamber of Commerce printed hundreds of thousands of copies of a report called "Communist Infiltration in the United Sates: Its Nature and How to Combat It," which included a lengthy section on Communists in the labor movement and why they had to be defeated. "Their demands are insatiable," it read, "because they thrive on trouble."

The strike wave came at a perilous time. The war had more than doubled the country's gross domestic product. Unemployment in mid-1945 was practically nonexistent, but the sudden end of the war threatened all of that. "Conversion" to a peacetime economy was the catchword of the

year in 1946. It meant demobilizing millions of servicemembers, dismantling or retrofitting thousands of factories, and finding housing for a wel-
ter of young families (and some 100,000 homeless veterans). Everyone
expected a depression—after the experience of the 1930s, it was a learned
response. At the end of 1945, Henry Wallace, still the secretary of commerce, predicted that domestic output would drop by $40 billion in the
coming months.

Truman tried to appease both sides. He called for collective bargain-
ing and higher wages. He urged unions to commit to a temporary mora-
torium on work stoppages. But the strikes continued—General Motors,
the coal industry; at one point in 1946 a million people were on picket
lines simultaneously. When A. F. Whitney, the president of the powerful
Brotherhood of Railroad Trainmen, came to the White House to inform
the president that his and the other railroad unions planned to strike the
next day, Truman signed an executive order to seize and operate them.
The unions went on strike anyway, effectively shutting down the U.S.
transportation system. Truman demanded emergency legislation to draft
the striking workers into the Army. Finally, Whitney and the rest backed
down, and settled on Truman's terms.

Conservative Republicans and Southern Democrats got in their licks
too. On the first day of the new Congress, in January 1947, they submitted
seventeen bills to limit labor rights. Over the next decade HUAC would
hold more than a hundred hearings covering Communism in the labor
movement. Representative Fred Hartley Jr., a Republican from New Jersey, warned that "a single communist in a position of power within the
labor movement could act under the direction of Russian agents so as to
seriously hinder this country's ability to defend its people and wage war
against its enemies." Soon after, he and Senator Robert Taft cosponsored
legislation packed with provisions restricting labor rights, among them
the requirement to sign anti-Communist affidavits. The bill sailed through
Congress with strong bipartisan support and even overcame a presidential
veto. It became law on June 23, 1947.

Speaking to reporters in May, Hartley had said that even many union
members supported his bill, because it gave "more rights to the individual worker than they ever had before." That was overstating things. But it

was an open secret that a number of moderate union leaders supported the anti-Communist provision. The war had merely suspended what, by 1941, had been an incipient civil war between the left and moderate wings of the labor movement. By the time Taft and Hartley got their bill together, Walter Reuther had effectively barred Communists from leadership positions at the United Auto Workers. Joe Curran had done the same at the National Maritime Union. "If I had my way," added Lewis, who had since left the CIO and turned against his former left-wing allies, "not a single Communist would belong to any labor union in the United States."

Even more so than Philip Murray, the head of the CIO, it was Walter Reuther of the autoworkers who drove the incipient campaign against Communists within the CIO's ranks. He was as charismatic and ambitious as Bridges but different in every other possible way. Redheaded and perpetually boyish, he neither smoke nor drank, unlike practically every other union leader at the time. In person he could be a bit cold and formal, lacking Bridges's sardonic wit. "He looked more like a junior executive than a labor activist," wrote his biographer Kevin Boyle, and in fact Reuther had spent just a few years on the factory line before transitioning to full-time union work. In between, he and his brother Victor traveled through the Soviet Union, arriving with bright-eyed curiosity and leaving convinced that Communism was a dead end.

Reuther was solidly liberal and a supporter of extending the New Deal, but he saw the Communist Party as an authoritarian scam, a sort of mass cult that drew in workers with its rhetoric, then exploited them to promote the interests of a foreign power. He was a founding member of Americans for Democratic Action, the liberal anti-Communist group, and remained one of its most vocal members. "Communism is in perpetual war with what democracy preaches, for it cannot abide the sanctity of the individual or the interplay of honest differences," Reuther proclaimed. He also felt personally burned by party members. At the CIO's 1938 Michigan convention, while he was still a rising figure in the UAW, he had formed a caucus with several Communist officers to remove the union's unpopular president—only to discover them huddled with another faction, working out a deal to keep the man in place in exchange for more influence in the union. "If you carry through this double-cross," Reuther thundered, "then count me on the other side, not only in this fight, but from here on out!"

Reuther was a man of his word. Already in 1940, long before other moderates came out against Communists in their ranks, he urged the UAW to purge them. He took control of the union at its 1946 convention, in Atlantic City, winning by a slim 114 votes out of 8,761 cast, on a nineteen-point plan that included barring Communists from its payroll. Fistfights erupted; a potted plant was overturned. The left-wingers called him a reactionary, but he didn't care: During his first year he fired dozens of Communists and suspected party members from the national union offices, then took aim at the locals. He was the first to insist that his union officers sign affidavits, and by the end of the year dozens of liberal leaders from across the CIO followed suit.

Things came to a head at the CIO's 1949 convention, held in Cleveland in late October. The 1948 presidential race, in which Henry Wallace's progressive campaign split the liberal-left coalition into two warring camps, had also cracked open the long-simmering tensions between centrist and left-wing unions. At the convention Murray and Reuther mounted the podium inside the city's Public Hall, a vast, smoke-filled auditorium, to declare a purge of its Communist-led unions. "The Communist program for labor is a program for destruction," Murray thundered to thousands of gathered delegates. Reuther concurred. "We have come here to cut out the cancer and save the body of the CIO."

Ostensibly, the dividing issue was whether a union's leadership was willing to sign the affidavits, mandated by the Taft-Hartley law, swearing they were not Communists. The largest of the Communist-led unions, the United Electrical Workers, had refused to sign them, and had already accepted its fate by announcing it would no longer pay dues to the CIO. Others, like the Farm Equipment Workers, likewise refused to sign and were sure to be kicked out soon. Bridges and his leadership had grudgingly signed the affidavits, even though the union's rank and file was full of Communists. Would the signatures be enough to save them from being expelled from the CIO?

Late one night Bridges stepped out of the stuffy auditorium, plucked up his suit collar against the November wind coming off Lake Erie, and walked across the street to Murray's hotel suite. He found the CIO boss and his advisers seated around a coffee table. Reuther was there too. So was James Carey, who used to run the United Electrical Workers but was kicked out when he tried, and failed, to rid it of Communists.

Bridges began to plead his case. He was no Communist, he said, and Communists did not control his union. Carey rushed over, got right in his face. "You're a goddamn liar, Bridges."

He held his ground. "So now we have reached the point where a trade union, because it disagrees on political matters with the national CIO, can be expelled."

"All I can say, Harry, is that your halo is on crooked today," said Reuther, sitting beside Murray.

Bridges couldn't believe that Murray was willing to eject so many unions at once, nearly a quarter million CIO members, some 20 percent of its total ranks. To Bridges, the great achievement of the CIO was its ability to unite the entire left under a single banner, then use the collective strengths to push a single agenda. Sure, he conceded, there were divisions. Bridges denounced the government's massive relief program for Europe—the Marshall Plan—after Murray had endorsed it. Murray had thrown the CIO's support behind Harry Truman and the Democrats during the 1948 race. Most of the left-wing unions, including Bridges and the longshoremen, had broken with his decision and backed Wallace. But Bridges figured that exiling left-wing unions would sap the organization of its strength at precisely the moment when big business and other anti-labor interests were gathering strength.

The affidavits were obviously a trap, he argued, a device concocted to undermine the union movement. But Murray and Reuther's position was never really about the affidavits, and Bridges knew it. It was about control. Bridges insisted on independence and autonomy for his longshoremen at a time when Murray, Reuther, and others were centralizing power. At war's end, Bridges had called for a no-strike pledge across the movement, just as dozens of unions were preparing for work stoppages. He called out fellow unions when they fell behind on issues like racial and gender equality in the workplace. To Bridges, talk of Communism was just an excuse to purge leaders who did not follow Murray's agenda. But to Murray, the intransigence from the left-wing unions could only mean one thing: They were in the tank for Moscow, and were more loyal to international Communism than they were to the American labor movement. The left-wing unions, Communist-run or not, had to go, including Bridges and the longshoremen.

The tragedy is that they were both right. Many of the Communist union leaders were indeed under the spell of Moscow. Many of them, though far from all, did not have the best interests of the movement in mind, but rather imagined it as a vehicle to revolution. Murray had a point in concluding that they were unreliable, if not inimical, to American labor. But Bridges was also right. The fight was not only about Communism; it was about centralizing control behind the CIO leadership. Murray and Reuther were using the immediacy of the Cold War and the onset of the Red Scare as an excuse to clean house and solidify their power.

By 1949 Bridges's legal troubles had returned. Hoover and the FBI had never dropped their insistence that Bridges was a top figure in the West Coast Communist Party. This time the government tried a different tack: It accused Bridges and two associates of conspiracy to commit perjury during the previous trial, when they claimed that he had not been a Communist. Bridges's trial on the West Coast was in full swing just as that of Alger Hiss came to its conclusion in New York. The Red Scare was shifting into a higher gear, and it was fanciful to assume that Bridges would escape the trial without a scratch. Still, he was shocked when, on April 4, 1950, the jury found him guilty and the judge sentenced him to five years in prison. Then he stripped Bridges of his citizenship. (The Supreme Court overturned the conviction and reinstated Bridges's citizenship in 1953.)

Bridges's conviction gave Murray the permission he needed to take the final step against the longshoremen. On August 30, the CIO's executive board voted 41 to 2 to expel the union's 75,000 members, along with the 5,000 members of the Marine Cooks and Stewards Union. When Murray announced the end of the purge a few days later, the CIO had cut 700,000 workers adrift. Bridges accepted the decision with his usual insouciance. "That will save us a lot of headaches, being free from that lousy outfit," he said.

Strangely, even as Bridges sustained heavy fire from the CIO and the Justice Department, he was making great strides toward peace with West Coast shipowners. After a pair of strikes, one of which ran through the summer and most of the fall of 1949, costing the companies $4 million a day, the two sides reached a sweeping agreement on time off, work stoppages, and arbitration that kept peace on the docks for another twenty-five years. Corporate negotiators found Bridges forthright, dependable, and admirable in his complete commitment to his members' interests. "He wants American free enterprise, American capitalism, to work," wrote *Fortune* magazine, with no lack of respect. Though Bridges eschewed political labels, his point of view by the late 1940s was more like that of a British Labour Party leader or a German Social Democrat than a burn-it-down radical. The director of one shipping company, who should have despised Bridges, praised him as a reliable negotiator who was simply "doing his best to get as much for the members of his union as he possibly could." And after several more years of fighting, Bridges won an appeal for his conviction and got the Department of Justice to drop its campaign against him.

The impact of the Red Scare on the American labor movement was immense and tragic. In purging its left wing, Murray removed many of the movement's most visionary leaders, the ones who saw unionism as being about not just wages and hours, but a different social order. They dreamed of an economy structured not by the needs of corporations, but the needs of workers. They dreamed of racial and sexual equality, at a time when many conservative union leaders maintained segregated memberships. And while some of them did follow the Soviet line, very few of them, by 1949, were committed Communists. Most were like Bridges—admiring of Communists, but not party members, and not beholden to its dictates. Bridges stood at the crux of the great divide in the American labor movement, and his career, both before and after the purge, shows what it might have become.

11

I Have in My Hand a List

Amid all the drama of the Hiss conviction and the fireworks at the CIO convention—not to mention the continued frenzy over the Soviet Union's first atomic bomb—few people noticed when, on February 9, 1950, an obscure, first-term senator from Wisconsin made a dinnertime speech to a meeting of the Women's Republican Club of Ohio County, based in the river town of Wheeling, West Virginia. Joseph McCarthy didn't want to be there, but he was doing his duty to the National Republican Congressional Committee, which every February sent its members on speaking tours to celebrate Lincoln's birthday and dish out partisan red meat to the party's loyal rank and file. Wheeling was just the first stop for McCarthy; afterward he intended to go west, to Reno, Salt Lake City, Las Vegas, and tiny Huron, South Dakota. McCarthy had recently hired a former reporter, George Waters, as a speechwriter, and as one of his first assignments had him write up two drafts to deliver that evening. One was a snoozer on foreign policy, the other a barnburner charging that Truman's State Department harbored 205 security risks. At almost the last minute, McCarthy chose the second.

Subversion was not a new theme for the senator. Elected in 1946, he had joined other first-time Republican candidates in attacking Truman on the issue, as well as his hapless Democratic opponent. In 1948, reacting to the Smith Act arrests, he told a colleague that "any man who joins the Communist Party, knowing that it is dedicated to the overthrow of the government by force, is guilty of treason the moment he joins it." Calling anything he didn't like "Communist" was second nature to him:

He used the slur against a housing project in Queens, New York, and accused the Madison, Wisconsin, *Capital Times* of having a "pro-Moscow slant." There is a story that McCarthy only landed on Communism as an issue when, at a dinner in January 1950 with Father Edmund Walsh and two other associates, he had fished around for issues to lift his sagging political fortunes. Walsh, an influential Jesuit who had founded the School of Foreign Service at Georgetown University, had reportedly suggested McCarthy go after Communism in government. Perhaps he did. But by then it had long become part of his talking points.

Given the tenor of the times, none of that was noteworthy; by 1950 it was the sort of thing that any conservative Republican was expected to say. The difference with McCarthy's Wheeling speech was its specificity. It was one thing to declare, offhand, that the State Department was pro-Communist. It was something else entirely to allege, as McCarthy did, the exact number of Communists actually working within it.

McCarthy always denied uttering the infamous sentence "I have in my hand a list," the line that seemed to encapsulate the Red Scare in just seven words. A local radio station recorded the speech, but the only copy was erased. Still, a reporter at the meeting wrote it down, and if it wasn't the exact wording, the point was the same: The senator said he had incontrovertible evidence that there were hundreds of people like Alger Hiss in the government. It was also not true. He had no list, not in his hand, not back in Washington. It was only a hair's breadth from a lie. There was indeed a list of sorts, from 1946, when then–Secretary of State James Byrnes had written to an Illinois congressman about the department's progress against accused security risks. It had identified 284 potential cases, and 79 had been removed. By the math, that meant 205 remained—as of 1946. McCarthy had not bothered to ask how the cases had been resolved, or even whether they had all involved charges of Communist subversion, and not one of the department's many other red flags, like alcohol abuse. Nor did he much care for consistency: He cited 207 at a stop in Denver, then 57 "card-carrying members" in Reno.

McCarthy had arrived in the Senate in early 1947 as something of a curiosity, having come out of nowhere to defeat one of the chamber's liberal lions, Robert La Follette Jr., in the Republican primary. He was just thirty-eight, a farm boy made good, climbing from small-town Wisconsin to Marquette Law School and a circuit court judgeship. He had volunteered for the war, and despite what his enemies said later, served with distinction—though he also burnished his record by claiming to have been part of a bomber crew, when in fact he was simply allowed to ride along a few times. The story earned him the nickname "Tail-Gunner Joe."

He built his campaigns against La Follette, and then against Howard McMurray in the general election, on personal attacks and innuendo, and trounced McMurray almost two to one. But he had struggled to make himself heard in the august Senate. He had ideological allies but few personal friends. He never set up a permanent home in Washington, crashing in spare bedrooms and on sofas, leaving his belongings scattered in closets across the city. He did not respect the Senate norms or Republican leadership. He drank at the wrong times, appearing inebriated at hearings, and spoke out on issues when the leadership wanted cub senators like him to keep quiet. His colleagues, like a wolf pack eager to separate from an ailing beta, hoped he would be one and done, out of office by 1952.

In large part because of his obscurity, the first reports of McCarthy's allegations in Wheeling did not appear in the national newspapers until several days later, and then as page 5 squibs. It was only when the State Department responded to the charges that reporters started to take serious notice. John Peurifoy, a deputy undersecretary of state, asked McCarthy to produce the names. The senator promised he would do just that, and more, when he returned to Washington.

One of the amazing things about the phenomenon that McCarthy and his associated "ism" would soon become is how, from the very beginning, reporters, congressmen, and other anti-Communists recognized him as a con man. "Sewer Politics," declared a Washington Post editorial on February 14, 1950, in describing his allegations. Even the American Legion, usually eager to jump on any allegation of un-Americanism, was skeptical. "When called upon to provide details I fear he fell down in so doing," wrote its commander. "In the opinion of many people he has gotten himself out on a limb."

It didn't matter. By the spring of 1950 McCarthy was a front-page fixture, and would remain that way for four years. In history he has gone down as a monster, so extreme in his willingness to tell Big Lie after Big Lie that he has become synonymous with the Red Scare itself. He is at the same time remembered as an aberration, a wild man, a singular cause of America's temporary national hysteria. But while he was certainly the best-known of the red-baiters, he was in fact a symptom of the era, not its cause. And if he shouted more loudly and crudely than others, in substance he did not say anything that virulent red-baiters like HUAC's John Rankin or J. Parnell Thomas had not already been saying for years. He was the era's uncomfortable id and a locus in the network of politicians, activists, columnists, and true believers who made the Red Scare possible. His significance lay in his unique ability to braid the two strands of the Red Scare—the culture war and the politics of Cold War security—into a single cord.

McCarthy's big moment came on February 20, 1950. He had promised to reveal all from the Senate floor. The Democrats tried to block him by leaving the chamber, thereby denying him a quorum and shutting down the proceedings. But by evening his allies had succeeded in wrangling enough of their Republican colleagues for the senator to begin. It was a preview of the way McCarthy would operate for the next four years: He rattled off cases but no names, describing lurid instances of dangerous subversives but offering no way to fact-check him. One person he described as a close associate of Harry Bridges; another, he said, had intervened with "a well-known general" to get yet another Communist hired to a sensitive position. "I do not believe that President Truman knows about them," McCarthy said. "I cannot help but feel that he is merely the prisoner of a bunch of twisted intellectuals who tell him what they want him to know."

The Democrats sat exasperated. "Will the senator tell us the name of the man for the record?" demanded Scott Lucas of Illinois, the majority leader, who had been trying to adjourn the Senate all evening.

"The senator can come to my office as soon as I finish and receive the names," McCarthy said—but only, he added, if that's what the entire Senate wanted. "The question is too important for either the senator from Illinois or the senator from Wisconsin to make the decision."

Instead, the next day, bleary-eyed after McCarthy's marathon speaking session ended close to midnight, the Democratic leadership huddled in Lucas's office. By now the press had caught a full whiff of McCarthy's scent, and they were making him an overnight star—and a potential problem in the upcoming midterm elections. The solution, Lucas decided, was to expose him, to take him seriously and give him a platform, and thereby enough rope to hang himself. The Senate would create a committee to examine his charges. Millard Tydings, a conservative Democrat from Maryland, would be its chairman. Lucas seemed oblivious to the possibility that the rope he was offering McCarthy would end up around his own neck.

What drove reporters' interest in this man McCarthy? He was probably lying, they all knew. But after Hiss and Coplon, who could be sure? And as some reporters were already learning, there was a train-wreck quality to the senator that turned the press corps into rubberneckers: He dressed like a slob, ate like a slob, talked like a slob. He invited reporters into his hotel room while he changed, tossing off quotes while he shaved down his five o'clock shadow in a sleeveless undershirt. He knew how to stoke the ardor of desperate journalists by feeding them zinger quotes right before deadline, so that they did not have enough time to verify them, but couldn't afford not to publish them. On a level few of his colleagues were even aware of, McCarthy understood what made the media tick—that salaciousness, not profundity, drove the front page. "McCarthy was a dream story," said Willard Edwards, who covered McCarthy for the *Chicago Tribune*. "I wasn't off the front pages for four years."

There was something deeply, uncomfortably but recognizably American about McCarthy, especially in that first decade after World War II. He liked to say that McCarthyism was "Americanism with its sleeves rolled up," and in a way he wasn't wrong. Even Americans who detested his politics recognized in him a culture that validated the unthrottled American, back from the war and determined to live life on his terms. He worked hard—in a sense, he never stopped working, even when he was three drinks in by lunch. He said what was on his mind. He slapped backs and gladded hands. He was the cartoonish version of the postwar American man, a real-life predecessor to Ralph Kramden and Archie Bunker. He gambled, he drank incessantly, he harassed women. His diet followed the national postwar appetite, but to an excess unimaginable even in those health-unconscious times: two cheeseburgers and a milkshake at lunch with a slice of apple pie topped with more cheese for dessert; a slab of steak for dinner, slathered in butter and sauce and flanked by greasy side dishes; and all of it washed down by copious amounts of alcohol, usually Scotch and soda, or brandy, or a duet of vodka martinis.

McCarthy arrived in Washington as part of a Republican wave that broke over the country in 1946. Many of his fellow newcomers in the Senate were drawn from the party's hard-right wing: John Bricker of Ohio, William Knowland of California, and William Jenner of Indiana joined the likes of Kenneth Wherry of Nebraska, Styles Bridges of New Hampshire, and Robert Taft of Ohio to form an anti-Europe, anti–New Deal, anti-Communist bloc. They were there not just to oppose Truman but to roll back everything his predecessor had achieved. And not just the policies of the New Deal, but the broader culture that the New Deal and the 1930s had ushered in.

They had grown up thinking that America—real America, at least— meant small farm towns where government stopped at the mailbox, led by a white, male, business elite that bowed to no one save the local clergy. White, conservative Christianity was the bedrock of their worldview and their guiding light in politics. They had never stopped believing in such a country, and they were determined to get it back. They lashed at Democrats and left-leaning elites as anti-American, allegedly forcing alien ideas onto a country that in their minds was still the domain of conservative, Protestant white men. Another of their ranks, Hugh Butler of Nebraska, put this worldview succinctly when he lashed out at Secretary of State Dean Acheson: "I look at that fellow, I watch his smart-aleck manner and his British clothes and that New Dealism in everything he says and does, and I want to shout, 'Get out! Get Out! You stand for everything that has been wrong in the United States for years!'"

If during his first few years McCarthy's Republican colleagues had looked at him skeptically, even if they agreed with him ideologically, that all changed after Wheeling. Almost all of them admitted that, for all his shortcomings, McCarthy was the savior they had been looking for. Following the unexpected disaster of the 1948 presidential campaign, the party concluded that its greatest mistake was not leaning into ardent anti-Communism as an issue. By 1950, Truman had done an adequate job of neutralizing the matter—prosecuting Hiss, Coplon, and the Smith Act defendants; establishing loyalty boards; unleashing J. Edgar Hoover. The Republicans suspected there was more to be said, but how? McCarthy showed them. With his signature grandiose style, he wedded the cultural and the geopolitical, the anti–New Dealism reactionism and the embrace of security at all costs. He showed how, during the Cold War, the longstanding, deep-seated hatred of progressivism on the right could be twinned with the newfound fear of Soviet Communism to create a whirlwind of political hysteria and recriminations.

So when McCarthy came begging for material to back up his charges, colleagues gladly opened their doors. Richard Nixon let him sift through his voluminous files. Veteran senators offered advice on how to deal with Millard Tydings, the Maryland Democrat who would now chair the committee looking into McCarthy's charges. And Taft, the very conservative but widely respected minority leader, gave McCarthy cover by defending him to the press.

The pro-McCarthy forces were not limited to Capitol Hill; in fact, few did more to boost McCarthy's image than a conservative journalist named George Sokolsky. Often referred to as "the high priest of militant anti-Communism," Sokolsky wrote a syndicated column, "These Days," which appeared in more than 320 newspapers. Practically every week he defended McCarthy and attacked his enemies. He funneled him reports, speeches, and gossip. Behind the scenes, Sokolsky acted as a sort of employment office for McCarthy, staffing the senator's office with true believers. He was the glue that kept disparate corners of the anti-Communist right linked to McCarthy's office. Even after many of McCarthy's allies abandoned him, Sokolsky stayed true. "My own attitude is of course naturally very pro McCarthy because to some degree I may be responsible for the difficulties he got into," Sokolsky wrote in a 1954 letter to Roy Brewer, a conservative labor leader in Hollywood. "After all, he was fighting our fight in the best way he knew how and just as we encouraged others to perform in this battle, we encouraged him." When Brewer, a McCarthy skeptic, pushed back, Sokolsky doubled down: "I, who believe in his methods because I was among those who helped devise them, am certain that no other methods will succeed in eliminating particularly spies within our society. Our laws are so rigged that the due process of law works entirely in their favor."

J. Edgar Hoover too saw something in McCarthy, at least at first. They were both unmarried workaholics with similar leisure interests. They ate at the same restaurants, and bet at the same racetracks around Baltimore. Hoover cultivated the Senate newcomer, even inviting him to give the keynote speech at the 1948 FBI Academy graduation. He gave his approval when McCarthy hired former FBI men to his staff. But Hoover also recognized McCarthy as a risk, a blustering showman whose wild-card antics contrasted with the meticulous professionalism of the FBI. He resented McCarthy's appropriation of an issue that Hoover had done too much to corner, and feared that if the senator fell, he could take anti-Communism as a whole with him. As a result Hoover played coy, offering McCarthy verbal support but encouraging the Justice Department to refuse his requests for files on the supposed security risks he intended to name on the floor of the Senate.

The Tydings Committee began its hearings in the Senate Caucus Room on March 8, 1950. In another, more reasonable moment, they would have been the cemetery of McCarthy's political career. Despite all the Republicans offering to help, he came in with no plan, and the Democrats knew it. Senator Tydings, without letting McCarthy make an opening statement, began the proceedings by demanding the names to go with the cases he had touted. McCarthy parried wildly, promising that the truth would come out in due time. He tossed out names of alleged Communists with abandon. A woman named Dorothy Kenyon, never before identified as a security risk, was the first. She was a New York lawyer who had worked alongside New Deal agencies on women's and consumer rights, but by 1950 was in private practice. She had long ago signed her name to several petitions in support of various left-wing causes, but she was otherwise uninvolved with anything approaching a Communist front, let alone the party itself.

When she appeared before the committee a few days after McCarthy brought up her name, she set the senators straight—though McCarthy himself was noticeably absent that day, as he often was when he wasn't introducing new charges. "Senator McCarthy is an unmitigated liar," Kenyon told reporters. The committee subsequently cleared her name, but her career as a public servant would never recover. "A Poor Beginning," editorialized *The New York Times* about the first few days of hearings. "Senator McCarthy of Wisconsin may have more to tell, and he deserves a chance to complete his story. It must be said, however, that it is off to a feeble start."

It was the space between those two poles—recognizing the emptiness of McCarthy's charges, yet insisting that he had a right to make them—through which the senator drove. Ignoring his failure on Kenyon, he moved on to other names and accusations: Philip Jessup, a diplomat and former chairman of the American Council of the Institute of Pacific Relations; Gustavo Durán, a United Nations official; Esther Brunauer, a State Department official who liaised with the U.N. and other international bodies. All of McCarthy's targets came to Washington to offer robust defenses before the committee. But none of it mattered, because by the time they arrived McCarthy had already moved on to other people, other charges.

Truman thought McCarthy was showing himself the fool they all knew him to be. So did Dean Acheson. At a press conference, the secretary of state made light of the proceedings, and McCarthy's persistent attacks on him—among other jabs, the senator insisted on calling him the "Red Dean" of American Communism. The secretary opened with a joke about a fight between Communists and anti-Communists. Eventually, Acheson said, the police arrive to break up the fight, clubs swinging, saying they were all under arrest. When one man protests, insisting he is an anti-Communist, an officer barks, "I don't give a damn whether you're a Communist, an anti-Communist, or what kind of Communist you are. You're under arrest!"

The gathered reporters laughed. As the Tydings hearings wore on, it seemed likely that McCarthy would fade out, that he would run out of names and that the public would grow tired of him. That the furor that began in Wheeling, West Virginia, in February would sputter to a close in Washington, D.C., a few months later.

12

A Government Within the Government

McCarthy was clearly in a bind. He was flailing before the Tydings Committee, barely keeping ahead of the Democratic chairman and managing to do so only by bouncing from one unsupportable accusation to another. He needed to land a punch. Finally, in a speech on the Senate floor on April 25, nearly three months into the hearings, he found his opportunity. Weeks earlier, McCarthy said, he had given Senator Tydings the criminal record of a man working for the State Department. Yet Tydings, McCarthy alleged, had done nothing about it. "Is the senator aware of the fact that I gave the complete police record of this man to the senator from Maryland, this man who was a homosexual?" McCarthy said. "The record shows—it is the police record, senators should understand—that he spent his time hanging around the men's room in Lafayette Park."

Tydings interjected. The purpose of the committee, he said, was to hunt Communists, not—in his words—"homos." McCarthy, he charged, was just trying to shift the subject. Why focus on gay men when the goal was to weed out Communists?

"I do not know which is the worst," retorted William Jenner, a conservative Republican from Indiana and an ally of McCarthy. "Does the senator?"

Less than an hour later, Senator Kenneth Wherry of Nebraska, another McCarthy ally, took to the floor. The man in question had been forced to resign as soon as McCarthy brought up his record. "It is my belief that had the senator from Wisconsin accomplished nothing more than that one thing, it would be worth the effort, the chagrin, the embarrassment, the charges, and all the smear to which he has been subjected," Wherry said. "I am proud to be associated with a man who is doing his level best to clear this country of Communists and moral perverts in the government." McCarthy, it seemed, was getting results.

Though none of the senators identified the man in question, his name was Carmel Offie, and while not a public figure by any stretch, he was all but certainly the highest-ranking openly gay man in the federal government. By the time of his ouster, he had worked his way from entry-level clerk in the U.S. embassy in Honduras to the top civilian ranks in occupied Germany. In 1948 he became one of the earliest hires to the CIA's clandestine branch. He was an ardent anti-Communist and one of the country's most effective spymasters in the heady, dangerous early days of the Cold War. The government cut him loose at a time when it needed him most, simply because of his sexual orientation. His story is worth recounting, not just as one of McCarthy's many targets but as one of the highest-profile casualties in the anti-gay campaign that would come to be known as the Lavender Scare.

While the majority of Americans had long considered homosexuality a sin, they had also considered one's sexuality a personal matter, to be dealt with discreetly, save for the occasional police raid on a gay bar or bathhouse. But the tumult of World War II had opened up new opportunities, and visibility, for gay men and women in America. Thousands who had lived in small-town isolation were suddenly thrown together in the military, or in wartime boomtowns like Washington. It was, the historian John D'Emilio wrote, "a national coming-out experience." And for a time after the war's end, it seemed like that crack in the doorway might remain, or even open wider.

The conservative turn that followed put a brutal end to those small hopes. So did the Red Scare. As in other areas of American life, anti-Communist fervor was both a catalyst and symptom of the return to traditional, rigid gender roles, and with it a hard turn against homosexuality as a threat to the older ways. It was bad enough, politicians declared, that gay men and lesbians were moral perverts and sexual predators. Now, they were supposedly national security threats. They were allegedly subject to blackmail. Those in the closet were by their very nature, such politicians said, liars. Their very presence in an office or a military unit was said to drag down morale. And their allegedly large numbers on the public payroll was attributed to their membership in a worldwide gay cabal that, according to Admiral Roscoe H. Hillenkoetter, the first director of the CIA, operated as a "government within the government." Guy George Gabrielson, the chairman of the Republican National Committee, said that "sexual perverts who have infiltrated our government in recent years" were "perhaps as dangerous as the actual Communists." Here again was the intertwining of two forms of paranoia: the fear that an anti-American elite was secretly running the country and the absolutist rush to security at all costs brought on by the Cold War.

The historian David K. Johnson estimates that more than five thousand people were fired or forced to resign as security risks because of their sexual preference, and an untold number more who either left before they were discovered or decided not to enter government in the first place. Others, like the writer James Kirchick, put the number much higher, to as many as ten thousand—nearly as many as were pushed out for being Communists or fellow travelers.

Carmel Offie was born in 1909 in Sharon, Pennsylvania, near the Ohio border, the son of working-class Italian immigrants. He moved to Washington when he was seventeen, and despite his lack of a college degree, soon found a job as a clerk in the Foreign Service. He served in Honduras, then Moscow, climbing the ranks thanks to his work ethic, his innate sense of diplomatic politesse, and a certain amoral view of the world that made him useful to a string of superiors who took him under their wing. William Bullitt, the ambassador to Moscow, relied on Offie to procure him fine French wines and other delicacies considered unobtainable under the Soviets. When Roosevelt promoted Bullitt to ambassador to France in 1936, Offie went along. Once more, he bloomed: In October the Marquis and Marquise de Polignac, whom Bullitt called "the greatest snobs in France," threw a party in Offie's honor at Maxim's restaurant. When John F. Kennedy and his brother Joe came through Paris in 1938, they sought out Offie to entertain them.

After the Germans captured Paris in 1940, Bullitt hoped to be named ambassador to the rump French government based in Vichy. Instead he found no new posting on offer. For that he blamed Sumner Welles, the patrician deputy secretary of state and a confidant of the president, who Bullitt believed to be a rival. True or not, Bullitt vowed revenge. Welles had a predilection for propositioning male sleeping-car porters for oral sex; Bullitt got ahold of the details in 1943, drew them up in a pamphlet, and had Offie distribute them around Capitol Hill. Bullitt then went to Roosevelt with a fait accompli: Congress would now have to investigate, and to avoid embarrassment the president had no choice but to ask Welles to resign.

Less than a month later, Offie was himself arrested after propositioning an undercover vice cop in Lafayette Square, a swatch of greenery on the north side of the White House that was a popular site for gay cruising. Fortunately for him, Cordell Hull, the secretary of state who had hated Welles and appreciated Offie's role in his dismissal, interceded before news of the incident leaked, and before Offie was charged. He was quietly shuffled out of the country.

Offie was also lucky that Washington was in the middle of a war, and willing to overlook such indiscretions. The city had changed immensely since he had first arrived, going from sleepy Southern town to the nerve center of an emerging global superpower. From a metropolitan population of 700,000 in 1930, it would reach 1.4 million in 1950. For the gay men among them, the city was a haven of relative tolerance: gay and gay-friendly bars proliferated in the neighborhood north of the White House, while parks like Lafayette became popular nighttime destinations. "I made more new friends, had more sex, and thought less about the stigma of being queer between Pearl Harbor and V-J Day than at any time in my life," recalled one gay War Department employee.

Offie went to work in occupied Italy, then Germany. He ingratiated himself with generals by throwing lavish parties at his Frankfurt home. He thought nothing of hopping a plane to Italy to secure a wheel of Gorgonzola. His superiors, at least, thought highly of the man: In 1946 they secured him a Medal of Merit—not long before he was caught trying to smuggle bundles of cash back to the United States. He was sent home.

If he felt crestfallen, it didn't last long. The Office of Policy Coordination (OPC), a new clandestine service nominally under the State Department and intended to combat Communist advances across Central and Western Europe, came calling. Its director, Frank Wisner, knew Offie by reputation, and realized that his special skills and deep knowledge of the grayer corners of Europe would come in handy. Offie went back to Frankfurt, officially to handle refugee issues but in fact to find, among the displaced, those men and women who might return to their Eastern homelands as spies. After the office was shifted to the CIA, Offie persuaded the agency to fund Radio Free Europe, and even procured transmitters to broadcast pro-American propaganda into Soviet-controlled territory. Under a secret operation code-named Paperclip, he fished out German scientists and former officers, including Nazis and war criminals, who could be of use in the coming clash with the Soviet Union.

Never shy, Offie was growing arrogant, and increasingly willing to express his sexuality in ways that made his buttoned-up colleagues blush. He would rub his nipples during office conversations, and jokingly compared his bedroom to "the playing fields of Eton." Coworkers grew uncomfortable, and resentful. "Who was it that said about Offie that either he was going to be secretary of state some day or his body was going to be found floating down the Potomac River?" recalled a fellow diplomat.

He made enemies at the wrong time. The tolerance of wartime Washington was giving way; homosexuality was increasingly considered not just a personal issue but a public menace. Domestic panics abounded: crime, pornography, gambling, juvenile delinquency, even comic books, all of which fed blaring headlines, congressional hearings, and B-movie plot lines. In 1946 the Washington city government declared that solicitation and lewd conduct could result in a felony charge, and a bolstered vice squad blanketed parks and wooded areas at night. The next year the U.S Park Police announced a "sex perversion elimination campaign," which in its first fourteen months resulted in 543 arrests, including 65 in a single night in Lafayette Park. And in 1948 Alfred Kinsey published his book *Sexual Behavior in the Human Male*, which reported that 37 percent of men had experienced a homosexual encounter to orgasm, and that 10 percent were exclusively homosexual. Rather than catalyze greater tolerance, the Kinsey Report helped set off a campaign of repression, nowhere more so than in the federal government.

The infrastructure for rapidly cashiering gay men and lesbians in the federal government was already in place. In 1941, on the eve of America's entry into World War II, the Army adopted a policy to eliminate "homosexual proclivities" from its ranks, with only moderate success. The FBI had opened a "sex perverts in government file" in 1942. A rider attached to the 1947 State Department funding bill gave the secretary of state absolute power to dismiss employees believed to be subversive, security risks, or homosexual. Secretary George Marshall established a Personnel Security Board, charged with removing State Department employees found guilty of "habitual drunkenness, sexual perversion, moral turpitude, financial irresponsibility, or criminal record." The board forced out thirty-one people under those categories in 1947, twenty-eight in 1948, and thirty-one in 1949.

The emerging politics of homophobia coincinded with the growing animosity toward Washington, especially toward the diplomatic corps. The State Department had long been the target of anti-gay slurs; one common attack on the East Coast elite was its supposed lack of manliness and virility—which at the time were tightly linked to one's heterosexuality—and the State Department was that elite's highest bastion. Congressmen openly referred to State Department clerks as "cookie pushers," "powder puffs," and "pinkos," a double entendre attacking both their sexuality and their alleged political allegiances. Journalists played their part as well: One writer, warning of the "sisterhood in our State Department," wrote that "in American statecraft, where you need desperately a man of iron, you often get a nance."

In October 1949, Offie made a pass at an agent from the Army's counterintelligence corps while the two were meeting at the OPC's headquarters, located in a nondescript temporary building at 17th and Constitution. The agent reported Offie to the CIA's internal security office, and eventually someone passed the report—along with a copy of the police blotter from his 1943 arrest—to McCarthy.

Offie might still have kept out of sight, and kept his job, were it not for the February 1950 testimony of Deputy Undersecretary John Puerifoy of the State Department. He was appearing with Secretary Acheson before an appropriations subcommittee, ostensibly to discuss the department's upcoming budget. Senators Styles Bridges and Pat McCarran, two of McCarthy's closest allies, both sat on the subcommittee, so the subject naturally turned to the State Department's alleged failure to clear out subversives. Bridges asked Peurifoy how many employees under investigation had resigned in recent years.

"In this shady category that you referred to earlier, there are 91 cases, sir," Peurifoy responded.

McCarran, his interest piqued, asked him to clarify what he meant by "shady category."

"Most of these were homosexuals, Mr. Chairman," Peurifoy said—hoping, it seemed, to emphasize how few actual Communists worked in the State Department.

Coming just weeks after McCarthy's speech in Wheeling set off a new phase in the Red Scare, Peurifoy's offhand comment ignited a new phase in the Lavender Scare. Journalists and Republicans seized on the number 91, not as evidence that the State Department was doing its job, but as proof that all the gay-baiting comments about "cookie pushers" were justified. McCarthy was especially eager to exploit the opening. Weeks before he alluded to Offie on the Senate floor, he was already peppering his appearances before the Tydings Committee with references to an allegedly vast number of "perverts" still working in the State Department. To no avail, Tydings implored his colleagues to "stop the continual heckling about homosexuals and other matters of that kind and let us get down, first, to the matter of investigating any possible disloyalty." But McCarthy and his allies were a step ahead of the chairman: In Red Scare Washington, homosexuality and Communism were two parts of the same thing, and they would do everything they could to exploit that link.

Peurifoy's revelation and Offie's ouster in early 1950 moved homosexuality from the sidelines to the center of the national security hysteria. Even as the Tydings Committee continued to examine McCarthy's charges that spring, two separate subcommittees convened to study whether gay men and women posed a threat to the national interest.

The first was led by Senator Wherry, who considered himself "the expert on homosexuality in the State Department," a bold claim for a former undertaker from Pawnee City, Nebraska. He was known for his stubbornly isolationist views and gift for political malapropisms—"chief joints of staff," he once said. "The distinguished Senator from Junior." Wherry was also among the most diehard believers in the fundamental threat to American life posed by homosexuality. He promoted the unproven claim that the Nazis had compiled a list of gay American officials, which fell into Soviet hands after the war and now offered a blueprint for blackmail. "Only the most naïve could believe that the Communists' fifth column in the United States would neglect to propagate and use homosexuals to gain their treacherous ends," Wherry said.

Along with Wherry's frequent grandstanding comments to reporters, his hearings made headlines after Lieutenant Roy Blick, the head of the Washington police vice squad, estimated that there were 5,000 gay men and lesbians in the city, and that 3,750 of them worked for the federal government. The lieutenant's math was fuzzy, but by the time anyone got around to checking it, the numbers had become conventional wisdom, a concrete assessment of the "threat" Washington faced.

Another star witness was Harry B. Mitchell, the head of the Civil Service Commission, who told the subcommittee that of the ninety-one employees cited by Deputy Undersecretary Peurifoy, twenty-two had easily found jobs in other government agencies. Wherry, incensed, demanded action, and Mitchell complied. Along with the twenty-two names, he drew together arrest lists from the D.C. police and the FBI, culling the names of nearly 180 additional federal employees. Mitchell then forwarded the names to dozens of government offices, demanding action. The Smithsonian Institution, the War Claims Commission, even the Post Office turned on their gay and lesbian employees. After Mitchell sent the list to the Agriculture Department in May 1950, 11 employees were immediately fired. Several months later, the FBI combined its "sex perverts in government" file with its database on sex offenders, creating a voluminous list from which J. Edgar Hoover selectively leaked tidbits to congressional allies and friendly police departments. Meanwhile, a seminar for federal managers, titled "Perversion Among Government Workers" and led by Robert Felix, director of the new National Institute of Mental Health, proved so popular that extra sessions had to be added.

The State Department moved especially quickly. Two staff members in Washington focused on the issue full-time, and every chief of mission was tasked with cleaning out their respective embassies and consulates. The department built a list of 3,000-plus names of suspected homosexuals, and checked new applicants against it. In June 1950, some 130 employees at the U.S. mission to occupied Germany were sent home as security risks, including "two homosexuals" and "eight to ten habitual drunkards." Eight months later, four "confessed homosexuals" were sent home from the consulate in Hong Kong, and in October 1951 four gay embassy workers in Seoul were forced to resign. By 1953 Carlisle Humelsine, who had succeeded Peurifoy as deputy undersecretary of state, was able to report to Congress that of the 654 people let go because of loyalty or security concerns in the previous five years, 402 had been gay men. Unlike employees dismissed as disloyal or security risks, those dismissed for being gay had no way to appeal the decision.

Despite Alfred Kinsey's insistence that homosexual experimentation was common, the department took a zero-tolerance approach: Even a single incident marked one for dismissal. The result was more than a loss of employment. Names were shared with the private sector, making it hard to find another job. Even worse, it often meant exposure to friends, family, spouses, children, an absolutely devastating outcome for closeted homosexuals. Andrew Ference, an administrative assistant at the U.S. embassy in Paris, underwent two days of interrogation in August 1954. The next day his roommate and lover returned home to find Ference dead of self-asphyxiation. Peter Szluk, a security officer for the State Department who investigated allegedly gay employees, later told an interviewer that "the only thing I regret in my campaign to rid the State Department of that type of individual was when within minutes, and sometimes maybe a week, they would commit suicide. . . . One guy, he barely left my office and he must've had this thing in his coat pocket—and boom!—right on the corner of 21st and Virginia."

While the focus of the Wherry hearings, and the Lavender Scare generally, was on gay men, women did not escape undiscussed. The early twentieth century had seen more opportunities for women to receive professional training, but when they applied for jobs at law firms and accounting departments, they found the doors still closed. Whatever chances they did have to advance were shut down by the mass unemployment of the Great Depression, when women were often the first to be fired. But Washington was different: Though the New Deal was run primarily by men, the mounting demand for economists, labor experts, sociologists, and lawyers, not to mention armies of secretaries, made Washington a rare bright spot for women in the 1930s and '40s. Among them was Charlotte Tuttle, a Vassar and top-ranked Columbia Law graduate who nevertheless faced dim prospects of finding a job with a private firm; instead, right out of school in 1934, she joined the Department of the Interior, where she worked to ensure that Native Americans benefited from federal policy. There were countless others like her—11 percent of the lawyers at the National Labor Relations Board were women, at a time when women constituted just 2 percent of lawyers nationwide. The "bright young things" of the New Deal, it seemed, were also bright young women.

Like many of their male counterparts, these women—and women nationwide—were not satisfied with punching a clock. They often saw their work for the federal government as the realization of the progressive values that had motivated the student left in the 1930s. As a student Tuttle had been active in the League for Industrial Democracy and declared herself a socialist, ideals that guided her at the Interior Department. Thousands of other women like her focused on issues ranging from civil rights, consumer protection, and conservation, to social welfare. A common, collective identity connected many women who had turned to public service, an understanding that their work had meaning beyond their own self-interest.

Not surprisingly, women in Washington got caught by the turn against progressivism during the late 1940s. So-called G-girls, for "government girls," were ripe targets for easy misogynistic slurs—that they were sexually promiscuous, slept their way up the career ladder, and connived among themselves, and with gay men. "Our capital is a femmocracy, a community in which the women not only outdo the men in numbers, but in importance," wrote the Hearst journalists Jack Lait and Lee Mortimer in their tawdry 1951 exposé *Washington Confidential.* The book sold 150,000 copies in its first three weeks, topped *The New York Times* best-seller list, and sold millions more as a paperback. In its success the book did much to poison the nation's attitude toward Washington, and in particular its gay and female workforce. Naturally, the authors linked women in the workforce to communism, alleging that Soviet agents enticed "sex-starved government gals," who in turn lured single men with their feminine wiles. Lesbianism was a frequent subtext, if not the text, of such charges: One anonymous informant told the Wherry hearings of a Russian plan to lure "women employees of the State Department under their control by enticing them into a life of lesbianism," using "erotic demonstrations" where "many are garbed in rich oriental costumes to help get into the spirit of things."

The Wherry subcommittee was just the warm-up, to test whether there was enough of a "risk" to justify a full-on investigation into the presence of homosexual employees in the government—though it was a foregone conclusion that there was. The next committee was significantly larger, with five senators and a three-person staff. It was led by Senator Clyde Hoey, a North Carolinian whose manners were considered old-school even at the time. He tried to keep one of the senators, Margaret Chase Smith of Maine, from attending many of the sessions, for fear that the content was inappropriate for feminine ears. She insisted, and played an active, and unblushing, role in the proceedings.

Hoey kept his hearings low-key, and drew praise for avoiding McCarthyesque headlines. But the testimonies were no less sensational in their content. Among the highlights was Admiral Hillenkoetter, the new CIA director, who unspooled the story of a closeted gay officer in the Austro-Hungarian Army before World War I. The officer, Alfred Redl, ran the imperial military's counterintelligence branch. The Russian army, one of Austria's many foes, supposedly discovered his secret, and set up an ambush to blackmail him. Redl ended up passing reams of secret documents to the enemy, including plans for the invasion of Serbia, a Russian ally. Finally discovered in 1913, he shot himself. Redl's story, as Hillenkoetter told it, illustrated the blackmail risks posed by gay men and women. It was also the only useful historical example anyone could find. All the rest, and there were only a handful, had complicating details and extenuating contexts. (So did Redl's, it emerged later—evidence showed that he was spying for the money, and it's likely his handlers didn't even know he was gay.)

Hillenkoetter then offered twelve distinct reasons why, in his mind, homosexual employees were security risks, including susceptibility to blackmail, an overactive emotional imagination, vulnerability to interrogation, and a mutually supportive "fraternity" that makes one gay man eager to help another regardless of national allegiance. Failure to root them out wherever they are found, Hillenkoetter concluded, is like "placing a weapon in the hands of our enemies and their intelligence service, and the point of that weapon would probably be aimed right at the heart of our national security."

Not all witnesses agreed with Hillenkoetter. Other agency heads dismissed the concern entirely. "Since it is possible, according to our understanding of medical and psychiatric opinion on the subject, for a homosexual to lead a normal, well-adjusted life, we do not consider that such a person necessarily constitutes a bad security risk," Howard Colvin, acting director of the Federal Mediation and Conciliation Service, told the committee. "We believe that each such case would have to be decided on its own merits." Dr. Leonard Scheele, the U.S. surgeon general, told the senators: "We are not just a hundred percent male or a hundred percent female, no matter who we are." And homosexuals, he said, are no more susceptible to blackmail than thieves or philandering husbands.

Hoey, in his final report, dismissed such nuance, concluding that even "one homosexual can pollute a government office." Republicans saw the issue as a timely diversion from the Tydings Committee and its revelations about the emptiness of McCarthy's campaign. The Tydings hearings, Senator Jenner said, were in fact revealing "an army of sexual perverts who are engaged in the filthy immorality of blackmail and degradation."

Most major newspapers agreed on the need to flush out the "colonies of such persons," as the *Washington Post's* editorial board put it in May 1950. "There are several good reasons why persons of this proclivity should be excluded from the government service," it went on. "If the government is justified in rejecting applicants on the ground of insufficient educational qualifications, or for various habits such as a tendency to talk too much when under the influence of alcohol, it is also justified in excluding them because of homosexuality."

That fall three aides to Truman warned him in a memo not to ignore the issue of homosexuality in the government. "Although the matter is frequently discussed in whispers behind hands," they wrote, "a number of responsible persons have advised that . . . the country is really much more disturbed over the picture which has been presented so far of the government being loaded with homosexuals than it is over the clamor about communists in the government."

13

The China Lobby

The frisson over the Offie dismissal and the resulting investigations into homosexual employees in the government gave Joe McCarthy the sort of boost he needed in the face of public efforts to delegitimize him. For a moment, senators and reporters began to say that maybe the Wisconsin senator was onto something after all. And even if not, he was, in his own darkly comic way, exciting to watch. Senate hearings tended to drone on, their conclusions foregone and their daily proceedings predictable. The Tydings hearings were different, thanks to McCarthy. No one knew where he would go next, not even McCarthy. Sensing he had run out his string on the original eighty-one (now reduced to fifty-seven) names but eager to keep the momentum going after his Offie revelation, he tossed his entire list aside and offered up a single name as the key to the entire conspiracy. "I am willing to stand or fall on this one," he said. "If I am shown to be wrong on this, I think the subcommittee would be justified in not taking my other cases too seriously."

The name belonged to Owen Lattimore, a professor at Johns Hopkins who had occasionally advised the State Department. Lattimore was a China scholar of some renown, and had spent years in the country beside President Chiang Kai-shek and his Nationalist government as it fought its losing battle against the Communists under Mao Zedong. He was also an outspoken progressive and an admirer of the achievements of the Soviet Union. But to McCarthy, he was the "architect" of America's failure to keep Communists from taking over China, "the top Russian espionage agent," and the puppet master behind Secretary of State Dean Acheson, he told a press conference, a point he hammered before the Tydings Committee. "I am absolutely convinced beyond any doubt that if the committee sees that file they will agree with me wholeheartedly that I have perhaps understated the case rather than overstated it."

McCarthy had no evidence against Lattimore, but he claimed it was all there, in the FBI files—though he conceded that he hadn't seen those, either. He put the onus on the White House, demanding that Truman open them. "It is up to the president to put up or shut up," he told reporters, and Tydings asked for them as well. But the president, with Hoover's backing, refused, and as a concession sent the FBI director to the committee instead. Hoover defended the secrecy of the files, but added, in no uncertain terms, that there was no evidence Lattimore was a Communist. When confronted with the director's statement, McCarthy could only mutter that he knew something Hoover didn't.

To the untrained eye, Lattimore might have seemed a random choice for McCarthy to throw into the Tydings proceedings, just one more name pulled out of his conspiratorial hat. But in fact it showed just how much the senator had come under the sway of a loose coalition of businessmen, politicians, ideologues, retired generals, and journalists who collectively believed that the primary front in the world war against Communism was not in Europe, but rather in East Asia—and that Roosevelt, Truman, and the American political establishment had sold out the region to the Soviets. They were called the China Lobby, and their collective influence in the late 1940s and '50s acted like a sort of dark matter during the Red Scare, shaping policy and politics, boosting and destroying careers in ways that even many insiders did not appreciate. In 1950, they enlisted McCarthy.

The China Lobby, strictly speaking, did not exist. It was not a formal organization; there was no letterhead, no membership list, no dues to be paid. Yet there was no denying that its members not only shared interests, but also information and rumors; they wrangled each other jobs and awards; they dined together and traveled together; and in doing so created a web of relationships that they used to confront and destroy their ideological enemies, real or imagined. The Red Scare may have started with the fear of Russian aggression in Europe, and it may have been sustained by the fear of Russian espionage and atomic weaponry. But much of the motivation, the resources, and the ideological organization that kept it going into the 1950s was centered halfway around the world. To the China Lobby, Europe was old news, the site of last year's battles hot and cold. The future, they insisted, lay in the Pacific.

The lobby's unofficial leader was a textile tycoon named Alfred Kohlberg. He had made his fortune importing cloth and finished items from China, first from his hometown of San Francisco, and later from the headquarters of Kohlberg Textiles, a mid-rise tower on 37th Street and Fifth Avenue in Manhattan, at the heart of the city's Garment District. He was beetle-browed and balding, with what one reporter called a "warmthless smile." By far his best seller, in this pre-Kleenex era, was the handkerchief, which he proudly branded as Kohlkerchiefs and sold in practically every convenience store, pharmacy, and department chain in America. *The New York Times* called him the largest textile importer in America. He called himself the "sole proprietor of the China Lobby."

Kohlberg's business empire in China gave him more than profits— it also gave him insights. By the late 1930s he employed or contracted 100,000 workers, and he hired advisers who mined that network for rumors, trends, and the sort of small tidbits of news that might foretell a dramatic change afoot. Thanks to that network, he grasped, earlier than most, just how significant the Communist movement was in China. During World War II he grew especially close to the anti-Communist General Chiang and his charismatic, Wellesley-educated wife, Soong Mei-ling, often known to Americans as Madame Chiang. Kohlberg paid for hospitals behind the Chinese front lines, and lobbied Washington for military aid to the Nationalists.

Kohlberg was just one of many leading figures in America who admired Chiang and the Nationalists. The publisher Henry Luce put Chiang on the cover of *Time* magazine for a stunning ten issues. Senator Knowland of California, a future Republican majority leader, spoke so adamantly on Chiang's behalf that wags started calling him "The Senator from Formosa," the island, now known as Taiwan, to which Chiang fled after the Communists conquered the mainland. Others, particularly Midwestern senators with little foreign policy experience, were simply bowled over by

Chiang as a Chinese version of George Washington, his chest full of medals and his speeches full of pleas for freedom and independence.

Such senators came to be known as Asia Firsters. Europe was complicated and confusing, with enemies who had been allies and allies who had been enemies. It was also the domain of the East Coast elite, of Wall Street and Washington. Asia seemed a blank slate, and therefore a place to impose moral absolutes: Chiang vs. Mao, democracy vs. Communism. "I believe very strongly," said Senator Robert Taft, "that the Far East is ultimately even more important to our future peace than is Europe." Asia was the future, but also the past. For all their talk about supporting Chinese Nationalists, what the China Lobby dreamed of was a supplicant, a China flush with labor and consumers and pliant politicians. Kohlberg called it "the China that was." The fight over China became another extension of the cultural conflict that had been brewing for well over a decade among New Deal progressives, the Washington Establishment, and conservative Republicans. And it was on the subject of East Asia that this long-simmering conflict would find new energy with the injection of Cold War politics and a justification for its wildest conspiracy theories to take root.

Kohlberg was in San Francisco when he read about McCarthy's February 20, 1950, speech on the Senate floor announcing his campaign to unmask Communists in the government. He immediately called the senator's office to schedule a meeting, then booked a flight to Washington. Over a two-hour dinner at the Mayflower Hotel, a few blocks north of the White House, Kohlberg gave the senator what he later called a "super cram session" on China. He had been waiting for someone of McCarthy's stature and outspokenness to catch on to the treasonous plots within the State Department. Now Kohlberg was going to tell him just what that treason involved.

Not everyone, it turned out, agreed with the China Lobby's ideas about East Asia. True, on paper, Roosevelt and Truman both supported Chiang in his fight against the Communists. Between 1945 and 1949 the United States sent the Nationalists some $2 billion in aid, mostly in weapons, the equivalent of about $25 billion in today's money. The money represented over 50 percent of the Chinese government's budget, significantly more than the United States gave to any European country following the war. But both presidents were skeptical about Chiang's chances, doubts fed by the State Department's even more critical rank and file. Virtually to a man, every diplomat who spent time in China came back withering in his assessment of the Nationalist government. It was fatally corrupt and thoroughly incompetent, wasting American fortunes while steadily losing ground to the Communists, who were in contrast unified, capable, and popular. "None seem soft, flabby, or indolent," wrote one such diplomat, John Service. "This vitality is not only physical; it is also intellectual."

Service was one of a bevy of mid-level State Department officials— John Paton Davies, O. Edmund Clubb, Raymond Ludden, John Carter Vincent—who had grown critical of the Nationalists as the Chinese Civil War restarted following World War II. They were joined by academics like Lattimore and John Fairbank, at Harvard, and journalists like Theodore White of *Time*. Together they were known as the China Hands, a term passed down from the era of British colonialism but which, in its current usage, meant something close to the opposite: The China Hands insisted there was no going back to the imperialism of before, and that the Chinese people had to determine their own course forward, regardless of what the Alfred Kohlbergs of the world wanted.

The China Hands were realists. Communism might be inevitable in the country, but Soviet dominance was not. The China Hands understood the differences between Stalin and Mao, between the Soviets and the Chinese. They believed that Mao could become an Asian version of Yugoslavia's Josip Broz Tito, a socialist at odds with Moscow and, as an enemy of their enemy, something of an ally of the West. Getting to that point, though, meant reducing America's commitment to Chiang, in practice if not in policy. As the Communists drew closer to victory in 1949, the China Hands became more vocal in their beliefs that Washington had to disengage from Chiang, and find a way to work with Mao.

Kohlberg saw things very differently. As he told McCarthy over dinner, the China Hands were not neutral observers of Chiang's looming defeat— they were, he said, actively encouraging it. In 1946 Truman sent George Marshall, not yet secretary of state, to negotiate an agreement between Chiang and Mao; when he returned empty-handed, Kohlberg and the China Lobby declared that his real mission had been to undermine Chiang by treating Mao as his equal. The impression grew stronger when in the summer of 1947 Marshall, now in charge of the State Department, sent General Albert Wedemeyer on a fact-finding trip to China. Wedemeyer, an adamant anti-Communist, likewise returned empty-handed, but he did bring stories fed to him by Chiang and his allies about American perfidiousness. Wedemeyer praised Chiang during a Senate hearing that fall, calling him "a fine character." When asked if he thought the United States had kept its promises to the Nationalists, he replied, "No sir, I do not."

The belief that Marshall and the State Department had sold out Chiang tied into, and seemed to support, the broader conspiracy theory about the pro-Communist tilt of the Democratic White House. The original sin came in 1945 at the Yalta summit, where Roosevelt, Churchill, and Stalin had met to start planning for the postwar era. Roosevelt, it was asserted by Kohlberg and others, ceded Poland and China to Stalin. Some said he had been conned and outmaneuvered by the Soviet leader. Kohlberg saw a plot by Roosevelt's top advisers, if not the president himself, to clear the way for global Communist control. The fact that Alger Hiss was among the U.S. delegation at Yalta added to the intrigue, even though Hiss had worked assiduously to block a Soviet plan to get a separate vote for each of its sixteen republics at the United Nations. "The real 'China Lobby,'" Kohlberg liked to say, "is the pro-Communist lobby within the State Department."

His message to McCarthy was clear: American foreign policy in East Asia was governed not by the president or secretary of state, but by obscure diplomats like John Service. They in turn took their direction from Lattimore, who, in Kohlberg's telling, had a direct link to Moscow. There was no evidence, just a string of wild leaps in logic. Lattimore had worked for the Office of War Information during World War II and, in that capacity, accompanied Henry Wallace, then the vice president, on a 1944 tour of China and Siberia. Wallace, China, the Soviet Union—Kohlberg insisted that the linkages were plain for anyone sufficiently clear-eyed to see it. Lattimore was obviously the connection point connecting the Russians, the Chinese, the State Department and, via Wallace, the American Communist Party. In a 1947 letter to Senator Styles Bridges, the New

Hampshire Republican, Kohlberg wrote that Lattimore was "dangerous to American security" and had been "consciously scheming" to deliver China to the Soviet Union.

China was an enormous nation góing through immense changes. The Communists' mass appeal was not so much their ideology as it was their promise to free the country of Western domination. But Kohlberg and the China Lobby wouldn't hear it. "Rather than acknowledging that the transformation of China was being wrought primarily by indigenous forces," wrote John Paton Davies, another China Hand, "most Americans felt that, surely, some force outside of China must be responsible for so untoward a turn of events. International Communism masterminded from conspiratorial Moscow was a ready explanation."

Kohlberg did not limit his finger-pointing to the government. He had long been a member of an organization called the Institute of Pacific Relations, an international, quasi-academic research network with an American subsidiary based in Washington. Over the years its ranks included everyone and anyone interested in China at the highest levels of business and academia, including, among others, Kohlberg, Luce, and Lattimore. The institute had always had a left-wing bend to its work, and by the early 1940s many of its conservative supporters, like Kohlberg and Luce, began to drift away. Kohlberg became convinced that the institute was not just a think tank but the linchpin of a vast campaign to turn over China to the Communists. "I soon saw that the center of the conspiracy was the Institute of Pacific Relations," he told a reporter in 1952. "The I.P.R. people had infiltrated the State Department, the O.W.I., the Treasury, and the intelligence services of the armed services."

In 1944 he wrote an eighty-eight-page pamphlet offering what he said was incontrovertible proof that the institute was an arm of Moscow. "You have allowed your staff to become almost 100% percent red," he wrote to the board several months later. He said he had a list of names, but he refused to provide it. In 1947 he demanded the board allow him to present his case. Instead, the institute's entire membership took a vote on whether to let him, and he lost, 1,163 to 66. He promptly quit. "I tried to clean out the I.P.R.," he said in 1952. "Instead they cleaned me out."

Kohlberg had already founded his own organization, the American

China Policy Association, and after leaving the institute founded his own magazine, *Plain Talk*. In 1946 he gathered sixty-two intellectuals to sign a document he called the Manchurian Manifesto. It claimed that the United States had agreed at Yalta, "behind China's back," to "secret provisions" allowing Russian troops to occupy the northern Chinese province of Manchuria during the last months of World War II, therefore giving them a base from which Stalin could support Mao's army. As a result, with the Communists at the advantage, Truman and the Americans had a moral obligation to support Chiang. "We must stand firm for justice in China," it read. The statement itself was hard to argue with. The Soviets had in fact occupied Manchuria, and were now running it as a protectorate, a worrisome turn of events regardless of who won the Chinese Civil War. But in its conspiracy-mongering, the statement also established a black-and-white division: Either you believed that the administration had sold out China, or you were part of the problem—and, in the mind of Kohlberg and others, part of the conspiracy.

Kohlberg funded a series of other anti-Communist groups—the Committee of 100, the American Jewish League Against Communism—and offered start-up money to political entrepreneurs looking to go into the red-hunting business themselves. But his real influence was as a facilitator and cheerleader of the Red Scare. He wrote voluminously, constantly, sending letters to highly ranked friends and enemies several times a week. "I myself count it a day lost when I do not see a letter Mr. Kohlberg has written to the President, or to Khrushchev, or to Allen Dulles, or to J. Edgar Hoover, or Mrs. Roosevelt, or de Gaulle, or Churchill, or you, or me, Copy to the New York Times, the New York Herald Tribune, the CIA, etc.," wrote one of his young admirers, William F. Buckley Jr.

Kohlberg was on a first-name basis with Richard Nixon. He traded intelligence and documents with Ben Mandel, a former Communist who worked as a senior adviser for both HUAC and McCarthy. He provided a link between hardcore anti-Communist Jews like George Sokolsky and Mandel and anti-Semites like Jack Tenney, the former California politician who had run his own version of HUAC in the state legislature before leaving to publish a fringe, hate-filled newsletter. He filled *Plain Talk* with innuendo and rumor and his own ranting essays, and sent copies to hundreds of prominent conservatives, free of charge. His constant correspondence meant that far-flung anti-Communists were kept up to speed on one another's doings, making him the primary interchange tying them all together.

Not every anti-Communist conservative was a conspiracy theorist, far from it. But many of the most outspoken were. Kohlberg stood in the front ranks. In a 1949 letter to several members of Congress, he asked whether the downsizing of the U.S. military after the buildup during World War II was "done deliberately to leave Western Europe militarily naked before the Russian Bear?" He believed the Soviets did not just influence American foreign affairs; they controlled it. He filled his letters to friends, foes, and strangers alike with leading questions: Who stopped General George Patton from capturing Germany's uranium mines? Who ordered a cache of surplus weapons, reputedly headed for Chiang, destroyed?

It was inevitable, then, that a man as full of wild conspiracy theories as Alfred Kohlberg would connect with a man as desperate to find them as Joe McCarthy. Kohlberg knew that for all his wealth and effort, his message could only get so far. He needed a megaphone. And he needed someone to wield it with abandon. "Although I know you are a Wisconsin farm boy, I hope there is enough Irish in you to enjoy a good fight," Kohlberg wrote McCarthy in a pep talk of a letter in June 1950. "With the mountains of evidence you have . . . you can't lose." He saw in McCarthy the same sort of quality he treasured in himself—what he would call a fighting spirit, what their opponents would more likely call a dangerous disregard for the truth. Kohlberg saw McCarthy as a useful idiot, "with guts enough and dumb enough" to say things that most politicians never would. He filled the senator's open mind with conspiratorial questions, like who blocked Eisenhower from driving on Berlin at the end of World War II, and what was really agreed to at Yalta. "McCarthy is a great guy," he said in 1952. "Practically everything he said will be proven. What I gave McCarthy was what I'd been sending the newspapers for years."

The news from Korea came to the president late in the evening, just after 10 p.m., on June 24, 1950. Truman was back home in Independence, Missouri, visiting his family and attending to some personal business. He was sitting in his library when the phone rang. It was Dean Acheson, calling from his farm in Maryland.

"Mr. President," Acheson said, "the North Koreans have invaded South Korea."

Truman flew to Washington the next day. Acheson met him at the airport. The invasion was a surprise but not wholly unexpected; tensions between the two countries had been rising for months. But the Americans had not taken them seriously, and in a January speech Acheson had, to his immediate embarrassment, skipped over Korea in his list of American interests in East Asia that the country was willing to defend. Yet as it became clear, over the following days, that the South Koreans could not defeat the North themselves, Truman committed U.S. troops to the fighting. The Korean War, which would last three years and kill 36,000 Americans, had begun. Truman's daughter, Margaret, later recalled that her father "made it clear, from the moment he heard the news, that he feared this was the opening of World War III."

To some on the left, the Korean War offered a silver lining, in that it gave Truman an opportunity to stand up to the Communists in North Korea and their patrons in Moscow. "McCarthyism will have a hollow sound when applied to the government that stood up to the Russians," opined the editors of *The Nation*. But to the China Lobby and its allies, the war was a vindication, and a catalyst to step up their attacks on the administration: Acheson and Truman, they shouted, had betrayed China, and now South Korea. They had withdrawn troops from the peninsula, and given all but written approval to the North's patrons in Beijing and Moscow that it was okay to attack. The significance of "who lost China," a debate which had roiled Congress and the conservative press for almost a year, suddenly shifted from the hypothetical to the real. Had the United States acted to prevent the Communist takeover in China, Kohlberg and others argued, then the war in Korea would never have happened. In Congress, Senator Knowland demanded that Acheson resign.

Acheson did not resign, and over the coming weeks and months the country returned to its wartime footing. Tens of thousands of soldiers, sailors, Marines, and airmen flowed into South Korea, eventually halting the North's relentless advance at the cost of thousands of military and civilian lives. For most of the public, war should have meant a return of political unity, at least in foreign policy. People still believed the myth that politics stopped at the water's edge, especially in a time of war. Many politicians disagreed, and they used the conflict to extend their red-baiting attacks on the White House and the State Department. Joe McCarthy was among the loudest. Having latched on to Owen Lattimore and the China Hands that spring as his lifeline during the Tydings hearings, he exploited the outbreak of fighting in Korea as hard as he could. "American boys are dying in Korea" because "a group of untouchables in the State Department sabotaged" aid efforts to the Nationalist Chinese, he railed.

Harry Bridges was still arranging his appeal when North Korea invaded the South. Suddenly, his status as the king of the West Coast dockworkers became a national security issue. Despite Bridges's strident support for the American military during World War II and the absence of any evidence that he might get in the way now, the Department of Justice persuaded a judge to revoke his bail, on the premise that he might call for a general strike, shutting down the ports from which American troops and war matériel issued. Bridges spent almost three weeks in prison, not for anything he had done, but for something that his enemies fantasized he might do—a clear violation of his basic human rights, regardless of his citizenship status. The day he went to jail more than ten thousand workers across the Pacific Coast walked off the job in protest, including four thousand sugar plantation workers in Hawaii.

Even though Truman threw everything America had into the fighting, his critics called for more, and derided anything less as giving in to the Communist march across Asia. They talked of using atomic weapons to push back the North's advance. They demanded that Chiang and his forces in Taiwan be allowed to fight alongside the Americans, something the White House resisted. "Will we continue appeasement?" asked Senator Bridges of New Hampshire. "Now is the time to draw the line." In September 1950, General Douglas MacArthur, commander of U.S. forces in the region, made a daring, game-changing amphibious landing at Inchon, on the peninsula's central western coast, that allowed the Americans and South Koreans to rapidly recapture the territory lost at the start of the war, and then some, as they pushed deep into North Korea. Republicans demanded still more—a drive to the border with China, perhaps beyond. And they were already setting the tone in case the White House flinched, linking any recalcitrance to the Communist-infested foreign policy establishment. "The Hiss survivors association down at the State Department who wear upon their breast the cross of Yalta are waiting for Congress to go home before they lift the curtain on the next act in the tragedy of Red appeasement," Representative Hugh Scott of Pennsylvania said just days after the victory at Inchon.

The war in Korea, it was becoming clear, was about so much more than just Korea. It was a chance to rev the engine of anger over China, to expand the scope of anti-Communist hysteria, and to define the Democrats as weak on security, foreign and domestic. Korea seemed to validate the legitimate criticism of the White House, that it had failed to take Communism in East Asia seriously, which in turn opened the door to wilder accusations: that the administration had done it on purpose, in fact that the Democrats going back to the earliest days of Roosevelt had been selling out the country to the Soviets. In this upside-down world, reasonable, establishment voices were cowed or silenced, and men like Joe McCarthy were suddenly calling the shots.

14

The Russians Are Coming!

At almost the same time that North Korea invaded its southern neighbor, Communists made another surprise attack, this time in the central Wisconsin town of Mosinee. Before the sun was fully in the sky on May 1, 1950, they had captured the town hall, arrested the mayor, and begun placing civic leaders in a wire-enclosed prison camp. Roadblocks went up and patrols went out, rousting residents from their sleep and ushering them into the central square, which had been hung with a banner reading "The State Must Be Supreme Over the Individual." Anyone entering town was required to show identification. Carl Gewiss, the chief of police, refused to cooperate, and was taken away to be executed. In school, students were forced to wear red armbands. A proclamation announced that all industries had been taken over by the party, and that all churches and labor groups had been abolished. At 10:15 the mayor, still in his pajamas, issued a statement from a stand in the renamed Red Square. "In all humility," he said, the Communists had conquered tiny Mosinee.

The idea to stage a mock invasion—locals called it a "pageant"—came from the American Legion, which wanted to warn small-town America about the risk of a Communist takeover and, in the words of one planner, to "elevate the debate to reach minds we hadn't reached." They chose Mosinee because the local paper was owned by a fellow Legionnaire. The "coup," manned by eighty-five Legionnaires, was led by two former Communists: Ben Gitlow, who had helped found the Communist Party of the U.S.A. and later offered himself as a freelance anti-Communist consultant, and Joseph Z. Kornfeder, who had been a party leader in Detroit. Kornfeder played the commissar who accepted the mayor's surrender, and held a pistol to his back as he spoke. To reinforce the realism of the demonstration, every restaurant in town served black bread and potato soup for lunch.

Mosinee was "liberated" by the American Legion that evening. As it did, the mayor collapsed from a stroke, and a local minister suffered a heart attack. This time, it was not an act. Both died a few days later. "The townspeople are terribly sad about the deaths," said the editor of *The Mosinee Times*. "But they feel that their demonstration for democracy was in no way dimmed or altered."

No one was surprised by the Mosinee coup; it had been planned for months, and discussed openly (perhaps too openly—the day before, actual Communists from Milwaukee and Chicago had snuck into town and plastered it with party leaflets and copies of *The Daily Worker*). Dozens of national reporters were on hand to watch, and 1,200 newspapers ran articles about it in the coming days. Other Midwestern towns soon copied it. In June the northwest Iowa town of Hartley, even smaller and more remote than Mosinee, held "Communist Rule Day." Again, clergy and town leaders were rounded up, though this time starting at a more civilized 1 p.m., in part because of a heavy rainstorm that morning. The mayor was "executed," and Communist books, pamphlets, and flags distributed. Chamber of Commerce members, acting as commissars, gave speeches. The mass performance ended at 5 p.m., giving way to a bacchanal of patriotism in which the offending books and flags were burned in a massive bonfire.

The Red Scare may have been heating up in Washington for years, but it was in the summer of 1950 that it came to a boil nationwide. It was no longer a political issue; it had become a cultural one. Stoked by McCarthy at home and Korea and Soviet nukes abroad, a generalized fear seeped into the country's every corner—its movies, its churches, its offices, its libraries, even its toy chests. Along with that fear rose a narrow view of patriotism and Americanism, one very different from the 1930s, with its celebration of diversity, its commitment to progress and equality—a vision that, not coincidentally, had made room for Communists, women, labor, and African Americans to claim equal standing alongside white Northern European men.

Things were very different in 1950. Especially in the country's interior, the end of the Depression and then the war signaled an intense desire to return to America status quo ante—"before the New Deal had empowered labor unions, before air travel had shrunk the Atlantic Ocean into a pond, and before scientists had ever thought about developing intercontinental ballistic missiles to catapult atomic warheads into their midst," wrote David Halberstam in *The Fifties*, his panoramic survey of the era. It was an America in which the Chamber of Commerce gentry ruled civic life, and dissenting ideas—about capitalism, about civil rights, about women's rights—were kept at the fringes and eyed suspiciously. In the South, white supremacy, ever present, reared up even more violently in the face of civil rights advances under the New Deal and during the war. Racist groups like the Ku Klux Klan worked alongside state and town governments not just to oppress Black Southerners, but to reassert a white, Southern culture, bereft of civil rights activism and liberal ideas, that in their minds had once dominated the region.

In the Midwest, the *Chicago Tribune* told millions of readers, many far beyond the paper's home turf in northeastern Illinois, how to think about and respond to a changing world. It was the leading conservative outlet of its day, led by Colonel Robert McCormick, the *Tribune's* isolationist, anti-Roosevelt publisher, adamantly opposed to everything and everyone to the left of Robert Taft. He ordered that in the *Tribune*, all New Deal agencies be labeled "so-called," to question their legitimacy, and demanded that agonizingly objective wire copy from the Associated Press be rewritten to reflect his ultraconservative beliefs, then published under the AP logo. McCormick's support for Taft kept the senator in contention for the Republican presidential nomination for three cycles, starting in 1944, and his tepid support for Thomas Dewey helped keep him out of the White House in 1948.

Millions of Americans longed for this old, mythic America. Communism, foreign and domestic, offered an invaluable foil. Abroad, war with the Soviets loomed, and if Americans were not vigilant, many came to believe, that war might take place on their soil. Just as alarming, they were told a similar threat lurked at home. Communists, clever and unbounded by good old American morals, were always and everywhere wheedling their way into the country's political and economic life. They were supposedly taking over labor unions and Boy Scout troops, state political parties and parent-teacher associations. Their agenda was hidden. Perhaps they were a fifth column, ready to open doors for Soviet invaders. Or maybe they planned to subvert the country themselves, to turn it into a socialist republic from the inside. If, in the 1930s, "it could happen here" meant that fascism could take over America just as it had in Europe, by 1950 the same phrase raised fears that what had befallen Russia, Poland, and China could happen in America. In places like Mosinee, Communism was often less of an actual threat than a stalking horse for something else: change from the white, male, conservative culture that had historically defined wide swaths of the country.

Many of the best-known stories and names from the Red Scare era center in places like Washington and Hollywood, and they give the impression that the period was mostly about fights in Congress and the courts. But the Red Scare was just as significant in town squares and American Legion halls, in the movies people watched and the books they read, in what the historian Richard Fried called "the fine dust" of anti-Communism. It was not necessarily the driver of the great changes pushing postwar society to the right, nor was it merely a symptom. It was a catalyst of forces already afoot. It might have been inevitable that as Americans back from the war sought to tighten community bonds and find meaning in a changing world, they would turn to religion; church membership shot up from 64.5 million in 1940 to 114.5 million in 1960. But it helped enormously that those churchgoers believed themselves under threat from godless Communists preparing for war in Moscow—and lurking just outside the chapel doors.

The Red Scare also helped refashion gender roles in the 1950s. Though tens of thousands of women went to work for the New Deal agencies during the 1930s, the economic and social status of most American women did not change until World War II. Rosie the Riveter was just one of millions of women who entered the workforce to take the jobs of men off at war. By the start of the war 30 percent of women were working. At the war's end, the number of working women had doubled, to some 60 percent, even though three quarters of those women were married. A third had children younger than fourteen. The shift was reflected in the culture. In the 1930s, movies were full of strong, independent female characters— not just as wives but as workers, friends, and lovers. Despite morality codes, divorce was considered acceptable, if the cause was clear. In *His Girl Friday*, released in 1940, Rosalind Russell and Cary Grant, a divorced pair of journalists, compete for scoops on equal terms. Russian women were celebrated in newsreels for working in the country's fields and factories, or even fighting alongside men.

Such movies were out of fashion by 1950. Women were being pushed from the workforce by employers eager to hire returning veterans, and by a culture that rapidly ejected ideas about gender equality and women's independence in favor of ideals about motherhood and the nuclear family. The historian Elaine Tyler May called it "domestic containment." Accordingly, Soviet women were now disparaged, or pitied, for having to work outside the home. So too were independent women—working, unmarried past a certain age, or worst of all, working while raising children. They might not be Communists themselves, but they were said to be under the thrall of an idea rooted in something now considered deeply anti-American.

Patriotic civic organizations were a central part of postwar American life, and by 1950 many of them—the Daughters of the American Revolution, the Knights of Columbus—had committed themselves to fighting Communism. None came close to the reach and influence of the American Legion. By 1950 there were 3.5 million members of the Legion, spread across more than eleven thousand posts. As part of its longstanding Americanism initiative, in 1947 the Legion distributed 120 million pieces of patriotic literature, reaching 10 million homes a month. Not a paramilitary, it was more than just a civic group. Its members, all veterans, saw themselves as something like an extension of the government, serving as its eyes and ears, but also going further into vigilante actions like pickets and boycotts. It was especially close to the FBI: Hoover spoke regularly at its conventions, and saw to it that a former agent was made a liaison with the bureau. The Legion obliged, and passed a regular flow of tips and rumors to Hoover's field offices.

The Legion pushed most of its efforts through its Americanism Commission. Founded in the early 1920s and still in operation decades later, the commission historically focused on civic engagement, pairing with groups like the Boy Scouts and the National Education Association. But for decades it had a dual mandate to combat what the Legion saw as anti-democratic and alien ideologies, a charge it took up aggressively in the late 1940s. The commission members collected reams of personal information about anyone suspected of harboring even a modicum of liberal sentiment. They passed it along, down to the local posts and up to the FBI. In the early 1950s the commission ran nationwide protests against the touring company of Arthur Miller's play *Death of a Salesman*, because of Miller's well-known progressive beliefs. At the other, local extreme, in 1954 it ran a campaign against a supposedly leftist candidate for a seat on a parent-teacher association in the Manhattan neighborhood of Yorkville—hardly ground zero for revolution.

New organizations sprouted up. In 1951, a group of women in Chicago formed the founding chapter of the Sixth Column, a patriotic group intended to counter the Communists allegedly lurking in neighborhood civic groups and schools. When organizers in tiny Poseyville, Indiana, started their own branch, three hundred people, almost a third of the town, showed up in the high school gymnasium for the first meeting.

In September 1949 a Belgian-born, Yale-trained sculptor and Republican activist named Suzanne Stevenson founded the Minute Women of the U.S.A. Like the men in the American Legion, Stevenson was concerned about the supposed steady creep of Soviet Communism into America's schools and churches, and she wanted a way for its women to take up the fight as well. "The world cannot be safe without good women," she said. The Minute Women, armed with their beliefs in God and free enterprise, rapidly took root among middle-class suburban housewives nationwide, with concentrations in the wealthier districts of Texas, California, and Maryland, as well as Stevenson's home state of Connecticut. Within three years she boasted of 500,000 members—the Houston chapter alone had 500, one of several militantly anti-Communist citizens organizations in the city.

Stevenson, née Silvercruys, was the daughter of a baron and ran the organization like a monarch, appointing and replacing chapter leaders at will. She called herself "Sizzling Sue" and "The Paul Revere of the Fairer

Sex," and carried an oversized copy of the Constitution on her speaking tours. She instructed her followers to act in secret; better, she told them, to appear as individual, concerned Americans rather than part of a nationally coordinated organization. In Houston their views went out every Sunday evening on a radio program called *Minute Women Calling for Liberty.* And while Stevenson herself denounced anti-Semitism, it crept into her organization, often through its sanctioned reading lists that included works by hatemongers like Gerald L. K. Smith.

The leaders of the Minute Women branches rarely met in person; instead, Stevenson told them to communicate by phone trees, and to operate in small cells. She had them write letters to studio executives promising pickets outside movies starring blacklisted actors. Some sixty women in the Houston chapter were married to doctors, and in letters to their congressmen they echoed their husbands' contention that Truman's plan for national health insurance was a Communist plot. Borrowing directly from advice dispensed by the U.S. Chamber of Commerce, Stevenson told members—"trained listeners," the chamber called them—to plant themselves in audiences gathered to hear a speaker suspected of left-wing tendencies, then heckle the person in what would appear as a spontaneous patriotic uprising. They flooded City Council meetings to oppose public housing. Stevenson instructed the mothers of young children to peruse their school libraries, and gave them a list of subversive books to haul before the school board. It was an easy task in conservative Houston, where Minute Women nearly took over the board itself.

What the Minute Women considered "Communist" broadened over time. Progressive education was definitely a target. So was civil rights talk—the Houston chapter protested a speech at the University of Houston by Rufus Clement, the president of Atlanta University, a historically Black institution, claiming his ideas about racial equality made him politically suspect. They drove out the new president of the university, W. W. Kemmerer, after he invited a white proponent of school integration to speak on campus. They managed to ban a United Nations–sponsored writing contest from public high schools, and in 1953 forced out deputy superintendent George Ebey, who had promoted the contest, as too "controversial."

By the early 1950s it was practically a requirement for any organization, no matter how small or how apolitical, to take a stand against Communism. In October 1950 a national conference of college fraternities called on every campus chapter to commit to fighting Communism in America's universities. A year later the board governing realtors in New Orleans voted overwhelmingly against Communism, and insisted that anyone who wanted a license take a vow of loyalty to the United States, apparently out of fear that they might otherwise sell Big Easy homes to Soviet subversives. And in 1951, the American Bar Association voted to expel all members who belonged to the Communist Party, and called on state and local bars to do the same.

When the federal government seemed to be moving too slowly, state and local governments took the initiative: In July 1950, in a bid to crack down on civil rights activists, the city of Birmingham outlawed the Communist Party; the state of Alabama followed soon after. Governments as large as Los Angeles County and as small as McKeesport, Pennsylvania, required all Communists within their limits to register.

Anti-Communism was everywhere. It was even in bubble gum. In 1951 the Bowman Gum Co. of Philadelphia released "Fight the Red Menace: Children's Crusade Against Communism," a set of forty-eight cards featuring, among other things, a ghoulishly green Mao Zedong and a "Visit from the Secret Police," showing blue-uniformed thugs roughing up a frightened family. Toys, especially for boys, took on an olive-drab complexion: Alongside the standard cowboys and miniature construction vehicles, playrooms abounded in green Army men, realistic plastic rifles, and lithoghraphed tin tanks.

Anti-Communism was all over the country's book racks as well. Frank Morrison Spillane, better known by his nickname Mickey, was a Brooklyn-born, New Jersey–raised comic book writer who, after getting out of the Army in 1947, bought a small house in upstate New York and sat down to write a novel. He needed money to pay for his young, growing family, he said. The result, composed over just nine days, was *I, the Jury*, a violent potboiler of an introduction to the world of Mike Hammer, private detective. The book sold 3.5 million copies by 1953 and established Spillane as one of the best-selling authors of the 1950s.

Hammer took on all comers—femme fatales, gangsters, random thugs—but he returned, time and again, to Communists. Spillane himself hated them; he was deeply religious, and a close friend of Ayn Rand. In another book, *One Lonely Night*, Spillane has Hammer kill forty Communists with a machine gun; Spillane had reportedly started with eighty, but his editor persuaded him to halve that. "I killed more people tonight than I have fingers on my hands. I shot them in cold blood and enjoyed every minute of it," Hammer says. "They were Commies." Spillane was not making an ideological point. To him, Communists were just one more set of bad guys. They were "soft as horse manure and just as dumb," but somehow also wily and conniving. His Communists acted like gangsters, or, if need be, silky seductresses. They were his all-purpose baddies, and his readers could not get enough. *One Lonely Night* sold three million copies. At the end of the decade, Spillane had written six of the ten best-selling books of the 1950s. Mike Hammer was a Commie killer, and Americans loved it.

With violent anti-Communism spilling from the nation's bookshelves, it was only a matter of time before actual rocks were thrown and skulls were cracked. In July 1950 anti-Communists in Houston waited until midnight to launch a fusillade of bricks at the apartment of the chairman of the Texas state Communist Party. They accidentally hit the neighbors' windows as well. The next morning the target's landlord forced him to move. Around the same time, a band of veterans, rounded up by a thirty-two-year-old laborer named Frank Zaffina, attacked six workers as they exited a Chrysler assembly plant in Los Angeles. They beat three of them badly. But Zaffina, who thought his targets were Communist activists, had received some bad intelligence: In fact, they were just everyday laborers, and veterans too. "I guess it isn't right," he mused the next day, "to take the law into your own hands."

On the surface, America in the early 1950s was *I Love Lucy* and Levittown and bowling leagues and bobby socks. Underneath it was seething, fearful, angry. Those who wanted more change—feminists, civil rights activists, antiwar organizers, gay people—were not just out of tune with the times; they were, of a sudden, considered dangerous to the commonweal. Violence was inevitable. In 1953 a fellow prisoner attacked

Robert G. Thompson, one of the Smith Act defendants, with a lead pipe over his Communist affiliations. A year later William Remington, who went to prison for perjury after Elizabeth Bentley accused him of being a Communist, was also assaulted in prison, and died a few days later. As with Thompson, Remington's assailant said he wanted to kill a red. The country was going feral.

15

The Pink Lady

Millard Tydings, the pugnacious Democrat from Maryland who oversaw the 1950 committee that introduced Joe McCarthy to the country, should have been able to seal the Wisconsin senator's fate after the hearings ended that July. McCarthy had dominated headlines but had failed to prove a single thing against a single person. Truman had eventually allowed the committee to review the State Department's security files; they found nothing to support the charges that the American diplomatic corps was rife with spies—though McCarthy claimed the files had been "raped and rifled." Tydings's final report was scathing, accusing the senator of lying, playing reckless with people's lives, and running roughshod over Senate decorum. That, the Democrats thought, should have been the end of that.

But McCarthy had never been playing to his colleagues. His base was far beyond Washington, in the Midwest communities where the *Chicago Tribune* was gospel and the New Deal was an epithet, and where millions of people saw McCarthy as a fighter, taking on a corrupt government at great risk to his own career and safety. He had the backing of the American Legion and the Veterans of Foreign Wars. His fellow senators saw the wave of popular support too, and heard about it in mail bags that came into their offices stuffed with pro-McCarthy correspondence. By mid-1950, it was clear that one's public standing on the right was measured by one's allegiance to McCarthy. He was in demand as a speaker, not just by local Republican groups and Legion posts but by the likes of carpet wholesaler conventions and medical conferences. After Tydings's report appeared, it was not just McCarthy's fellow conservatives who came to his defense, but establishment stalwarts like Senator Henry Cabot Lodge Jr. of Massachusetts, who sat on the Tydings Committee. They countered that Tydings had politicized the hearings from the beginning, that McCarthy had never had a fair shot. They refused to sign off on the report, calling it "inconclusive."

Tydings and the Democrats wanted to get back to normal, to push past the scandals around Hiss and the Smith Act trials to discuss things like national health care and security aid to Europe, issues of substance that also happened to be their political bread and butter. They wanted to go back to 1948, when President Truman triumphed in his election by establishing himself as the candidate of reform and progress and the Republicans—and by extension their candidate, Thomas Dewey—the "do-nothing" party. What they did not understand, and what McCarthy and many of his Republicans allies did, was that there was no turning back, that a new urgency, a budding hysteria was overtaking American politics. The 1950 midterms were fast approaching, and this time the Republicans were not going to leave the arrow of anti-Communism in their quiver, even if it meant abiding, or embracing, Joe McCarthy.

Not every Republican played along. Among the few to speak out against McCarthy was Margaret Chase Smith, an independent-minded senator from Maine. She had been, she told reporters, initially open to McCarthy's charges. But the more she listened, the more she realized how dangerous he was. On June 1, 1950, she rose in the Senate to deliver a speech she called a "declaration of conscience," and invited other Republicans to sign on. The Democratic Party, she said, was indeed weak on the global Communist threat. "Yet to displace it with a Republican regime embracing a philosophy that lacks political integrity or intellectual honesty would prove equally disastrous to this nation," she went on. "The nation sorely needs a Republican victory. But I don't want to see the Republican Party ride to political victory on the Four Horsemen of calumny—fear, ignorance, bigotry, and smear." It was a powerful statement, and it won her praise from editorial boards nationwide. But only six other Republicans signed on, and three of those backed out after the outbreak of the Korean War a few weeks later. Another senator, Wayne Morse, later switched parties.

Tydings released his report on July 18, 1950, by which point America was already committed to the Korean War, and the public's fear of nuclear conflict with the Soviet Union was ratcheting ever higher. Only the day before, the FBI had arrested an engineer in New York named Julius Rosenberg on charges of giving America's atomic secrets to the Soviet Union; three weeks later, agents arrested his wife as well. Both were former members of the Communist Party. Though their trial would not start until early the next year, news coverage of their arrest was everywhere that fall, shading every election, at every level, into a referendum on the nation's safety against the "red menace." Realtors were pitching homes in far-away, exurban towns, at the edges of major metropolitan areas, for their safe distance from atomic blast zones. Contractors did a brisk business building backyard bomb shelters.

In September Congress passed, over Truman's veto, the Internal Security Act, which essentially outlawed the Communist Party while at the same time requiring all members of "subversive" organizations to register with the government—so that, in the event of an emergency, they could be rounded up and placed in detention camps. Plans for such camps were drawn up by the FBI. The Tydings report was simply swamped by an anti-Communist wave. In a perilous world, McCarthy's antics mattered less than his position on the right side of the fight.

He was in high demand as the midterm election season kicked in. During October and November McCarthy made thirty-two speeches in fifteen states in support of Republican candidates. He took a particular interest in two races—the reelection of Scott Lucas, the Senate majority leader, in Illinois and Tydings in Maryland. In Illinois, he appeared beside Lucas's opponent, Everett Dirksen, and promised that a vote for the Republican was a vote against the "Commiecrat Party." He was particularly vicious toward Tydings, not only stumping for his opponent, a newcomer named John Marshall Butler, but funneling him money as well. Through a thinly disguised intermediary, he distributed a doctored photo of Tydings alongside Earl Browder, the former Communist leader.

Among the many beneficiaries of Red Scare hysteria that fall was Richard Nixon, the California representative who had made himself a national name through his seat on HUAC and his dogged pursuit of Alger Hiss. Now, he was running for Senate. It was the right time: The Korean War was raging, the Truman administration seemed adrift, and Americans were finally showing a sustained eagerness to move on from a generation of Democratic control over the federal government. Nixon was the smiling young face of the Republican Party waiting to take their place. He was among the few politicians who could speak in two registers at once: He could red-bait like McCarthy, then call for careful, measured respect for civil liberties as well as any card-carrying member of the ACLU. No wonder he drove Democrats crazy.

His opponent, Helen Gahagan Douglas, had the sort of résumé that might have carried anyone into high office during the height of the New Deal. She was born into wealth and gifted with quick intelligence, attending Barnard but leaving without a degree. She went into acting, tripping the lights of Broadway during the 1920s and marrying an equally charismatic actor, Melvyn Douglas. She was said to be the second coming of the actress Ethel Barrymore and "ten of the twelve most beautiful women in the world." In the 1930s the couple had joined the armies of talent moving west, to Hollywood, and moving left, into progressive causes, including the Anti-Nazi League. They became active in Democratic politics, and friends with the Roosevelts. Helen joined the Democratic National Committee and in 1944 won a seat in Congress, representing part of downtown Los Angeles.

Douglas's celebrity preceded her to Washington, and she used it to get out in front on progressive causes. She supported the United Nations and civil rights, and she opposed loyalty checks and the Truman Doctrine. She voted against the Taft-Hartley bill to regulate unions and the Mundt-Nixon anti-Communist bill. Her record was clear, and in a conservative midterm year an easy target for Nixon to attack.

In his memoirs, Nixon insisted that is all he did. "I felt that the best strategy was to let her record do my work for me," he wrote. "Throughout the campaign I kept her pinned to her extremist record." But that's not the entire story. Nixon's campaign strategist, Murray Chotiner, persuaded him to go much further and smear his opponent as a fellow traveler. After Alger Hiss's conviction in January 1950, Nixon had given a widely covered speech in the House, a sort of victory lap in which he tore into the Democrats, Truman, and Acheson. He received hundreds of letters full of praise for his words, and urging him to take the fight against domestic Communism much further. That was all he had needed to hear.

The Republicans had tried red-baiting in their 1946 midterm campaigns—Representative B. Carroll Reece of Tennessee, the party's chairman at the time, had declared "a fight basically between Communism and Republicanism"—but their successes in the House and Senate were due to a variety of factors, domestic Communism being a marginal contribution. Two years later, Thomas Dewey had largely refused to attack President Truman as soft on Communism, much to the dismay of the party's right wing. But that was before the fall of China, before the Soviets got the bomb, before Hiss and Coplon and Foley Square and McCarthy and Korea. Red-baiting was not just an option by 1950; it was practically required of Republican candidates.

An early demonstration of anti-Communism's power came in the Florida Democratic primary in May, in which Representative George Smathers defeated Claude Pepper, the liberal incumbent. "Red Pepper," Smathers and his adjuncts claimed, had been endorsed by *The Daily Worker* newspaper and sought to protect Communists by voting against a string of anti-subversive bills. In a primary that the journalist David Brinkley called "dirtiest in the history of American politics," Smathers's allies circulated a forty-nine-page report called *The Red Record of Senator Claude Pepper*, which linked the incumbent to a string of Communist front organizations, often on the thinnest of evidence and without any context. Written by a former FBI agent and funded by an anonymous donor (or donors), the book went out just a week before the election, to every corner of the state, in a shipment that weighed nine tons. Pepper hit back, but Smathers trounced him on primary day, 55 percent to 45 percent.

The Republicans took note. "If Helen is your opponent," Representative Karl Mundt wrote to Nixon, "something of a similar nature might well be prepared." Once Douglas dispatched the Democratic incumbent in the primary, that is precisely what Nixon did. In a radio address at the start of his general-election campaign, Nixon promised "no namecalling, no smears, no misrepresentations." He was careful not to call Douglas a Communist.

Rather, he called her "pink," a "fellow traveler," a species more dangerous than Communists because they were more numerous and more likely to climb into positions of power. He and his adviser Chotiner first compiled a lengthy analysis of Douglas's voting record, showing the many times that she had been on the same side as her far-left colleague Vito Marcantonio, the New York City representative who had close ties to the Communist Party. "Why has she followed the Communist line so many times?" Nixon asked one audience. Many of those votes were procedural or noncontroversial, and on several Nixon had voted alongside them. But the report didn't mention that.

Nixon hired a woman named Edna Lonigan, a statistician and right-wing ideologue who believed that Douglas, the Democrats, and even many Republicans were Communist agents. The fruits of her opposition research were distributed on pink paper, a choice that Chotiner said was coincidental but went well with Nixon's new sobriquet for his opponent, the Pink Lady. Nixon did not, as it is often said, call Douglas pink "right down to her underwear"—that clever turn of phrase was uttered by a third-party candidate in the same race. But the sentiment, a two-pronged, sexualizing dig at Douglas's politics and her gender, ran through the entirety of Nixon's campaign that fall.

Nixon's attacks catalyzed the public. Hecklers began to show up at Douglas's events, shouting names and demanding to know whether she was a Communist. Melvyn Douglas, on tour for the play *Two Blind Mice*, frequently found protesters marching outside the theaters, warning audiences about the Communist—or husband of a Communist—performing inside. "The fabricated stories came at me like a mudslide; I couldn't keep up with it," Douglas wrote in her memoir.

Nixon continued his attacks as the summer turned to fall. He lumped in Douglas with the China Hands, baselessly suggesting that she shared the blame for Chiang's defeat. "Mrs. Douglas aligned herself with the Lattimore clique in the State Department which adopted the appeasement policy in Asia that led to Korea," Nixon said in early October. Then he added, "This action by Mrs. Douglas had been established to have come just two weeks after William Z. Foster"—the head of the American Communist Party—"transmitted his instructions from the Kremlin to the

Communist national committee." She was guilty by coincidence of timing, a tactic torn straight from the McCarthy playbook.

Nixon trotted to victory that November, defeating Douglas with
59 percent of the vote. His triumph was part of a wave of Republican
wins on an aggressive anti-Communist platform, fueled by McCarthy
and his allies. In Maryland, Millard Tydings, who had been a 10 to 1 favorite, lost to a political newcomer. In Illinois another McCarthy enemy,
the Democratic majority leader Scott Lucas, lost to Everett Dirksen. Mc-
Carthy was declared a kingmaker. "McCarthyism, be it an incomparable
epithet, is simply today a very considerable force in the Congress of the
United States. And it seems to be here to stay," wrote *The New York Times*,
calling McCarthy "the most politically powerful first-term senator in this
Congress."

Nixon did not win simply by red-baiting. He was a much better
candidate—better prepared, more energetic—and ran a much better campaign. Douglas was peripatetic, unfocused, unable to land counterpunches.
Nixon also had much deeper pockets. He drew nationwide support, especially from the Texas oilmen who were fast becoming the main source of
financial support for right-wing Republicans. His win made him a national
figure and marked him as a future leader of the party. But his decision to
smear Douglas came at a price. Long before a slush-fund scandal nearly derailed him from the 1952 presidential ticket, and decades before Watergate,
his red-baiting tactics marked him as a politician willing to do anything to
win. Anti-Communist hysteria had gripped the nation. It's no excuse to say
that for candidates like Nixon, there was really no alternative.

16

Running with the Hounds

The FBI had first come to Julius and Ethel Rosenberg's apartment on the morning of June 16, 1950. The couple lived with their two very young sons in a one-bedroom in Knickerbocker Village, a housing development on Manhattan's Lower East Side. Julius met the agents at the door, and insisted they remain there while he finished shaving. Could he let them in? they asked. No, he said, calmly, not without a warrant. He did agree to accompany them to Foley Square for questioning. At no point along the way did he give any hint that he knew what was happening. It came as a shock to him when, during the interview, an agent asked, "What would you say if we told you your brother-in-law said you asked him to supply information to the Russians?"

"Bring him here," Julius said, recovering quickly. "I'll call him a liar to his face."

The agents let Rosenberg go, but he must have realized that he was already in their net. On the street he saw a newspaper headline announcing that David Greenglass, his wife's brother, had been arraigned that morning on charges of espionage. Julius quickly found a lawyer. Then he waited, a whole month, until Judge F. X. McGohey—whose prosecution of the Smith Act defendants in 1949 had won him a District Court seat—signed a warrant for his arrest. Agents returned to the Rosenberg apartment on the evening of July 17 and took Julius away in handcuffs. Ethel was arrested less than a month later.

Based on the testimony of Greenglass and his wife, Ruth, the Rosenbergs were charged with conspiracy to commit espionage. They had, the government contended, received documents that Greenglass stole from his job as a machinist working on the atomic bomb and passed them to the Soviets. It was, J. Edgar Hoover later said, "the crime of the century." Their trial, in the spring of 1951, became another Rorschach test for one's views on Communism, the Cold War, and the Red Scare: Their alleged crimes either vindicated those who, like Joe McCarthy, believed that Communism was a mortal threat to America and required every means available to repel it; or the trial, justified or not, proved how far down the hole of political hysteria the country had fallen.

Julius Rosenberg grew up ensconced in the Jewish immigrant world of the Lower East Side. He went to New York's City College, at the time a prestigious institution among the city's working-class Jews, where he majored in electrical engineering. It was the 1930s, and he was surrounded by the swirling politics of the left. He took interest in the case of Tom Mooney, a labor activist whose imprisonment for his role in a 1916 bombing in San Francisco made him a martyr on the left. Many thought Mooney had been framed, and he was the subject of campus marches and protest songs. Julius connected with Mooney's plight, and the people he encountered as he learned of it. He was smart, talented, but adrift, intellectually and spiritually, in an ailing capitalist system that many people around him in the 1930s said could not be fixed. He found succor and focus in the Young Communist League, where he met Ethel. They married the same year he graduated college, 1939.

The next year Julius took a job at Fort Monmouth, New Jersey, the home of the Army's Signal Corps, which carried out cutting-edge research on radar, sonar, and other technologies. He joined the Federation of Architects, Engineers, Chemists and Technicians, a Communist-linked professional organization. In 1942 a friend in the party introduced him to a Soviet intelligence agent, and soon Rosenberg was funneling him top secret schematics and other documents, working through a courier named Harry Gold.

The Rosenbergs quit the party in 1943, a common tactic among those who were to be used for espionage. They remained members of the underground, as so-called submarine Communists. Julius expanded his operation, going from a solo project to a full-blown spy ring. Most of his network also worked at Fort Monmouth, but not all. One member, Morton Sobell, worked at a General Electric plant in Schenectady, New York, and provided detailed plans for radar and guidance systems. After David Greenglass was hired to work in the high-explosives unit of the Manhattan Project, at Los Alamos, New Mexico, Julius brought him in as well. And while Greenglass's information on the atomic bomb drew the most attention from prosecutors and the press, Rosenberg's network collected all manner of secret documents, including antiaircraft radar systems and schemes for the P-80, America's first regular-production jet fighter.

Why did Julius do it? Many spies worked for money; the Soviets preferred it that way. It was cleaner. Those who worked out of ideological passion were harder to parse, and could turn at any time, especially if they got wind of what was happening in the Soviet Union. That's what happened to Whittaker Chambers. Rosenberg too did it for the cause, but he never wavered. Even when he was on death row, he believed he was on some level innocent. It wasn't just that he thought he had been helping a wartime ally, as many onetime spies did. He believed he was being convicted of capitalist crimes in a capitalist society, one that would soon pass into history as America followed Russia into the Communist future. He had been helping that process along, something he believed could not be a crime.

The Army never caught on to Rosenberg's spy work, but it did find out about his past party membership, and it discharged him in 1945. He went to work, for a time, at Emerson, an electrical engineering firm, then opened his own machine shop in New York City with Greenglass.

Then, in early 1950, things began to unravel. Even during the war, Army counterintelligence and the FBI had suspected that there was a Soviet program to infiltrate the Manhattan Project. Elizabeth Bentley, back in 1945, had offered tantalizing but inconclusive clues, mostly code names and unprovable hearsay. She had even mentioned a contact named Julius, though she didn't know his last name. In February 1950 British authorities arrested a physicist named Klaus Fuchs, who had worked at Los Alamos, for stealing atomic secrets. Under interrogation, he identified his courier as Harry Gold. The FBI quickly arrested Gold, who just as quickly named

David Greenglass as his source. And Greenglass, arrested in turn, named Julius Rosenberg.

Historians continue to disagree on what role Ethel played in all this. Before he died in 2018, Morton Sobell told the reporter Sam Roberts that she had almost no role at all. She had been present, and maybe offered a hand here or there, but had no substantive involvement. "She knew what he was doing," he said, "but what was she guilty of? Of being Julius's wife." Others point to the frequent references to her found in the Venona transcripts, the top secret Soviet transmissions decoded by American intelligence in the 1940s. "Soviet archival documents also show that Ethel Rosenberg hid money and espionage paraphernalia for Julius, served as an intermediary for communications with his Soviet intelligence contacts, provided her personal evaluation of individuals Julius considered recruiting, and was present at meetings with his sources," wrote a group of five historians in a 2014 article for *The Weekly Standard*.

It's a slightly different question, though, to ask about her role in the acts for which she was charged. At first, Greenglass had mostly left his sister out of his story. He said he had passed off documents to Julius on the street, and that his own wife, Ruth, had assisted in preparing them. Ethel had merely helped secure the connection between Julius and David, and had been aware of what they were doing. But then Greenglass switched his story. In front of the grand jury, he said that the handoffs had taken place inside the Rosenbergs' apartment, and that Ethel had typed up his notes. This new account is what led to her arrest. And it was a lie. After confessing, Greenglass, who also spoke to Roberts, told the reporter he was simply corroborating what his wife had already told the authorities— which was a lie as well. "So what am I going to do, call my wife a liar?" he said. "My wife is more important to me than my sister."

Government investigators surely realized that he was lying. But as the historians Ronald Radosh and Joyce Milton describe in their canonical account of the case, *The Rosenberg File*, Greenglass had given them what they needed: a wedge to use against Julius to get him to name the rest of his ring, as well as his Soviet contacts. "There is no question . . . if Julius Rosenberg would furnish details of his extensive espionage activities it would be possible to proceed against other individuals," J. Edgar Hoover wrote in a memo to Attorney General J. Howard McGrath on July 16, 1950 (Tom Clark, McGrath's predecessor, had moved to the Supreme Court in 1949). "Proceeding against his wife might serve as a lever in this matter." When that didn't work—when they arrested her, and Julius still didn't talk—only then did they decide to raise the possibility of execution. During a closed appearance before the Joint Committee on Atomic Energy, one prosecutor said that "the only thing that will break this man Rosenberg is the prospect of a death penalty or getting the chair, plus that if we can convict his wife, too, and give her a stiff sentence of 25 to 30 years, that combination may serve to make this fellow disgorge and give us the information on those other individuals. I can't guarantee that."

"He is pretty tough, isn't he," said Senator Brien McMahon, Democrat of Connecticut, the committee chairman.

"It is about the only thing you can use as a lever on these people," the prosecutor replied.

The Rosenberg trial began on the morning of March 6, 1951, in Room 107 of Foley Square, the same downtown Manhattan courthouse where Alger Hiss, Judith Coplon, and the Communist Party leadership had been tried, just over a year earlier. Representing the government was U.S. Attorney Irving Saypol, who had worked on the Hiss, Coplon, and Communist leadership trials. He was a dour, unfriendly man, with a chiseled jaw and bushy eyebrows. He was so committed an anti-Communist that he often declined to shake hands with defense attorneys representing accused party members. (Later, as a judge, he once found a lawyer in contempt for wearing a brown suede hat in the courtroom, calling it "grotesque" and a "flamboyant turban.") Among his assistants was a young, recent graduate of Columbia Law School named Roy Cohn.

The trial lasted just over three weeks, but in that time Saypol managed to blur the lines between the actual charges against the Rosenbergs and the much more serious crime of treason, of which they were not accused. In his opening statement, he said that their actions took place during wartime, which would be an exacerbating factor were it not for the fact that the Soviets were American allies at the time. He said the Rosenbergs "have committed the most serious crime which can be committed against the people of this country," which might have been the case but was not what they were charged with. And he repeatedly mentioned that they had been members of the Communist Party, an irrelevant point that drew repeated rebukes from the judge, Irving Kaufman, because it might well bias the jury.

Bizarrely, the Rosenbergs' own lawyer, Emanuel Bloch, helped Saypol advance his implicit charge of treason. While Cohn examined Greenglass, he introduced a replica of the atomic bomb schematic that Greenglass had given to Rosenberg, then asked that it be admitted as evidence. Bloch immediately objected—to ask that it be impounded to keep it secret from "the court, the jury and counsel."

"That is a rather strange request coming from the defendants," Saypol said.

"Not a strange request coming from me at the present," Bloch replied.

Judge Kaufman was all too happy to comply. A few minutes later, as Cohn began to ask Greenglass about the schematic, Bloch asked to approach the bench, so as to be out of earshot of the jury.

"Despite the fact that the Atomic Energy Commission may have declassified this," Bloch said in a hushed tone, "I was not at all sure in my own mind, and I am talking privately, whether or not even at this late date this information may not be used to the advantage of a foreign power."

He asked for the examination to move forward in camera—that is, with the press and public removed from the courtroom. Kaufman agreed, at first, but after the reporters protested he let them back in. Still, the damage was done: Bloch's actions underlined, and perhaps exaggerated, not just the significance of the schematic but the nature of the Rosenbergs' crime.

Once the two sides rested, it took the jury little time in finding the couple, and Sobell, guilty. The jury even drew out its deliberations so as not to make it seem like it was rushing. "My opinion is that your verdict is a correct verdict," Kaufman told them. "The thought that citizens of our country would lend themselves to the destruction of their own country by the most destructive weapon known to man is so shocking that I can't find words to describe this loathsome offense." Kaufman had reserved for himself the decision on whether to find them subject to the death penalty. He held a number of confidential, likely improper conversations with Saypol and his team, as well as with Department of Justice and FBI officials. The bureau and much of the department in Washington was against the death penalty for Ethel—some believed it was simply wrong to execute a young mother, while others, including Hoover, worried that doing so risked a public backlash. But in New York, both Saypol and Cohn pressed Kaufman hard for a double death penalty, and the judge agreed.

A week later, Kaufman rendered his sentence. He began by noting that the Espionage Act, under which they were charged, allowed for a maximum of twenty years, unless the country was at war, in which case the death penalty was permissible. And indeed, he said, the country had been at war—again sidestepping the inconvenient fact that the Soviets and Americans had not been at war with each other. "Citizens of this country who betray their fellow countrymen can be under none of the delusions about the benignity of Soviet power that they might have been prior to World War II," he said. "The nature of Russian terrorism is now self-evident. Idealism as a rationale dissolves." But that was anachronistic, and untenable as an argument—either the Rosenbergs were guilty of actions during the war, when, by Kaufman's logic, one might still be idealistic about Russia's intentions, or they were guilty of actions now, when the United States and the Soviet Union were not at war.

Kaufman complained at length about the insanity of a law that provided for a maximum peacetime penalty of twenty years in prison for stealing atomic secrets. And though he recommended that Congress change that law, he also made it clear that he was going to go beyond what was allowed. "I consider your crime worse than murder," he said, addressing the defendants, who sat staring, stony-faced. "Plain deliberate contemplated murder is dwarfed in magnitude by comparison with the crime you have committed. I believe your conduct in putting into the hands of the Russians the A-bomb years before our best scientists predicted Russia would perfect the bomb has already caused, in my opinion, the Communist aggression in Korea, with the resultant casualties exceeding 50,000 and who knows but that millions more of innocent people may pay the price of your treason. Indeed, by your betrayal you undoubtedly have altered the course of history to the disadvantage of our country." He said he had searched his conscience for mercy, and found none. "It is not in my power, Julius and Ethel Rosenberg, to forgive you," he said. "Only the Lord can find mercy for what you have done." With that he sentenced them to death, to be carried out the week of May 21, 1951.

The Rosenbergs' supporters insisted that they were the innocent victims of a fascist state. But many more Americans thought they got what they deserved, and that their crimes proved the venality of domestic Communism and the rightness of the Red Scare. For decades, those who believed in their innocence were called pinko leftists. Those who believed them guilty were called McCarthyites. But, as with most things, the truth lies in between.

The government's case, as it was presented to the public in 1951, was largely circumstantial, and rested primarily on the testimony of Ethel's sister and brother-in-law, the Greenglasses. What the government could not say was that even more evidence sat, unused, in the Venona decryptions. When they were finally opened in 1995, the Soviet cables documented how Julius had run his ring, and its persistence up until his arrest, evidence that might have quieted some of his defenders. At the same time, the government did not admit that during the grand jury investigation that led up to the Rosenbergs' arrests, David Greenglass had completely changed him testimony. It was not until 2001 that he confessed to his lies. Then, in 2011, Morton Sobell, in his interview with Sam Roberts of *The New York Times*, finally admitted that yes, he and Julius had been spies for the Soviets. The Rosenbergs' orphaned sons, who had long insisted on their father's innocence, ultimately came to believe in his guilt, though not in the justice of their death sentence.

But even this gradual, damning accretion does not tell the full story. From early on, the government had known not only that Julius's network was much larger than it revealed in court, but that Ethel's role in it was much smaller than it charged. These disparities were related. Prosecutors were using her to get to him, hoping that the thought of his wife dying alongside him would be enough to make him talk—or, at least, enough to make her talk. Executing either was never the real goal. The government believed that Julius Rosenberg was the centerpiece in a much larger web of Soviet espionage, and that he could provide them with a map to it. The couple weren't even prosecuted correctly: They were charged with conspiracy under the Espionage Act of 1917, but found guilty of treason—even though, to do so, the prosecution was supposed to present two separate witnesses for each of the twelve "overt acts" listed in the charge, which it did not. "The government framed a guilty man," Roberts concluded in his book about Greenglass, *The Brother*. The real question, then, is not whether the Rosenbergs were guilty. It is how the government ended up executing two people when so few of those involved in the case thought they deserved to die.

At the same time the Rosenberg trial was reaching its conclusion, the Supreme Court was considering the final fate of the ten Communist Party leaders convicted at Foley Square under the Smith Act, whose case on appeal was known as *Dennis v. United States*. In their appeal strategy after their trial in Foley Square, in late 1949, the Communist Party leadership had bet on a Supreme Court much different than the one they found in 1951. Two of the court's stalwart civil libertarians, Frank Murphy and Wiley Rutledge, had been replaced by two vocal defenders of the government, Tom Clark and Sherman Minton; alongside Chief Justice Fred Vinson and Associate Justice Stanley Reed, they formed a solid bloc of deference to the executive branch. Under justices like Murphy and Rutledge, in combination with the liberals Hugo Black and William O. Douglas, the Smith Act case might have been reversed. But not now..

Less clear was the opinion of Felix Frankfurter, a famed Harvard Law professor who had made his name as a staunch advocate of progressive causes in the 1920s and '30s. He defended left-wingers during the first Red Scare and helped found *The New Republic* magazine, a fortress of liberal opinion. He was a leading figure in the defense of Nicola Sacco and Bartolomeo Vanzetti, two Italian immigrants convicted and ultimately executed for murder, in 1927, charges that Frankfurter believed were ideological and unsupportable. Even after he settled in Cambridge, he was known as one of the most influential figures in the New Deal for his mentorship and promotion of his prize students into positions of early authority in the executive branch, including Dean Acheson, presidential adviser Thomas Corcoran, and Alger and Donald Hiss—a group collectively known as Frankfurter's Happy Hot Dogs.

Frankfurter's progressive fans were legion, and they cheered when, in 1939, Franklin Roosevelt named him to the Supreme Court. But Frankfurter soon disappointed. In his first significant majority opinion, he weighed whether a school could force two Jehovah's Witness children to pledge allegiance to the American flag, even though their religion expressly prohibited displays of patriotism. Much to the distress of his progressive friends, Frankfurter ruled that national unity was the "basis of national security," and that the government's interest in promoting patriotism outweighed the children's religious freedom. But he also argued that the court had only limited power to intervene in "the subtle process of securing effective loyalty to the traditional ideals of democracy, while respecting at the same time individual idiosyncrasies." To do otherwise, he wrote, "would, in effect, make us the school board for the country. That authority has not been given to this court, nor should we assume it."

The decision marked Frankfurter as the voice of judicial restraint on the court, the heir to two previous titans of the doctrine, Justices Oliver Wendell Holmes Jr. and Benjamin Cardozo. It also, somewhat unfairly, earned him a reputation as a judicial conservative. Frankfurter's views had not changed. The role of the law in a liberal society, he felt, was to adjudicate disputes between competing values, not to favor one value over the other. There was also a practical side to Frankfurter's thinking: During the 1930s, the court's then-dominant conservative bloc had sought out and destroyed numerous federal programs, interfering in a way that Frankfurter believed was antidemocratic. Better, Frankfurter thought, for the courts to stay out of such fights whenever possible.

Now he was confronted with a similar question regarding the Smith Act case. He was sure that the act was a faulty, even dangerous law. But was it his place to make that decision, if the law was otherwise constitutional? Justice Stanley Reed, for one, thought it was not, and told Frankfurter so. "My position is that a teaching of force and violence by such a group as this, found by this jury, is enough at this period of the world's history to make the protection of the First Amendment inapplicable," Reed wrote, urging Frankfurter to join him in upholding the convictions. The logic of absolute security imposed by the Cold War, Reed argued, should trump considerations of civil liberties. Even the slightest risk of violent subversion justified putting the defendants in prison. Chief Justice Vinson agreed. "If the government is aware that a group aiming at its overthrow is attempting to indoctrinate its members and to commit them to a course where by they will strike when the leaders feel the circumstances permit," he wrote in his decision, "action by the government is required." Like Reed, he was unbothered by a strong conviction to protect civil liberties.

Frankfurter found himself caught between his dual commitments to civil liberties and judicial restraint, under the pressure of his colleagues who believed that perilous times rendered that question moot. Ultimately, he joined the majority in upholding the convictions, but could not bring himself to agree with Vinson and Reed's Cold War reasoning. "We need not decide how we would adjust these interests were the initial decision ours," Frankfurter wrote in a concurring opinion to the 6–2 decision, handed down on June 4, 1951. "It is not. It is enough that we cannot say that Congress has exceeded constitutional bounds in concluding that a combination such as the conviction established in this case is subject to punishment." He clearly felt uncomfortable with his conclusion, because he hurried to add, "Much that should be rejected as illiberal, because repressive and envenoming, may well be not unconstitutional."

Frankfurter's decision alarmed his liberal friends. Two of his fellow justices also took issue. Lacking evidence of subversive actions, the crime, William O. Douglas wrote in his dissent, "depends not on what is taught but on who the teacher is. . . . Once we start down that road we enter territory dangerous to the liberties of every citizen." Hugo Black raised the brightest red flag. From the beginning, he wrote in his dissenting opinion, the case had been driven by fear, not justice, as frightening a threat to the rule of law as one could find in a democratic society. He could only hope that the fear would subside before permanent damage was done to the body politic. "Public opinion being what it now is, few will protest the conviction of these Communist petitioners," he wrote. "There is hope, however, that in calmer times, when present pressures, passions and fears subside, this or some later Court will restore the First Amendment liberties to the high preferred place where they belong in a free society."

A few months later, Columbia University invited Douglas, an alumnus of its law school, to sit at the head table during a celebratory dinner for one of his former law school classmates, Governor Thomas Dewey. The two-time presidential candidate centered his speech on the court, and with Douglas sitting a few feet away, he attacked it for falling short in its share of the anti-Communist crusade. Having failed to take advantage of anti-Communism in the 1948 presidential race, Dewey was making up for it now. He did, however, have to give the court credit for its Smith Act decision. "Never, never did I dream that the Court would have the guts to send those Communists off to prison."

The room filled with applause. Douglas quietly folded his napkin and walked out. He was disgusted to see such a supposedly sophisticated crowd fall prey to hysteria. "It was sad that educated lawyers would think that sending the miserable defendants in *Dennis* off to prison had saved the country," he wrote in his memoirs.

With the Smith Act decision, the Court signaled that it was now on the side of the red hunters, that, in the words of Douglas, it was "running with the hounds." Less than a month later, in August 1951, the FBI arrested 17 second-tier Communist leaders, and over the next six years it would arrest 128 more. All were charged under the Smith Act. None were shown to have done anything more than discuss Marx, organize picket lines, and do what they could to publicize their revolutionary ideas. Lacking the fireworks and protests of the first Smith Act case, the trials took on a routine, almost perfunctory tone, with the same evidence presented, the same professional witnesses on the stand, and the same sense that it was all a fait accompli. Prosecutors rarely bothered to suggest that the Communists presented an imminent threat—because, according to the Vinson court, there no longer needed to be.

The court fed the hysteria in other cases as well. In *Garner v. Los Angeles Board of Public Works*, decided on the same day as *Dennis*, fifteen low-level employees of the city of Los Angeles had refused to sign an affidavit, required by the state of California, in which they were supposed to promise they were not members of the Communist Party, and had not been for the last five years. They were fired. The law applied to everyone from police officers to garbage men, and struck many, even at the time, as an unnecessary intrusion into the political views of employees who had no reasonable relationship to national security. But Justice Clark, responding for the majority, was unbothered, writing that the provisions "are a reasonable regulation to protect the municipal service." Frankfurter, this time, joined Douglas and Black in dissent.

"Douglas and Black dissenting" became the watchword in the Red Scare cases, with Frankfurter occasionally joining. Another 1952 case involved three immigrants whom the government sought to deport because, at one point or another, each had joined, then left, the Communist Party. The court upheld the deportation, leaving Black apoplectic. The country, he said, was in more "desperate trouble on the First Amendment than it has ever been, much worse than during the Palmer Raids" of the late 1910s, during the first Red Scare. In all these cases, including those where Frankfurter himself dissented, the majority's guiding approach was deference to the other branches when it came to national security—even though it was the court's job to balance those issues against civil liberties.

Perhaps the most egregious case was that of Dorothy Bailey, a Black woman who had gone to work as a clerk for an obscure federal agency, the U.S. Employment Service, in 1939. She was laid off in 1947, then reinstated a few years later. Since she was technically a new hire, she was examined by a loyalty review board, which had been created in between her two periods of employment. A confidential informant had told the FBI that Bailey had been a secret member of the Communist Party in the mid-1930s, leading the board to bar her from government employment. Bailey admitted to attending a party meeting once, out of curiosity, but she flatly denied ever joining. She was involved with civil rights, having protested the segregation of Black and white blood at a Red Cross center, and she retorted that the snitch must have been someone unhappy with her activism. But the board refused to let her confront her anonymous accuser, or even review the evidence behind the allegations.

Bailey appealed. The D.C. Court of Appeals agreed that her treatment was unfair, and that she had in effect been convicted without a trial. But it ruled that, especially in light of the world situation, the courts should not encroach on the president's power to police the government's employees—even when that power led to unfair outcomes, like hers. The Supreme Court split on the case, 4–4 (with Clark abstaining, since he had been attorney general at the time of her firing). That meant the decision against Bailey would stand.

17

Naming Names

Hollywood had been one of the first places seared by anti-Communist witch hunts, all the way back in 1947, and by 1951 the film industry was in the full grip of the Red Scare. Message films were out, lighter fare was in. "You might say the popular phrase out here now is 'Nothing on the down-beat,'" one screenwriter told Lillian Ross of *The New Yorker*. Ayn Rand's *Screen Guide* offered a map for avoiding suspicion and keeping one's job. Actors and writers who had gladly signed petitions, chipped into fund-raisers, and proudly marched against fascism were suddenly afraid that the country's new Savonarolas would discover their former courageous stands and out them as Communist sympathizers. It had been easy, even socially advantageous, to take a political stand in the 1930s. Now that the Hollywood Ten—the screenwriters, directors, and producers who had re-fused to discuss their Communist affiliations with HUAC—were on their way to jail, such courage was harder to come by.

Anti-Communism was especially powerful in Southern California, where the veneer of liberalism lay over a rock-hard substrate of law-and-order conservatism. The Los Angeles Police Department had an eager and aggressive "red squad" that kept copious files on suspected Communists and fed the information to the FBI and HUAC, which had kept up its steady pace of inquisitions into all corners of American life, even as Mc-Carthy had pushed its witch-hunting off the front page. As early as 1946, the city board of education was investigating charges of Communist in-doctrination in public schools. In 1948 the Los Angeles County Board of Supervisors instituted a loyalty test for all government workers, and in 1950 it required all members of the Communist Party to register. (Not to be outdone, the cities of Los Angeles and Santa Monica passed identical loyalty tests, also in 1948.)

The first, and easiest, thing to do was to turn on the Hollywood Ten. Cutting them off professionally and socially was an immediate way to show one's anti-Communist bona fides. Former friends refused to take their phone calls, and they crossed the street when they saw them coming down the road. Antipathy among directors, producers, and actors, who tended to be more politically conservative, was predictable, but even the Screen Writers Guild, once reliably progressive, refused to support their defense. In 1953 the guild would go even further, agreeing to let producers refuse credit to writers who admitted to past membership in the party or refused to answer HUAC; the agreement remained in effect until 1977.

In late 1947, Tom Clark, still the attorney general, had indicted the Ten for contempt of Congress, and they had surrendered to a U.S. marshal in downtown Los Angeles a few days later. In January 1948 they had returned to Washington to stand trial. Dalton Trumbo and John Howard Lawson went first, and were quickly convicted in April 1948. The remaining eight had agreed that they would accept the decisions in the Trumbo and Lawson trials as their own, and lean on the chance of an appeal. While they waited, they went on a near-continuous speaking tour, picking up what support and funds they could find. They joined forces with the Joint Anti-Fascist Refugee Committee. In June 1948 Trumbo and Lawson hosted a fundraiser for the committee, and members of each group toured the country together, giving speeches against HUAC, which they labeled "Deadline for Freedom" rallies.

Most of them, even Trumbo, their sardonic ringleader, really had believed in a Hollywood ending—that their cases would make it to the Supreme Court and be vindicated. In June 1949 an appellate court found against them. Since the question was about contempt of Congress, it was an easy decision, since the courts, especially at the time, gave the legislative branch wide discretion to enforce its own rules. But the appeals court went further, injecting politics and ideology into its decision. "Neither Congress nor any court is required to disregard the impact of world events, however impartially or dispassionately they view them," its chief judge wrote. In April 1950, the Supreme Court refused to take up the case, and in June, the Ten began to surrender themselves to the Department of Justice to serve their sentences, in most cases for a year.

On their way, they retook some of their previous status as martyrs: A thousand people gathered at Penn Station, in New York City, to see Trumbo and Lawson on their way to Washington, and into the federal penal system. "Jack and I had the rather grotesque experience of being carried aloft through the crowd like a pair of startled, sacrificial bullocks on their way to the altar," Trumbo wrote in a letter to his wife, Cleo. "There were speeches and FBIs and harried Pennsylvania officers, the latter as eager to have us downstairs in quieter surroundings." At least one of the writers, Ring Lardner Jr., had some comic, cosmic consolation: Serving time alongside him at Danbury, Connecticut, was his former tormentor, HUAC chairman J. Parnell Thomas, who in the meantime had been convicted of fraud.

When they finally emerged from prison, in late 1950 and early 1951, the Hollywood Ten found their lives upended. They couldn't get work, at least not under their own names. They couldn't get bank loans. It was bad enough that old friends turned newly cold. In Hollywood, social connections are a conduit to employment. Without their networks, writing gigs, once as plentiful as salmon in spawning season, completely disappeared. After getting out of prison, one of the ten, Lester Cole, had to settle for a job writing copy for the Sealy Mattress Co. Another, Herbert Biberman, earned $100 a week as an assistant buyer for the Pacific Coast Textile Co.

Between November 1948 and June 1950, when he went to prison, the screenwriter Alvah Bessie had made just $4,200, or about $54,000 in today's dollars—not nearly enough to support his family. Neighbors, once friendly, sneered at his wife as she walked along South Crescent Drive in Beverly Hills, where they were renting a small duplex apartment. Only one child among the dozens on their block was allowed to play with his four-year-old daughter. A community that had once accepted, even valorized, men like Bessie now shunned them.

At least the Hollywood Ten knew they were on the blacklist, and why. Over the next decade, hundreds of others would see work disappear, friends turn away, and calls go unanswered, for reasons they did not always understand. All it took was a rumor about someone being a little too eager to back the 1945 strikers, about being a little too early in her anti-Nazism, about being seen one time too many in the company of a known Communist like Lawson. Hollywood being a fickle place, where careers rocket up and collapse just as quickly, it might not be clear, right away, why an actor's work had suddenly dried up. They might go months, a year even, before a friendly producer or an old agent finally tipped them off—a revelation that often led to an absurd sense of comfort. "At first, I didn't realize what it was," recalled one actor. "It seemed outrageous to have been quietly burned that way. But still, I was greatly relieved to hear the news—it was not that I had lost either my looks or my ability, as I half-believed!"

Walter Bernstein, who had been a staff writer at *The New Yorker* before turning to scripts, found out one day in 1950 why he had stopped getting work from a friendly CBS executive. At first, the executive said it was because Bernstein was being paid too much. Then it was because the show he wrote for, *Danger*, was going in a new direction. One morning the executive took him to an empty bar and told him the truth. Bernstein was on a list. If he wrote again for the studio, it would have to be under an assumed name. And even that was a huge risk for the executive to take—most writers were shut out completely.

Scores of writers, actors, and artists, suddenly unable to find work in the United States, moved to Mexico City, where in the 1950s a lively community of left-leaning Americans took root, mingling with local intellectuals and Europeans who had settled there while fascism overtook their own homes. Trumbo and his family were among the many who made the trip. He continued to write under a pseudonym, but soon found it a grind—everything he did was unofficial and under the table, a hard thing to manage from some two thousand miles away. He moved back to Los Angeles after two years.

Some were given a chance by their studios to come clean by naming names. Another screenwriter, Bernard Gordon, recalled how the head of security at Warner Brothers pressured him to talk—first as the good cop, then as the bad cop. "Look, Gordon. You know why you're here," the man told him in one meeting. "We want you to think about your own situation, your own interests. We want a little cooperation from you, and it's all over. Understand?" Gordon refused, and found himself blacklisted immediately. Still others were required to demonstrate their newfound anti-Communism by joining and promoting right-wing groups like the Motion Picture Alliance.

Several writers, starting with Trumbo, accused the studios of anticompetitive collusion by agreeing to bar them from writing. Trumbo and the Hollywood Ten might have had a case—they were explicitly named in the Waldorf Statement, the 1947 document that inaugurated the blacklist. But for the rest, there was no proof. There was never any singular "blacklist." Rather, there was a whisper network linking executives and columnists and groups like the American Legion, carrying unfounded innuendo and clear warnings to stay away. It was the result of a risk-averse herd mentality; once word got out that a writer or actor was tainted, no one wanted to touch them. Studios, Walter Bernstein wrote, "wanted to be left alone to make money. If a condition of that was a blacklist, the price was trifling."

Even as the blacklist shut down careers, it opened new opportunities. Groups like the American Legion and the Legion of Decency, a Catholic organization, established or expanded beachheads in Hollywood as investigators and consultants, judges and executioners. The American Legion kept a list of "acceptable" and "unacceptable" films and actors, and organized protests and boycotts against those that didn't clear the bar. *The Hollywood Legionnaire*, the newsletter serving the American Legion posts around the film industry, included a running list of movies and plays to protest; the January 1952 edition called for action against *Death of a Salesman*, *A Streetcar Named Desire*, and *A Place in the Sun*. Legion members duly showed up outside studios and theaters with placards and harsh words.

The Legion of Decency sent representatives to the studios to read over scripts and sit in on film shoots—and the studios welcomed them, so afraid were they of crossing Hollywood's new, self-appointed censors. "We've worked very closely with the Catholic Church, doing it the way they want it done," Victor Fleming, who was directing a film about Joan of Arc, said. "We want to be sure all these artists don't get a bum steer."

While directing *The Treasure of the Sierra Madre*, John Huston found just how invasive and pernicious these new arbiters could be, and just how easily the studios found it to accept their pro-American strictures. The movie was supposed to open and close with a subtitle: "Gold, Mister, is worth what it is because of the human labor that goes into the finding and getting of it." But the executives at Warner Brothers axed it because of the word "labor," and whatever that might imply. "That word looks dangerous in print, I guess," Huston told Lillian Ross, of *The New Yorker*. "You can sneak it onto the sound track now and then, though."

Before a studio hired a writer or an actor, inquiries were made. A producer would call the Hollywood American Legion post for an off-the-record briefing. Films were analyzed for questionable content, and even the slimmest, most absurdly bad-faith readings of a script raised concerns. The sci-fi hit *The Day the Earth Stood Still* was at one point at risk of being yanked because, in one scene, the alien Klaatu dismisses humans as "stupid," a description the local Legionnaires found dangerously close to Communist propaganda.

The result was a flood of anti-Communist films. In the late 1940s and early '50s, the Soviets were not yet the pop-culture enemy they would become. For now the evil emanated closer to home. Eager to curry favor with HUAC and the American Legion, studios pumped out films with unsubtle titles like 1949's *I Married a Communist* (also known as *The Woman on Pier 13*) and 1951's *I Was a Communist for the FBI*, based on the real-life story of Matt Cvetic, a Pittsburgh laborer who spent over six years as a mole within the local Communist Party branch. *Big Jim McLain*, released in 1952, featured John Wayne as a HUAC agent hunting subversives in Hawaii. That same year saw the release of *My Son John*, starring the estimable Helen Hayes, about a mother who suspects her son is a Communist. Hayes's presence was not enough to balance the onus of its anti-Communist larding; the film, wrote critic Bosley Crowther of *The New York Times*, was "so strongly dedicated to the purpose of the American anti-Communist purge that it seethes with the sort of emotionalism and illogic that is characteristic of so much thinking these days. . . . Not only does it heroize the image of the ranting, song-singing patriot who distrusts and ridicules intellectuals as dangerous perverters of youth, but it falls in completely with the assumption, which has become so perilously prevalent, that guilt is evidenced by association, so far as politics are concerned." None of these films was especially good, though *My Son John* did, somehow, earn an Academy Award nomination for best writing.

The closest anyone came to an official blacklist appeared in June 1950, under the unsubtle title *Red Channels: The Report of Communist Influence in Radio and Television*. The document was the product of a company called American Business Consultants, which had been established in 1947 by three ex-FBI agents, with funding from Alfred Kohlberg, the textile importer and unofficial head of the China Lobby. It amassed hoards of documents related to hundreds of people and groups even an inch to the left of the center, from the NAACP and the *Bulletin of the Atomic Scientists* to Langston Hughes and Dorothy Parker. The company put itself forward as essentially an anti-Communist detective agency: For five dollars a report, it would do a deep scrub of an employee or job candidate's background, looking for anything subversive, progressive, or hinting at pro-Communist leanings. Its clients included some of the biggest TV and radio sponsors of the era, like Du Pont, General Motors, and R.J. Reynolds. It also published *Counterattack*, a weekly "newsletter of facts to combat Communism," that kept subscribers up to date on the latest Communist machinations. Its editors had little compunction about publishing rumors and hearsay; even its verifiable facts, like who signed an anti-Franco petition in 1937, were freighted with innuendo.

Red Channels collected its findings on names in the film industry, but it was a hit far beyond Hollywood. American Legion posts bought copies to know which movies to picket and where to direct letter-writing campaigns. The superintendent of schools in Newark, New Jersey, bought copies to put in the city's libraries and give to its educators. "Teachers should know something about the subversive action going on under our noses," he said. A supermarket chain in Syracuse, New York, urged its shoppers to boycott products from the sponsors of shows written by or starring anyone listed in *Red Channels*. After Bernstein and several other writers for *Danger* appeared in the book, the chain's owner taped a sign beneath a stack of Amm-i-dent toothpaste, one of the show's sponsors. "Would you buy this toothpaste if you knew the money was going to the

Communist Party?" below which he placed two boxes, labeled yes and no, with a notepad and pen to mark votes. Within weeks, stores around the country were doing the same.

American Business Consultants was not the only player in the game. After its first flush of success, one of its founders left to start his own company, Aware, which released its own newsletters similar to *Counterattack*. The American Legion's Americanism Commission published suspicious names in its magazine *The Firing Line*. Several Legion posts supplemented *The Firing Line* with their own newsletters, most notably *The Vigil*, published by the Hollywood American Legion. Yet another, similar group, the Wage Earners Committee, was itself a sort of front, getting money surreptitiously from anti-union studio executives.

Among the worst of the copycats was Myron Fagan, a second-rate playwright in the twilight of his career who, in 1950, published a pamphlet called *Documentation of the Red Stars in Hollywood*. Along with fingering actors and writers as Communists—usually with no proof—he also took shots at *Counterattack*, saying that it was too soft and did not reveal the full extent of what he alleged was an all-out plot to take over America's entertainment industry. It was a sign of the times that anyone took Fagan seriously: He was already an outspoken conspiracy theorist and America Firster, with a long history of smearing the New Deal and Franklin D. Roosevelt in the most fantastical ways imaginable—The United Nations was a Communist front, he said, and Roosevelt had secretly promised to cede Europe to Stalin. No one took him seriously until he found the one issue on which, for a time, no one could afford to ignore him.

Extremist hacks like Fagan helped the likes of American Business Consultants look good. They pretended to responsibility and fair dealing. Theodore Kirkpatrick, one of the ex-FBI agents who founded the company, told *The New York Times* that he would be happy to publicize any anti-Communist actions taken by people listed in his publications. By way of example, he touted the playwright Irwin Shaw, who after seeing his antiwar play *Bury the Dead* listed in *Counterattack* offered to have it permanently withdrawn from production.

Red Channels listed 151 TV and radio stars and their purported connections to the Communist Party. The evidence was typically slim and vague:

The entry for the composer Aaron Copland, for example, claimed that he was "affiliated" with eleven fronts and suspect groups, a "supporter" of three more, and a signer of three suspect statements, including a welcome scroll presented to the Russian composer Dmitri Shostakovich during a 1949 visit to the United States. It also dinged him for writing a piece called "Into the Streets May First," which the report described, vaguely, as a "mass song."

Copland was lucky; his name was already well established, his legacy secure. But to read *Red Channels* today is to peruse a long list of stymied careers and thwarted ambitions. Jean Muir had been a promising stage actress when she was cast in mid-1950 as a lead in the TV version of a popular radio program, *The Aldrich Family*. Her career was about to take a big step up. Then came *Red Channels*. Like Copland, most of Muir's entries were as a "supporter" or "signer" of various progressive groups and causes. But she had also spent six months as the vice president of the Congress of American Women, which the attorney general had listed as a subversive organization (while progressive in its leaning and open to Communist members, the group also counted liberal and moderate women in its ranks). NBC, the network behind *The Aldrich Family*, was inundated with letters, as was the show's sponsor, General Foods. The network quickly dropped Muir from the show. Her career derailed, she eventually moved to Missouri to teach theater at the all-women's Stephens College in Columbia.

Not all networks were so craven. Despite protests that the entertainer Gypsy Rose Lee was listed in *Red Channels*, ABC refused to fire her as the emcee of an upcoming game show. On the other hand, in January 1951 CBS required all its 2,500 regular employees to sign a loyalty pledge swearing that they had never belonged to the Communist Party or any of the groups listed as subversive by the attorney general.

Blacklisted actors like Muir had little option but to leave the industry to wait it out until the storm passed or find other work entirely. Precisely because they were stars, government authorities and their self-appointed adjuncts in the American Legion continued to hound them. Walter Bernstein, the screenwriter, recalled one actor friend (he declined to give his name) who struggled to find a job and finally settled for working as a cashier at a butcher shop. That is, until the day two government agents visited his new boss to ask if he knew what sort of man he had hired. After they left, Bernstein's friend was fired on the spot—though the owner, out of some modicum of shame, sent him home with a few lamb chops.

Writers had it a bit easier. In TV, they could join a writers' room and contribute uncredited material. They could pick up odd jobs as script doctors, work fed to them by sympathetic producers and directors. Most of the time, they got by under pseudonyms or fronts—real people who, like Christian in *Cyrano de Bergerac*, passed off the blacklistee's work as their own, while also passing along the bulk of the commission. Dalton Trumbo maintained more than a half dozen fronts. In the years between his contempt conviction and his time in prison, Trumbo wrote five screenplays, for $126,000 ($1.65 million in today's money), and "in each instance I used the name of some friend who was at least somewhat known in the motion picture industry, which is to say, the story was by the friend and I had no connection with it whatever." The friends received a third of the money, Trumbo the rest. Such ruses became necessary when CBS and other studios insisted that its producers meet with screenwriters in person, to verify they weren't dealing with a blacklistee working under an assumed name. These arrangements were also risky of course, and at times comical. Bernstein received compliments for scripts he didn't write. And he once found a writer he barely knew claiming falsely that he was his front, hoping to generate interest in his own mediocre scripts. "I did not know whether to be flattered or enraged," Bernstein wrote.

The blacklisted writers also had each other. Without agents, it was up to them to find their own opportunities, a task made harder by the omerta against hiring them. They shared what they could—tips, connections, even gigs. They loaned one another money. In 1954 several banded together to make a film about a mineworkers' strike called *Salt of the Earth*. It too was blacklisted. Mostly, they commiserated, and created a community after the rest of Hollywood had shunned them. "Surprisingly, we laughed a lot," Bernstein recalled. "No matter how horrendous the story, we could usually find some dark humor in it. Maybe it was because many of us were Jewish. We specialized in the hilarity of doom."

Jean Muir's defenestration by NBC demonstrated the power of *Red Channels* and the fear it instilled in studios, TV networks, and corporate America. By late 1950, a purge was on across the TV and radio industry, driven by the marketing firms that linked them with advertisers. "I think Miss Muir's case is only the beginning of what we're going to face," one TV executive told *The New York Times*. "The 'Red Channels' book is now the Bible up and down Madison Avenue." As one producer told Bernstein, "We cannot take any chances. We quarantine everyone in the book."

But American Business Consultants wanted to take things further, to close the circle. So did the studios. The various lists were long and many; there was simply too much talent at risk to blacklist them all. So the company offered another service, for an additional fee. In addition to identifying possible risks, it would also help clear those it had named if they made what it considered a good-faith effort to denounce their past. It was, in short, a racket. "It all had an efficient circularity," Bernstein wrote. "First make the accusation; then offer protection against what you had created."

Over time, a network of so-called clearance agents emerged. An apologetic actor might first approach American Business Consultants, or the union leader Roy Brewer, or the columnist George Sokolsky, who had established himself as an arbiter of such cases. These men would tell the potential blacklistee to write a letter of confession, usually addressed to a studio head and vetted by these self-appointed intermediaries. The designated intermediary—often Sokolsky or Brewer—would then share copies with the others in their network, debating its sincerity and checking it against lists like *Red Channels* to make sure the writer was coming clean about everything. Typically Brewer, who succeeded John Wayne as head of the Motion Picture Alliance for the Preservation of American Ideals in 1953, had final say; if he approved, he would meet with studio executives to get the letter writer back to work. The clearance network took its task extremely seriously, in language and deed that bring to mind a Spanish inquisitor. "The onus is on these people, who have transgressed against their neighbors, to do something on their own to demonstrate their change of heart, if any," wrote one of the founders of American Business Consultants in a letter to Brewer in 1953.

There was a formula to writing such letters. The supplicant needed to say that he or she had been duped—that they didn't know the group they were joining or the petition they were signing was a Communist front.

They needed to swear they had never joined the party, and that they were adamantly, violently opposed to Communism. They needed to be humble in their apology and aggressive in their denunciation. They didn't have to name names, but it helped if they could. The more abject and self-critical, the better. The Black singer Lena Horne, in her 1952 clearance letter to Brewer, went so far as to blame her dalliance with Communism on her psychological reaction to racial prejudice. "I had begun to realize that I was being classified as a 'lucky Negro,'" she wrote. "This became a very heavy burden resulting in an inferiority complex," which, she said, made her vulnerable to the party's appeals. Brewer was at first unpersuaded, and decided to oppose letting Horne appear on TV. A long, pleading conversation with the singer followed, and Brewer changed his mind. Horne stayed off the blacklist.

At the height of the Red Scare, the clearance network wielded immense, unchecked power over the lives of tens of thousands of Hollywood workers. In a November 1952 letter from Brewer to Jim O'Neil, publisher of the American Legion's in-house magazine, he explained how the network divided the letters into four tiers, with only the first being acceptable. The others required various degrees of revision and coaching, though for now they would be marked "unacceptable" and their agents and studios informed. In an attached list, Brewer wrote that Marlon Brando, Kirk Douglas, Rita Hayworth, and Henry and Phoebe Ephron (the screenwriter parents of Delia and Nora) had written passable letters, while the actor and producer John Houseman, the screenwriter Norman Corwin, and the script editor Bernard Smith had not, and needed to revise their work before he would clear them.

Red Channels was, by its own standards, fairly accurate; if it said an actor had, for example, given money to the Joint Anti-Fascist Refugee Committee in 1943, he probably had. The same could not be said for the weekly *Counterattack*, which was rife with errors and outdated information. Nor did American Business Consultants, its publisher, claim otherwise: It said explicitly that it was merely repeating publicly available information, not attesting to its accuracy. It was up to the accused to correct the record. In March 1948 the Academy Award–winning actor Fredric March, a frequent target of smears going back to the Dies Committee, sued American

Business Consultants for libel, claiming *Counterattack* had called him a Communist; his wife, the actress Florence Eldridge, filed an identical suit on the same day. They asked for $250,000 each but settled for a retraction.

Eventually all of Hollywood fell in line. George Sokolsky, the fervent anti-Communist and widely syndicated columnist, was an active node in the network. His papers, held at the Hoover Institution archives at Stanford, overflow with statements from the likes of Lena Horne, Vincent Price, and Edward G. Robinson, pouring out their sins. Even as stalwart a liberal as John Huston eventually came around. In one abject letter, desperate to clear his name, the two-time Academy Award–winning director of *The Maltese Falcon* and *The Treasure of the Sierra Madre* ate crow, pleading that he had loaned his name to organizations he later learned were considered unsavory by the government. "In so doing, I was unwittingly following the Communist party line, and giving unconscious aid to subversive elements without our country. To the extent that this occurred, I am profoundly regretful."

Another operator who found fortune in the folly of the blacklist was the lawyer Martin Gang. He took on clients looking to clear their names, then, for a fee, walking them through the process. By most accounts, Gang hated the blacklist. "Somebody had to go to bat for them and I did," he told one interviewer. He became their advocate and envoy to HUAC, *Red Channels*, Sokolsky, and the studios, finding out what his clients needed to do to clear their names, then coaching them on how to write a sufficiently remorseful letter, on whether to speak with the FBI, and, in more than a few cases, whether to testify before HUAC. Gang saw himself as a laborer dismantling the blacklist, brick by brick, name by name. Others, including some of his clients, saw him as one of the blacklist's most valuable enablers, giving it credence when it should at all times have been denounced.

Among his many clients was the actor Sterling Hayden. A high school dropout from a wealthy New Jersey family, Hayden's first career was at sea; by twenty-two he was captain of his own ship. He would have been happy to stay there. But he had the sort of looks that belonged on-screen—six foot five, blond, chiseled—and after his photo ran on the cover of a maritime magazine, Paramount offered him an acting contract. "The Most

Beautiful Man in the Movies," the studio bragged. Hayden despised Hollywood and longed for a reason to leave. When the United States entered World War II, he joined the Army, then the Marines, and eventually found himself working for the Office of Strategic Services, the forerunner to the CIA. He parachuted into Nazi-controlled Croatia, rescuing downed Allied pilots and acting as a liaison with the Communist partisans under Tito. (Coincidentally, Walter Bernstein, as a wartime correspondent for *Yank* magazine based in Italy, interviewed Hayden and even sneaked into Yugoslavia to interview Tito.)

Hayden's experience with Tito's Communists stuck with him after he returned to Hollywood, and he joined the party in 1946. For a brief time, he was a hardened comrade, standing ramrod straight and imposing at Communist Party meetings and helping to organize the guilds during the labor strikes. But he left after six months, because, like so many others who toyed with membership, he got tired of the constant discipline and hours-long study sessions. Hollywood, he decided, was more fun than spending one's nights debating Marx and Engels.

Eventually those six months caught up with him. In 1947, during the HUAC hearings of the Hollywood Ten, Hayden joined the Committee for the First Amendment in Washington. He sat alongside Humphrey Bogart and Lauren Bacall in the hearings, and denounced the proceedings to reporters later. Whispers began to get around that he was a former party member; in fact, his presence was one reason why the Committee for the First Amendment returned to Hollywood before the hearings ended. Things quieted for a while, but in 1951 the rumors returned, and HUAC called him to testify. Hayden rang up Martin Gang.

Hayden was having marital trouble, and he feared that if he didn't cooperate, the FBI would make sure he lost custody of his children. He and Gang wrote to Hoover for advice, then visited the FBI field office in Los Angeles. He wanted to come clean, to testify, even name names. "I would like to avail myself of this opportunity to congratulate you both on the decision you have made," the special agent in charge told them.

Quietly, HUAC was also getting back in gear to take on Hollywood. Word got around that new, public hearings were coming. In Hollywood, the news hit like the announcement of a sequel nobody wanted to a movie nobody had liked in the first place. The truth was, HUAC was desperate. Thanks to the heat of the Cold War, Congress had continued to renew its mandate, and to supply it with funds. But it had been years since the Hollywood Ten fireworks, since Nixon nabbed Hiss. And now McCarthy had made the Senate, not the House, the place to be to watch anti-Communist action.

During the fall of 1950 a number of actors came to HUAC in executive session in an attempt to head off being called under oath later. Edward G. Robinson, known for his gangster roles in the 1930s, appeared in late October before a panel of HUAC investigators. He swore that he was not a Communist, despite appearing in *Red Channels* for his membership in such shady organizations as the Hollywood Democratic Committee.

Robinson's testimony was not enough for HUAC, whose former and current Democratic chairman, John Wood of Georgia, was eager to recapture the spotlight won and held by his predecessor, J. Parnell Thomas. And by late 1950, it was a much brighter, larger spotlight. The 1947 hearings sufficed to coverage by print and newsreel; now, millions of Americans had TV sets, giving Wood an unprecedented platform. And the Red Scare had only gotten hotter: Alongside Joe McCarthy, Senate and House candidates ran and won their races in November 1950 on staunch anti-Communist platforms, promising more hearings, more investigations, and more legislation to root out so-called subversives wherever they were found. In January 1951 Wood announced that Robinson would be called back to HUAC, in public, as part of a renewed investigation into Hollywood. This time they would go after the glamourous fish—actors and actresses; no more pointy-headed (and, to the public, largely obscure) screenwriters.

The first subpoenas went out in mid-February. Robinson got one. So did the actor Larry Parks, the actor and director Howard da Silva, and the Academy Award–winning actress Gale Sondergaard, whose husband, Herbert Biberman, was one of the Hollywood Ten. Fourteen more were soon added to the list, the first batch of dozens to be called over the next year. The witnesses would first appear in executive session, away from the cameras and press, where they would be asked if they were, or had ever been, a member of the Communist Party. If the answer was yes, they would be asked for names of anyone else they knew from Hollywood who had been members with them. If they gave good enough answers—if they offered up high-profile names, if they gave salacious details, anything that might catch a reporter's ear—the committee would schedule them for a public appearance.

Of course, the witnesses could refuse to talk. Back in 1947, the Hollywood Ten had relied on their First Amendment rights to free speech—or, in their case, not to speak. That had not worked out well for them. This time, witnesses were counseled to plead the Fifth Amendment, asserting their right not to speak in a way that would incriminate them. But this brought its own problems. Since the Communist Party was not illegal, admitting to membership was not, strictly speaking, incriminating. Plus, taking the Fifth was, to all the world besides a courtroom, as good as an admission of guilt. Otherwise, why take the Fifth? As Wood explained to one recalcitrant witness, "If you say" the question about party membership "would incriminate you, it leaves one conclusion in my mind and in the mind of every other fair-minded person within sound of your voice."

One reason was to protect friends. According to the Supreme Court, taking the Fifth was not an à la carte situation. One either said nothing, or one had to say everything. So even if a witness had nothing incriminating to say about their own past, as soon as they started talking, they would be forced to discuss the affiliations of other people. Over time, witnesses started to use what their lawyers called the "diminished Fifth"—testifying about their own past, but refusing to say anything about people they knew. The committee, not eager to make martyrs by charging more witnesses with contempt, at times allowed it. The playwright Lillian Hellman, a well-known progressive who had told Chairman Wood in a diffident letter answering her subpoena that she would "not cut my conscience to fit this year's fashion," used the diminished Fifth in her May 1952 testimony. To her surprise, the committee did not press contempt charges—though she was blacklisted by Hollywood and Broadway anyway.

Many witnesses chose the easy path and named names. By 1951, they figured, there were no more secrets: HUAC and everyone else who looked knew who had been a Communist. The subpoenas, the executive sessions, the spotlights—they were all part of an absurd ceremony intended to generate heat but little light, except what was cast back on the ambitious men on the committee. With the witnesses' livelihoods in the balance, it was hard not to take the offer.

Larry Parks, a rising star best known for playing the lead in two biopics about the singer Al Jolson, was the first called by HUAC in 1951 and the first to name names. In a March executive session, he confessed to being a party member from 1941 to 1945, but then begged the committee not to force him to name others. He was a pathetic sight, clearly there under duress. "I don't think it is fair to people to do this," he said once he got to the public session, his cheeks streaked with tears. "I don't think this is American. I don't think this is American justice." Finally, he named names. Parks's testimony didn't save him when, in early May, Columbia canceled his contract. Though he picked up some film roles over the next decade, mostly in Britain, his career was over. He ended up working in real estate.

Gale Sondergaard, who had won the first-ever Oscar for supporting actress in 1936, took the witness chair after Parks that same day but refused to follow his lead. "A blacklist already exists," a defiant Sondergaard said in a letter to the Screen Actors Guild, explaining her noncompliance. "It may be widened. It may ultimately be extended to include any freedom loving non-conformist or any member of a particular race or any member of a union—or anyone." She was immediately exiled from Hollywood and did not appear on-screen for another twenty years.

Newspapers ate it up. By now, Communism had joined murder, celebrity sex, and organized crime as surefire headline fodder, and the renewed chance to pair it with Hollywood was irresistible. The editorial board of the *Los Angeles Times* demanded more, including testimony from every member of the Committee for the First Amendment, which had defended the Hollywood Ten almost four years earlier and included stars like Will Rogers, Humphrey Bogart, and Lauren Bacall. "A whole galaxy of Hollywood names has been drawn under suspicion by the various inquiries and the committee owes it to the public and to the great majority of decent, self-respecting and patriotic Americans who work in Hollywood to clear up the matter," the paper editorialized after Parks testified. No one wanted to hear Roy Brewer when he testified before HUAC that, in fact, the party's influence in Hollywood had cratered after the 1947 HUAC hearings. The *Chicago Tribune* was outright giddy. "The 'Witch Hunt' Keeps Turning Up Witches," one headline read.

Out of the 110 Hollywood figures called before HUAC that year, 58 of them opted to cooperate. According to an analysis by the historians Larry Ceplair and Steven Englund, they offered up an average of 29 names each, or 902 in all, ranging from the 155 named by the screenwriter Martin Berkeley to the 6 named by the playwright Clifford Odets. Some stars did not wait to be called; their lawyers told them that the best way to clear any suspicions was to volunteer to testify. One of those, Sterling Hayden, appeared before HUAC on April 10. Martin Gang had coached him on what to say. "It was the stupidest and most ignorant thing I had ever done in my life," Hayden said of his time in the party, prostrating himself before the committee. Gang also instructed him to name names. Hayden did his best to limit the damage, citing just two people, both of whom had already been identified as suspected Communists. Otherwise, he pleaded ignorance—most party members, he told the committee, used aliases, which was true, but also hard to believe he didn't recognize members in the tight-knit, celebrity-ridden world of Hollywood.

Hayden was not blacklisted, but he was emotionally broken. He kept acting, but he stayed away from Los Angeles, living for long stretches on houseboats in Paris and Sausalito, California, north of San Francisco. Work was good, mostly Westerns, easy money—which made him hate it even more. "I swung like a goon from role to role," he wrote in his best-selling memoir, *Wanderer*. The work came in a steady stream, often from studios happy to have a cooperative star on their bill. "They were all made back to back in an effort to cash in fast on my new status as a sanitized culture hero." His best roles were still far ahead of him—General Jack D. Ripper in *Dr. Strangelove*, Captain McCluskey in *The Godfather*—but Hayden never forgave himself for testifying. "I don't think you have the foggiest notion of the contempt I have had for myself since the day I did that thing," he told his psychiatrist.

HUAC's procedures this time around were streamlined. Along with Chairman Wood, most of the committee's membership had changed. Richard Nixon and Karl Mundt had moved up to the Senate. John Rankin had left the committee. The new men were just as eager for the anti-Communist spotlight as before, but now they smoothed their act with a professional, dispassionate sheen. Witnesses were filed in and out with brute efficiency, so as not to permit disruptive speechifying. This time, no one was subjected to contempt charges; the threat of the blacklist was incentive enough to cooperate. There were exceptions, though: Dashiell Hammett, a screenwriter and best-selling author of noir classics like *The Maltese Falcon*, served six months in prison for contempt after refusing to name his fellow members of the bail fund of the Civil Rights Congress.

With the Hollywood left in disarray, there would be no Committee for the First Amendment to speak on Hammett's behalf. In fact, groups like the Screen Actors Guild, once stalwart in its opposition to the blacklist, made it clear that it would not stand by unfriendly witnesses. In a response to Gale Sondergaard's resistance, the guild wrote, "If any actor by his own actions outside of union activities has so offended American public opinion that he has made himself unsaleable at the box office, the Guild cannot and would not want to force any employer to hire him."

Among the committee's biggest catches was the director Edward Dmytryk, a member of the Hollywood Ten recently released from his prison sentence for contempt. With the help of his lawyer, he wrote an affidavit confessing his past membership in the Communist Party, swearing that he had not been a member at the time of the HUAC hearing, and attesting to his intense "allegiance and loyalty" to the United States. He got out in November 1950, and by the new year he was meeting with Roy Brewer, Ronald Reagan, and other leaders of Hollywood's new conservative establishment. They told him to go to HUAC.

On April 25, Dmytryk did more than confess to his membership in the party and name names. He aligned himself fully with HUAC's driving belief that the Communist Party had wanted to "control the content of motion pictures" and turn Hollywood into a massive propaganda machine. Two weeks later he recounted his political journey in an article for *The Saturday Evening Post*. The left-wing press attacked him as a patsy, but early the next year, Columbia offered him a four-film contract.

Dmytryk's appearance was a model for how former Communists could cleanse themselves before HUAC and the American public. HUAC staff had worked with him and his lawyer to fine-tune his statement. He claimed that he had joined the party out of a misguided belief that it was the right thing for America. But after he realized he was wrong, and that the party was a treasonous, duplicitous organization, he had turned against it with that same patriotic passion. Gone unsaid was the other reason he was there—to escape the blacklist.

It would be wrong to assume that craven self-interest was the only motive behind testifying; the desire to avoid the blacklist was an inescapable incentive, but few people saw it as the only reason. Most, including Dmytryk, really did have deep-seated differences with the party and its members, even resentments. The novelist and screenwriter Budd Schulberg had quit the party after it demanded that he make significant changes to his novel *What Makes Sammy Run?* Though it became a best-seller and made his name as a rising literary star, the Communist press tore into it as insufficiently revolutionary. Schulberg had good reason to be bitter. Whether he needed to name sixteen people during his testimony, as he did, is a slightly different question.

The same could be said for the director Elia Kazan. Like many directors and writers caught up in the HUAC maelstrom, he had begun his career in the heady world of left-wing theater in 1930s New York, in his case with the progressive Group Theatre. He had been in the party, and believed in the power of theater to spread the message of Communism. But he drifted, resigned his membership in 1936, and sooner than most found himself disagreeing not just with the tactics of Marxist theater, but with the entire Communist project.

Kazan was also immensely successful, more so than almost anyone else HUAC called to the carpet. He was one of the twentieth century's greatest directors, and arguably the greatest to operate on both stage and screen. His direction on the New York stage had brought Arthur Miller's early plays to global acclaim. In Hollywood he had quickly defined himself as a craftsman of prestige films like *A Tree Grows in Brooklyn*, *Gentleman's Agreement*, and *A Streetcar Named Desire*. He was still working on the last of those when in late 1951 the head of 20th Century Fox called him to his office in New York. He gave Kazan a statement to sign. It said that not only had he been in the party and would testify fully before HUAC, but that he gave the studio the right to cancel his contract if the committee was unhappy with what he told it.

At first, Kazan refused. But the pressure mounted. The liberal producer Darryl Zanuck, sympathetic to his plight, urged him to sign. "Name the names," Zanuck told his friend. "Who the hell are you going to jail for? You'll be sitting there and someone else will sure as hell name these people. Who are you saving?" Finally, Kazan folded. His career was in the balance. But he also decided that Communism's moral corruption obviated any obligation to his former comrades. He reasoned that if he were a director in the Soviet Union, and those men were sitting in judgment of him for some concocted ideological crime, they would not hesitate to condemn him.

Kazan first appeared before HUAC in January 1952. He arrived a half hour early. In a private session, a committee staff member asked if he would name names. Kazan said he would not. The staffer urged him to reconsider. Kazan said no again. It was all so mortifying. "A film director could not have devised a more humiliating setting for a supplicant," he wrote in his autobiography. But the committee was not happy, and now the head of 20th Century Fox reached out. Kazan, he said, had disappointed him. Did he still want to work in Hollywood? At this point, Kazan felt he had no choice. He returned to the committee on April 10, and this time named the Communists he had worked with in the Group Theatre, nearly twenty years before, adding the names of several affiliated artists and hangers-on. "I have come to the conclusion," Kazan told the committee, "that I did wrong to withhold these names before, because secrecy serves the Communists and is exactly what they want. The American people need the facts. . . . It is my duty as a citizen to tell everything I know."

Had that been all he said, Kazan would have still been attacked by his former friends and many current fellow liberals, especially those who didn't face the same impossibly difficult choice he did. But his break might have been forgotten had he left his statement in the HUAC hearing room. The historian Daniel Boorstin named names, for example, but did so quietly, and later became the librarian of Congress. Lucille Ball hemmed and hawed, not wanting to take the Fifth but averse to answering questions about why she had registered to vote Communist in 1936; that too became a footnote. But Kazan earned the lasting enmity of Hollywood by taking out a full-page ad two days later in *The New York Times*. He did not just explain his position; he excoriated his former friends. He hyperbolized his time in the party, calling it a "taste of the police state," and he demanded that liberals join him in fighting Communism. The experience, he said, "left me with an abiding hatred of Communist philosophy and methods and the conviction that these must be resisted always."

It was all too much. His former collaborator, Arthur Miller, would barely speak with him afterward. Before he had testified, Kazan invited Miller to his home in Connecticut and, during a walk in the woods, told him what he was likely to do. Now, after the *Times* ad, Miller was livid. In July he cut all professional ties with his old friend, and announced that Kazan would not be directing his next play, a historical work about the Salem Witch Trials. He called it *The Crucible*, and it became one of the signal artistic statements against the hysteria of the Red Scare era. Miller was later denied a passport and called before HUAC; he testified but, relying on a promise from the committee, refused to name names. He was convicted of contempt anyway, though he won an appeal in 1958.

Kazan's next project, a script by Budd Schulberg, was *On the Waterfront*, the story of a longshoreman, played by Marlon Brando, who ends up turning on the corrupt bosses who run the docks of Hoboken, New Jersey. It was another huge success, perhaps Kazan's best-known film, but it was widely seen as an attempt to explain and valorize his own decision to turn (both Kazan and Schulberg denied that such thoughts ever entered their conversations). Kazan was a sufficiently brilliant director that even his many, many enemies could not keep him from getting work—including later classics like *East of Eden* and *Splendor in the Grass*. But he never lived down what many in Hollywood concluded was a deep betrayal of their industry at a time when it, and the country, were under ideological attack. At the 1999 Oscars, when Robert De Niro and Martin Scorsese presented Kazan with a lifetime achievement award, scores of actors in the audience refused to applaud—including many who had been infants when Kazan named names.

18

The China Hands

Whether it was Hollywood, HUAC, or Joe McCarthy, the anti-Communist hysteria of the early 1950s drew much of its dark energy from the ongoing war in Korea. After the United States under General Douglas MacArthur pushed all the way to the North's border with China, the Chinese had jumped into the fighting at the end of 1950, driving the Americans back on their heels. The Chinese soldiers, tens of thousands of them, had come pouring over the hills in the evening of November 1, ceaseless waves of grenades and machine gun fire and men coming out of the night, catching the Americans and South Koreans by complete surprise. The attack was probably inevitable: With good reason, Mao Zedong feared that the Americans would not stop at North Korea, and would soon invade China. And even if they didn't, an American presence at his border would cause all manner of problems for a Communist leadership still consolidating its control over a vast nation. China's entrance into the war changed it from a containable conflict—what the United Nations euphemistically called a police action—to a regional war, with potential to further draw in the Soviet Union, which was already supplying weapons to both China and North Korea. If Americans had worried about the war before, they were now liable to be terrified.

Once again, MacArthur bounced back. At the cost of tens of thousands of casualties and the temporary loss of Seoul, the South Korean capital, by June 1951 he fought the Chinese and North Korean forces to a standstill around the middle of the peninsula. The next two years of the war would see the combatants expend untold lives on control of a few miles in either direction, with the conflict coming to resemble the trench warfare of World War I. To some, MacArthur was a narrow-minded egotist who had wasted American blood on a series of battlefield blunders; to others, he was the only thing standing in the way of Communist victory in Asia.

There was no mystery to MacArthur's appeal: His martial arrogance, jutting chin, fierce drive, and outspoken hatred of Communism made him a darling of the American right and a foil to Dwight D. Eisenhower, the establishment's favorite general, whom both parties were courting as a presidential candidate for the upcoming 1952 election. Eisenhower, who had led the Allies to victory in Europe during World War II, then left the Army to become president of Columbia University, was a man who respected civilian authority and moved easily among the bankers and lawyers that dominated the centrist wing of the party. He looked good in uniform, but just as good in a suit, or in golf togs. No one could imagine MacArthur in civvies. He was imperious, militant; he had led the United States to victory over the Japanese, then ruled over them as an occupying overlord. And he had always been an Asia Firster—his father, Arthur MacArthur Jr., had been governor-general of the Philippines, where young Douglas had first deployed after graduating at the top of his class from West Point.

MacArthur had never been popular with members of the Truman administration, Secretary of State Acheson especially, but also General George Marshall and other top military brass. Marshall, a man of impeccable decorum and absolute fealty to the country's civilian leadership, considered MacArthur a dangerous showboat. Acheson, who felt that MacArthur's weakness was his predilection for surrounding himself with sycophants, recalled in his memoir a story Marshall told him. Marshall and MacArthur were at a conference during World War II, and MacArthur had started a statement with the phrase, "My staff tells me . . ." Marshall, without missing a beat, cut him off. "General, you don't have a staff; you have a court."

MacArthur's court extended to Congress: The bad blood between the general and Acheson had led Senator Kenneth Wherry of Nebraska, a MacArthur supporter, to accuse Acheson, during his 1945 confirmation hearings to be undersecretary of state, of having "blighted the name" of the general in his opening remarks. Wherry tried to torpedo the nomination, and got eleven other senators to vote with him.

The general's followers were not just impressed with his success and stature; they swooned over his rock-ribbed commitment to the sort of black-and-white anti-Communism they felt was dangerously lacking in Washington. While Truman and Acheson and the whole East Coast Establishment talked and talked about containment and economic aid and mutual defense, MacArthur pushed for military rollback, the idea that the West could, and must, force the Communists out of their postwar gains in Eastern Europe and, increasingly, Asia. To him, the West would lose the Cold War unless it was willing to turn it hot. He was a man of action, and promised success, his backers believed, if only the White House would unleash him. MacArthur's wartime headquarters in Tokyo became, in effect, a satellite headquarters for the China Lobby and the hardcore anti-Communist right.

His chief of intelligence, Charles Willoughby, was a case in point. Born Adolph Karl Weidenbach, Willoughby was a proud German immigrant—specifically Prussian, he insisted—and he cultivated a Teutonic accent and demeanor, imperious and bombastic, arrogant toward his underlings yet utterly servile to his boss. MacArthur half-jokingly called him "my lovable fascist." Willoughby believed that any dissent was not just wrong but Communist-inspired. "American Communist brains," he wrote in a letter to the House Committee on Un-American Activities in 1950, "planned the communization of China." He fed rumors and his own slanted opinions about MacArthur's critics to the FBI, Kohlberg, and McCarthy. In Japan in the late 1940s, he launched his own miniature HUAC, investigating anyone and everyone—officers, diplomats, journalists—he thought might cross the general. Willoughby was later accused of downplaying the risk that China would enter the war to halt MacArthur's northward advance. Some went so far as to say that he had "falsified the intelligence reports" and that "he should have gone to jail." (He was also accused of falsifying his family history and parts of his academic record.) After retiring from the Army in 1951, Willoughby established himself as an unofficial go-between linking the U.S. military and the Franco dictatorship in Spain.

Rather than diminishing MacArthur's standing, China's devastating entry into the war, followed a few weeks later by Republican gains during the 1950 midterm elections, emboldened him and his supporters. He demanded more resources, more troops, and above all more authority. Anything less, including a negotiated settlement, would be appeasement. "To give up any part of North Korea to the aggression of the Chinese Communists would be the greatest defeat of the free world in recent times," the general wrote in a November 8, 1950, cable to the Joint Chiefs of Staff back in Washington. "Indeed to yield to so immoral a proposition would bankrupt our leadership and influence in Asia and render intolerable our position both politically and militarily."

MacArthur chafed under limits imposed on him by Washington, and he said so publicly. He began to give orders to his generals that went far beyond the scope of executing Truman's commands. He refused to answer cables suggesting a cease-fire, then released his own public statement calling for a wider war—the news of which, when it reached the White House, sent the president into a fit. "I was ready to kick him into the North China Sea," Truman recalled. "I was never so put out in my life." On April 11, 1951, he relieved MacArthur of his command. "I deeply regret that it becomes my duty as President and Commander-in-Chief of the United States military forces to replace you," he said in his official statement. In private, he reportedly said, "I fired him because he wouldn't respect the authority of the President. I didn't fire him because he was a dumb son of a bitch, although he was, but that's not against the law for generals."

Truman's decision set off a wave of recriminations in Washington. Senator Taft, the Republican leader, called for the president to be impeached. Others accused him of being part of a Communist conspiracy. "I charge that this country today is in the hands of a secret inner coterie which is directed by agents of the Soviet Union," said Senator William Jenner of Indiana. "Our only choice is to impeach President Truman." MacArthur returned to America a hero. Half a million people greeted him in San Francisco. He addressed a joint session of Congress, where he attacked those "who for varying reasons would appease Red China." He threw out the first pitch at a New York Giants game and received a ticker-tape parade in Manhattan; at 7.5 million people, it was among the largest in New York history. People of influence considered him a likely Republican candidate for president. Everywhere he harped on the same theme: The real threat to national security came from within. "It is not from threat of external attack that we have reason to fear," he told a crowd in Houston. "It is from those insidious forces working from within."

The MacArthur boom faded by late 1951. Generals rarely make good politicians, and the man later known as the American Caesar was no exception. He lacked a common touch; beyond his jutting chin and give-'em-hell politics, he had nothing to say about the state of the nation or its challenges. National health insurance? Education? The budget? As he made the rounds of the Republican Party leadership, it became clear to them that he lacked not just an education in such issues, but any interest in learning about them. And he paled in comparison with Eisenhower, who came across as a Renaissance Man in comparison, and who was currently buttressing his cosmopolitan bona fides as president of Columbia. MacArthur went on to speak at the 1952 Republican National Convention, but shorn of his uniform, he was a much diminished, much obviously embittered man. His few delegates swung to Senator Taft, always the preferred choice of the Midwestern right.

McArthur receded, but the damage of his removal remained. It had been a Hobson's choice for Truman: He had to relieve the general, but in doing so he helped ensure that his public approval ratings, already abysmally low at about 27 percent, would stay there for the rest of his term. The blast radius extended beyond the White House. The general's removal was jet fuel for the conspiratorial, red-baiting right, who now had McCarthy as their no-holds-barred man in the ring. The Wisconsin senator called for Dean Acheson and George Marshall to be impeached. Marshall especially: Like Eisenhower, he was loved by the establishment and hated by the Republican right; unlike Eisenhower, he had been a member of Truman's cabinet. McCarthy understood this, and the opportunity it afforded him. In June 1951, he ran across a group of reporters as he headed out of his office. Where was he headed? they asked. The Senate floor, he replied, to unveil "a conspiracy so immense and an infamy so black as to dwarf any previous venture in the history of man."

Marshall was not only beloved by the East Coast Establishment. He was the namesake of the Marshall Plan, which poured $13.6 billion ($174 billion in today's dollars) into Western Europe after World War II and bolstered anti-Communist governments across the continent. He was strictly, adamantly nonpartisan and absolutely correct in his demeanor; one of the only times he showed his displeasure at Truman was when the president referred to him by his first name. His loyalty was to the status quo, the consensus, and the office of the presidency—and that made him an enemy of the McCarthyites.

McCarthy didn't invent the case against Marshall. Precisely because he was a conventional general willing to cede the floor to diplomats and civilians, the hard right frequently lambasted him as weak and ineffective in the face of the Soviet menace. It was no secret that Marshall loathed MacArthur, and that he had advised Truman to relieve him. But it was McCarthy who elevated the attacks on Marshall to front-page news. When he entered the Senate chamber that afternoon, he carried with him a sixty-thousand-word speech, every syllable a frontal assault on Marshall. Hubert Humphrey, a liberal, first-term senator from Minnesota, tried to persuade his Democratic colleagues to leave the chamber, thus denying McCarthy a quorum, but it was too late. As usual, McCarthy introduced himself as the burdened bearer of bad news, a truth-teller aware of his painful duty. "I realize full well how unpopular it is to lay hands on the laurels of a man who has been built into a great hero," McCarthy said. "I very much dislike it. But I feel that it must be done if we are to intelligently make the proper decisions in the issues of life and death before us."

He presented his case as a laundry list of indictments against the general. "It was Marshall who enjoined his chief of military mission in Moscow under no circumstances to 'irritate' the Russians. . . . It was the State Department under Marshall . . . that sabotaged the $125 million military aid bill to China in 1945. . . . It is Marshall's strategy for Korea which has turned that war into a pointless slaughter." These were not just mistakes, McCarthy insisted. "If Marshall were merely stupid, the laws of probability would dictate that part of his decisions would serve this country's interest." Rather they were the result of Marshall's membership, alongside Truman and Acheson, in a triumvirate that both controlled the U.S. government and carried out the bidding of Moscow. "What is the objective of the great conspiracy? . . . To diminish the United States in world affairs, to weaken us militarily, to confuse our spirit with talk of surrender in the Far East and to impair our will to resist evil. To what end? To the end that we shall be contained, frustrated and, finally, fall victim to Soviet intrigue from within and Russian military might from without."

The speech took McCarthy all afternoon to read, and it was later printed as a book, *America's Retreat from Victory*. Liberal newspapers and some centrist Republicans denounced the senator. But most Republicans, including their leader in the Senate, Robert Taft, kept quiet, at least in public. McCarthy was powerful, so powerful that he could defame one of America's most respected figures from the Senate floor and get away with it.

In the unwritten laws of Washington physics, every political action has an equal and opposite reaction. Truman, aware of the political damage he sustained by removing MacArthur, had to find a way to balance it. And so, one by one, the China Hands in the State Department began to fall. The president did not explicitly order their purge. But he stood by as they were investigated, smeared, and fired. Each story is its own tragedy; together, they constitute an astounding act of self-injury by the U.S. government, denying itself a cadre of experts at the opening of a new, complicated, and dangerous era of American engagement in East Asia.

The diplomat John Service was the first to go. He had been born in China, in 1909, to missionary parents. He stayed there until leaving for college, at Oberlin—after which he returned to China, and soon joined the Foreign Service. He had traveled around China during World War II, gathering insight into the Nationalist and Communist forces. He was out-spokenly critical of Chiang Kai-shek's Nationalists, and perhaps naïvely impressed by Mao Zedong's men. He had also made the mistake of lending some of his reports to Philip Jaffe, the left-wing editor of the journal *Amerasia*, and he had been placed under investigation after the FBI raided its offices in 1945.

After Service was cleared, he was assigned to MacArthur's headquarters in Japan. But the China Lobby remembered his name, and with the fall of Chiang to the Communists in 1949 and the onset of the Korean

War a year later, they came after him. He was one of 14 people McCarthy named in 1950—out of the 205 he had originally cited, in his West Virginia speech—as "a known associate and collaborator with Communists." The Senate cleared him quickly, but on December 13, 1951, a review board found "reasonable doubt as to his loyalty." Secretary Acheson, knowing what Truman wanted, fired him the next day.

Service fought back, claiming that the board had no right to supersede the Senate. He eventually took his case to the Supreme Court, which in 1956 found unanimously in his favor. He returned to the Foreign Service, but any hopes of restarting his career were long passed. His final posting was to the U.S. consulate in Liverpool. He retired in 1962.

At least Service got a second chance. Another leading China expert, John Carter Vincent, was less fortunate. He was a Kansas native, tall, mustachioed, and natty in his dress, formed from the Acheson mold. He was quick with languages and perfected his Chinese before he arrived in the country for his first posting. Like Service, he grew increasingly skeptical of the Nationalists' ability to hold the country, and said so in his dispatches to Washington. He was an architect of George Marshall's ill-fated mission to China in 1946, after which he served in diplomatic posts in Switzerland and Morocco.

Vincent was called back to Washington in 1952 to face charges that he was secretly a Communist, having also been named by McCarthy during the 1950 hearings before the Tydings Committee. He vociferously denied it under oath, calling himself a "Wilsonian Democrat"—that is, a moderate. A State Department Loyalty Review Board cleared him, but in early 1953 a similar body under the Civil Service Commission voted 3 to 2 that there was "reasonable doubt as to Vincent's loyalty to the United States." John Foster Dulles, who became secretary of state in January 1953, fired him.

There were other China Hands, more than a dozen cases of men unfairly driven from their work because they ran afoul of McCarthy and the China Lobby. Perhaps the most shocking case was the dismissal of John Paton Davies. Like Service, he had been born in China, in 1908, came to the United States for college, then immediately returned. He joined the Foreign Service in 1931. Again like Service, he wrote critical assessments of the Nationalists paired with glowing reports about the Communists. "We should not now abandon Chiang Kai-Shek," Davies wrote in one memo. "But we must be realistic. We must not indefinitely underwrite a politically bankrupt regime. We must make a determined effort to capture politically the Chinese Communists rather than allow them to go by default wholly to the Russians." At one point in 1943 he was on a cargo plane when the engine failed; the crew, Davies, and sixteen other passengers parachuted into the jungle, and over the next month he led them to safety. For his courage he received the Medal of Freedom.

Davies later admitted that he had been naïve about Mao's intentions, but he insisted he had never been a Communist sympathizer. In fact he was known in the department for his strong stand against the Soviet Union, endorsing the sort of aggressive rollback policy that many in the Truman White House resisted. One reason he was so critical of Chiang was his concern that if the Nationalist leader managed to beat back Mao, Stalin would swoop in to crush him. Still, after World War II ended and the Chinese Civil War resumed, Davies was among the first people accused of undermining support for Chiang. It emerged that he had been a part of the planning for a secret, unexecuted CIA operation to develop intelligence from inside China—the details of which McCarthy and his allies distorted to charge Davies with trying to infiltrate Communist agents into the United States. After years of such baseless attacks, a State Department review board ruled that while his loyalty was assured, his career at the State Department was "not clearly consistent with the interests of the national security." After Secretary Dulles fired him, he moved to Lima, Peru, where he became a woodworker.

The China Hands were scapegoats two times over. The China Lobby and McCarthy targeted them for "losing" China, then for undermining American security at home, knowing that while they could never take down an Acheson or a Marshall, they could pick off any number of lower-level diplomats. The fact that there was never any evidence to support their claims mattered little, either to the accusers or, all too often, to the press that covered them. In fact, many reporters bought into the idea that a small group of Americans was responsible for the results of a civil war in the largest nation on earth. "Throughout the fateful years in China, the American representatives there actively favored the Chinese communists," wrote the syndicated columnist Joseph Alsop in 1950, in *The Saturday Evening Post*. "They also contributed to the weakness, both political and military, of the National government. And in the end they came close to offering China up to the communists, like a trussed bird on a platter."

Nor did the lack of evidence seem to matter to their superiors. Vague euphemisms like "not clearly consistent" with American interests did not mean they were disloyal or security risks; such verbiage masked the fact that they were political sacrifices. Acheson, Truman, Dulles, and so many others who could have come to their defense simply did not. Acheson had tried it once, with Alger Hiss, and gotten burned. And the administration had already expended its capital sacking MacArthur. The China Hands had to go. Such was the cruel logic of the Red Scare.

19

Terror by Index Cards

Despite his kingmaker work during the 1950 midterms, McCarthy was still a first-term senator, and an unpredictable one, so the Senate Republican leadership was wary of giving him too much institutional power. But it gave him some, and he used it immediately, and vindictively. As soon as McCarthy was placed in charge of assigning seats on the Government Expenditures Committee, in early 1951, he removed Margaret Chase Smith of Maine, who had dared to speak out against him on the Senate floor in June 1950, from the powerful investigations subcommittee to a backwater spot overseeing government reorganization. He denied it was an act of retribution, cheekily telling reporters that she had been "promoted."

People who should have known better fell under McCarthy's spell; he moved so fast, and claimed such authority, that even many skeptics believed that he had to be offering at least a kernel of truth. As he grew in prominence, his personal habits became more exaggerated: He ate faster, wolfing down burgers and shakes and steaks. He salved his ulceric stomach with handfuls of baking soda and half sticks of butter. He rose late, went to bed after midnight, filled his off hours with poker games that only the most daring would join. "You get to the point where you don't care what McCarthy's got in the hole—all you know is that it's too costly to stay in the game," one frequent opponent told *Time*. Even as he launched witch hunts, he believed he was the victim of one himself. He hinted to crowds that he was risking his life to bring them the truth. He had a habit of turning on the faucet and tapping his pencil eraser on the receiving end of a phone, tactics, he insisted, to confuse wiretaps.

He encouraged supporters to send money, and he claimed to receive a steady flow of letters enclosing wads of small bills. More important, he encouraged all "patriotic Americans" to send him tips, amassing an unofficial army of informers he called the "loyal underground." The attention went to his head. If McCarthy was erratic before, after the 1950 midterms he was positively unhinged. After a dinner party at Washington's Sulgrave Club, he assaulted the columnist Drew Pearson in the coatroom. Pearson had criticized McCarthy frequently and viciously, even suggesting that the perpetual bachelor was a closeted homosexual. A full-on brawl was avoided thanks to intervention by, of all people, Senator-elect Nixon, who dashed in, shouting, "Let a Quaker stop this fight." McCarthy, panting and pushing his receding hair back in place, said, "You shouldn't have stopped me, Dick."

The story shocked the establishment, but McCarthy's fans loved it. They thought Washington was soft, and he was the only one willing to fight, literally. He filled his speech with violent rhetoric. He would "kick the brains" out of an opponent, he said. "If you will get me a slippery-elm club and put me aboard Adlai Stevenson's campaign train," he said about the 1952 Democratic presidential candidate, "I will use it on some of his advisers, and perhaps I can make a good American out of him." His justice was frontier justice, his tools the fist, the club. He often carried a gun, for personal protection, he insisted, though what that meant, and what it would take to make him shoot, he left unexplained.

Sexuality, and homosexuality in particular, was a frequent subtext of his attacks, when it wasn't the text itself. At a June speech before the Fifth Marine Division Association, at the Statler Hotel in New York, McCarthy attacked both Acheson—"the Red Dean of Fashion"—and Marshall, accusing them of selling out millions of Asians to Communist slavery. "I am afraid I will have to blame some of the roughness in fighting the enemy to my training in the Marine Corps," he told the gathered veterans. "We weren't taught to wear lace panties and fight with lace hankies."

Throughout 1951 and into the 1952 presidential campaign season, McCarthy attacked with abandon. He became a part of the political landscape, a reliable source for outrageous quotes and a bellwether for the insanity of the moment. Facts, accuracy, and consistency did not matter.

On August 8, 1951, he promised to release the names of twenty-nine security risks currently or formerly in the State Department; the next day
he offered just twenty-six, including old favorites like John Service and
Philip Jessup, the chairman of the Institute of Pacific Relations. But there
was no there, there—whatever documents he claimed to have in his pos-
session, he never gave them to the State Department. He relied on a circular argument: He had evidence that the State Department was riven
with spies, but he could not reveal it or hand it over to the government,
because, he said, the government could not be trusted, since it was full of
spies. Whenever it seemed like he was about to get caught in his own web,
he made another, even more outlandish charge. In September 1951 he
told a gathering of Marine veterans in Savannah, Georgia, that "there are
members of Congress and the Senate who have members of the Communist party on their staffs"—a charge that he did not substantiate.

President Truman, who had no fear about getting into the muck with
McCarthy, regularly lashed his buffoonish anti-Communism as the greatest
asset the Soviets had. He called him "pathological" and a "character assas-
sin." McCarthy gave back as good as he got. "It would be a waste of time
trying to impeach Truman," he said on *Meet the Press* in June 1951, raising the possibility that he might try it anyway against his cabinet. "What
we should do is impeach some of the crimson cliques surrounding him,
some of his advisors, specifically Dean Gooderham Acheson." When the
president kept up the criticism, McCarthy dismissed it, saying he was "too
busy" to sue him. "The louder they scream, the more I know they're hurt."

McCarthy was perpetually one step ahead of his pursuers. Through
1951 and 1952 he fought a war of attrition with Senator William Benton, a millionaire Democrat from Connecticut, who accused McCarthy
of all manner of offenses: lying to Congress, corruption, "sneak attacks"
against the State Department. McCarthy took to calling Benton a "mental
midget" and a Kremlin stooge. Benton introduced a resolution to expel
McCarthy from the Senate for violating a list of norms and rules; despite
being taken up by a subcommittee and covered extensively in the press,
the motion languished. Meanwhile McCarthy sued Benton for $2 million,
charging slander. He had no intention of winning, only flipping the narra-
tive. He didn't pursue the suit, and Benton lost his reelection race in 1952.

And while another subcommittee, investigating McCarthy's intervention in the Tydings-Butler race of 1950, called his actions "despicable," once more nothing came of it. In January 1952 a twenty-four-year-old American in Switzerland, Charles Davis, sued McCarthy for $100,000 after he was convicted in a Swiss court of "political espionage" on McCarthy's behalf. Davis claimed McCarthy paid him $200 a month to spy on American government employees in Europe, including John Carter Vincent, then serving as minister to Switzerland. McCarthy admitted to encouraging Davis but never paying him, and that case also sputtered out.

In private, relatively moderate members of the anti-Communist right, like Nixon, would worry that McCarthy's bloviation was giving them a bad name. And certainly, in the long run, that's what happened. But not at the time. McCarthy's vocal denunciations were the melody laid over a steady beat of HUAC hearings, federal loyalty probes, American Legion boycotts, and an expanding Hollywood blacklist. The logic worked inverse to what Nixon feared: McCarthy might be overstating things, but the sheer volume of his charges seemed to prove there was something there.

And he acted with the explicit support of the Republican Senate leadership. Robert Taft was always careful to keep a modicum of distance between McCarthy and himself: After McCarthy's attack on Marshall, Taft told reporters, "There are certain points in which I wouldn't agree with the Senator." But he also insisted, in interviews, that McCarthy was "fully justified" in his assault on the State Department. Taft was even more encouraging in private. "If one case doesn't work out, bring up another," he told McCarthy in March 1950. Two years later, the party's shorthand for its 1952 campaign theme was K1C2—Korea, Communism, Corruption.

Steadily, McCarthyism became part of the conservative mainstream. The party's pro-Chiang right wing had been attacking Marshall and Acheson for years. But his berserker assaults made it possible for the party's leadership to get on board. By mid-1951 the party was roundly calling for Acheson to resign, or be impeached. And the Senate made McCarthyism a bipartisan affair: A 1950 law, the Internal Security Act, established the Senate Internal Security Subcommittee; chaired by Pat McCarran, a Democrat, it became a platform for McCarthy's attacks, and a way to give them an official, somewhat sanitized gloss. McCarran had already been in the Senate for eighteen years, and was something of a McCarthy before the fact. He defended the Spanish dictator Francisco Franco, attacked immigrants, hated the United Nations, and claimed that Communists were behind the New Deal.

McCarran kept his new committee busy: He picked up McCarthy's campaign against the Institute of Pacific Relations and the China expert Owen Lattimore, and brought in the former Communist Louis Budenz as a friendly expert witness. He claimed Communists were attempting to infiltrate the Boy Scouts. McCarran had the standing and influence to make his punches land: Lattimore was indicted for perjury (three long years later, the charges were dismissed). McCarran could be crude, but he was no showboat, and he kept a relatively low profile. Some conservatives liked to claim that the McCarran Committee was doing anti-Communism right, in contrast to McCarthy. But the truth was, they were all of a piece.

McCarthy did his offensive best to contribute to a Republican presidential victory in 1952. Taft was his man, but when the Ohio senator's campaign faltered and collapsed at the party's national convention, in Chicago, he dutifully lined up behind the nominee, Eisenhower. While running for his own reelection, McCarthy worked as an attack dog for the Republican, going after Adlai Stevenson, the Democratic candidate, as the epitome of everything wrong with liberalism: cerebral, out of touch, soft on Communism. It was the standard Republican line that year, but McCarthy added his special touch, most famously slurring Stevenson as "Alger—I mean, Adlai." Such was his overwrought insistence on Stevenson's pro-left leanings that he persuaded many people to ignore the Democratic candidate's own aggressive anti-Communism: Backed by Americans for Democratic Action, Stevenson supported loyalty tests, the Smith Act trials, and barring suspected subversives from the classroom.

Eisenhower had never cared much for Communists, but he didn't care for McCarthy and his ilk, either, especially after their attacks on General Marshall. He wanted to make his distaste clear during the campaign—on a swing through Wisconsin in fact. An anti-McCarthy speech was written, and debated heatedly among Eisenhower's advisers. "I was privileged

throughout the years of World War II to know General Marshall personally, as chief of staff of the Army," the draft read. "I know him, as a man
and a soldier, to be dedicated with singular selflessness and the profound-
est patriotism to the service of America. Here we have a sobering lesson
of the way freedom must not defend itself" (underlining in the original).
After McCarthy joined the tour in Peoria, Illinois, the former general told
him to his face what he was going to say. "If you say that, you'll be booed,"
McCarthy told him. Eisenhower was unfazed. "I've been booed before,
and being booed doesn't bother me," he said.

But after days of being pushed by advisers and Wisconsin's Republican
governor, Walter Kohler Jr., Eisenhower caved, and removed any reference to Marshall from his speech. In Green Bay, he even gave McCarthy
a tepid endorsement, encouraging voters to elect the entire Republican
slate. Later, in Milwaukee, a reporter asked about his stand on McCarthy.
Eisenhower equivocated. He agreed on the problem of Communists in
government, he said, and understood McCarthy's motivation. "The differences apply to method," he said.

Standing a few feet away, McCarthy smiled. "I'm not unhappy about his
statement," he told reporters afterward.

Eisenhower was running to "clean house," and not just of Communists. After twenty years of Democrats in the White House, the country
seemed to want change, but at the same time stability. Eisenhower, in his
very being, promised calm competence, from both parties. There was an
expectation that a Republican victory would silence McCarthy by changing the atmosphere in Washington. "It is this paper's hope and belief that
McCarthyism would die overnight if Eisenhower were elected," *The Washington Post* editorialized. McCarthy, for one, seemed to agree. "Now it
will be unnecessary for me to conduct a one-man campaign to expose
Communists in government," he said days after the election, in which
Eisenhower trounced Stevenson. Running with the standard Democratic
postwar playbook, Stevenson had asked, in a campaign poster, whether
voters wanted to return to the "Party of Hoover," as in Herbert, under
which it listed "bread lines," "homeless," and "banks closed," or the "Party
of Roosevelt," as in Franklin D., under which it listed "high wages," "better
homes," and "social security." But by 1952, millions of young voters had

no memory of the Hoover years, and even Roosevelt seemed like a distant memory. More immediate was the "Party of Truman," which the Republicans cast as corrupt and weak, especially on security, including domestic Communism. Truman had time and again tried to ignore the Red Scare, or else neutralize it with steps such as loyalty tests and prosecutions, only to see it roar back in headlines and Republican stump speeches.

Eisenhower took 55.2 percent of the vote to Stevenson's 44.3 percent, and even captured several Southern states—including Texas, Tennessee, and Virginia—that had been reliably Democratic since the end of the Civil War. He was the first Republican to capture the White House in twenty years. Americans elected him for all sorts of reasons, but the impression that the Democrats had failed to take on Communism at home was a major one. "We have a new president who doesn't want party-line thinkers or fellow travelers," McCarthy told reporters. "He will conduct the fight."

McCarthy's mystique was rooted in "documents," a word he wielded like an incantation. Not just his documents, but "the" documents, as if there were a bedrock set of records and memos and names that, if they were just made public, would seal his case. In a Washington overrun with bureaucracy, and in an industrialized country where records, memos, and the information they contained were the common currency among thousands of corporations, government offices, and civic organizations, his claim to know the secrets hidden in the files seemed unassailable. He was never without them—notes tucked into his jacket pockets, reams of paper crammed into his briefcase. After all, people liked to believe, documents didn't lie, even if McCarthy played fast and loose with them.

It was a time of lists. Everyone had them. There was the Hollywood blacklist, *Red Channels*, *Counterattack*, and all their many copycats. The FBI had its own vast collection of data, decades worth, spilling over with rumors and hearsay but also carefully documented observations by agents sent to tail suspects, or just the merely suspicious. It was run by the General Intelligence Division and overseen by hundreds of clerks laboring twenty-four hours a day over millions of index cards. They kept track of "radicals," foreign nationals, leftists, rightists, and many in between. A subset of those cards was part of the so-called custodial detention system, which in the event of a war would be used to make mass arrests of suspicious characters, who would be placed in detention camps without due process. But even without a war, just knowing that the FBI records existed, and that if you have ever signed an anti-Franco petition or joined a front organization in college you were probably in them, was enough to keep people in fear. "None of these persons today has violated the specific Federal law now in force and effect," J. Edgar Hoover said of the files. "But many of them will come within the category for internment or prosecution as a result of regulations or laws which may be enacted in the event of a declaration of war." Representative Vito Marcantonio, the stalwart defender of the hard left in Congress, called it "terror by index cards."

The Red Scare was a cultural phenomenon, but it was also a sprawling bureaucratic construction, with lists at its center. Hoover and the bureau vacuumed up material from a broad range of sources far beyond their own agents: State-level bureaus of investigation, local police red squads, patriotic organizations like the American Legion—some 100,000 informants all fed what they knew into the bureau's files. Hoover protected those files jealously and rarely gave back in return, even as he encouraged his sources to keep pumping out information. McCarthy would have killed to get his hands on them; so would HUAC and any number of corporate security officials. The demand for information was endless. The result was a proliferation of local and private lists to fill the intelligence gap.

The Department of Justice set the tone. Truman's attorney general, Tom Clark, had naïvely intended his list of subversive organizations to be used only by federal agencies. But the list was public information, and in no time states and cities began passing their own anti-subversive laws that incorporated the attorney general's list for use in scouring their own agencies for subversives, down to obscure posts that by no stretch of the imagination might allow a conniving Communist to threaten domestic security: departments of motor vehicles, fish and wildlife services, beauticians' licensing offices. Several states used the attorney general's list to police real estate agents and undertakers; in Indiana, professional wrestlers had to take loyalty oaths that they had never been a member of a listed group. In New York State, one had to clear the list in order to fish in a public reservoir. In Chicago, for a time, people with a connection to a group on the attorney general's list were barred from public housing. Schools—public and private, college and primary—used the lists to vet educators, administrators, even in some cases custodial staff.

Private employers followed suit: At first, and with some encouragement by the federal government, the list was used to exclude "subversives" from sensitive jobs with defense contractors and power utilities. But soon all manner of businesses were using them as well, usually not out of any real fear of subversion, but as a means of patriotic virtue signaling, to announce that no Stalin lover would ever be allowed to shuffle papers at the Acme Widget Co. In a 1972 interview, more than two decades after he compiled the original list, Tom Clark, by then a former Supreme Court justice, seemed shocked that it had ever been abused. "It was a time of some hysteria," he said, with heavy emphasis on the "was," as if the mood of the moment was all that he needed to explain away his own role in it all.

Once the attorney general's list got out into the public, freelance investigators built their own databases around them, in an early version of what later generations would call "doxing." With Clark's list in hand, a group like the American Legion would set to work, digging into the personal histories of private citizens to come up with incriminating material, then sell their findings for a fee. Along the way they might throw in addresses and phone numbers. Enterprising individuals would do the same. Among the first to get into the business was a retired major general named Ralph Van Deman. Born in Ohio in 1865 and trained at Harvard to be a surgeon, he switched career paths early on and joined the Army. Van Deman was ill-fitted for combat—ungainly, poor eyesight—but brilliant at intelligence gathering, a skill he honed on deployment in the Philippines after the Spanish-American War. Stationed in the United States during World War I, he restarted a derelict Army division, the Military Intelligence Section, and created a network of 350,000 domestic informants to aid the government's anti-subversive campaign. His achievements during the war earned him a reputation as the father of American military intelligence.

Van Deman retired from the Army as a major general in 1929, but not from intelligence. His work during World War I had put him in contact with a paramilitary group called the American Protective League, and in the 1930s he used those connections to start collecting names and information on what he considered domestic subversives. "Working feverishly as he had during the war, he soon built a semiprivate agency that left the other patriotic groups in the dust," wrote the historian Roy Talbert. Based out of his home in San Diego, Van Deman fed his information to all who asked: the FBI, HUAC, police squads. He specialized in teachers—he could tell you where hundreds of California educators had studied, what campus groups they had joined, even what they said in class. He wasn't precious with his material, either. If another freelancer needed intelligence on a possible subversive, Van Deman was happy to help. When he died in 1952, Army intelligence agents swooped in to collect his files. It took them nine days to pack it up. All of it was incorporated into the military's own expanding collection of information on American citizens.

Van Deman may have been the first American to make a career as an anti-Communist list maker, but the greatest of all was J. B. Matthews. Over the course of three decades he made the unlikely transit from a difficult childhood in small-town Kentucky to Christian missionary abroad to socialist firebrand to, finally, a die-hard anti-Communist who joined McCarthy's staff in June 1953. Sturdily built and tall, he loomed over a room less for his physical than his intellectually aggressive presence. He had a professorial, combative air that teetered on the edge of imperiousness and, at the same time, betrayed the eternal self-consciousness of a country boy eager to prove himself to his cosmopolitan friends. Like the China Lobby's Alfred Kohlberg, with whom he carried on a decade-long friendship, Matthews was not well known outside the circle of anti-Communists, and for that reason he has also been largely forgotten by history. But the Red Scare could not have happened without him.

Joseph Brown Matthews was born in 1894 in Hopkinsville, an agricultural town in southwestern Kentucky. His world was rough-and-tumble; he witnessed a murder when he was six. He was a precocious child, and went off to college at a time and in a place where most of his cohort stayed to work the fields. Afterward he served as a missionary on the Southeast Asian island of Java for six years, then returned for graduate school at Drew University, Columbia, and Union Theological Seminary. He received degrees with high honors from each; though none was above a master's, his scholarly demeanor led people to call him "Doctor" the rest of his life.

Matthews had hoped to join the ministry, and taught for a period at Scarritt College, a Methodist institution in Nashville. He also deepened his involvement with left-wing politics. He stumped for the progressive Wisconsin senator Robert La Follette during his 1924 run for president, and he promoted racial integration on the Scarritt campus and in his home. Locals could abide his views on the presidency but not on race. Eventually he was forced to leave Scarritt, and Nashville.

Matthews moved to New York in 1929, where he joined a string of progressive groups and fronts, often at the top echelon. At different times, he was the chair of the U.S. Congress Against War and of the American League Against War and Fascism. He was never a Communist Party member, but he visited the Soviet Union five times between 1927 and 1932, and was given to spouting Communist-flavored zingers like "bourgeois democracy is a fig leaf to hide the naked realities of the capitalist system," uttered during a 1933 speech at Madison Square Garden. He spoke the firebrand language of the truly committed. "J.B. Matthews would always be one who believed more than one who doubted," the journalist Murray Kempton wrote. "His view of the intellectual all along has been the believer's revulsion from the doubter, and the recruiting sergeant's discontent with the immobilized."

His loyalty to the left was not to last. In his 1938 memoir, *Odyssey of a Fellow Traveler*, Matthews explained that, like Whittaker Chambers and so many others, he had finally realized the horrors that lay behind Communism and switched sides. But many observers then and later speculated that his reasons were more pecuniary. To support his family, Matthews had taken a job as an executive with a consumer research company; when the staff went on strike, he found their demands so repellent that he snapped. *Time* wrote that the experience of dealing with the strikers was so searing that Matthews "regarded himself as the victim of a Communist plot."

Whatever the cause, Matthews quickly became a celebrity in anti-Communist circles. In 1938 he was the first former Communist to testify about the party before HUAC. Among other bits of right-wing catnip that he offered to the committee, Matthews suggested that the Roosevelt administration and the New Deal were riven with Communists. He joined the HUAC staff soon after, and as Chairman Martin Dies's right-hand man he fed the committee's appetite for high-profile witnesses and blaring news coverage. Matthews grew more conservative as the 1940s passed. He had voted for Alf Landon, the Republican candidate for president in 1936, but refused to vote for Wendell Willkie in 1940 or Thomas Dewey in 1944 or 1948, deeming them both insufficiently conservative. Long before figures like Whittaker Chambers or Joe McCarthy came on the scene, Matthews was there, telling anyone who would listen that America was threatened by a vast conspiracy burrowing within.

Matthews was also an inveterate hoarder, and beginning in the 1930s he amassed a paper mill's worth of left-wing letterheads, court filings, press releases, and back issues of *The Daily Worker*, the Communist Party's primary publication. He pored through every page, looking for names and affiliations. From there he compiled a database, linking thousands of names to hundreds of organizations and causes, all of which, he asserted, were secretly in league with the American Communists and Moscow. He went beyond the attorney general's list, which he found inadequate. Where it listed a few hundred, Matthews counted more than a thousand subversive organizations. Nor did he worry too much about what qualified someone to be placed on his list—sometimes all it took to get on it was co-signing an amicus brief in the name of an appellant he considered too left-wing. His list eventually ran to 2,100 pages, which he had bound and published by the Government Printing Office after leaving the Dies Committee. *Time* called it "probably the largest private file on U.S. Communists and suspected Communists." It was full of errors and unsubstantiated rumors, and the GPO soon stopped printing it. But hundreds of copies got out, and they became prized possessions among red hunters—their book of spells, as it were.

Matthews didn't always wait for a knock at his door to spread what he knew. In December 1948 he wrote a flurry of letters raising concerns about the cast and stage crew of *All My Sons*, Arthur Miller's play about a corrupt defense contractor. "There is something rotten somewhere and it is not in the state of Denmark," Matthews said. He had written voluminously for Communist organs like the cultural review *New Masses*; now he wrote just as often for right-wing outlets like *The American Mercury*. People listened: A December 1951 article he wrote for the American Legion magazine, "Did the Movies Really Clean House?," helped reignite HUAC's interest in Hollywood.

Matthews served as a hub, connecting journalists, congressional staffers, industry executives and other freelance red hunters. He worked closely with the American Legion, who made him a regular feature at its increasingly frequent anti-subversive conferences, held at first just in Washington but eventually in cities around the country. He was also an ideologue, among the more dedicated of the anti-Communists. But like many others, he found a way to put his hard work and hard beliefs to making money. After he left the Dies Committee, he took a job with Hearst, the publisher, where he served as an in-house research bureau supplying material to right-wing columnists like George Sokolsky and Westbrook Pegler. Professional red-baiters like Jack Tenney, the former state legislator in California, relied on Matthews to investigate political enemies. During the blacklist, Hollywood studios and TV networks hired him to run background checks on stars, and potential stars.

At other times Matthews became one of many professional witnesses called before state and local anti-subversive committees, always for a hefty fee, plus expenses. When he had tapped all the possible clients among the red-baiting right, he went even further afield, selling chunks of his list to white supremacist and anti-Semitic groups. Even some anti-Communists grew wary of him. "He is not to be trusted," wrote Freda Utley, herself an ardent anti-Communist conservative. "Always double-crossing his own friends." Her skepticism proved unpersuasive—after the 1952 elections, Joe McCarthy hired Matthews to his staff, overnight making him one of the most influential red-baiters in the country.

McCarthy's new post following the Republican takeover of the Senate in 1952 was as chairman of the obscure Committee on Government Operations. It was supposed to be a sort of quarantine, giving him absolute

control over a supposedly powerless corner of the upper chamber. But
Robert Taft, the new Senate majority leader who placed him there, mis-
calculated. The Committee on Government Operations had a permanent
investigative subcommittee, and McCarthy made himself chairman of
that as well. It had a mandate to look into any part of the government it
wanted, and McCarthy intended to push that responsibility as far as he
could. He brought in several new staffers, including Matthews and Robert F. Kennedy, the younger brother of his new Senate colleague John F.
Kennedy. Their father, Joseph Kennedy, was a longtime supporter of the
fellow sharp-elbowed Irish American, sending McCarthy campaign con-
tributions and showing up in Washington to offer political advice. Mc-
Carthy was a regular presence at the Kennedy compound in Hyannis Port
and a regular part of the lineup in family softball games. He was even
there at Robert Kennedy's 1950 wedding to Ethel Skakel in Greenwich,
Connecticut.

McCarthy's most consequential hire was a rising-star lawyer from New
York named Roy Cohn. The son of a liberal judge, he had climbed briskly
through the city's elite educational institutions—Fieldston, Horace Mann,
Columbia University and its law school—then gone to work for the U.S.
Attorney's Office for the Southern District of New York. He had shot
through school so fast that he had to wait two years after receiving his
law degree to meet the age requirement for the bar exam. Once he did, he
made a name as a crusading anti-Communist prosecutor, with a hand in
many of the big cases of the late 1940s and early '50s, including the Smith
Act and Rosenberg trials. All the while, Cohn became a fixture on New
York's nightclub scene, with a regular table at the Stork Club, which he
used as a base to cultivate reporters and columnists. He came to Washington to seek his fortune, and after a brief stint at the Department of Justice
he had his friend George Sokolsky introduce him to McCarthy. The senator hired him immediately.

Among the anti-Communist right, it was a perfect match. Even Sokolsky had long worried that McCarthy was too loose a cannon, that he was
more interested in the trappings of power than the reasons why he had it.
He was disorganized, slovenly, and prone to mistakes. Cohn was none of
that. He was committed to the cause. He was a legal wizard. He was fo-

cused. But he was also a distillation of everything that men like Sokolsky loved about McCarthy—his viscousness, his vindictiveness, his willingness to lie. In ways large and small, Cohn became the chief executive of McCarthyism, Inc., determining the senator's targets, writing his talking points, and pushing him further than even he might have chosen to go.

PART III

20

Positive Loyalty

Joe McCarthy liked what he saw in the Eisenhower administration. The new president had run on a promise to clean up Washington, which, to McCarthy at least, meant rooting out the Communists he claimed were burrowed within the federal government. "Now it will be unnecessary for me to conduct a one-man campaign to expose Communists in government," McCarthy told reporters days after the 1952 election.

Eisenhower certainly talked a good game. Although no one expected him to be lenient on the Rosenbergs, who had been convicted of passing nuclear secrets to the Soviet Union in 1951, he repeatedly voiced his belief in the rightness of their death sentence. "By their act these two individuals have in fact betrayed the cause of freedom for which free men are fighting and dying at this very hour," he said a few days after his inauguration, in a statement rejecting one of their many pleas for clemency. And almost immediately, Eisenhower began planning a new, more powerful internal security system to replace Truman's loyalty program.

The incoming secretary of state, John Foster Dulles, particularly impressed McCarthy and his allies. Though he was a member of the so-called Dewey wing of East Coast Republicans—Princeton; Sullivan & Cromwell, the whitest of white-shoe law firms; the grandson and nephew of secretaries of state—and even though he had been a mentor to Alger Hiss, Dulles worked hard during the campaign to build ties to McCarthy, Styles Bridges, and other conservative senators. Among his first steps in office was to select Scott McLeod, a former FBI agent and close aide to Bridges, as his head of Bureau of Security and Consular Affairs, adding

"Personnel" to the office title and empowering him to oversee loyalty tests and sniff out subversives. In his inaugural address to State Department employees, just days after Eisenhower had given his own to the nation, Dulles demanded not just an absence of suspicious activity in their past but demonstrations of "positive loyalty." By April, he and Eisenhower had crafted their executive order to replace Truman's loyalty program. Chief among the changes was to replace "loyalty" with "security"—a seemingly semantic alteration that in fact opened wide new avenues for the invasion of personal lives. Loyalty and disloyalty imply intent. But even a loyal employee can be a security risk if, for example, they drank too much, or slept around, or simply talked too much to strangers.

Eisenhower's order, in the works since Inauguration Day, required an expanded security apparatus to implement it. McLeod was the ideal choice for the job—"an almost perfect distillation of the McCarthyist mindset," wrote his biographer, the journalist Todd Purdum. With his bushy crew cut and horn-rimmed glasses, McLeod looked like any of the millions of efficiency engineers and mid-level executives stocking the nation's postwar corporate sector. And in a way, that's what he was: brutally effective, dedicated to his task, uninterested in its political ramifications. In his confirmation hearing, he called himself an "eager beaver." When asked which jobs he considered the most sensitive, he said every single one—and that he would go deep into the lives of even the lowest-ranking State staffers. He fired employees with abandon, including twenty-four suspected of "homosexual" tendencies in the first three weeks. "McLeod's was a name used to frighten babies," wrote Edward Corsi, who worked on refugee issues at the State Department during the mid-1950s.

Still, none of Eisenhower's efforts kept McCarthy happy for long. He made noises about opposing two of Eisenhower's foreign policy nominees, Walter Bedell Smith as undersecretary of state and James. B. Conant as U.S. high commissioner for Germany. He ended up voting for them, but the new president understood the momentary opposition as a shot across the White House lawn. McCarthy then announced hearings into Voice of America, a news service within the State Department. He told reporters he wanted the same thing Eisenhower did, to rid the department of supposed subversives. But no one was fooled. "McCarthy

Poses an Administration Problem: His Wide Swings Are Hitting Dulles and the State Department Routine," read a *New York Times* headline on February 22, 1953.

What McCarthy failed to grasp was that for all of Eisenhower's stalwart talk about security and standing strong in the Cold War, he was not at all interested in joining the hard right's long-running war on the progressive left. Like most of America by 1953, Eisenhower had come to accept the tenets of the New Deal, and along with it the expansive powers of the federal government. During his two terms he would expand Social Security, create the National Highway System, sign the National Defense Education Act, and defend domestic agencies from Republican attempts at budget cuts. He was no progressive, but like progressives he believed in the fundamental goodness of government and its workers, and its power to improve the lives of their fellow citizens. He detested those who, like McCarthy, saw nefarious plots and secret government cabals behind every agency doorplate. In this sense Eisenhower's election signaled the beginning of the end of the Red Scare, the moment where the cultural and the national security impulses that drove it forward began to diverge.

The senator and the president were headed for a clash, and it didn't take long to arrive. At the same time Dulles was wooing McLeod, he asked the diplomat Charles Bohlen to be ambassador to the Soviet Union. The country had been without one for months, and after Joseph Stalin's sudden death at his dacha outside Moscow on March 5, 1953, filling the embassy's executive position became a top priority. Bohlen was a perfect choice: universally respected in Europe, coauthor of the Marshall Plan, and, under Truman, minister to France. He had been at Dean Acheson's side, way back in 1947, as the two plotted an emergency response to the Greek crisis. But there were also rumors about his sexuality. Bohlen and his wife were close friends with Carmel Offie, who had worked with him in Paris and sometimes spent nights at their Washington home. It was Bohlen who had put Offie on the radar of Frank Wisner and the Office of Policy Coordination, after Offie's gray-market dealings in Europe had gotten him sent home from Germany. Bohlen's brother-in-law, Charles Thayer, a consular officer in Germany, was rumored to be a Communist and a homosexual. And anonymous tipsters told the FBI—and eventually McLeod too—that Bohlen was likely gay himself.

By 1953 it was gospel in official Washington that gay men were security risks, and Eisenhower and Dulles's promise to clean house at the State Department had extended to what they deemed "moral perverts." McLeod was happy to go along. Using an investigative manual with nearly ten pages about identifying and removing homosexual employees, he taught his team how to look for "any unusual traits of speech, appearance and mannerisms" that might betray same-sex feelings. "The campaign toward eliminating all types of sex perverts from the rolls of the department will be pressed with increased vigor," he told Congress, and at the end of the year bragged that ninety-one had been "separated," or about one every three days.

At first, McCarthy and his Senate allies focused their opposition to Bohlen on his time in the Roosevelt-Truman White House. As soon as Eisenhower announced his nomination, they opened fire with charges that Bohlen had been a key part of the "surrender" at the Yalta summit in 1945. Bohlen had in fact urged Truman to cede Eastern Europe to the Soviets; it was clear, he argued, they would take it anyway. He was just being realistic, but that didn't make him look any less like an appeaser, if not an accomplice to a geopolitical crime, in the eyes of McCarthy and his allies. Bohlen, McCarthy thundered, "was too important a part of the old Acheson machine in the State Department to properly represent the administration, especially in this key spot."

Then came the results of an FBI probe into Bohlen's background, which strongly implied a history of homosexual indelicacies. In his own report to Dulles, McLeod declared him a security risk. The secretary dismissed the suggestions, and testified in Bohlen's favor before a closed hearing of the Senate Foreign Relations Committee. A few days later, the committee approved Bohlen's nomination 15–0. The next day, McLeod offered to submit a resignation letter. Dulles refused it.

The Bohlen fight moved to the full Senate, where McCarthy's allies pounced. Pat McCarran, the conservative Democrat from Nevada who had led the Senate subcommittee on internal security until 1952 and now sat as its ranking Democratic member, declared the nomination to be the "acid test" showing that the new president's State Department was no different than Truman's. The White House closed ranks. McCarthy tried three times to meet with McLeod, and three times was told he was unavailable—evidence, the senator said, of yet another conspiracy. He demanded that Bohlen take a lie detector test. And he insisted that the full Senate see Bohlen's FBI file. Thinking quickly, Dulles arranged a compromise: Republican Senate Majority Leader Taft and Democratic senator John Sparkman of Alabama, his party's vice presidential nominee in its recent, losing run for the White House, could review a synopsis based on the files, and report back on their impressions. He also persuaded Bohlen's brother-in-law, Charles Thayer, to resign—a bitter pill for the young, promising diplomat to swallow, but swallow he did out of family loyalty. When Taft and Sparkman returned with nothing, the full Senate confirmed Bohlen, 74–13.

A few weeks later, as Bohlen was preparing for his new role, Dulles asked him how he and his family were planning to get to Moscow. Bohlen said he would go first, and his wife would follow once she had closed up their house.

"Oh, don't you think it would be wiser for you and your wife to travel together?" Dulles asked.

"For God's sake why?"

"Well, you know, there were rumors in some of your files about immoral behavior and it would look better if your wife was with you."

Bohlen thanked him for the suggestion, then headed to the Soviet Union alone.

On the surface, the Bohlen fight looked like a loss for McCarthy. Even normally friendly senators like Taft had turned against him. But he had won something. Eleven of the thirteen nay votes came from the president's own party, while more Democrats (thirty-nine) than Republicans (thirty-four) voted aye. And by fighting to the end, McCarthy had shown that he was nobody's foot soldier—that he would strike wherever he felt like it. He came away from the Bohlen fight as an adversary of the administration, a split that he did nothing to heal.

By the time of the final vote, McCarthy had already moved on, and was deep into his campaign against his next target, Voice of America. The agency had been founded during World War II to spread pro-American news and information, a job that took on new import with the erection of the Iron Curtain. Transmitters went up along the eastern edge of Western Europe, broadcasting into the new Soviet puppet states. But the agency was undermined by tensions between those who wanted it to act like the BBC, offering objective news in a bid to highlight the strength of a free press, and those who wanted a more aggressively propagandistic model. The partisans of the latter approach fed rumors about pro-Communist infiltration within the agency to George Sokolsky and other sympathetic columnists, who in turn urged McCarthy to investigate.

McCarthy didn't need to think it over. Roy Cohn had convinced his boss to bring on his friend, the hotel heir G. David Schine, as an unpaid assistant, and they took on the Voice of America investigation as their first big assignment. The two spent weeks lining up witnesses from Schine's luxury apartment at the Waldorf Astoria hotel, in New York. No one, including McCarthy, could ever explain what qualified Schine to serve under him; his single claim to expertise on the Soviet issue was a short book—a pamphlet, really, called *Definition of Communism*—that he wrote and had placed like a Gideons Bible in the bedside drawers of every hotel in his father's chain. He was there, it seemed, mostly to keep Cohn company.

The Voice of America hearings, held in downtown Manhattan, were a bust. An investigation into the suspiciously inefficient placement of powerful radio transmitters got bogged down in technical details. Cohn's witnesses proved unreliable, even pathological, when placed before a microphone, bearing out for all to see what should have been obvious from the beginning: The accusations about Communist infiltration were simply rehashed versions of petty intra-department squabbles and power grabs.

As always, by the time the hearings sputtered to a close, in March 1953, McCarthy had found a way to distract attention from the failure. He turned to another State Department agency, the Overseas Library Program, which had dozens of outlets across Europe, open to the public as a means of publicizing America's commitment to free speech. Secretary Dulles had already issued new guidance limiting what books the libraries could offer, telling staff to pulp hundreds of titles by Communists and progressives. Some simply burned them. But the conflagrations didn't keep McCarthy from charging that the department's libraries still held thirty to forty thousand "dangerous" books. The count was likely inflated, and included titles like *The Maltese Falcon*, of interest only because its author, Dashiell Hammett, was a noted leftist—a form of bibliographic guilt by association. McCarthy demanded hearings.

Before they began, he allowed Cohn and Schine to undertake a whirlwind fact-finding tour around Europe to see just what these libraries contained. They visited both U.S. and Russian-sponsored institutions, and compiled a list of which authors appeared in both—as if a copy of *Huckleberry Finn* found in a Soviet House of Culture somehow proved that Mark Twain was a Communist. They looked into personnel too: After they flew through Frankfurt, Cohn charged that Theodore Kaghan, stationed in the city as part of the U.S. High Commissioner's Public Affairs Division, had "once signed a Communist Party petition." Kaghan then dismissed the two as "junketeeting gumshoes." The State Department called him home and fired him.

Reporters followed the pair wherever they went, noting their hijinks. In Munich they were seen swatting each other with newspapers as they ran through a hotel lobby. They left their rooms strewn with empty liquor bottles and disemboweled newspapers. They ran up enormous food and shopping tabs, charged to the local embassy or consulate. Rumors surfaced that they were closeted lovers—rumors that Cohn did little to dispel when, upon checking in and declining an offer to share a room, joked that "we don't work for the State Department."

McCarthy opened his hearings into the overseas libraries in April 1953. During fifteen sessions running to July, he called a string of professional ex-Communist witnesses, including Harvey Matusow, an expert witness from the Smith Act trial whom McCarthy had recently hired as a staff assistant—and who, in a disaster for the anti-Communists, would later go to prison for perjury and recant almost all his testimony. The witnesses not only fingered authors for the mildest of left-wing tendencies, but raised alarms about why particular anti-Communist books were not included on the library shelves. One witness, Freda Utley, who had made her own study of U.S.-backed libraries in West Germany, complained that she easily found nine novels by Howard Fast, while anti-Communist books were often catalogued in imposing sections like "Europe" or "Labor and Capital," making them difficult to find. McCarthy demanded that Dulles himself "run down the purchase orders" for the offending books. The secretary did as he was told; several agency officials were fired as a result, and the libraries' director and his assistant resigned. America was safer knowing that impressionable European youths would no longer be exposed to Fast's *Lord Baden-Powell of the Boy Scouts* and other allegedly subversive books.

None of this made the president happy. "If Eisenhower could have had his own way in dealing with Joseph R. McCarthy, he would have ignored the senator completely," wrote his close adviser, Sherman Adams. But he had no choice—McCarthy was everywhere, and getting stronger. "In the early part of the Eisenhower administration, a visitor from another civilization would have been forced to conclude that in the United States the measure of political virtue was the number of unworthy civil servants a government managed to dismiss," wrote the journalist Richard Rovere. Eisenhower didn't have a strategy for dealing with McCarthy, just a stern refusal to engage with him. "I will not get into the gutter with that guy," the president would say, and hope that his own steady hand would deprive the demagogue of a platform.

By summer, McCarthy was wielding his committee like a shotgun, firing wildly at targets as far apart as the Government Printing Office, the CIA, and the Atomic Energy Commission. He barked at witnesses who refused to admit to past affiliations, calling them "Fifth Amendment Communists." When a few of his colleagues worried to him privately that his campaign might backfire for the administration, he denounced them in public. On August 29 he stood before five hundred American Legionnaires gathering in St. Louis, dressed in his own Legion uniform. "My good friends, when we start saying we will not uncover threats to the country because of embarrassment, we can decide on that day that this nation has not long to live," he told them.

If other Republicans wanted McCarthy to tone it down a notch, no one wanted him to stop. Stalin might have been dead and the Korean War, after three bloody years, might have been grinding to a draw, but the Red Scare was still good politics. McCarthy's comments came less than a week after Senator William Jenner, the new chairman of the Internal Security Subcommittee, released a report declaring that legions of Communist spies remained in the government: "The Soviet International organization has carried on a successful and important penetration of the United States government, and this penetration has not been fully exposed." Not to be outdone, on September 1 Attorney General Herbert Brownell declared Communism "a greater menace now than at any time."

And why not? Red-baiting had become practically a national pastime. In New York, the state government fired a water-quality investigator because he refused to discuss whether he had been a Communist in the past. The Democratic governor of Texas, Allan Shivers, called for Communists to be executed. Legislatures in Massachusetts, Pennsylvania, and Illinois voted to outlaw the Communist Party. The New York City welfare commissioner announced a campaign to root out leftists from his department's ranks. Dozens were let go, including an assistant case supervisor in Brooklyn who had refused to appear before an inquiry into possible past Communist affiliations; the commissioner not only fired her, but canceled her pension as well. And in Baltimore, a used car salesman spent his own money to erect an eight-foot-tall monument to Joseph McCarthy outside his showroom. On the back it read, "Senator Joseph R. McCarthy, Statesman."

All of this took place while the Communist Party, already enfeebled by its own infighting, publicly imploded. What had been a vibrant, ecumenical movement in the 1930s and early 1940s had contracted into brittle, paranoid sectarianism that often seemed more interested in punishing its own members than in finding new ones. Gone was the "romance" of American Communism of Vivian Gornick. Adherence to party doctrine was everything, and divining the latest orders from Moscow occupied much of the membership's time. In 1946 Stalin had ordered communist parties to run their own campaigns for office, only to apparently change his mind and direct them to burrow into existing left-leaning political organizations. For two years the party tied itself in knots trying to follow his tortuous directives. (In fact by then Stalin didn't care what they did, having largely written off the American Communist Party as an instrument of revolution.)

Internal fighting occupied more and more of the party's time. Even the tiniest alleged offense set off hours of meetings, trials, and confessionals. One member who served watermelon at a party was expelled for the offense of "white chauvinism." Others were disciplined for Trotskyism, Browderism, the slightest whiff of doctrinal disagreement with whatever shape the party line took that day. "The American Communist Party became an Orwellian caricature of itself, disintegrating from within even as it was being destroyed from without," Gornick wrote. In 1946 the screenwriter Albert Maltz dared to challenge the party diktat that art's only value was as a tool for revolution. "I have come to believe that the accepted understanding of art as a weapon is not a useful guide, but a straight-jacket," he wrote in *New Masses*. The article hit the Hollywood branch like an incendiary bomb. John Howard Lawson called an emergency meeting, with Maltz in the hot seat. Howard Fast attacked him in *The Daily Worker*. Finally, Maltz gave in, and like a Soviet functionary before a Stalinist court, he admitted to a long list of thought crimes. Lawson magnanimously let him back into the branch, but the damage was done. Dozens left, disenchanted. The Maltz affair exposed the postwar party as a hidebound, doctrinaire propaganda machine. "They were walking toward a common grave," Murray Kempton wrote, "hating one another."

It was a cruel irony: The postwar party was hardly the sort of organization that could resist a growing force of government and social repression, but also, for that same reason, hardly the sort of threat that anti-Communist zealots imagined it to be. According to a *New York Times* article entitled "American Communist Party Is a Shell of Its Old Self," by the beginning of the 1950s the party was on the verge of collapse, and would disappear completely were it not for the revenue generated by government agents subscribing to *The Daily Worker* in order to keep tabs on it.

How Red Are the Schools?

Among the witnesses subpoenaed during Joe McCarthy's Voice of America hearings in the spring of 1953 was Julius Hlavaty, a forty-six-year-old math teacher from New Rochelle, New York. Hlavaty was born in Piestany, a town in the Austro-Hungarian Empire that now sits in western Slovakia, and immigrated to New York City in 1921. His family was poor, but the New York schools treated him well: After graduating from the prestigious DeWitt Clinton High School, in the Bronx, he was accepted by Harvard but couldn't find enough scholarship money to attend, and so went to City College, then to Teachers College, at Columbia University, for a doctorate in mathematics education. By the time McCarthy called him to Washington, Hlavaty was the chairman of the mathematics department at the Bronx High School of Science and widely considered one of the best math teachers in America.

A year before Hlavaty's appearance, a producer with the Slovak-language section of Voice of America asked if he would record a statement about his immigrant experience and subsequent career for the radio, to be broadcast in Slovak across Central Europe. He gladly agreed. He was proud of what he had achieved in the United States, and grateful for the opportunities his adopted country had provided him. At the time, no one asked about his political leanings. Hlavaty was registered with the progressive American Labor Party, and may have been a member of the Communist Party in his youth. Someone—it was never revealed who—heard about the broadcast, knew of his alleged party affiliations, and tipped off McCarthy's office.

The first of the hearings took place in Washington, but McCarthy soon moved them to Foley Square to be near Voice of America's Manhattan offices, home to its Eastern European desks where Hlavaty had recorded his talk. He appeared on the afternoon of March 13, 1953. Renowned around the halls of Bronx Science for his sartorial finesse, he wore a pin-striped suit with a textured white handkerchief in his breast pocket. He kept his white hair slicked back, and looked more like a British stage actor or a continental industrialist than a high school math teacher. Ostensibly, he was there to talk about his broadcast, and anything suspicious he might have noticed about Voice of America. But the only thing McCarthy wanted to hear about was his past. Was he a member of the Communist Party? Not now, Hlavaty said, though he refused to talk about his former politics. Had he registered as a member of the American Labor Party? McCarthy asked. He had, Hlavaty replied, though he didn't see why his private political opinions were any business of the subcommittee's.

Hlavaty had no illusion about what was really going on, or what would soon happen to him. By this point, in 1953, McCarthy's routine was predictable. "I may say that it seems to me that my name tomorrow is going to be spread over all the newspapers in the country and what I said here, which would be the strongest defense that I would have, will not be in there," he told the committee. "What is happening here today means, if not actually, potentially, the end of a career, which I with all modesty can say was a distinguished career in education."

The senators were unmoved. Everett Dirksen, the McCarthy ally from Illinois who had toppled the Democratic majority leader in 1950, asked whether Hlavaty thought Communists should be allowed to teach. Hlavaty said he agreed with something Senator Robert Taft had said recently. To the surprise of many conservatives who considered the Ohio Republican a stalwart man of the hard right, Taft had said he was okay with Communists in the classroom, as long as they kept their political opinions outside it. Dirksen felt otherwise. "No matter what your competence may be in the field of mathematics," he lectured Hlavaty, "I think there is a subtle influence it goes out from your conduct and your identity with organizations." Hlavaty conceded that some students had, in fact, started wearing pocket squares and boutonnieres, just like he did, but that he doubted whether his influence extended much beyond that. They went back and forth like this for an hour before McCarthy dismissed Hlavaty in frustration.

Three weeks later, Hlavaty was called before the New York City Board of Education, in downtown Brooklyn, and fired for insubordination. The board had recently ruled that anyone refusing to cooperate with Congress would be considered unfit to teach, and summarily ousted. A week after that Hlavaty's wife, Fancille, a teacher in the Westchester, New York, suburb of New Rochelle, was also fired. On her last day in school, she told her students she had taught in the city's schools for nine years, and that during that time she had "nothing to hide." But things were changing. "Inquisitions into a person's private beliefs, particularly of their distant past, are a danger," she told them. She then packed up her things and left.

The Hlavatys were just two among many hundreds of teachers nationwide hounded out of the profession in the late 1940s and early 1950s by school boards, congressional committees, and ad hoc "citizens" groups, many of whom were working in close collaboration. Countless more were cowed into silence by the threat of summary recriminations for teaching "controversial" material, left the profession early, or never entered it to begin with—all at a time when the baby boom was driving demand for thousands more teachers, and the technological challenges posed by the Soviet Union necessitated more teachers like Julius Hlavaty to prepare the next generation of physicists, mathematicians, and engineers.

Teachers were not the only ones targeted: Libraries and librarians were attacked for the books they carried, college professors were quizzed on the content of their lectures, and everyone from deans to janitors were forced to sign loyalty oaths. What constituted "controversial" material was left to the accuser: It could be a book by a suspected leftist, a civics lesson that sounded insufficiently enthusiastic about the free market system, or even an off-the-cuff remark in favor of civil rights. One witness told the Senate Internal Security Subcommittee in 1953 that Communist teachers were using one particular film to indoctrinate students—though the film, *Races of Mankind*, was based on a 1943 U.S. Army pamphlet by the anthropologists Ruth Benedict and Gene Weltfish to educate soldiers about the evils of Nazism.

Parents encouraged their children to report anything questionable they might have seen or heard in their classroom, introducing gossip, misunderstandings, and petty recriminations against unpopular teachers as fodder for investigations. The hunt required constant vigilance, said the eminent philosopher and ardent anti-Communist Sidney Hook. "No one indoctrinates when he is under observation," he wrote in *Time* in 1953. "Except in its crudest forms, indoctrination in the classroom can rarely be detected save by a critically trained observer who is almost continuously present." Better, he and many others concluded, to ban anyone with even a hint of radicalism in their past.

Perhaps it was inevitable that schools would become a Red Scare battleground. Education has always been contested ideological terrain in America, whether it was over who got to attend or what they were taught. And in the 1950s, the fear of Communist subversion was just one more chapter in the postwar hysteria over the country's youth. Comic books came under fire for their violence and racy content, leading to Senate hearings in 1954 and the adoption of strict content codes by the industry. The scourge of juvenile delinquency, better reflected in movies than reality, caused no end of pearl-clutching. But the fear of Communist subversion went further. Conservative critics had long charged that the very idea of free, publicly supported education was itself socialistic. Now, suddenly, in the form of teachers like Julius and Fancille Hlavaty, they seemed to have found their proof. "Propaganda for New Deal doctrines, socialism, and the 'welfare state' is being poured into American high school children in massive doses," claimed the *Chicago Tribune*. "The public schools have been and are now being used for partisan politican purposes," said the Sons of the American Revolution at the 1951 annual meeting. "The minds of our children are being filled with propaganda to lead us gradually and deceptively into a social welfare type of state." Such grandstanding seemed to work: A 1953 Gallup poll found that 66 percent of Americans opposed letting even former Communists teach in public schools.

Teachers unions and professional organizations largely fell in line. At its 1949 convention, the National Education Association, the country's largest teachers union, voted to bar communists from its ranks, and it adopted a resolution that "the responsibility of the schools is to teach the superiority of the American way of life." The organization built ties with anti-Communist activist groups like the National Citizens Commission for the Public Schools and the National Congress of Parents and Teachers, and through its Defense Commission undertook dozens of investigations into allegations of Communist "infiltration" of schools around the country. Even the more progressive American Federation of Teachers shrank from the moment: At its 1952 meeting in Syracuse, five hundred delegates voted overwhelmingly for a declaration that the union would not defend members found to be Communists.

Especially in big cities, teachers of the early 1950s were indeed a progressive bunch. Better educated and more worldly than the average American, many had come of age in the 1930s and early '40s, and had drunk deeply of the progressive ideas abounding in schools of education at the time. A few had become Communists; a handful still were. And for a while, they had been able to bring their ideas to their classrooms—not Communism itself, but ideas that Communists shared with the broader left, about civil rights, women's rights, labor, and foreign affairs. When the culture turned against those progressive ideas, America's teachers were among the biggest targets.

By the time Julius Hlavaty appeared before the Board of Education in April 1953, New York City had become the epicenter of the Red Scare in education. The city's teachers had long leaned to the left, especially with the influx of Jewish educators starting in the early twentieth century, who in many cases came from communities where Communism was widely accepted, like central Brooklyn and Manhattan's Lower East Side. By the 1930s the Communist Party had established its own beachhead in the profession, with an especially strong presence in the Teachers Union, the leading labor organization for city schools and public colleges. A conservative backlash was quick to form. From 1940 to 1942 two Republican state legislators, Assemblyman Herbert Rapp and Senator Frederic René Coudert Jr., held closed-door hearings that, in their secrecy and low standards of evidence, presaged the HUAC and McCarthy inquiries: Hostile witnesses were forced to name names, and informers were allowed to speak with anonymity. The Board of Education fired anyone who did not cooperate, as well as anyone identified as a subversive by two or more witnesses. More than forty teachers, mostly at City, Queens, Hunter, and Brooklyn Colleges, lost their jobs, including the first Black man hired to the faculty at City College, Max Yergan, who taught "Negro History and Culture." When two witnesses accused him of being "liberal" and "progressive," his contract was not renewed, with no chance for appeal.

The focus on teachers picked up again in the later stages of the Red Scare. In 1949 New York State passed the so-called Feinberg Law, which made membership in any group on the attorney general's list of subversive organization grounds for dismissal. A year later the New York City Board of Education began "trials" against teachers suspected of Communist sympathies, as well as anyone who refused to cooperate with its investigations. Among the first was a substitute elementary school teacher in the Bedford-Stuyvesant neighborhood of Brooklyn named Mildred Flacks. She took the Fifth Amendment, refusing to answer questions on the grounds that she might incriminate herself, and was immediately fired. "Is there evidence that she taught her little ones that D stood for *Das Kapital* or that two plus two added up to surplus value?" quipped I. F. Stone in his weekly column.

Another teacher, Irving Adler, led a group of union members in a suit against the Board of Education, reaching the Supreme Court in 1952. But the court, in a 6–3 decision, ruled that teaching was a privilege, not a right, and that the interests in keeping Communist influence out of impressionable young minds outweighed the teachers' First Amendment rights. The court's two stalwart liberals, William O. Douglas and Hugo Black, predictably dissented. Teachers, they said, had no recourse under the law to explain why they had belonged to a subversive group. "Youthful indiscretions, mistaken causes, misguided enthusiasms—all long forgotten—become the ghosts of a harrowing present," the pair wrote in a scathing minority decision. "Any organization committed to a liberal cause, any group organized to revolt against an hysterical trend, any committee launched to sponsor an unpopular program, becomes suspect. These are the organizations into which Communists often infiltrate. . . . A teacher caught in that mesh is almost certain to stand condemned. Fearing condemnation, she will tend to shrink from any association that stirs controversy. In that manner, freedom of expression will be stifled." As the majority made clear, though, there was no room for such protections or distinctions in the Cold War.

The proceedings, which ran regularly into the late 1950s, were the worst form of guilt by association. The notion of pedagogical subversion—that teachers, by virtue of their private political opinions, would sway young minds—was just that, a notion, built on broad-brush, often fantastical ideas about how education worked and how educators did their jobs. No teacher was ever found advocating Communist ideas in the classroom— or even, for that matter, outside the classroom. Certainly none was found engaged in subversive activities against the government. It was an enormous loss for the profession and a self-inflicted wound by a country that, in other respects, was eager to get out ahead of the Soviets in educational achievement and technological prowess. Julius Hlavaty was typical in this respect: There was a strong correlation between strong progressive views outside the classroom and excellence in teaching inside it. After all, few people enter the profession for money or fame. They are driven by a passionate vision for education and how it can change the world, especially in public schools. In the early 1950s, such a vision could get a person fired.

Of course, the absence of overt subversion did little to allay the truly paranoid, who insisted that Communist influence worked in more subtle and sinister ways. Anti-Communist watchdog groups emerged everywhere, some national in scope, others hyperlocal. In Scarsdale, New York, an investment banker named Otto Dohrenwend became convinced that Communists were on the verge of taking over the public schools of his wealthy Westchester suburb, just north of New York City. In 1948 he founded the Scarsdale Citizens Committee and began burrowing into the affairs of the town's schools, calling out suspect books, investigating teachers, and criticizing curriculums. After a New York psychologist spoke at the Scarsdale High School career day, Dohrenwend sent his fellow residents a four-page flyer accusing the man of being a Communist sympathizer and a former instructor at a Communist-sponsored college. He demanded to know who on the school board had invited him. "The tragedy of the board's laissez-faire attitude is that it paves the way for further infiltration of our schools," Dohrenwend wrote. "No wonder it keeps on happening here!!!"

Eventually, the community's education leaders, including the Parent-Teacher Association, had enough. Four principals wrote a public letter that, without naming Dohrenwend specifically, said that his constant attacks threatened to fatally undermine the Scarsdale education system. "Unless the forces that are establishing fear, raising doubts and undermining confidence can be met and resolved, there can be no future for the good name of our schools," they wrote. Some 1,500 parents showed up for a raucous school board meeting in May 1952, in which an anti-Dohrenwend slate was elected, along with a statement declaring that there had been no "Communist infiltration" in Scarsdale.

Scarsdale was a rare bright spot. In most parts of the country, people like Dohrenwend won the day. Local groups like his received significant support from national organizations with anodyne titles like the National Council for American Education, founded by a far-right activist named Allen Zoll. During the 1930s Zoll had founded an anti-Semitic, pro-fascist group called American Patriots. It was considered so extreme that the military refused his application for civilian intelligence training during World War II. Zoll's new group established itself as an arbiter for patriotic education and as a watchdog against subversives. He pumped out a steady stream of pamphlets with titles like "How Red Are the Schools?" "Progressive Education Increases Delinquency," "They Want Your Child," and "Red-ucators at Harvard." He created a blacklist of sorts, keeping track of ousted teachers and circulating them to his subscribers around the country, to prevent educators from relocating to a new state and reentering the profession. And he developed a running list of subversive books, insisting that school and public libraries get rid of them immediately. Hundreds followed his orders; one library, in Oklahoma, even burned its suspicious texts, out of expediency or stridency or both.

The crackdown on books represented another front in the war on subversion in schools, a domestic version of McCarthy's assault on overseas libraries. Once more, novels by left-wing writers like Howard Fast and Dashiell Hammett were banned, not because of their content but because of their authors. An attempt to purge the school libraries of Marin County, California, failed, but the public schools agreed to quarantine several titles, so that pupils could only read them under a teacher's supervision. After a 1952 survey of school libraries, *The New York Times* concluded that "a concerted campaign is under way over the country to censor school and college textbooks, reading materials and other visual aids."

In 1951 a conservative activist named Lucille Cardin Crain, who edited a prominent journal called *The Education Reviewer*, wrote an essay excoriating *American Government*, a standard textbook in hundreds of high school civics courses. Its author, Frank Magruder, a professor at Oregon State College, had committed such sins as advocating for the United Nations Charter and referring to impoverished people as "underprivileged" and "unfortunate." The popular right-wing radio commentator Fulton Lewis Jr. read Crain's review and amplified it, and by early 1952 the book had been banned in Houston, Little Rock, and the entire state of Georgia, among dozens of other places. In banning the book in Georgia, administrators removed some thirty thousand copies from schools and libraries. It was clear that many of its critics had never read *American Government*, concluded *The New York Times*, because in places where board members were forced to examine it after appeals by parents, they usually allowed it back on the shelves.

Countless school districts also barred "controversial" guests from speaking on campus. The board of education in Washington, D.C., kept a blacklist of proscribed speakers, filling it with anyone whose name appeared in a HUAC investigation, for any reason other than as a friendly witness. Often a rumor or simple accusation was enough to get someone blacklisted: The school board in Englewood, New Jersey, rescinded an invitation to the civil rights leader Mary McLeod Bethune after a tipster called in, saying she was a Communist. She denied ever joining the party, but was nevertheless forced to speak at a nearby private college instead.

Groups like the National Council for American Education encouraged parents and students to act as informants, reporting back even their slightest suspicion about a teacher or principal. Did they talk a little too much about labor rights? Did they speak out a little too loudly against segregation? Did they criticize Joe McCarthy? In California, the state education commissioner urged the American Legion to report "to me any evidence concerning subversive activity it may have respecting any person connected with the public schools." School districts also got help from Washington: Through its "Responsibilities" program, the FBI allowed administrators to request information on suspicious teachers or job applicants. According to the historian Beverly Gage, by 1955 the bureau had fulfilled nine hundred such requests.

For teachers, the profession had become a police state. "The law inevitably turns the school system into a spying project," wrote Justice Douglas in his dissent in the *Adler* decision, focusing on New York's anti-Communist law but describing the broad, repressive environment it encouraged nationwide. "Regular loyalty reports on the teachers must be made out. The principals become detectives; the students, the parents, the community become informers. Ears are cocked for tell-tale signs of disloyalty."

All of this—the vigilantism, the censorship, the loyalty investigations— had an immense effect on teacher morale. Thousands left the profession in the early 1950s, or didn't join in the first place. Most of those who remained kept their heads down, and shied away from important if controversial subjects. In a poll of Houston teachers, 58 percent said they felt pressure from outside groups to alter their curriculum, and 40 percent said they felt their job was at risk because of their political beliefs. A 1953 survey by the National Education Association found an overwhelming reluctance on the part of teachers to discuss such "controversial" topics as civil rights, universal health care, capitalism, and sex. "Far more to be feared than any radicalism in our schools is the tyranny that would force education into a straight-jacket of regimented conformity," said Reverend Walter Tunks, the rector of St. Paul's Church in Akron, Ohio, at the National Education Association's 1953 convention in Miami Beach. "That is the real threat to our American way of life."

It was inevitable that many of the same people who went after teachers would also attack college campuses. During the 1930s, these places had been a seedbed of the intellectual, technocratic elite that had driven so much of the progressive change now being assailed. Already in 1948 the Joint Legislative Committee on Un-American Activities, the "mini-HUAC" established in Washington State by State Senator Albert Canwell, opened investigative hearings into subversive professors at the University of Washington. Using tactics borrowed directly from HUAC, the committee interrogated dozens of faculty members and administrators. Three professors lost their jobs, and dozens of others had their careers derailed by lingering suspicions inserted into their personnel files.

By the turn of the decade more than a dozen states had barred Communists from teaching at public colleges and universities, as had scores of private colleges. Almost every state instituted some form of loyalty oath, none more aggressively than California. The state already required all professors and instructors to sign a pledge of allegiance, but in 1950, under pressure from the state legislature, the University of California adopted an additional oath, forswearing belief in subversive ideas and membership in any subversive organization, and as usual "subversive" was largely undefined. Thirty-one employees refused to sign, and in August the Board of Regents fired them. They were saved only when Republican governor Earl Warren, an alumnus and ex officio member of the board, stepped in to force a compromise: a loyalty oath for all state employees, whether at the universities or not.

In most cases, universities and administrators went along. In 1953 the American Association of Universities, a group representing thirty-seven of the country's top educational institutions, issued a statement declaring that no Communist should be allowed to teach in a college classroom, and demanding that any academic called to testify before a government committee should speak honestly and fully—no Fifth Amendment allowed. Several university presidents, including James Conant of Harvard, issued blanket statements barring Communists from their faculties. "America's colleges and universities," wrote the historian Ellen Schrecker, "had given Joe McCarthy and the members of HUAC a say over selecting their faculties."

It was perhaps inevitable that HUAC would single out Harvard for special treatment. It was not only the best-known and most prestigious university in the country, but it and its law school were the alma mater of so many of the liberals and progressives who had helped build out the New Deal, from President Roosevelt down through Felix Frankfurter and Dean

Acheson to Alger Hiss. For many of the cultural warriors who had been railing against Communist subversion since the 1930s, Harvard was the pinnacle of the Eastern elite who, in their minds, were rapidly driving the country to the left. (Harvard was hardly a fortress of pro-Communist sentiment; in a 1949 poll of faculty taken by *The Harvard Crimson*, more than two thirds agreed that "Communists should not be employed as teachers.") In 1953, HUAC held a series of hearings that all but explicitly targeted Harvard University, and got several prominent academics, including the literary scholar Granville Hicks and the historian Daniel Boorstin, both of whom had attended Harvard during the 1930s and dabbled in Communism, to name names.

They testified to the existence of a Communist cell on Harvard's campus at the time, involving students and professors, including one who remained on faculty, a physicist named Wendell Furry. Both HUAC and McCarthy called Furry to testify. At first he declined to speak, citing his Fifth Amendment right against self-incrimination. Then, during televised hearings in 1954, he agreed to discuss his own past as a Communist, but he adamantly refused to name names. Congress voted him in contempt. The new Harvard president, Nathan Pusey, defended Furry, and he managed to avoid prison time. But the episode demonstrated the ambition of congressional investigators to reach into the highest levels of American education, and the fact that, for the moment, there was little to stop them.

After being attacked by Senators McCarthy and Dirksen in Washington and losing his job at Bronx Science, Julius Hlavaty suffered a further indignity. His sole book, a student primer called *Review Digest on Solid Geometry*, was added to a list of titles to be removed from government-sponsored overseas libraries. In an acid-flecked letter published in *The New York Times*, Hlavaty wrote that his book "consists exclusively of questions, problems, and solutions in solid geometry, logarithmic and trigonometric tables, and reprints of past examinations in solid geometry. Yet it has been thought important to notify all United States libraries abroad to ban this apparently 'dangerous' and 'controversial' work."

Other books on the list included the novels of Howard Fast and the poems of Langston Hughes, two authors who had likewise refused to discuss their political beliefs before Congress. As was the case in school libraries at home, those abroad were rarely told to remove works with actual subversive content; there weren't any. Rather, the edict from the State Department was to sequester books by anyone suspected of Communist affiliation, or who had taken the Fifth Amendment before Congress. Even a minor connection to a book was enough; *The Selected Works of Tom Paine* was removed because Fast had edited it. The use of the Fifth Amendment, a department representative told reporters, "Has created a public impression regarding these authors which, justified or not, raises serious doubts as to whether their works contribute to the purposes of the program." When that same official labeled such books "controversial," reporters pressed him to define the term. He could not.

Libraries around the world followed suit, removing copies of more than three hundred titles by dozens of writers. A worldwide survey by *The New York Times* found that the policy was inconsistently carried out. Books were burned in Tokyo, but merely set aside in a locked room in Sydney. A book by *New York Times* reporter Walter Duranty that was removed from the more than forty Amerika Haus libraries across West Germany was left on the shelf in Vienna. An overzealous librarian in Buenos Aires removed not just proscribed titles like *The Maltese Falcon* but Whittaker Chambers's aggressively anti-Communist *Witness* too.

Though all this happened on President Eisenhower's watch, even he was taken aback by the federal government's foray into censorship. In June 1953 he traveled to Hanover, New Hampshire, to deliver the commencement address at Dartmouth College. "Don't join the book burners," he told the gathered students and families. "How will we defeat communism unless we know what it is, and what it teaches, and why does it have such an appeal for men, why are so many people swearing allegiance to it? . . . They are part of America. And even if they think ideas that are contrary to ours, their right to say them, their right to record them, and their right to have them at places where they are accessible to others is unquestioned, or it isn't America."

22

A Race for Death

President Eisenhower may have clashed with Joe McCarthy over the Bohlen nomination, and he may have been offended by the book-burning zeal of his countrymen, but he was in other ways just as militantly anti-Communist as they were. He agreed that Communism was both a global challenge and a domestic problem, and he believed that his two predecessors had done too little to stop it. He urged his attorney general, Herbert Brownell, to expand the list of subversive organizations. And his executive order to replace Truman's loyalty program with his own greatly expanded the scope of investigations into the federal workforce.

The biggest test of Eisenhower's commitment to Red Scare justice came in mid-spring 1953. Julius and Ethel Rosenberg had received their death sentences in 1951, but a string of appeals had stretched through the intervening two years. Now it was clear that their time was running out, and that their executions, at Sing Sing prison in Westchester County, were fast approaching. Eisenhower was adamant in his position that the pair had to die as punishment for their crimes. But almost as soon as he took office, he began receiving appeals from around the country and overseas, arguing that a groundswell of support for the Rosenbergs made the cost of carrying out the sentence too high. They had two children who would be left orphans. Commuting their sentences and remanding them to life in prison, several of Eisenhower's advisers told him, could win him enormous credit with moderate voters at home while demonstrating to millions of people around the world that American justice was both firm and merciful. The events of the Red Scare so far—the Hiss trial, the Smith Act case, the riots in Peekskill—had already done much to weaken America's position in the battle for the world's hearts and minds during the early Cold War. Now came the Rosenbergs.

It had taken time for the shock of the Rosenberg verdict to translate into action among their supporters, both at home and overseas. During the trial and their appeals, the Rosenbergs' supporters had believed that there was so little evidence to convict them, too many holes in the case, too many questions about the seemingly damning testimony of David Greenglass, Ethel Rosenberg's brother. And many in the United States had been cowed by the overwhelming, bloodthirsty elation that had swept the country after the verdict—millions of people who had paid little attention to the trial rejoiced in the streets when they heard about the sentence.

There was also the issue of Judaism. The Rosenbergs, David Greenglass, Morton Sobell, Klaus Fuchs, and most of the other members of Julius's espionage ring were Jewish. So too were Judge Samuel Kaufman, District Attorney Irving Saypol, and Saypol's assistant Roy Cohn. The core of the Rosenbergs' supporters included many Jews as well. For that reason some shrank from leaping to their defense after the verdict, wary of aligning themselves with condemned traitors at a time when anti-Semitism was blatant and rampant, and the memories of the Nazi era were still fresh. "Among the grown-ups, two compelling questions were unspoken," the journalist Sam Roberts wrote, recalling his own impressions of the era as a boy in New York. "Less than a decade after the Holocaust, how could Jews have done this to America? And how could America have done this to Jews?"

Slowly, though, the progressive press began to take up their cause. In a widely read series of articles, the journalist William A. Reuben dissected the prosecution in *The National Guardian*. Others wrote stinging take-downs of Saypol and Kaufman. Grassroots groups like the National Committee to Secure Justice in the Rosenberg Case, founded by one of the couple's neighbors in Manhattan, steadily gained followers. As the couple and their lawyers pressed their last appeals, their innocence became a new orthodoxy on the left. The Rosenbergs were the "first victims of the American fascist state," the refrain went, and anyone who disagreed, or even questioned their defense, was accused of being a McCarthyite.

The irony is that McCarthy himself had little to do with the case. Of course he supported the verdict, and cheered the sentence. But he had never done much more than cheerlead. What mattered more to him was the ongoing war in Korea, the precedent of spies like Alger Hiss, and above all the government's conviction that the drumbeat toward their death would force one or both of the Rosenbergs to start talking about their connections to the Soviet spy apparatus. The FBI placed a mole in the cell next to Julius Rosenberg at the House of Detention in Manhattan, where he was being held until his transfer to Sing Sing. The mole was there to glean whatever information he could, but also to act as a sensor of sorts, allowing the FBI to gauge whether Julius was any closer to talking.

He wasn't. Though the mole accumulated a few scraps of information, his reports made it clear that Rosenberg was convinced of his innocence, without remorse about his actions, and sure that the government would relent. Ethel was no less steeled, even when it became clear that she would never see her children again. "She called our bluff," William P. Rogers, the deputy attorney general, later told Roberts.

If many Americans remained convinced of the Rosenbergs' guilt and the rightness of their sentence, the belief was not shared in Europe. There too their case had taken time to catch the public's attention, but by mid-1952 a pro-Rosenberg movement had taken hold. Posters featuring an enormous, grotesque, smiling caricature of Dwight D. Eisenhower, with electric chairs for teeth, began popping up on walls around Paris, drawn by a renowned left-wing cartoonist named Louis Mittelberg. Like millions of other French citizens, Mittelberg had admired Eisenhower as a liberating general during World War II, but had soured over the president's insistence on executing the Rosenbergs. By summer's end reproductions of Mittelberg's image were everywhere—not just on posters but aside editorials, on handbills passed out at protests, and on placards carried along Avenue Gabriel in Paris, in front of the U.S. embassy.

That fall translated transcripts of the Rosenberg trial finally landed in France. To people already sympathetic to the cause, the documents made clear what they already believed: that the trial was a scam, that David Greenglass had perjured himself, and that the United States was preparing to execute two innocent people. The French Communist Party took up the cause, as did the Comité Français de Défense des Rosenberg, founded in December 1952. The former rallied the far-left base, while the Comité developed a broader following among the French political center. Between December 1952 and the Rosenbergs' execution the following June, there were eighty rallies in Paris alone, filled with flyers showing the doe-eyed Rosenberg boys and papered with pamphlets quoting a letter Ethel wrote from prison: "We are not martyrs or heroes and we don't want to become them. We are young, too young for death. We ardently want to see our two sons, Michael and Robert, grow and become men."

There was a geopolitical aspect to the French embrace of the Rosenbergs. France was still years from reckoning with its role in the Holocaust, but awareness and guilt were there, barely submerged. So was a steady anti-Americanism on the left, fueled by the Cold War and wounded French cultural pride. The Rosenberg case, it seemed, put America in its place, showing that it too was savagely anti-Semitic and, below its superficial promise of freedom and the rule of law, a proto-fascist state. The philosopher Jean-Paul Sartre called the case a "a legal lynching which smears with blood a whole nation," connecting it to America's other great sin of slavery and white supremacy. Others called it the American Dreyfus Affair, referring to the 1894 case of a Jewish officer in the French army wrongly accused of passing secret documents to the Germans. The French Communists were especially exercised by this angle, because the fall of 1952 saw a series of anti-Semitic purges of the Czechoslovak Communist Party in Prague, and the Rosenbergs offered a distraction. Jacques Duclos, the French party chairman, went so far as to say that while "the conviction of U.S. atom spies Julius and Ethel Rosenberg was an example of anti-Semitism . . . the execution of eight Jews in Czechoslovakia last week was not."

Sympathy for the Rosenbergs was not limited to the Communists. By late spring 1953 some 150 non-Communist deputies in the French Assembly had signed a petition for clemency, as had hundreds of French priests and clergy. In a call with John Foster Dulles, Jean Monnet, the French diplomat then overseeing the European Coal and Steel Community (a forerunner of the European Union), told him the Rosenberg case was "the most troublesome issue affecting relations between the United States and Europe."

The French response worried American diplomats, especially during the transfer of power from Truman to Eisenhower. On May 15 Douglas Dillon, the new ambassador to France, wrote an "eyes only" telegram to Dulles. "I am deeply concerned with long-term effect of possible execution of Rosenbergs on French opinion," he began. By then Cohn had joined the McCarthy staff, and had just completed his whirlwind tour through Europe with Schine. "Nothing could be better calculated," Dillon wrote about the trip, "to convince waverers that the Rosenbergs, if executed, will be victims of what the European press freely terms McCarthyism."

Dillon pleaded with Dulles—and by extension Eisenhower—to consider clemency, in the interest of national security. The president did give the issue thought, and his archives are full of meeting transcripts, reports, and letters generated by the White House during the first six months of 1953.

"The actions of these people have exposed to greater danger of death literally millions of our citizens," Eisenhower wrote to Clyde Miller, a friend from his time as president of Columbia. "The very real question becomes how far this can be permitted by a government that, regardless of every consideration of mercy and compassion, is also required to be a just government in serving the interests of all its citizens." And against Dillon's concern, he asserted the need to push back against Communists' belief that "free governments—and especially the American government—are notoriously weak and fearful and that consequently subversive and other kind of activity can be conducted against them with no real fear of dire punishment on the part of the perpetrator." The president would not budge.

The White House was not the only part of Washington where the politics of the Cold War and the high drama of the Rosenbergs collided. The case was tearing the Supreme Court apart.

For much of the time since the couple's conviction in 1951, the nine justices had watched with no small amount of trepidation as the case climbed its way up toward them through the appeals process. Although

Truman had appointed his friend Fred Vinson as chief justice in an effort to bring consensus and comity to the court, he had barely managed to achieve the former and had failed utterly at the latter, though the justices' fierce animosities had remained largely hidden from the public. The prospect of considering the Rosenberg case threatened to blow it all into the open.

The court had already rejected attempts by the Rosenbergs' lawyers to hear their appeal. Now they were set to be executed on June 19. Three days before that date, Justice William O. Douglas arrived at his chambers at 11 a.m. to find four lawyers for the Rosenbergs, plus three from the government, waiting with yet another attempt. Though he was known as a liberal, Douglas was an odd pick for a last-ditch effort by the lawyers to save their clients. While the couple's plight seemed to awaken something of the old progressive fighter in Felix Frankfurter, Douglas had refused to join in his colleague's willingness to consider their appeals, and instead had joined the majority in denying them a hearing. This was the same man who had written so many dissents in Red Scare cases, standing up for civil liberties during a turbulent time. Frankfurter, never a fan of Douglas, thought he knew what was going on: Douglas, he believed, was a politician at heart, having even considered leaving the court to become Roosevelt's running mate in 1944. He heard the bloodthirsty calls for the Rosenbergs' death, and perhaps had been on the receiving end of one too many angry letters sent to him after his Red Scare dissents. In Frankfurter's mind, Douglas had bent to the anger of the Red Scare.

But then, in late May, Douglas began to change tack. He sent around a memo explaining that he now thought that the prosecutors in the Rosenberg case had biased the jury by commenting favorably on the arrest of one of Julius Rosenberg's accomplices. The defense lawyers sensed an opening. After all, what other chance did they have?

Sitting in Douglas's office, they presented a novel argument: The Rosenbergs had been tried under the wrong law. The Espionage Act of 1917, which had been used to convict them, did not cover atomic secrets; the 1946 Atomic Energy Act did. And that law said that for someone to be sentenced to death, the government had to prove that they had done so with the explicit intent to harm the country, which the Rosenbergs had not. And even then, they could only be convicted with the jury's recommendation, which had not been offered in the case. The lawyers also pointed out that potentially helpful testimony from David Greenglass had been impounded and not shown to the Supreme Court during previous attempts to get an appeal to them. The lawyers were not asking Douglas to agree to hear the case; they only asked for a stay of the execution so the court could consider their argument.

Douglas was impressed, but unsure what to do. "The question was analogous to the case in which, while a burglar was entering a house, the penalty for burglary was lightened," he wrote in his memoirs. "Which penalty should be applied, the heavier one or the lesser one?" He stayed at the court building until 1 a.m., wary of leaving while hundreds of reporters, photographers, and protesters milled around outside. He went out a back door and drove to Chief Justice Vinson's apartment. Should he grant the stay? The chief justice said no. Douglas called Frankfurter a few hours later; Frankfurter told him to ignore Vinson and trust his instincts. Just before noon the next morning, Douglas issued the stay. Then he got in his car, heading west toward his boyhood home in Yakima, Washington, for a few days of rest. He may have avoided the crowd around the Supreme Court Building, but word was out about the appeal. Before he left he received an anonymous telegram from Yakima: "If you grant the Rosenberg's [sic] a stay, there will be lynch party waiting for you here."

Douglas made it to the Pittsburgh suburbs before stopping at a motel for the night. It was June 17, 1953. He was unloading his car, listening to a symphony on the radio, when a news flash cut in. Vinson had called a special session, for the following day, to consider Douglas's stay. The chief justice had consulted Attorney General Brownell and had decided on the session without trying to track down Douglas first, let alone wrangle the five votes usually needed to call it. Douglas threw his bags back in the car and hurried back to Washington. He made it just in time for the session.

The justices fought all that day and into the next. "This is a race for death," Justice Black said. "This will be a black day for the Court. I plead that it not be decided today." Clerks several offices away said they could hear Frankfurter yelling. The most that could happen, he said, was for the case to be sent back to the lower courts to consider these new points—not a full reprieve. "The Rosenbergs were behind bars; they could be executed in October as well as in June," Douglas wrote, siding with Frankfurter and Black. But the other six justices could not be moved. The justices vacated the stay.

The court announced its decision on the morning of June 19, the day the Rosenbergs were scheduled to be executed. One of their lawyers, Fyke Farmer, sped through rush-hour traffic to Black's house in Alexandria, Virginia, hoping the one judge who had always sided with them would somehow come through at the last minute, though he knew not how. Accounts differ on what happened next. Farmer later said he found the Black home empty, the justice at the hospital for elective surgery. But one of Black's biographers, Roger Newman, said the justice was not only at his home, but out back, playing tennis with his daughter, Martha Josephine. She went in to answer the door, then came back to tell him what Farmer wanted.

Black, standing on the court in his tennis shorts, his racket dripping limply from his hand, broke down. "I can't do it," he cried. "Josephine, tell them I can't do it."

Shut out by the courts, the Rosenberg lawyers made one last effort to win them a little more life. Their executions were scheduled for 11 p.m. on Friday, after sundown and therefore during Shabbat, the Jewish holy day. Their lawyers asked the Bureau of Prisons for a few days' delay; instead, officials moved up the time, to 8 p.m., just before sunset.

Julius went first, and was pronounced dead at 8:06. Minutes later, Ethel was strapped to the same electric chair, which had been swiftly mopped of her husband's urine. It took five shocks over almost five minutes before she died.

In Paris, Rome, Berlin and dozens of other foreign cities, thousands of pro-Rosenberg protesters had gathered in plazas and churches to wait into the night for the news. They rioted the next day. One person was shot in Paris. Workers in Italy went on strike, and someone threw a brick at the U.S. embassy in Dublin. Thousands of their supporters marched two-by-two around the Treasury Building in downtown Washington, hoping to catch the attention of President Eisenhower in the White House next door. Thousands more denounced the execution in Manhattan's Union

Square. But there could be no doubt where the feelings of the country lay. Passersby yelled at the demonstrators in Washington to "Go Back to Russia!" South of the White House, police had to fight to separate a mob of seven thousand from attacking the pro-Rosenberg pickets. As news of the executions went out across the radio, drivers across the country honked their horns in celebration. Hecklers surrounded a few dozen protesters standing vigil outside the federal courthouse in Los Angeles and shouted "Jew blood gonna fry," recalled the blacklisted screenwriter Bernard Gordon.

The mood inside the Supreme Court was somber, dejected. Whatever illusion of consensus Vinson had managed to maintain in Communist-related cases had shattered, leaving the justices despondent, especially those who had tried in vain to halt the executions. Frankfurter called it "the most anguishing situation since I have been on the court" and wrote in his dissent that "perfection may not be demanded of law, but the capacity to counteract inevitable, though rare, frailties is the mark of a civilized legal mechanism." Douglas, for once, agreed with his nemesis. "I know of no more serious danger to our legal system than occurs when *ideological* trials take place behind the façade of *legal* trials," he wrote.

23

A Dry Crucifixion

No single case illustrates the overwrought zeal for security during the Red Scare—or the willingness of petty men to abuse it to their own ends—than that of the physicist J. Robert Oppenheimer. Having shepherded the atomic bomb into existence and use, he stood as a colossus over the emerging scientific-industrial complex of the early postwar era. The Manhattan Project, which he had directed from his isolated mesa-top office in Los Alamos, New Mexico, united many of the world's top scientists from the University of Chicago, Berkeley, UCLA, and a dozen other campuses with the virtually inexhaustible resources of the U.S. military. Some 130,000 people worked on the project, which in just a few years cost $2.2 billion ($38.2 billion in today's dollars), an almost unimaginable sum for a government whose entire budget in 1940 had been $9.5 billion. Almost all that work had been under Oppenheimer's direction. He exemplified the harnessing of high-theory science and its rapid application through the awesome power of the federal government. Even his rumpled porkpie hat achieved iconic status: For their inaugural issue in May 1948, the editors of *Physics Today* put the hat on the cover, alone, without a caption because none was necessary.

Tall, spindly, sallow-cheeked, with ice-glinting eyes, Oppenheimer seemed to hail from another planet, though he was one of the few native-born Americans among the country's new atomic clergy. He spoke with precision and grace about not just the latest developments in physics but literature, Freudian theory, and Hindu philosophy. There was a tragic romance about Oppenheimer, a sense that he had been given great intellectual

gifts and now had to bear the awful consequences of their employment—
he was, by his own estimation, "a destroyer of worlds," a loose translation
of a line from the Bhagavad Gita, which he had read in the original San-
skrit. He was also imperious, arrogant, and pedantic. He had a habit of
cutting people off in the middle of a sentence, then completing it for them.
And if he stated those sentences better and with more nuance than the
original speaker might have ever hoped to do, that did not make his trans-
gression any more forgivable. Later, after his humiliations, he was able to
recast himself as a humble, wronged man. But those who knew him, knew
better. His friend and fellow physicist Victor Weisskopf said Oppenheimer
was "impressed by their need to come to him," they being everyone from
hordes of students to Senate select committees. Another, less friendly associate, the mathematician John von Neumann, quipped that "some people
profess guilt to claim credit for the sin."

Oppenheimer had spent much of his youth in worlds apart from the
everyday. The son of wealthy secular Jews in Manhattan, he had grown
up amid his family's Van Goghs and well-stocked libraries. He raced
through Harvard, graduating summa cum laude in three years, followed
by doctoral work in Germany. He later said that during these times that
he rarely picked up a newspaper and never owned a radio. He was by his
own admission unaware of the world around him, even as Europe began
its descent into fascism. That began to change after he took up a teaching
post at the University of California, Berkeley, and fell into the Bay Area's
vibrant progressive scene. He supported the 1934 dockworkers' strike and
met the labor leader Harry Bridges at a party. He backed the progressive author Upton Sinclair's 1934 run for governor and, with several other
professors, gave $1,500 to buy an ambulance for the Republican forces in
Spain. He joined the executive board of the ACLU's California chapter. He
later joked that he probably signed up with every Communist front group
on the West Coast. It was a political promiscuity he later attributed to his
own naïveté, but it was not so different from that of other progressives
during the heady, early days of the New Deal era. If Oppenheimer was a
fellow traveler, there were many other people traveling with him.

Oppenheimer insisted that he never joined the Communist Party,
and despite extensive efforts, the FBI could never find proof otherwise.

(Later scholarship by John Earl Haynes and Harvey Klehr, among others, drawing on evidence unavailable until after Oppenheimer's death, makes a strong claim that he was in fact a party member, likely in secret and only for a few years in the late 1930s and early 1940s; more to the point, Haynes and Klehr conclude he was definitely not a spy, and no compelling evidence exists to show otherwise.) He did, however, have many Communist friends, and until the mid-1940s clearly sympathized with them, even after he was chosen to lead the Manhattan Project team. His wife, Kitty, was a party member; so was a girlfriend, Jean Tatlock, and his brother Frank. At Berkeley he became close friends with a dashing professor of French literature, Haakon Chevalier, an open party member who, in about 1943, suggested to Oppenheimer that he might use his new position with the government to garner information useful to America's Soviet allies. Oppenheimer demurred, but he failed to report Chevalier's approach to his new government handlers.

Oppenheimer never hid his progressive leanings, nor his connections with left-wing radicals. They were well known by General Leslie Groves, who oversaw the Manhattan Project for the government, and John Lansdale Jr., who ran security at Los Alamos; both nevertheless cleared him for work. In the late 1940s, as the Red Scare gathered steam, controversy seemed to pass Oppenheimer by. Even though the FBI had opened a file on him in 1941 and J. Edgar Hoover was convinced that he was a security risk, and even though HUAC had called him to testify in 1947 about security concerns around the atomic bomb program, he was allowed to proceed with his postwar work as a consultant for the Atomic Energy Commission. Oppenheimer played a critical part in a report, coauthored by Dean Acheson, calling for international control of atomic energy. In 1947 he came east to take up the directorship of the Institute for Advanced Study, in Princeton, New Jersey, at the invitation of one of its board members, the financier Lewis Strauss.

The politics of atomic warfare were changing. Since well before the atomic bomb's first test at a site Oppenheimer called Trinity, a group of Los Alamos scientists, led by the Hungarian émigré Edward Teller, had argued that the fission bomb, of the sort dropped twice on Japan, was just the beginning, and that a much more powerful fusion bomb was possible. It relied on hydrogen isotopes for its reaction and so was called a hydrogen, or thermonuclear, bomb, but at the time everyone called it the Super. Especially after the Soviets detonated their own fission bomb in 1949, Teller insisted that rapidly developing the Super was a matter of national, even planetary, life and death. Many in the military and Congress agreed, especially those who believed that a war with the Soviets was inevitable. Better to attack them first with a weapon of overwhelming proportion, they said, than to wait for them to attack with something similar.

Oppenheimer vehemently disagreed. The Super was an immoral weapon, he said. A single bomb could pack as much explosive force as a third of all the ordnance dropped during the entirety of World War II. But he also thought it impractical. All the resources put into developing a Super could go toward building a massive stockpile of fission bombs, he said. Oppenheimer was no pacifist: While he believed that using a Super would be suicidal, he approvingly foresaw the possibility of using small, tactical atomic bombs on a future battlefield, and made that point repeatedly, to anyone who would listen. Nor was Oppenheimer alone. Most of the scientists who had worked on the Manhattan Project were uncomfortable with the new world they had wrought and feared making it worse. But he was by far the most prominent, the best-spoken, and the most charismatic. It was only a matter of time before Teller and his other enemies decided he had to go.

Teller, rotund and thickly browed, had always been a dark, brooding presence among the atomic scientists at Los Alamos, and remained there to run it after Oppenheimer's departure. He brought an uncompromising zeal to his anti-Communism and, by extension, his work advocating for the Super. Anyone who disagreed was, in his eyes, not just an intellectual opponent, but a possible subversive. Even if they did not mean to undermine national security, their opposition to what he believed was the country's best interest made them a threat to it. He tried to draw Oppenheimer back to Los Alamos, but he declined; so did several other veterans of the Manhattan Project. Teller decided it was a conspiracy, that Oppenheimer was plotting against him, using his charisma to woo physicists away from the Super program.

Joining Teller was Strauss, a member of the Atomic Energy Commission board, the same man who had brought Oppenheimer to Princeton but who had since come to doubt his decision. A strictly observant Jew who grew up too poor for college and started adulthood as a shoe salesman in Richmond, Virginia, a conservative Republican who saw the world in black-and-white terms, Strauss looked contemptuously at Oppenheimer's wealthy, secular Jewish upbringing, his elite education, his progressive ideas and nuanced political perspectives. Strauss was brilliant, maybe not like Oppenheimer, but smart enough, and he added to that a genius for political infighting—"more elbows than an octopus," said one associate. He was an early partisan of the Super, and like Teller he brooked no dissent. "If you disagree with Lewis about anything, he assumes you're just a fool at first," wrote Joseph and Stewart Alsop in a damning book about the Oppenheimer affair. "But if you go on disagreeing with him, he concludes you must be a traitor." And Oppenheimer was not just a single dissenter, but the bannerman for the opposition. Strauss agreed with Teller.

Strauss left the Atomic Energy Commission in 1950 in a dispute with the Truman administration, but returned after Eisenhower appointed him its chairman—this despite the fact that Strauss had openly campaigned for Senator Robert Taft in 1952. Strauss made it clear that he intended to shake things up. He adopted the same "positive loyalty" position that John Foster Dulles was implementing at the State Department: Employees were considered a risk until they could demonstrate otherwise. And he fully bought into Eisenhower's distinction between loyalty and security. Much in the same way that a person in the Soviet Union could be "objectively" a class enemy, whatever their beliefs, Strauss believe that even a committed American patriot could be a dangerous security risk based on their behavior, their beliefs, even their positions on policy matters. Oppenheimer was doomed.

There were supporting players in the unfolding tragedy. William Borden was a staff aide to the Joint Committee on Atomic Energy who became something of a Javert to Oppenheimer's Jean Valjean. As a bomber pilot during World War II, flying over England, he had watched, stunned, as a German V-2 rocket rose from the Dutch coast and shot westward, moving so fast he felt like he was sitting still in his cockpit. Ever since, he believed that technology's headlong advancements would soon create a winner-take-all bounty for the country that achieved them first. For years Borden had been convinced that Oppenheimer was not just unreliable but an active Soviet agent. He pored over his security files, looking for the damning evidence. He continued even after he left government and went to work for a defense contractor in Pittsburgh. Borden amassed his findings—almost all of them repackaged pieces of well-known, well-worn revelations about Oppenheimer's distant past—into a three-and-a-half-page, single-spaced report, and sent it to J. Edgar Hoover at the FBI. "It seems reasonable to estimate that he is and for some years has been in a position to compromise more vital and detailed information affecting the national defense and security than any other individual in the United States," Borden wrote. "More probably than not J. Robert Oppenheimer is an agent of the Soviet Union."

Eisenhower read the report and was livid. What if McCarthy found it? The senator was already interested in Oppenheimer's story, and had made noises about opening an investigation. The president had held the senator at bay by dispatching Nixon to beg him off, telling him that the White House would soon take care of the matter. Now, Borden forced Eisenhower's hand. With more alacrity and open determination than he had brought against McCarthy, the president ordered a "blank wall" to go up between Oppenheimer and the Atomic Energy Commission. When Strauss suggested a special administrative hearing to decide a permanent solution for the atomic scientist, Eisenhower gave him free rein.

On the afternoon of December 21, 1953, Strauss invited Oppenheimer into his office, shut the door, and, with only a minimal effort to hide his glee, told the physicist what he had in store for him—though he maintained the fiction that his hands were tied by bureaucracy and the president. The irony was that Oppenheimer's security clearance was set to expire in a few months anyway. But Strauss wanted to do more than get rid of him; he wanted to debase him, humiliate him, ruin him so that he could no longer cast influence over atomic policymaking. Strauss offered to let Oppenheimer drop his clearance voluntarily, likely knowing that he was too proud and obstinate to say yes.

A few days later, FBI agents appeared at the Oppenheimer home outside

Princeton to confiscate boxes upon boxes of records. Strauss established a three-man panel to run the hearing, and picked its members. He allowed Oppenheimer to appear with a lawyer, but he also hired his own—not an AEC staff lawyer, but a fierce, feared prosecutor named Roger Robb. He permitted Robb and his team to review raw FBI data, including transcripts of illegal wiretaps. He did not afford Oppenheimer's team the same access; after all, Strauss insisted, this was not a trial but an administrative hearing. Even the judges—and really, that's what they were, judges—got to paw through the files, which, in their unprocessed state, contained all sorts of scurrilous rumors and twice-baked hearsay.

The hearing took eight weeks, but it was over before it began. Even the setting was tawdry: the stuffy second floor of a dilapidated temporary building at 16th Street and Constitution, right on the National Mall, one of dozens erected during the war and slated for imminent demolition. Except when he was testifying, Oppenheimer sat on a sagging old sofa, off to the side, a witness to his own execution. A parade of witnesses came in his defense—big names, like George Kennan and Leslie Groves. But none of it mattered. Tiny things became mortal sins; a recent dinner in Paris with his old friend Chevalier became proof that Oppenheimer was continuing in his radical-left ways; his failure to remember obscure, long-past details proved that he was covering up something big. Robb was relentless, and got Groves to admit that, if he were to consider Oppenheimer today for security clearance, he would deny him. The final shiv came from Teller himself: "If it is a question of wisdom and judgment as demonstrated by actions since 1945, then I would say one would be wiser not to grant clearance." As he passed Oppenheimer on his way out, he put out his hand and said, "I'm sorry."

The judges split 2 to 1. Ward Evans, an emeritus professor of chemistry at Northwestern known for spouting racist nonsense, surprised everyone by writing a fierce dissent. "They cleared him," he wrote, referring to Groves and the wartime military. "They took a chance on him because of his special talents and he continued to do a good job. Now when the job is done, we are asked to investigate him for practically the same derogatory information." The other two on the panel—Gordon Gray, president of the University of North Carolina, and Tom Morgan, an executive at the Sperry Corporation—gave four reasons for recommending revocation of Oppenheimer's clearance, including his "serious disregard for the requirements of the security system," his "susceptibility to influence," his opposition to the hydrogen bomb, and being "less than candid" during the hearing. The ruling was, Evans retorted, "a black mark on the escutcheon of our country."

To keep ahead of the Soviets, the Americans were employing German scientists who had worked for the Nazis during World War II. At the exact same time, they were excommunicating an American scientist who had done more than almost anyone else to help win that same war. Right-minded observers called it what it was, a farce, a self-inflicted wound to the nation, a harbinger of much worse. "When the winning side starts trying to outlaw the losers as 'security risks,' as happened in the China service and is now beginning to happen in the scientific-military world, one wonders what sort of people our future governments will attract," Arthur Schlesinger Jr. wrote in *The Atlantic*. But their voice mattered little in the face of a national security state that would not only permit no dissent, but destroy those who dared to offer it.

Strauss had what he wanted. As a twisted consolation prize, he arranged for Oppenheimer to keep his post at the Institute for Advanced Study, and even got him a raise. But Oppenheimer was forever severed from atomic research; he could not even casually discuss it with his former colleagues. He eventually quit the institute, and in the few years he had left—he died in 1967—lived mostly in a spartan cottage on St. John, in the U.S. Virgin Islands. Still the FBI hounded him. Agents followed him whenever he visited the mainland, and regularly interviewed people he might have encountered on the island. Some say he took the blow with equanimity. But one day a friend said to him that he'd been subjected to a "dry crucifixion." Oppenheimer retorted, "You know, it wasn't so very dry. I can still feel the warm blood on my hands."

PART IV

24

The Tonangeber

By late summer 1953, the Supreme Court was in tatters. Chief Justice Vinson, Harry Truman's backslapping drinking buddy, had struggled to build consensus among the eight other justices, but at the expense of judicial coherence and the protection of civil liberties—and for that he is remembered as one of the worst chief justices in the history of the court. He had failed to rally a consensus during the fractious Rosenberg appeals, and even gone behind Justice Douglas's back to undermine his motion to stay their execution. Now he was dead, struck down by a massive heart attack at his Washington apartment on September 8, 1953. Justice Frankfurter, who thought the chief justice intellectually unfit for the high court, would not miss him. Vinson's death, he told two of his clerks, was "the first indication I have ever had that there is a God." But if so it was a trickster deity, for Vinson left behind him a morass of thorny, potentially explosive issues, above all school desegregation and the Red Scare.

Speculation had it that President Eisenhower would fill the opening with a Catholic jurist, since the court had none at the moment and powerful supporters were urging him to. But Eisenhower and Herbert Brownell, his attorney general, resisted. Their priority was an establishment Republican, someone with clear political bona fides and strong leadership skills, "a man of broad experience, professional competence, and with an unimpeachable record and reputation for integrity." It was not long before the president and Brownell settled on a single name: Earl Warren, the governor of California.

Warren had been Eisenhower's runner-up choice for vice president, though Nixon had outmaneuvered him, a bitter experience that made Nixon into Warren's lifelong enemy. As a consolation, the president had promised to nominate Warren to the first high-level federal vacancy that appeared once his administration began. Eisenhower apparently thought that meant solicitor general, and didn't expect a Supreme Court seat to open instead. Now, Warren pressed his case, even cutting short a hunting trip to insist, in a call with Brownell, that the president fulfill his promise. And he flat out demanded to be made chief justice, rather than have Eisenhower elevate a sitting member of the court, then name Warren to fill his associate spot.

On paper, Warren had everything the president wanted. He was the popular third-term governor of the nation's fastest-growing state, having won reelection from majorities of both parties. Before that he had been state attorney general and Alameda County prosecutor, where he had developed a reputation for his strict commitment to law and order. As governor he had steered his state through the tumult of World War II, then harnessed the power of the war's bounty—a booming population, federal subsidies, manufacturing, advanced technology—to turn it into the world's most vibrant economy. He was by temperament and biography a rock-ribbed Republican: He climbed out of genteel poverty through hard work and integrity, and he expected the same from his family, friends, and constituents. But in practice he was quite liberal, even progressive. He believed that the role of government was to spread the wealth of the state through programs like expanded health care access, progressive taxation, and aid to the indigent. "He's a Democrat and doesn't know it," Truman said in 1948.

Warren was the son of Norwegian immigrants who had changed their surname from Vaare upon arrival in Los Angeles, shortly after the birth of his father in 1864. Earl, who did not have a middle name because his father said he was too poor to give him one, was born in Los Angeles in 1891 and grew up in Bakersfield, a farming town toward the southern end of the San Joaquin Valley. He was a proud product of the California public school system, from his local elementary through Berkeley and its law school. He was not an especially distinguished student, by his own admission, but he was a genius politician. He took inspiration from the progressive Republicans of his youth, especially Hiram Johnson, the wildly popular governor and senator who ran as Theodore Roosevelt's vice president on the Bull Moose ticket in 1912.

What Warren lacked in scholarship he made up in other forms of intelligence. He was tall, fully built, with an egg-shaped head framed by wire-rim glasses and a short shock of tow-head blond hair. He smiled, he bounded, he took control of rooms the second he entered them. He was a joiner and a natural leader; people gravitated to him, and he to them. If Joe McCarthy represented the era's male id, Warren was its ego: optimistic, civic-minded, living an upright life and believing in the best of people. There was a depth to Warren's conviviality, a bedrock belief in the importance of civil society to a healthy democracy. He insisted that people who came together with a spirit of mutual respect could solve anything, regardless of their differences. His energetic idealism was considered a bit corny, even at the time. But no one left his presence unimpressed with his conviction.

After a short stint in private practice and the Army, Warren went to work in the Alameda County district attorney's office in 1920. He was a law-and-order lawman, especially when it came to left-wing radicalism. Early on, he led the prosecution against a union leader with close ties to the newly formed Communist Party. The West Coast had been a hotbed of labor radicalism since the turn of the century, from Finnish loggers of the Pacific Northwest to stevedores in San Francisco Bay. Under California's Criminal Syndicalism Law, proving mere membership in the Communist Party was often enough to win a conviction. Warren, assigned to prosecute one such labor leader, overcame compelling objections about police misconduct to secure a fourteen-year sentence. He kept up pressure on local radicals, as well as substantial files, after becoming district attorney in 1925. He despised Communists, and took every opportunity to hunt them down, in the process winning acclaim from the state's business elite. In the 1930s he grew close with J. Edgar Hoover, who saw Warren as a valuable ally.

It was from that base that Warren launched his successful campaign for state attorney general in 1938. His election as California's chief law enforcement officer coincided with the onset of World War II and the likely inevitability of American involvement. Warren was no isolationist, and did what he could to encourage the expansion of the state's military-related industries—shipbuilding up north, aircraft factories around Los Angeles. Then the Japanese attacked Pearl Harbor.

Through the various fraternal organizations Warren had joined over the years, he was already linked to the thick strain of white nativism and anti-Asian racism that ran through California's elite. One such organization, the Native Sons of the Golden West, went so far as to call for Japanese Americans to be stripped of their citizenship, a motion Warren endorsed. When, in January 1942, calls began to go out for Japanese Americans to be moved away from West Coast cities and into detention camps, Warren came out fully in favor, a move not even J. Edgar Hoover supported.

Warren later claimed that he had studied the issue and decided as best he could, given what evidence he had at the harrowing time. It was indeed a frightening moment: Japanese submarines were said to be patrolling the West Coast, and in February 1942 one of them surfaced to fire a few dozen rounds at an oil field near Santa Barbara. But that was the Japanese navy, not Japanese residents or citizens. In fact there was no evidence, at the time or later, to suggest that Japanese people living in the United States, citizens or non, presented a threat to national security—a fact that Warren would have discovered if he had in fact studied the issue. Instead, he said, "The Japanese situation as it exists in this state today may well be the Achilles's heel of the entire civilian defense force." His reasoning was on its face racist, arguing that while Italian or German Americans could be readily understood and the spies among them sussed out, Japanese were inherently inscrutable, and therefore suspect. "We believe that when we are dealing with the Caucasian race we have methods that will test the loyalty of them," he told Congress that winter. "But when we deal with the Japanese we are in an entirely different field and we cannot form any opinion that we believe to be sound." He found it suspicious that they tended to live near critical infrastructure and work in agriculture, implying the possibility of not just individual disloyalty but a vast conspiracy.

He was far from alone in these beliefs, but that's the point. Warren got caught up in the hysteria—and as California's attorney general, he swiftly moved to do something about it. He lobbied Congress and the White

House to act, and on February 19, 1942, Roosevelt signed an executive order creating "exclusion zones" along the coast and authorizing the military to remove anyone from them that they wished. Evictions of Japanese and Japanese American residents began on March 24. Ultimately approximately 120,000 were sent to ten camps, their property was seized, and their civil liberties were effectively nullified. Warren's support never wavered.

Warren went on to win three elections to the governor's mansion and the Republican vice presidential nomination in 1948, alongside Governor Thomas Dewey of New York. By the end of the decade he was widely considered the best governor in America, by members of both parties. He was at the same time a moderate Republican, in line with the East Coast Establishment, and something wholly new, a small-d democrat who understood how to rally the disparate corners of his enormous state and the potential of an empowered, centralized government into one singular, world-beating dynamo.

There was nothing obvious in Warren's background to foretell his turn as chief justice and the nation's great tribune of civil liberties, and his wartime support for Japanese internment points in the opposite direction. But despite his record during World War II, there were clues. He had always believed deeply in the government's role to protect the "little guy," even when he was a prosecutor. He believed naïvely in the inherent rightness of law enforcement, so much so that he was willing to look away at minor infractions of civil liberties—because, he insisted, the police were there to protect the innocent.

Warren arrived at the Supreme Court in October 1953 as something of a blank slate. He did not have Felix Frankfurter's lengthy résumé of scholarly writings, or Hugo Black's estimable record as a trust-busting senator. He impressed his new colleagues as a proverbial hail-fellow-well-met, beaming with a slightly goofy but ever-winning smile as he shook their hands and said, "Hi, I'm Earl Warren!" He knew enough to show deference to Black, the senior justice, allowing him to run the first meeting of the justices during his inaugural term and assigning him one of their first big cases. And he asked Black for advice on what to read to prepare himself for his new role. "Aristotle on Rhetoric," the justice replied. Black was won over immediately. "I am by no means sure that an intelligent man with practical, hard common sense and integrity like he has is not as good a type to select as could be found in the country," he wrote in a letter to one of his sons.

When it came to the new chief, Frankfurter was even more effusive and self-aggrandizing than Black. Sixteen years before, Roosevelt had chosen Black over Frankfurter as his Supreme Court nominee, despite Frankfurter's strong support from progressives. To add to the insult, Roosevelt had then asked him to tutor Black in the finer points of constitutional law. (Roosevelt passed over Frankfurter again in 1938, naming Stanley Reed to the court, before finally nominating him in 1939.) Now Frankfurter took it upon himself to tutor his new chief. He blanketed Warren's desk with memos, suggested articles, and book chapters, along with notes complimenting him on even the smallest offhand comment made in conference. He looked past Warren's lack of scholarly heft to call him the "Tonangeber," German for "tone setter." Frankfurter, whose insistence on judicial restraint made him something of an odd duck on the court of the time, needed an ally, and saw Warren as an apt pupil in the ways of judicial deference to the elected branches.

Warren had a lot to learn, but he was no rube. He soaked up Frankfurter's instruction quickly, and in doing so shed much of his earlier naïveté, if not his idealism. Not long after he joined the court, the justices heard the case of *Irvine v. California*, in which police officers had illegally entered and wiretapped the home of a bookkeeper, gathering evidence later used to convict him. The issue was whether evidence gathered in violation of the Fourth Amendment, which prohibits warrantless search and seizure, could be used in court without violating the Fourteenth Amendment, which guarantees due process. The case was seemingly custom-built to appeal to Warren's law-and-order instincts, pitting an obviously guilty bookie against his beloved California legal system. Warren joined the majority in upholding the conviction. But he was bothered by the officers' misconduct, and joined Justice Robert Jackson, who wrote the decision, in recommending that the men be investigated by the Department of Justice. Warren was still thinking like a district attorney, still believing the system would correct itself.

But nothing happened. Political appointees at the Department of Justice also wanted action against the officers, but in the end no indictments emerged. Warren was dismayed. Here was an obvious violation of a person's constitutional rights, and the Department of Justice would do nothing to correct it. It was his first lesson that if the Supreme Court was going to uphold civil liberties, it would have to do more than defer to other branches and hope they do the right thing.

In one of his first Red Scare cases, Warren sided with the majority in upholding the right of the New York Board of Regents to deny a medical license to Edward Barsky, the former chairman of the Joint Anti-Fascist Refugee Committee. Like Helen Reid Bryan, another figure from the refugee organization, Barsky had gone to jail for refusing to give Congress his group's records. When he got out, he applied for a new license to practice medicine. But in the heat of the Red Scare, the licensing board had decided that no one affiliated with a subversive organization could be trusted to examine a patient's heartbeat or take a child's X-ray. Warren agreed with the majority opinion, which held that the control of licenses was "a vital part of a state's police power." Justices Douglas and Black, of course, dissented. "When a doctor cannot save lives in America because he is opposed to Franco in Spain," Douglas wrote in his dissent, "it is time to call a halt and look critically at the neurosis that has possessed us."

In both cases, Warren's instinct was to apply the law in favor of powerful government institutions. He always had. As prosecutor and attorney general, it had been his job to side with the government. As governor, he had built and managed vast public agencies. But now, on the court, he saw how those institutions, even when functioning as designed, could ruin lives. Maybe the New York Board of Regents had the power to prevent Barsky from practicing medicine. But in conversations with Justice Black, Warren began to wonder who benefited when it did. Certainly not Edward Barsky or his patients. And slowly, slowly, Warren began to come around. He did not ditch his commitment to law and order. What changed was his dawning awareness that the investigatory powers of Congress and the police powers of state and local governments were prone to abuse, and indeed were being widely abused during the Red Scare. And it was up to the courts to stop it.

25

Who Promoted Peress?

Dwight D. Eisenhower had come to the presidency as both a protector and a consensus builder. He took his mandate seriously: He would fight hard against Communism at home and abroad, but he would also accept the changes wrought by the New Deal and even extend them. This made him popular among establishment Republicans and even some moderate Democrats. But it put him increasingly at odds with his own party's right wing, not just the McCarthy types in Washington but millions of rank-and-file Republicans across the country. "This means eight more years of socialism," snorted one woman after Eisenhower defeated Robert Taft for the 1952 Republican convention.

Eisenhower was aware that his distaste for McCarthy and his wing of the party was politically problematic; in 1953 a large majority of Republicans still backed the Wisconsin Republican, and his popularity nationwide was above 40 percent. Eisenhower thought McCarthy was a "sorry mess." But he kept his displeasure private. "I have never indulged in personal indictment or attack," he wrote to his brother Milton. "To my mind, that practice smacks more of the coward and the fool than of the leader." In April 1953, he played a round of golf with Senator Taft, who began to lag halfway through and had to leave before the ninth hole. A medical exam found malignant cancer throughout his body, and he was dead by the end of July. Taft's death made Eisenhower the undisputed leader of the Republicans. It was now up to him to unite the moderate and right wings of his party—even if that meant sidelining McCarthy.

The president's approach would be to lie low and hope that an opportunity to strike appeared, ideally without being noticed. His first chance came in June, when McCarthy hired J. B. Matthews as the staff director for the Subcommittee on Investigations underneath the Committee on Government Operations, both of which were chaired by McCarthy. Matthews was already a veteran member of the McCarthy circle, brought in by Alfred Kohlberg of the China Lobby to provide the senator with names and research from his voluminous files, going back to his time working for Martin Dies and HUAC in the late 1930s. His arrival came soon after McCarthy had hired Karl Baarslag, the former director of the American Legion's anti-subversive activities, as a researcher, and not long after Roy Cohn joined as chief counsel. By all outward appearances, the McCarthy machine was only gaining strength. But McCarthy hired Matthews without telling his subcommittee colleagues, a clear breach of protocol. Worse, around the same time he was hired, Matthews published an article in *The American Mercury* declaring, in its first sentence, that "the largest single group supporting the Communist apparatus in the United States is composed of Protestant clergymen." Church leaders loudly protested; even conservative Southern Baptists cried foul. Overnight, Matthews became a liability. Several Conservative Republicans joined the rest of Congress in calling on McCarthy to fire him.

Eisenhower saw his chance. He had Vice President Nixon visit McCarthy in his office and persuade the senator that it was in his interest to ditch Matthews. McCarthy agreed, and offered to go right out and tell the Capitol Hill press corps. But then, following the president's instructions, Nixon kept the senator chatting for hours to keep him from making his announcement. Meanwhile, Eisenhower released a statement castigating the new hire. McCarthy was trapped: He couldn't back out of his promise to Nixon, but by going forward it appeared to all the world as though he was surrendering to the president. He dumped Matthews, handing the president a small victory.

The Matthews kerfuffle was just a warm-up skirmish before the main battle. It began at a nondescript military installation tucked just a few miles inland from the wide beaches of the New Jersey Shore. This was Fort Monmouth, headquarters to the Army's Signal Corps, a somewhat antiquated name for a unit tasked with conducting the military's radar and telecommunications research. As it expanded rapidly during the war, Fort Monmouth drew on the engineering talent coming out of New York City to staff its uniformed and civilian research staffs. As it did, rumors circulated about radical, pro-Soviet sentiment among some of the researchers—rumors that came with at least a whiff of anti-Semitism, since many of them were Jewish engineers who came to the Army after facing discrimination in the private sector. But the rumors did have some basis in fact: among those who passed through Monmouth's gates were Julius Rosenberg and Morton Sobell, both later convicted of atomic espionage. In 1951 the FBI investigated the fort's personnel and sent the Army a list of thirty-five potential security risks.

The Army claimed that it had the problem under control, and for a while it did. Most of the men named on the list were cleared, discharged, or transferred. But in mid-1953 someone leaked news of the list to McCarthy. It was an irresistible target. He had never been a fan of the Army; as a Marine during World War II, he had resented the way Army generals like Douglas MacArthur took credit for his own branch's successes. And poking at the Army was a way of poking at the president himself, an appealing prospect for the senator. McCarthy spent the summer gathering material, holding hearings on military training manuals, and subpoenaing a handful of civilian workers accused of subversion, yet still on the Army payroll.

His fishing expedition produced not a nibble, and in early October he and his new bride (and current secretary), Jean Kerr, left for a long honeymoon in the Bahamas. But just a few days after departing he came roaring back, his nuptial vacation cut short by a telegram from Cohn. McCarthy's investigators had uncovered "extremely dangerous espionage" at Fort Monmouth, it read. McCarthy landed in New York on October 13, and for several weeks his subcommittee—often just he and Cohn—grilled dozens of witnesses in an unused room at Foley Square. It was supposed to be a closed hearing, but every afternoon McCarthy would open the doors to a gaggle of reporters, feeding them increasingly dramatic reports of the proceedings inside. "If this develops as it has been developing it will involve the entire Signal Corps—and that goes beyond Fort Monmouth," he said on the first day. The Army conceded that there was a problem and promised, once again, to solve it, suspending a dozen employees within a week. But that only made the headlines bigger and drove McCarthy further. "McCarthy Charges Soviets Got Secrets," blared *The New York Times* on October 23. It seemed, for the moment, that he had struck gold: The Army was back on its heels, the public was following his every word, and best of all, he might actually find some Communists this time. He scheduled public hearings in November.

On November 6, 1953, just days ahead of McCarthy's hearings, Attorney General Brownell traveled to the Executive Club of Chicago. His plan— endorsed, with some hesitation, by Eisenhower—was to steal McCarthy's thunder with his own play at red-baiting. Standing before the city's business elite as they munched on a light lunch, he made a shocking announcement: President Truman had not only known about Harry Dexter White, the New Deal financial wizard accused of espionage before his untimely death in 1948, but had refused to act on what he knew even after repeated urging by J. Edgar Hoover. Brownell swung hard. "It is a source of humiliation to every American that during the period of the Truman administration the Communists were so strikingly successful in infiltrating the government of the United States," the attorney general said. A White House aide added to reporters, on background, that it was just the beginning—it was a "pretty good guess," the person said, that more such revelations about the Truman administration would be forthcoming.

Brownell's speech set off a firestorm. Representative Harold Velde, a retired FBI agent and the new Republican chairman of HUAC, subpoenaed Truman, the first time a congressional committee had demanded a president, current or former, appear before it. Truman shot back with a series of escalating counterattacks against Velde, HUAC, Brownell, and the White House, culminating with a televised address denouncing the attorney general for having "lied to the American people" and claiming that the FBI had in fact supported his decision not to go after White. "It is now evident that the present administration has fully embraced, for political advantage, McCarthyism," Truman said. "I am not referring to the senator from Wisconsin. He is only important in that his name has taken on a dictionary meaning of the word. It is the corruption of truth, the abandonment of the due process of law. It is the use of the big lie and the unfounded accusation against any citizen in the name of Americanism or security." And it would only get worse, he concluded. "This is not a partisan matter. This horrible cancer is eating at the vitals of America and it can destroy the great edifice of freedom."

The back-and-forth recriminations were not over. The next day Hoover appeared, in a surprise visit, before the Senate Internal Security Subcommittee, the body that was in some ways the upper chamber's equivalent of HUAC. The hearings were televised, so that viewers got a rare glimpse of the usually low-flying FBI director—"although often mentioned in the press, Hoover's picture rarely appears," noted *The Boston Globe*. With barely restrained words, Hoover calmly demolished Truman's claim. He insisted that "I felt it unwise for White to serve," and that he had said as much to the president. But Truman had ignored him, he said. Applause erupted. "The approval of the audience was the loudest of the day," the *Globe* wrote.

McCarthy piled on as well. He demanded, and received, airtime from the networks to respond to the president. But after lambasting Truman, he turned his guns on Eisenhower. In an interview, the president had insisted that his administration was making steady progress on removing subversive elements from the government, and that he expected "this whole thing will be a matter of history and of memory by the time the next election comes around" by the midterm elections, in November 1954. McCarthy decided to hit back. Eisenhower was, he conceded, doing "infinitely better than the Truman-Acheson regime, there is no comparison." But there were "a few cases where our batting average is zero—we struck out." The Republicans did not create the problem, he said. But Eisenhower, he went on, was dangerously naïve to think his job was done. "Now what are we going to do about it? Are we going to continue to send perfumed notes, following the style of the Truman-Acheson regime?"

It was, wrote top White House aide C. D. Jackson in a memo to the president, the day that McCarthy "declared war on Eisenhower." In his notes taken at a meeting a few days later, Jackson recalled telling the president that "the three little monkeys act was not working and would not work, and that appeasing McCarthy in order to save his seven votes for this year's legislative session was poor strategy, poor tactics and poor arithmetic."

Jackson urged Eisenhower to attack McCarthy by name, but still the president resisted. On December 2, 1953, he had Secretary of State Dulles give a press conference defending the administration's foreign policy, then followed it with his own, restrained statement on the "fair, thorough and decent investigations" under his new security order. The president reiterated his expectation that within a year subversion would no longer be an issue, so that he and Congress could move on to more important matters. He still hoped that McCarthy could be brought to reason, quietly, or just as quietly pushed to the side. That same month the president invited Senators McCarthy and Jenner, along with Representative Velde, to a White House lunch so that Brownell could brief them on everything the administration was doing to fight subversives. Eisenhower also ordered Nixon and William P. Rogers, the deputy attorney general, to nudge McCarthy into line. They brought him to Nixon's favorite vacation spot in Key Biscayne, Florida, where they wined him and dined him and suggested he move on to other subjects, like tax reform. But the senator would not budge. "Frankly," Nixon said, "we tried to mediate with McCarthy until we were blue in the face."

The new year of 1954 brought new demands from McCarthy and Cohn, who was increasingly manning the helm at the Subcommittee on Investigations. As part of the hunt for subversives at Fort Monmouth, he had already requested personal loyalty files of suspicious employees. Now he and McCarthy wanted to interrogate members of the Army Loyalty and Security Appeals Board, which had the responsibility of vetting personnel with question marks in their files. Eisenhower found the requests alarming: Not only were they asking to invade the privacy of likely innocent Americans by looking at their personnel files, but they were overstepping the line that separated the legislative and executive branches. In fact, Truman's 1948 order creating the loyalty boards had forbid their members from testifying about their findings before Congress. Brownell arranged a meeting in his office on January 21, 1954, with John Adams, the Army's chief counsel, to work out a response.

Halfway through the meeting, Adams dropped a bomb. David Schine, one of McCarthy's assistants and Roy Cohn's close friend, was being inducted into the Army, and having flunked the officer's candidacy test, he was bound to be assigned low-level work in some remote part of the country, or even overseas. Soon after Schine had received the news, Cohn began to badger Adams about giving Schine preferential treatment. According to Adams, Cohn's demands had started out ridiculous and grown steadily worse from there. He wanted the secretary of the Army, Robert T. Stevens, to make Schine his personal assistant. Adams said no. Cohn then suggested that Schine be made a West Point instructor; that too failed. The badgering continued. Once, when Adams was lecturing in Amherst, Massachusetts, he had to stop to take a call from Cohn, who insisted that he get Schine off kitchen duty the next day. Cohn started showing up wherever Adams happened to be. After finding him in Manhattan, Cohn offered to give Adams a ride to his train at Pennsylvania Station, then lobbied him about Schine as he weaved in and out of Midtown traffic. Adams gave not an inch, and eventually Cohn got so angry that he stopped the car in the middle of Park Avenue and ordered Adams to get out and walk. (McCarthy, it turned out, didn't much care for Schine, and told Secretary Stevens that he'd be happy if the Army sent him far away and "out of my hair.")

Adams's story, the men in Brownell's office decided, was just the sort of ammunition they needed to force McCarthy to back down. Cohn had clearly stepped over the line, and probably committed a crime in doing so. Best of all, Adams had kept meticulous notes. Brownell and Sherman Adams, Eisenhower's chief of staff, directed him to write up a detailed chronology, which they would present, in private, to McCarthy and Cohn.

But the senator had his own bomb to drop. In December, he and Cohn had learned of a Queens dentist named Irving Peress who had been drafted into the Army Reserves in 1952. He had refused to sign a statement, required by all military inductees, confirming that he had never joined an organization "advocating a subversive policy or seeking to alter the form of the government of the United States by unconstitutional means"—in short, that he had never been a Communist. But a series of bureaucratic snafus had led to his honorable discharge, scheduled for March 31, 1954, and a promotion from captain to major, based on his prior medical experience. It was, simply, a mistake of paperwork. But in McCarthy's hands, "Who promoted Peress?" became his new war cry.

McCarthy launched his latest campaign on February 18, once more at Foley Square. Peress was called, but he refused to answer questions, citing the Fifth Amendment. After he left the witness table McCarthy, the sole senator in attendance, called General Ralph Zwicker, the commander of Peress's last posting. Zwicker, a fellow Wisconsinite, was polite but evasive, offering the bare minimum of an answer to Cohn and McCarthy's questions.

"General," said McCarthy, "let's try and be truthful. I am going to keep you here as long as you keep hedging and hawing."

"I am not hedging," Zwicker said.

"Or hawing."

"I am not hawing, and I don't like to have anyone impugn my honesty, which you just about did," Zwicker said.

"Either your honesty or your intelligence," McCarthy retorted. "I can't help impugning one or the other."

McCarthy asked leading, loaded questions about whether the generals responsible for the Peress promotion should be stripped of their command. Zwicker refused to play along. As the hearing went on, McCarthy grew even more frustrated, then angry, until finally, red-faced, he burst. "General, you should be removed from command," he shouted. "Any man who has been given the honor of being promoted to general and who says 'I will protect another general who protects Communists' is not fit to wear that uniform."

Robert Stevens, secretary of the Army, erupted when he heard about the hearing. He called McCarthy and told him that he would not allow any more witnesses from the Army to appear before his subcommittee. McCarthy, unmoved, threatened to send subpoenas, setting off a constitutional crisis between the Congress and the White House. Stevens thought better of it, and after speaking with the other senators on the subcommittee, invited McCarthy to a compromise.

The meeting took place over lunch in the office of Senator Everett Dirksen, adjacent to Nixon's Capitol Hill suite. Stevens was a wealthy heir to a textile business who had proven himself a hard-nosed executive, but he found himself out of his depths against McCarthy. He had come to the parley determined to prevent more Army personnel from being called to testify, but over a two-hour meal of fried chicken and coffee he completely caved, leaving with a meaningless promise from McCarthy that he would treat future witnesses fairly. Nixon called the meal "one of the most controversial repasts of the 1950s." Reporters quickly dubbed it the "chicken lunch," with the double-entendre very much intentional. "Senator McCarthy achieved today what General Burgoyne and General Cornwallis never achieved—the surrender of the American Army," wrote *The Times* of London.

Stevens offered to resign, but Eisenhower just steamed. It was one thing for McCarthy to go after private citizens and civilian federal employees. But attacking the Army—his beloved Army—was too much. He had had enough of the hard-right senators who had made rabid anti-Communism a litmus test for loyalty. "We just can't work with fellows like McCarthy, Bricker, Jenner, and that bunch," he told his aides, referring to senators John Bricker and William Jenner, two close McCarthy allies.

The president tried to calm things with a March 3 statement to the press, admitting the Army had made some mistakes but reasserting his confidence in Stevens and the branch's top brass. "We must be unceasingly vigilant in every phase of governmental activity to make certain that there is no subversive penetration," Eisenhower said. Then he added, "In opposing Communism, we are defeating ourselves if either by design or through carelessness we use methods that do not conform to the American sense of justice and fair play."

Just two hours later, McCarthy offered his own televised address. He told viewers what he had always said, that he was being punished for telling the truth. But he would not stop. "If a stupid, arrogant, or witless man in a position of power comes before our committee and is found aiding the Communist Party, he will be exposed," the senator said. He didn't say Zwicker's name, but he didn't need to.

The line was drawn. On that day, "Ike really made up his mind to fight Joe from now on in," wrote his aide James Hagerty in a memo. On March 8 Eisenhower assigned Nixon to give a televised response to a recent jab by his 1952 opponent for the presidency, Adlai Stevenson, though in fact Nixon's speech would take aim at McCarthy. Nixon would not speak for another five days, not until March 13, 1954. By the time he did, the speech was all but ignored—little did the White House know how much would change by then.

The day after McCarthy's televised right hook at the president, a mild-mannered backbench senator from Vermont named Ralph Flanders took the floor of the Senate to give a "brief talk . . . in the nature of advice to the junior Senator from Wisconsin." Flanders, a Republican, hadn't coordinated anything with the White House, or with anyone else. McCarthy wasn't even on the Senate floor to witness him take the rostrum. But that did not prevent the folksy Flanders from unleashing a tongue-lashing the likes of which the chamber had not seen since the years before the Civil War, when heated arguments between Northern and Southern legislators sometimes broke out into violence.

Flanders had been quietly fuming over McCarthy's wanton behavior for years, but he had never spoken out—no one in his party had. Flanders was, finally, fed up. "To what party does he belong?" he asked of McCarthy. "Is he a hidden satellite of the Democratic Party, to which he is furnishing so much material for quiet mirth?" he asked. "He dons his war paint. He goes into his war dance. He emits his war whoops. He goes forth to battle and proudly returns with the scalp of a pink Army dentist. We may assume that this presents the depth and seriousness of Communist penetration in this country at this time." It was the first time since Margaret Chase Smith in 1950 that a Republican senator had spoken out against McCarthy. And the day wasn't over.

That evening came another shocker. Edward R. Murrow of CBS, perhaps the most respected figure in broadcast journalism, dedicated his evening show *See It Now* to an exposé on McCarthy. Murrow had quietly opposed the Red Scare for years, hiring blacklisted Hollywood writers to script historical documentaries. He had already gone after the American Legion. For months he had methodically gathered material on McCarthy. He and his producer, Fred Friendly, had personally paid for an ad promoting that night's program.

The broadcast drew on fifteen thousand feet of film to present the senator in his own words, speaking, cajoling, threatening, bullying. TV was still a new medium, and though millions of Americans were buying sets every year, many had still never seen McCarthy on film, only read about him in the newspaper alongside still, often posed photographs in the newspaper. This time they saw a different McCarthy: dour, stubbled, rumpled. Murrow offered only the minimum of commentary as the footage played on, until near the end of the program, when he reappeared on camera.

"His primary achievement has been in confusing the public mind, as between internal and the external threats of Communism," Murrow said of McCarthy. "The actions of the junior senator from Wisconsin have caused alarm and dismay amongst our allies abroad, and given considerable comfort to our enemies. And whose fault is that? Not really his. He didn't create this situation of fear; he merely exploited it—and rather successfully. Cassius was right. 'The fault, dear Brutus, is not in our stars, but in ourselves.'" He closed with his standard signoff, but it carried extra meaning that evening: "Good night, and good luck."

Murrow had worried about a backlash from advertisers, the public, and CBS executives. And negative, even threatening, mail did trickle into the CBS offices. But it was overwhelmed fifteen to one by letters and phone calls praising the broadcaster.

Two days later even more bad news came for the senator. On the morning of March 11, 1954, during a public hearing, Cohn and McCarthy had called a middle-aged Black woman named Annie Lee Moss, a veteran federal employee they accused of being a Communist agent. She appeared before the subcommittee swaddled in a thick black coat and frayed white gloves. She not only denied being a member of the Communist Party, but insisted she had only learned of its existence in 1948.

"Did you ever hear of Karl Marx?" Cohn asked.

"Who's that?" Moss replied as the audience laughed.

McCarthy had picked the wrong person to bully. The crowd sided with her immediately, as did the other senators. Stuart Symington, Democrat of Missouri, said that if she lost her job because of McCarthy, he would have one for her in his office. Somehow, Cohn then managed to make things even worse. He had tried to link her to a Communist named Rob Hall. But as the questioning rolled along, it became clear that the Rob Hall she knew was a different man, and that Cohn had called the wrong Annie Lee Moss. McCarthy, declaring her of no importance, left the interrogation halfway through. The embarrassing episode was all over the evening newspapers.

So too was news of the Adams chronology, released that afternoon. It listed forty-four instances of inappropriate actions by Cohn over eight months. It was detailed, precise, and damning. The Army, the White House, even Senator Dirksen suggested that McCarthy could make it all go away if he fired Cohn. But that wasn't McCarthy's way. The next day, March 12, he accused the Army of cooking up the chronology as blackmail. The Army held its ground. The only way forward, the Senate and White House quickly decided, was a hearing.

The White House and the Pentagon favored holding it before the Senate Armed Forces Committee, chaired by Massachusetts Republican Leverett Saltonstall, a stolid old-line conservative, though no fan of McCarthy. Saltonstall demurred—he was up for reelection that fall, and with a large pro-McCarthy faction in his state's electorate, he preferred to keep his name out of it. That left McCarthy's own Government Operations Committee as a venue, which, because he was chairman, presented its own difficulties. Surprisingly, McCarthy agreed to step down temporarily, in exchange for the right to cross-examine witnesses. In his place would be one of his dependable allies, Karl Mundt of South Dakota.

With its general counsel, John Adams, involved in the hearings as a witness, the Army went outside the Pentagon for a lawyer. At the suggestion of Governor Dewey of New York, Secretary Stevens hired a puckish Boston lawyer named Joseph Nye Welch. He had been born in Iowa and raised on a small farm. He had hardly ventured beyond the state until, upon graduating at the top of his class from Grinnell College in central Iowa, he was accepted to Harvard Law School. Afterward he joined the elite firm of Hale and Dorr, made partner while still young, and settled into a life as a quintessential white-shoe lawyer, handling antitrust and estate cases.

If E. B. White had ever needed a Boston lawyer to fill his books alongside his canoeing mouse-boys and talking pigs, he would have conjured up someone like Joe Welch. He stood six foot three inches and skinny as a maypole. He was balding, and kept what hair remained closely cropped. He reveled in his own eccentricities: He worked at a stand-up desk, owned more than two hundred bow ties, and considered it bad luck for a lawyer to enter a courtroom with a two-dollar bill in his pocket. He was a Republican but rarely voted. He was, he never tired of saying, "just a country lawyer," and while no one believed him, they let him get away with saying it, and that's what mattered to him. He was a surprisingly effective courtroom presence, and he knew how to play the part.

Upon arriving in Washington and setting up his temporary office at the Pentagon, Welch immediately grasped the single most important thing about the upcoming Army–McCarthy hearings. Though they were set up like a judicial process, with lawyers and cross-examinations, there was no judge, no jury, no verdict. The only arbiters would be the viewers watching at home, and their verdict on Senator McCarthy and his charges would be adjudicated in poll results and letter-writing campaigns. It didn't matter to Welch whether McCarthy was actually at fault. The key was to make viewers think he was. Performance, not legal theory, would determine the outcome. Welch's goal was to drag out the hearings as long as possible, knowing that the more viewers saw of the real Joe McCarthy—the sweating, fidgety, angry, rude McCarthy—the more they would turn against him. All Welch had to do was clear the path.

Karl Mundt took one final puff on his pipe, grabbed his ashtray—his preferred form of gavel—and on April 22, 1954, at 10:30 a.m. on the dot, slammed it down on his desk. It was the first day of the Army–McCarthy hearings. At the sound, the Senate Caucus Room and its seven hundred occupants fell silent. Hundreds had been waiting all morning to get in. Technicians had spent the night setting up TV cameras and recording equipment. The two sides—McCarthy and Cohn, the Army and Welch—had filed in a few minutes earlier. As Welch paused at the door to take in the shuffling, muttering crowd, a Capitol Police officer told him, "Don't worry, in three days there won't be 20 people here." He was wrong.

It was not the first televised congressional hearing, or even at the time the most watched—that distinction goes to the 1950–1951 hearings on organized crime, chaired by Estes Kefauver, a Tennessee Democrat. But the Army–McCarthy hearings are among the best-remembered, even decades later. They were, despite the complicated material, high drama. No one knew what might happen day to day, minute to minute. "On the way to the hearing room it was impossible to predict what would happen between 10 am and 5 pm; on the way back it was sometimes hard to believe what had happened," Welch wrote in *Life* magazine, after it was all over.

McCarthy dominated the proceedings from the start, needling and heckling, calling "point of order" twice as often as the other participants combined. He thought he had scored a major win early on, when on April 27 his staff produced a photograph showing Stevens standing alone alongside Schine—evidence, he claimed, to support his story that the Army secretary had been in effect holding Schine hostage, refusing to give him preferential treatment in the hopes that the senator might back off on his investigations. If Stevens knew Schine well enough to pose with him for a photo, surely, the senator claimed, he knew all about the politics behind the young man's plight.

Welch managed to get ahold of an uncropped version of the photo, which showed Stevens and Schine as just two men among many—hardly evidence that the secretary even knew who Schine was. But Welch was more interested in a different angle. Where did the photo come from, he asked the witness, Jim Juliana, one of McCarthy's closest aides. "A pixie?"

It was an odd question, and the crowd's attention perked up. Was Welch making a joke? McCarthy, suddenly flustered, interrupted. "Will counsel for my benefit define—I think he might be an expert on that—what a pixie is?"

"Yes, I should say, Mr. Senator, that a pixie is a close relative of a fairy," Welch replied. No one noticed whether he looked at Cohn as he spoke, but he didn't need to. Most people in the room knew the rumors about Cohn and Schine. In that deeply homophobic era, Welch's implication was clear. So was his strategy: Get under McCarthy's skin, make him lose his composure in front of millions of viewers.

McCarthy tried another tack, this time producing a copy of the 1951 FBI memo informing the Army of potential security risks at Fort Monmouth. Welch sidestepped its significance by demanding to know how McCarthy had come to possess such a classified document. McCarthy insisted that his source came from his "loyal underground" of anonymous admirers within the government, and that he could not betray them. He even doubled down a few days later, praising leakers as "individuals who have placed their oath to defend the country against enemies . . . above any presidential directive."

Finally, on May 17, Eisenhower had had enough. He issued an order forbidding any executive branch employees from testifying before the committee. At the same time, the president did not want the hearings to stop. Through his Senate surrogates, he deflected attempts to bring them to a close. The best, he knew, was yet to come; without Army witnesses to badger, McCarthy would implode.

The focus turned to McCarthy's staff, starting with Cohn. He sat under questioning for days, first from the subcommittee, then Welch. The Boston lawyer put Cohn through his paces, poking him about memos, dates, and other minute details that Cohn only half-remembered. Welch had already been baiting McCarthy in executive sessions, held outside the public view and kept classified for fifty years. The day before, during one such session, Welch had said: "Here is the thing about these hearings that begins to somewhat appall me. Looking at you, Senator McCarthy, you have, I think, something of a genius for creating confusion, throwing in new issues, new accusations, and creating a turmoil in the hearts and minds of the country that I find troublesome. And because of your genius, sir, we keep on, just keep on, as I view it, creating these confusions. Maybe I am over-impressed by them. But I don't think they do the country any good."

McCarthy just sat there, fuming. And Welch had more in store. Soon after the Army hired him, he had asked two young lawyers from his law firm to join him as assistants, James St. Clair and Fred Fisher. Both were recent Harvard Law graduates, and both would go on to estimable legal careers—two decades later, St. Clair would serve as Nixon's chief counsel during the Watergate hearings. At their first meeting with Welch, over dinner in Washington, he had asked them if there was anything in their pasts that might raise questions. Fisher said yes: During law school he had been a member of the National Lawyers Guild, one of the groups on the attorney general's list of subversive organizations. He had even founded a chapter with a man later revealed to be a Communist. Welch thanked him for his service, and suggested it was best that he return to Boston immediately.

It was a minor story, and not a secret one. *The New York Times* reported it on April 16, minus the bit about the Communist cofounder. Welch was worried that McCarthy would find out the whole story and blow it up. But he also knew that there were questions about Cohn's draft status, and whether he had used his influence to gain a deferment. So, early in the negotiations that set the ground rules for the hearings, Welch and Cohn had made a deal: Both Fisher's membership in the National Lawyers Guild and Cohn's draft status were off limits. According to Cohn, McCarthy knew of and approved the arrangement. It was Welch's bet that the senator, sufficiently angered, would be unable to keep his word.

Welch began his questions on the morning of June 9, 1954, by asking Cohn why, if he had damaging information about subversives at Fort Monmouth, he hadn't reported them immediately to the Army. Cohn said he couldn't recall why. But Welch pressed on: "Mr. Cohn, tell me once more: Every time you learn of a Communist or a spy anywhere, it is your policy to get rid of them as fast as possible?"

"Surely, we want them out as fast as possible, sir."

"And whenever you learn of them from now on, Mr. Cohn, I beg of you, will you tell somebody about them quick?"

Cohn was getting flustered, but he seemed to be handling the situation. It's unclear why, at that exact moment, McCarthy interjected.

"In view of Mr. Welch's request for the information be given once we know of anyone who might be performing any work for the Communist Party," the senator said, "I think we should tell him that he has in his law firm a young man named Fisher whom he recommended, incidentally, to do work on this committee, who had been for a number of years a member of an organization which was named, oh, years and years ago, as the legal bulwark of the Communist Party."

The room grew hushed. Senator Mundt squirmed. Welch stood, impassively.

"Whether you knew he was a member of that Communist organization or not, I don't know," McCarthy went on. "I assume you did not, Mr. Welch, because I get the impression that, while you are quite an actor, you play for the laugh, I don't think you have any conception of the danger of the Communist Party. I don't think you yourself would ever knowingly aid the Communist cause. I think you are unknowingly aiding it when you try to burlesque this hearing in which we are attempting to bring out the facts, however."

Mundt tried to interject. But Welch was ready. This was his trap. "Mr. Chairman, under these circumstances I must have something approaching a personal privilege," he said. Mundt nodded.

"Senator McCarthy, I did not know—" But McCarthy had turned away. Welch raised his voice. "Senator, sometimes you say, 'May I have your attention?'"

"I am listening to you," McCarthy said. "I can listen with one ear."

"This time I want you to listen with both, Senator."

"Yes." But then McCarthy turned to an assistant, telling him to prepare a news release on Fisher.

"You won't need anything in the record when I have finished telling you this," Welch said. "Until this moment, Senator, I think I never really gauged your cruelty or your recklessness. Fred Fisher is a young man who went to the Harvard Law School and came into my firm and is starting what looks to be a brilliant career with us." He explained how he had brought on Fisher, and how Fisher had been forthright about his past affiliations.

"So, Senator, I asked him to go back to Boston," Welch said. "Little did I dream you could be so reckless and so cruel as to do an injury to that lad. It is true he is still with Hale and Dorr. It is true that he will continue to be with Hale and Dorr. It is, I regret to say, equally true that I fear he shall always bear a scar needlessly inflicted by you. If it were in my power to forgive you for your reckless cruelty, I will do so. I like to think I am a gentleman, but your forgiveness will have to come from someone other than me."

The room was utterly silent. Everyone stared at McCarthy, waiting to see what the old bruiser would do. He could have dropped the issue, or apologized, and walked away with a flesh wound. But it wasn't his style to back out of a fight.

"May I say that Mr. Welch talks about this being cruel and reckless,"

McCarthy said. "He was just baiting; he has been baiting Mr. Cohn here for hours, requesting that Mr. Cohn, before sundown, get out of any department of Government anyone who is serving the Communist cause. I just give this man's record, and I want to say, Mr. Welch, that it has been labeled long before he became a member, as early as 1944—"

"Senator, may we not drop this?" Welch cut him off. "We know he belonged to the Lawyers Guild, and Mr. Cohn nods his head at me. I did you I think no personal injury, Mr. Cohn."

"No, sir," Cohn said.

"I meant to do you no personal injury, and if I did, I beg, your pardon. Let us not assassinate this lad further, Senator. You have done enough. Have you no sense of decency, sir, at long last? Have you left no sense of decency?"

McCarthy, it seemed, did not. "I know this hurts you, Mr. Welch. But I may say, Mr. Chairman, on a point of personal privilege, and I would like to finish it—"

"Senator," Welch said, "I think it hurts you, too, sir."

McCarthy pushed on. He just had to notch his point. He sputtered on about the National Lawyers Guild, trying to show that it was a Communist front. "Let me ask Mr. Welch. You brought him down, did you not, to act as your assistant?"

Instead of answering, Welch went in for the kill.

"Mr. McCarthy, I will not discuss this with you further," he said. "You have sat within six feet of me, and could have asked me about Fred Fisher. You have brought it out. If there is a God in heaven, it will do neither you nor your cause any good. I will not discuss it further. I will not ask Mr. Cohn any more. You, Mr. Chairman, may, if you will, call the next witness."

The crowd, silent until that moment, erupted in applause. Mundt's ashtray sat motionless for minutes before he began gaveling it, calling a recess. McCarthy, swiveling in his chair, asked "What did I do? What did I do?" to his assistants.

Welch, a handkerchief in hand, walked out of the caucus room. There was a tear in his eye—and, according to one witness, a gleam.

McCarthywasm

The hearings plodded along for another ten days after Welch's climactic confrontation with McCarthy, finally ending on June 17, 1954. In the course of 72 sessions over eight weeks, the subcommittee generated 7,424 pages of testimony, or some 2 million words, from 32 witnesses. Over 187 hours were broadcast on TV. And yet as soon as they ended, viewers and participants alike wondered what it had all been for. The committee had sought to discover whether McCarthy was putting undue pressure on the Army, or vice versa, but that was a question that a politically charged public forum like this one was unlikely to answer definitively. The proceedings were confusing, and the panel was too partisan to decide fairly. The concluding report, issued on August 31, criticized subordinates on both sides, finding that Roy Cohn had indeed pressured the Army on David Schine's behalf and that Adams had tried to block Senate investigations into Fort Monmouth. But it largely exonerated the principals, McCarthy especially.

Which is not to say the senator got off. In the end, Welch was right. The real verdict came from the public. All that airtime had allowed Americans to see McCarthy in action, and many did not like what they saw. The Gallup poll told the story: McCarthy began the year with 50 percent of respondents approving of his methods, and just 29 percent against. When the hearings ended, only 34 percent still sided with the senator, and 45 percent were opposed. The drop in approval gave his enemies a green light: Senator Flanders spoke again on June 11, this time calling on the Senate to oust McCarthy from his chairmanship of the Committee on Government Operations. The Republicans, now led by McCarthy's ally William Knowland, flatly rejected the suggestion, but there was too much weight—from the White House, from the public, from other Republicans—not to do something. Cohn resigned over the summer, and in July Flanders offered a new plan, this time to censure McCarthy for conduct that "tends to bring the Senate into disrepute"—not because of how he behaved during the Army–McCarthy hearings, but for his unrelated conduct during the 1952 investigation into his finances, led by Senator William Benton of Connecticut.

The Senate established a six-person committee to assess the charges. The committee beetled about for months, all through the fall, but there was no question about the outcome: McCarthy would eventually be censured. He might have avoided the blow, or at least softened it, with a show of contrition. Instead, speaking in November to 1,500 diners at a gala in his honor at the Pfister Hotel, in downtown Milwaukee, he said, "Regardless of what is done at this circus, whether I am censured, or am no longer chairman of my committee, I shall continue to do this job as well as I can til I die."

McCarthy's moment of prominence was passing. But his imploding popularity among the general public, and the mounting attacks from inside the Senate chambers, masked a persistent bedrock of support among his ardent followers. The fact that, even after the Army–McCarthy hearings, a third of Americans still supported him speaks to the strength of his conspiracy-minded populism. If anything, for millions, Senate opposition to his tactics only proved his claim that there was a massive, bipartisan plot in Washington, a pro-Communist cabal determined to quash anyone who tried to uncover it. In March 1954 McCarthy barnstormed the Midwest, drawing anti-Communist groups like the Minute Women and Legionnaires by the busload, alongside those from even more adamantly right-wing groups like Sons of I Shall Return and the Alert Council for America. The next month he came to New York, where Cardinal Francis Spellman and over a hundred police officers gave him a rousing cheer of support.

In June, when the *Chicago Tribune* sent a reporter to Wisconsin to test whether his support there held strong, the result was a definitive yes. The pro-McCarthy *Tribune* could hardly be expected to say otherwise, but the *Los Angeles Times* found similar results in an informal poll in central Pennsylvania. During the hearings two young conservatives, William F. Buckley Jr. and L. Brent Bozell Jr., published *McCarthy and His Enemies*, which defended the senator, excused his excesses, and lambasted his critics, writing in an elevated Brahmin style that gave his cause an intellectual gloss. It was a best-seller, and not just among the rural and blue-collar Americans who made up the senator's base. McCarthy was not for everyone, but his appeal remained deep and wide.

The looming censure vote turned McCarthy into a living martyr for those committed to the idea that a corrupt elite had taken over the commanding heights of American life. In November 1954 a group calling itself Ten Million Americans Mobilizing for Justice announced plans to collect 10 million signatures against the censure petition in ten days. They were led by a platoon of former generals alongside Charles Edison, the former governor of New Jersey and son of Thomas Edison. The group organized a rally at Madison Square Garden in late November that drew thirteen thousand McCarthy supporters. One of its leaders, Rear Admiral John G. Crommelin, addressed the flag-waving throngs, saying, "We believe that the power of Congress to investigate the executive is the first line of our internal defense against the hidden force. . . . Senator McCarthy is its primary target not because of his alleged contempt of the Senate. The hidden force must liquidate him for a much more practical reason. He is the one man left who—singlehandedly—has been able to rouse the people of the United States to the menace of the hidden force in their government."

Meanwhile hate mail poured into the offices of those senators, particularly Republicans, who had come out against McCarthy, no one more so than Flanders's. "Dear Commie Senator from Vermont" was a typical salutation, milder than many, which often dripped with foul language, eschatological damnation, and anti-Semitic tropes, regardless of the recipient's religious affiliation. Such letters offered an X-ray of what lay at the heart of extreme anti-Communism in America, and what could not be excised by a mere vote in the Senate.

On December 2, 1954, by a vote of 67 to 20, the Senate found that McCarthy had indeed violated its norms, back in 1952. It was a specific charge, and one that dealt with events already well in the past. The pro-censure ranks had also agreed to drop the demand that he lose his committee chair. It was a slap on the wrist, nothing more, but it added to the year's irreversible toll on McCarthy's reputation in Washington. He was no longer a feared demagogue among his colleagues. Six days after the censure vote, McCarthy broke openly with Eisenhower, accusing him of a "shrinking show of weakness" against Communist China and apologizing to voters for supporting the president in 1952. This time, even many of his fellow conservative senators abandoned him, siding with the president and denouncing McCarthy.

One afternoon in June 1955, a group of presidential advisers tramped through the early summer heat to a meeting at the White House. It was a routine affair, called to discuss upcoming legislation with the president. Among the items was a resolution criticizing the United Nations. It had been offered by McCarthy. The president paused, signaling a joke was forthcoming. "It's no longer McCarthyism," he said, "but McCarthywasm."

The president's advisers chortled politely. It wasn't his joke; it was making the rounds in Washington, and by then they had probably heard it a dozen times. The Democrats had won back the Senate the previous fall, and in January 1955 McCarthy had lost his perch atop the Committee on Government Operations. And without his bully pulpit, he had to rely on a diminishing circle of reporters and assorted Washington sycophants to be heard. He could still draw crowds back in Wisconsin and across the Midwest, but his currency in D.C. was next to worthless.

Eisenhower chuckled at his joke too, and not just because he enjoyed a good pun. Behind the scenes, he and his administration had played a significant part in the senator's political demise. Eisenhower had encouraged Army Secretary Stevens to pick a fight with McCarthy. He had then urged Senate Republicans to hold hearings, ostensibly to resolve the conflict but in reality to expose the worst of McCarthy to the public. When it looked like McCarthy and Cohn might actually draw blood by getting Army officials to admit they had tried to block his investigation, the president forbid the officials from testifying—thereby keeping the spotlight on the senator. And Eisenhower had resisted efforts by the Republican leadership, and even advisers within the White House, to bring the hearings to a close early.

Perhaps McCarthy's demise was inevitable, with or without the president's puppetry. There was always something provisional and momentary about McCarthy. He was a single senator throwing rhetorical haymakers, not a leader of a political faction. He never had power in an institutional sense; his potency was frustrating and frightening, but no one imagined him taking over the levers of government. Plus, the world had begun to settle down: Stalin died in March 1953; the Korean War ended three months later. The American economy was booming, and with it the public's sense of security and normalcy.

Eisenhower did something else to sideline McCarthy and his allies, something bigger than stage-managing a Senate investigation. From the beginning of his administration, the president had sought to co-opt anti-Communism, to sanitize it, and in doing so defuse the threat that the hard right posed to Roosevelt's expanded federal government, which he and the Republican establishment had long since come to accept, and even value. It was a maneuver that Truman had attempted, with his loyalty program, but had failed. It took someone with Eisenhower's martial bona fides to succeed.

The president had begun almost as soon as he was inaugurated, with his revision of Truman's loyalty program, as well as his considered, but ultimately resolute endorsement of the electric chair for Julius and Ethel Rosenberg. In a June 1954 speech he touted a long series of additional steps during his first two years in office, including the recent conviction of 41 Communist Party leaders under the Smith Act, two more party figures for espionage, and one for treason; the deportation of 84 "alien subversives"; the addition of 62 new groups to the attorney general's list; and the removal of 2,200 "security risks" from the federal government. "The constant surveillance of Communists in this country is a 24-hour, 7-days-a-week, 52-weeks-a-year job," he said.

He also encouraged Attorney General Brownell to pursue an amendment extending the provisions of the 1950 Internal Security Act, a bill that would give the federal government more power to investigate organizations suspected of harboring Communist members, even if the organizations were not themselves Communist run. The primary target was labor unions, and labor leaders pressed Democrats to respond. They did, and then some: On the morning of August 12, Hubert Humphrey, Democrat of Minnesota, introduced a substitute bill, the Communist Control Act, which would instead make membership in the Communist Party itself illegal, subject to up to $10,000 in fines and five years in prison. Congress had considered such a measure for years, but always backed off because it seemed too extreme. Even J. Edgar Hoover had opposed it, for fear it would drive Communists underground. Now, in 1954, it was not only under consideration, but it had been proposed by Senate Democrats. "I am tired of reading headlines about being 'soft' toward communism," Humphrey said in introducing the legislation. His fellow Democrats in the Senate agreed. Well-known anti-Communists like Henry Jackson of Washington and John F. Kennedy of Massachusetts signed on as cosponsors, and so did many liberals, like Herbert Lehman of New York and Paul Douglas of Illinois. "I think the time has arrived for all of us to stand up and be counted," said another, Mike Mansfield of Montana.

The bill declared the Communist Party to be "the agency of a hostile foreign power" and "a clear, present and continuing danger to the security of the United States"—a claim that its sponsors surely knew was ridiculous, given the party's well-publicized implosion. Humphrey claimed that the bill was in fact a measure to protect civil liberties, because it provided a legal framework for deciding whether someone was a party member. If you weren't a party member, he said, you no longer had to worry about baseless accusations that you were. But Humphrey was silent on the bill's effect on the civil liberties of actual party members. In any case the tactic of using a bad bill to stop a worse piece of legislation backfired when Republican senators insisted on merging the two. The whole thing became an incoherent mess when the two parties stripped the Humphrey section of enforcement, making party membership an unpunishable crime—though a crime nevertheless. Only two liberal Democrats opposed the combined bill in the House, and it passed unanimously through the Senate. Eisenhower signed the legislation on August 24, 1954, commending it as a weapon for "combatting the Communist menace in this country."

Looked at one way, McCarthyism was continuing without McCarthy, and with bipartisan support. Looked at from a slightly different angle, though, it appeared that both parties were lining up behind the president's logic: By taking ownership of the issue, they, the responsible ones, could deprive the hard right and the Red Scare of oxygen.

At the same time, Eisenhower maintained a relentless commitment to fighting subversion through constitutional means. "Protecting America includes also the protection of every American in his American rights," he said in a speech at Columbia's bicentennial celebration in May 1954. "Let us not lose faith in our own institutions, and in the essential soundness of the American citizenry lest we—divided among ourselves—thus serve the interests and advance the purposes of those seeking to destroy us." By taking on McCarthy while shoring up his anti-Communist credentials, Eisenhower offered the American public a stark choice in whom it wanted to lead the charge against subversion. By early 1955, the public's answer was clear.

Nothing changed overnight. Red-baiting was still good politics, even after McCarthy's fall. In January 1956 the Senate Internal Security Subcommittee, the upper chamber's chief Communist-hunting panel, had requested and received a record budget of $285,000 for the year, citing a "sharp revival in the fighting spirit of American Communists." It then turned its focus to newspapers, holding hearings that led to the firing and blacklisting of dozens of journalists at *The New York Times*, the New York *Daily News*, and other leading dailies. Anti-Communist activity continued at the state level too. In June 1955 the California Senate Committee on Un-American Activities released a report claiming that Communists had all but taken over the state's power utilities and other key institutions. In 1955 New York ruled that insurance brokers had to pass a loyalty test, and as late as May 1957 it required would-be anglers to take a non-Communist oath before casting into its rivers and lakes.

And yet by the mid-1950s, measures like these were beginning to feel like routine, almost bureaucratic, exercises in performative patriotism. The existential fear of world war had subsided, Eisenhower had co-opted the passion of the Red Scare, and McCarthy was gone. But in their wake they left a residue of hyper-loyalty, anti-dissent, and pervasive suspicion. On May 1, 1956, thousands of people gathered at the north end of Union Square Park in Manhattan. For decades, this had been the date and place for mass demonstrations by progressives, socialists, and Communists. Now the park was decked in patriotic glory, with red, white, and blue bunting and a sign renaming the park "Union Square, U.S.A." Manhattan borough president Hulan E. Jack said that the rally "reflects the continuing failure of Communism in its feeble attempt to spread its un-American propaganda in our nation." Not a single Communist showed up to protest.

The fact was, there weren't many Communists left to persecute. The party's leadership was either in jail, on trial, or deep underground. And only a few thousand remained out in the open, spread around the country in scared little clusters. The party, wrote the journalist and stalwart member Jessica Mitford, had long since become a "self-defense organization," no longer striving for revolution, or even change, but simply its own survival. Hounding by the FBI had taken its toll, but so had neglect from Moscow. "Oh for a shipment of Moscow gold," Mitford wrote.

In June 1956 news reached the West about a "secret speech" delivered by Stalin's successor, Nikita Khrushchev, before a closed-door session at the Twentieth Communist Party Congress in Moscow. He called it "The Cult of Personality and Its Consequences." He accused Stalin of all manner of crimes, above all deviation from the plumb line of Marxist-Leninism. News of the speech washed away virtually all that remained of the American Communist Party. The cognitive dissonance was simply too much. Howard Fast, already disenchanted, wrote his final column for *The Daily Worker* on June 3, 1956, then quit the party. Thousands followed him. The speech, coupled with the Soviet invasion of Hungary after a student uprising, made 1956 the final annus horribilis for American Communists. Only a few thousand remained, and no amount of demonizing and scaremongering could make them seem like the threat they had once appeared to be. *The Daily Worker*, which once claimed a circulation of 100,000, published its last edition on January 13, 1958. On that day it printed just 5,000 copies.

With McCarthy gone, Eisenhower in charge, and the Cold War stabilizing, cracks began to appear in the laws and rules and practices that made up the Red Scare—starting where it had begun, in Hollywood. More than anyone else, it was Dalton Trumbo who finally broke the crumbling blacklist. Writing under the alias Robert Rich, he won the 1956 best story Oscar for *The Brave One*, the story of a poor Mexican boy who raises a bull, only to see it sent off to fight in a corrida. At the last minute, thanks to the boy's efforts and the crowd's sympathy, the bull is allowed to live. The story was not intended as an overt allegory of the Red Scare, but its themes of individual courage, nonconformity, and the swaying opinions of the crowd track with Trumbo's own experience during the blacklist and his optimism about how it might end. In 1960 he admitted to writing the screenplay, not long after the director Otto Preminger (who had cast Joseph Welch, McCarthy's nemesis, as a judge in *Anatomy of a Murder*) announced that he had hired Trumbo to adapt Leon Uris's novel *Exodus* for the screen. In a June 1960 interview with *Variety*, Trumbo revealed that he had written thirty screenplays since the Waldorf Statement launched the blacklist in 1947, all behind the scenes. That same year he announced he had adapted Howard Fast's *Spartacus*, to be directed by Stanley Kubrick, a choice the director made after intense lobbying from the film's star, Kirk Douglas. Again, progress was uneven: In April 1960 Frank Sinatra, under considerable pressure from John Wayne and other Hollywood conservatives, fired Albert Maltz as a screenwriter for his film *The Execution of Private Slovik* over Maltz's Communist past (the movie ended up getting shelved).

Since there had been no official blacklist, there was no official end to it, either. The reason it lasted as long as it did was because everyone was waiting for someone else to make the first move. Even after Trumbo came in from the cold, others were still waiting. Hoops remained, and they had to be jumped through. The director Sidney Lumet and producer Carlo Ponti hired another blacklistee, Walter Bernstein, to write a script about a wartime love story, but they warned him that the executives at their studio, Paramount, might balk once it ran his name through the system. And they did, having learned that HUAC had a standing subpoena for Bernstein to appear before it. Paramount's top executives made his appearance a condition of his employment. But Bernstein told him that he would rather stay unemployed. Somehow, that defiance was enough to shock Paramount to its senses. The studio hired Bernstein a few days later. And suddenly, he was off the blacklist too.

A few desultory picketers from the American Legion appeared outside theaters showing Trumbo's films, but both *Exodus* and *Spartacus* were critical and commercial successes. Hollywood was happy to forget that the blacklist had even occurred, and the lucky few who had managed to remain on the industry's fringes, like Trumbo, were able to restart their careers; by the mid-1960s Trumbo was once more among the highest-paid writers in town. Bernstein even received an Oscar nomination for his 1976 script *The Front*, a viciously funny attack on the industry directed by Martin Ritt, who had also been blacklisted, and starring Woody Allen and the comedian Zero Mostel, yet another blacklistee.

The House Committeee on Un-American Activities continued its plodding pursuit of left-wing entertainers. In 1956 it found the playwright Arthur Miller in contempt after he refused to name names, a charge it repeated against the folk singer Pete Seeger. But here too the charges were largely for show; no one expected them to go to prison, and neither of them did. Francis Walter, HUAC's new chairman and a twenty-year House veteran, went after Hollywood, and newspapers, and professors, all the usual prey. But by 1956 the targets were getting fewer, and much less interesting. He was left to pick up the scraps, to play the greatest hits—which largely explains why the Black singer Paul Robeson was seated before him on June 12, 1956.

Since his appearance at the Peekskill concert in 1949 set off two bloody riots in the New York City suburbs, Robeson had been suffering through his own version of a blacklist. He rarely performed, and rarely spoke in public. Former allies like Eleanor Roosevelt had stopped inviting him on their TV shows and to their gala events. The government had confiscated his passport. Under the stress, his health had declined. Robeson battled recurring prostate infections and frequent bouts of depression. He wore glasses now, and the former star tackle on the Rutgers football team walked with a slight hunch in his back.

The subcommittee claimed it wanted to examine passport abuse by Communist sympathizers; more likely, it wanted the spectacle of poking at a wounded old bear. As press photographers clicked away busily, a committee staff member asked Robeson, "Are you now a member of the Communist Party?"

"Oh please, please, please," Robeson snapped. He had long ago lost access to the upper range of his voice, but his deep baritone was richer than it had been in his youth. "What do you mean by the Communist Party? . . . Do you mean a party of people who have sacrificed for my people, and for all Americans and workers, that they can live in dignity?"

The staffer asked if Robeson knew Ben Davis, the Black New York councilmember and Communist Party leader who had been convicted during the 1949 Smith Act trials. Yes, Robeson said, he did. "I say that he is as patriotic an American as there can be, and you gentlemen belong with the Alien and Sedition Acts, and you are the nonpatriots, and you are the un-Americans, and you ought to be ashamed of yourselves."

Walter, finally, had had enough. "The hearing is now adjourned."

"I should think it would be," Robeson said.

"I have endured all of this that I can," Walter said, with one final clack of the gavel.

That afternoon the committee unanimously voted Robeson in contempt, the first step in sending the aged singer to prison for his refusal to cooperate. But this time the full House did not go along. It did not even schedule a vote on the contempt motion. The next day Robeson's performance was on front pages across the country. For the first time in years, people were talking about Paul Robeson again.

27

Red Monday

By 1957 the United States was no longer the war-weary, shell-shocked nation it had been at the end of World War II. It had fully embraced its postwar role as a globe-spanning economic and military colossus, exporting its cars, clothes, and culture to every open market in the world. At home the housing crisis and labor unrest of the late 1940s seemed like a distant memory, replaced by ever-rising incomes and the mass consumption that came with it. Much of the credit went to President Eisenhower. In foreign policy, he had brought a level of sanity to the Cold War through his New Look strategy, which reconceived of the Soviet Union as a long-term, chronic challenge, as much economic and ideological as it was military. He talked of balancing military with domestic needs, and sought to contain military spending by shifting to a reliance on nuclear deterrence and covert operations.

Those came with their own repercussions, but for the time they allowed the president to rally the country behind a new, optimistic consensus about their place in the world. He achieved something similar at home by taking control of the anti-subversive issue and hammering on his efforts to wipe out the Communist movement, then isolating those politicians who, like Joe McCarthy, continued to insist that something deeper and more nefarious was afoot. Though it took a few years, by the time Eisenhower faced reelection in 1956, in a rematch against Adlai Stevenson, domestic Communism was a nonissue among voters.

Yet there was one task remaining. The years of anti-Communist hysteria left behind a new, powerful infrastructure for suppressing dissent, one that continued to wreak havoc even as the public seemed to have moved on. Communists were still being arrested and convicted under the Smith Act. Professors were still being forced to sign loyalty oaths, and fired if they didn't. In the same way that the legal tools deployed during the anti-radical campaign of the late 1910s became the framework for a much more thorough and terrifying campaign in the late 1940s, the legal apparatus erected by the Red Scare—the Smith Act, HUAC, loyalty oaths—remained in place, ready for another wave of zealots to turn against their political enemies. Only when these tools were demolished could the Red Scare finally come to an end.

On October 19, 1956, Chief Justice Earl Warren strode briskly into the main conference room of the Supreme Court, where his eight fellow justices were waiting, along with their array of clerks. It was a Friday before a beautiful, brisk fall weekend, the sort of day when work becomes an afterthought. But Warren was almost gleeful about the task ahead of him. He looked down at his notes, then up at the men arrayed around him. "Heigh ho, let's get to work," he said.

The case at hand involved a labor activist named Clinton Jencks, who lived and organized among the disenfranchised, largely Hispanic mineworkers of rural New Mexico. He had been convicted of perjury for signing an affidavit swearing he was not a Communist, only to have two witnesses attest otherwise. One of those witnesses had been Harvey Matusow, an ex-Communist who had made a career as a professional witness in Red Scare–era trials, and who had later been revealed as a serial liar. He had been in the party, but almost everything he said about it, including his supposedly unfailing recollections about the members he had encountered, he had made up. Even more critical to Jencks's appeal was the revelation that both witnesses had provided written reports on him to the FBI—reports that the government refused to provide to his defense lawyers. The case raised a question central to the workings of the Red Scare apparatus: the use of anonymous sources and secret evidence, kept from defendants in the name of national security. Was it Orwellian overreach, or a necessary precaution during a global Cold War?

One can imagine an earlier version of Earl Warren siding with the government. The one who had made his name as a law-and-order attorney general in California, the one who had excused the internment of Japanese Americans as a wartime necessity. But that Earl Warren was no more. This time, he said right away that he was in favor of overturning Jencks's conviction. He was bothered not just by the trial judge's unwillingness to let Jencks see the reports, but also by the judge's vague instructions to the jury. The judge had told them it didn't matter whether Jencks was an actual member of the Communist Party; it was enough to show that he had been an "affiliate"—a sympathizer. During the height of the Red Scare, guilt by association had been a surefire strategy, in courts and in Congress. Now Warren was determined to put an end to it.

It took three more meetings over nearly six months for the justices to reach a decision, and even then it was close, a 5–3 split, announced on June 3, 1957. Justice Tom Clark, who as Harry Truman's attorney general had established the government's list of subversive organizations, was livid in his dissent. He predicted that the ruling, which ordered courts to share most documents with defendants in such cases, would allow Communist subversives "a Roman holiday for rummaging through confidential information as well as vital national secrets." Anti-court animus boiled over in the mainstream. David Lawrence, the conservative editor of *U.S. News & World Report*, wrote that it was "treason's biggest victory." After a report by a committee of the American Bar Association criticized the decision, and Warren's leadership, the chief justice resigned from the organization in protest.

Still, the importance of the Jencks decision was clear to anyone who had not yet noticed the Warren Court's increasingly aggressive defense of civil liberties, especially when it came to issues of political expression. Earl Warren had led the court in its decision to strike down school segregation in *Brown v. Board of Education of Topeka*; now he was determined to dismantle the Red Scare. Even before the Jencks decision, he had been hard at work. He had already led the court in two separate cases involving progressive lawyers—Rudolph Schware and Raphael Konigsberg—who had been denied licenses based on their past Communist affiliations. The court sided with both of them.

Four of the most important decisions came on June 17, 1957—it was, in effect, the day the Red Scare ended. J. Edgar Hoover called it Red

Monday. The legal scholar Geoffrey Stone called it "the end of the Cold War in the Supreme Court," the day when "the Court handed down four decisions that reversed the course of Constitutional history." Each case undermined a different piece of the Red Scare infrastructure. In one, *Watkins v. United States*, the court found in favor of a Chicago union leader who had denied being a Communist before HUAC, but refused to name names, only to be found in contempt. The case struck most of the justices as deeply problematic, Warren especially. HUAC, he believed, had gone rogue, using its investigatory powers to harass and destroy. It had to be reined in. "There is no power to expose where the predominant result can only be an invasion of the private rights of individuals," he wrote in his decision.

Warren was equally exercised by the second case that day, *Sweezy v. New Hampshire*. Paul Sweezy was a Marxist economist who frequently lectured at the University of New Hampshire. In 1953 the state's attorney general subpoenaed him as part of an investigation into subversive activities among New Hampshire academics and activists. He asked Sweezy probing questions about his beliefs in the inevitability of socialism, his criticisms of capitalism, and the content of his campus lectures—all of which Sweezy refused to answer, citing his academic freedom. The state successfully charged him with contempt. Once again, Warren wrote a broad, impassioned opinion reversing Sweezy's conviction. "There unquestionably was," he wrote in his opinion, "an invasion of petitioner's liberties in the areas of academic freedom and political expression—areas in which government should be extremely reticent to tread."

A third decision, *Service v. Dulles*, was the culmination of a six-year fight by John Service, one of the original China Hands, over his dismissal from the State Department. The former diplomat alleged that Secretary Acheson had fired him out of a lack of political courage in the face of Alfred Kohlberg and the China Lobby, and that the actual findings of the various loyalty boards had left him cleared. It was true, Warren felt, that Acheson had the "absolute discretion" to dismiss Service. But that, the court said, did not mean that he was justified in doing so. Service was reinstated.

It was the final decision on that Monday that hit the hardest. In the weeks following the court's 1951 decision affirming the Smith Act convictions, the FBI had swept up dozens of second-string Communist leaders. Among those arrested were Oleta Yates, the head of the Communist Party in California, and thirteen other state functionaries. Even more than the Foley Square trial of 1949, the Yates case seemed to place the entire era under examination. The trial judge was a member of the American Legion who set bail at $50,000 each, or nearly $600,000 in today's dollars—a ridiculously high amount that underlined a belief that even lower-level Communists posed an immediate danger to national security. The case against the defendants was a carbon copy of the original Foley Square brief. After Yates refused to say whether she knew other suspected Communists, the judge had her jailed for contempt, in an un-ventilated cell in the middle of the summer.

Warren argued that the Smith Act had been abused; Justices Douglas and Black, the court's strongest civil libertarians, said they thought the Smith Act was unconstitutional. The four conservative justices voted to sustain. The remaining two, Justice Frankfurter and John Marshall Harlan II, were at first undecided. They found the whole trial distasteful but were wary of rejecting the Smith Act itself—and with it nearly one hundred high-profile convictions. Harlan, finally, found a way out for them both. He latched on to the idea that the judge had told the jury to decide whether the defendants had "organized" the Communist Party. Harlan argued that "organized" meant to "establish," and therefore to be a part of the creation, or re-creation, of the party in 1945—not as part of an ongoing process, as prosecutors and the judge had said. And if that were the case, then the act's three-year statute of limitations had lapsed long before the fourteen were arrested. Harlan's logic might seem semantic, but it had wide-reaching consequences. The Department of Justice announced soon after that it would drop all Smith Act cases, and in effect stop prosecuting violations of the act entirely. Earl Warren, the country's new champion of civil liberties, had finally snapped the keel of the Red Scare.

Future decisions, led by Frankfurter and Harlan, would pare back the *Sweezy* and *Watkins* conclusions, reaffirming HUAC's investigatory power and reasserting the government's broad authority to seek out subversives.

Yet such turnarounds did little to alter the court's fundamental position: that Congress had met the very real threat of Communist subversion with weapons ill-suited to the job, and it had abused them with little regard for the rights and livelihoods of American citizens. The Smith Act was moribund, the FBI thwarted, and red hunters everywhere put on notice that Earl Warren's Supreme Court was no longer their friend.

HUAC would drone on, flaccid and perfunctory, a stump for wingnuts and a fat target for a new generation of protesters. The acronym had once struck terror among progressives brought up in the 1930s; to their children it was a joke. After Khrushchev's speech, the committee released a series of reports under the title *The Crimes of Khrushchev*, in an attempt to bring fear of the Communist menace back into the hearts of everyday Americans. It didn't work: Scores of people protested, then rioted, outside San Francisco's City Hall during a visit by three committee members in May 1960; in a foretaste of the coming decade of activism and unrest, police turned fire hoses on students from Stanford and Berkeley. Two years later the committee subpoenaed members of the antiwar group Women Strike for Peace, who, rather than being cowed by the congressmen, assailed HUAC in flyers and speeches. Hundreds of members volunteered to give additional testimony, overwhelming the committee. At the hearing, Congressman Clyde Doyle tried to get one witness, Blanche Posner, to admit that Communists might have infiltrated the group without her knowing. "We are too bright for that," she replied, to the roaring approval of the crowd behind her. When she got up to leave, Doyle, ever the gentleman, thanked her for her appearance. "You are welcome, Mr. Doyle," she replied. "And thank you. You have been very, very cooperative." The hearings showed the committee at its worst: bullying yet ineffective. "By now," wrote the journalist Walter Goodman, "the committee was like a tiresome uncle who insists on telling his old ghost stories in broad daylight to nephews with other things on their minds."

Called before the committee in 1966, Jerry Rubin, cofounder of the Yippies, arrived dressed as a Revolutionary War soldier, handed out copies of the Declaration of Independence, chewed bubble gum, and mocked committee members with Nazi salutes. Rubin was just nine years old when the committee had first terrorized Hollywood; to him and millions of other baby boomers, HUAC was a venal vestige of a bygone era.

It never recovered. It changed its name to the House Committee on Internal Security in 1969, then shut down completely in 1975, when it was absorbed into the Judiciary Committee.

28

The Coal-Seam Fire

Joe McCarthy checked into Bethesda Naval Hospital on April 28, 1957, and died four days later. Then and later people said it was alcoholism that did him in, and there's no denying it was a contributing factor. But McCarthy had been unwell for years. His body was simply more fragile than he wished to admit, and he pushed it further than it could go. He suffered from shingles, ulcers, and gout, and likely major depression. His drinking and poor eating habits exacerbated his physical and mental unhealth, especially toward the end, when, after his 1954 censure by the Senate and his return to the chamber's back bench, he wiled away the lonely hours at home, sitting quietly beside his fireplace. He talked to friends about leaving politics, moving to Arizona, taking up cattle ranching and a small law practice. He and Jean adopted a daughter.

His death brought ironic benedictions and bitter recriminations. Former secretary of state Dean Acheson, when asked about his late antagonist, said simply, "De mortuis nihil nisi bonum"—of the dead, nothing but good. J. Robert Oppenheimer heard about McCarthy's death right before entering an auditorium at Harvard, where an overflow crowd of 1,200 waited to hear him deliver six lectures on "The Hope of Order." He silently walked up to the blackboard and wrote "R.I.P." The anti-Communist writer George Sokolsky, who had claimed to be the man most responsible for bringing McCarthy to the front page, now lashed out at those he believed had brought down the senator. In a column published a few days after McCarthy's death, Sokolsky wrote that "Senator McCarthy was hounded to death by the communists, their friends, their supporters, innocent dupes and those who were afraid that they themselves might be exposed." In Washington, two thousand people showed up for the senator's funeral service; four hundred more gathered in Los Angeles to bid him farewell, remotely.

Eisenhower had, as he had once joked, turned McCarthyism into McCarthywasm by embracing the issue of domestic security that had provided part of the energy behind the Red Scare. But as the lamentations over McCarthy's death made clear, he had succeeded only in part. The Republican Party's embrace of anti-Communist paranoia had, for a time at least, given the hard-right wing of the party an influential seat at the table, a taste of power that it would not soon forget, and which was only whetted by Eisenhower's decision to push it back once more into the political closet. The nostalgic, resentful, cultural paranoia that had arisen in response to the New Deal, and that finally found purchase during the dawn of the Cold War, remained burning in the hearts of millions of Americans. Without McCarthy they were easier to ignore in Washington, but they remained, fed by a steady diet of mimeographed newsletters, radio broadcasters, and small-town politicians who insisted that McCarthy had been right all along.

In death, McCarthy became only stronger, and the lines between his legacy and the political mainstream, and especially establishment Republicans, grew starker. Sokolsky and other pro-McCarthy journalists eulogized him as a victim of the Washington left, which by 1957, in their eyes, included Eisenhower. "The stinking hypocrite in the White House," wrote William Loeb III, the publisher of New Hampshire's *Manchester Union Leader*, had "worn down" McCarthy's "adrenal and other glands." The American hard right had taken his spectacular fall in 1954 as a signal that things were worse than they thought. They had truly believed everything he said. Maybe not every accusation; maybe they understood that he shot from the hip and occasionally missed. But they believed in his message: America was in thrall to an atheistic, Communistic conspiracy in Washington that could only be destroyed by courageous, even reckless, truth-tellers like McCarthy. When he died, Eisenhower and the rest of the establishment told themselves that the conspiratorial populism McCarthy embodied died with him. It did not. His death convinced his adherents that a more thorough makeover of the political right was in order, even if it would take decades to achieve.

McCarthy's death hit Alfred Kohlberg especially hard. The grand master of the China Lobby had been one of the senator's great champions, and McCarthy was the congressional horse on whom he had placed all his bets. Kohlberg had stuck with him even as McCarthy grew toxic among all but the most diehard conservatives. He had brought him to speak in New York in July 1954, at a gala honoring Roy Cohn after he resigned from the senator's office. As the pall of Communist paranoia began to lift, many of its fair-weather followers, like Richard Nixon, quickly distanced themselves from their previous stridency. Others, like Kohlberg, doubled down, convinced that the rise of Eisenhower and the fall of McCarthy were part of the same plot.

In the early 1950s he had struck up a correspondence with a Massachusetts confectioner named Robert Welch. Welch had worked for his brother's candy manufacturer, the James O. Welch Co., best known for inventing Sugar Daddies and Junior Mints, then tried to use his prominence as a business leader as a stepladder into Boston-area Republican politics. He ran unsuccessfully for lieutenant governor in 1950, and tried, again unsuccessfully, to win a delegate spot at the 1952 Republican National Convention. He was not unusual among conservatives in being deeply disturbed by events in Asia—the Communist takeover, the Korean War, the removal of General MacArthur. But like Kohlberg, Welch took things much further. He had dropped out of Harvard Law School, he said, because he thought its faculty was too far to the left. The New Deal, he came to believe, was merely a tool to open the country to Communist takeover. It was only logical that he would see the same radical machinations behind America's foreign policy. He backed Robert Taft for president in 1952, and when Eisenhower bested the senator for the nomination, Welch quit the Republican Party. Taft's defeat, Welch said, was "the dirtiest deal in American political history."

Welch began writing. Like Kohlberg, he was prolific and unfiltered. Treatises, newsletters, articles, and short books flowed forth. In 1952 Henry Regnery, a conservative publisher, released his book *May God For-*

give Us, in which Welch wrote, "It is my utterly sincere belief that, through whatever puppets activate to exert their combined insidious pressures, MacArthur was fired by Stalin." The book offered Welch's map for what he believed was a Communist plot to turn America into a socialist dictatorship, and he drew lines linking Hollywood, Roosevelt, the New Deal, Acheson, and the China Hands in one vast network. The tome, which *The New York Times* dismissed as "pure polemic," sold more than 100,000 copies.

Welch's extremism may have distanced him from the Eisenhower administration, but it won him powerful friends among the Republican Party's hard right. He was especially close to Senator William Knowland of California, who had become majority leader after his party's sweeping victory in November 1952. It was Knowland who first told Welch the story of a young Baptist missionary and U.S. intelligence agent, John Birch, who had been killed by Chinese Communists in 1945. Welch saw in Birch the embodiment of all his hopes and fears: The death of a young patriot at the hands of evil Communists seemed to foretell the fate of the ignorant West, but at the same time the strength of Birch's ideals (or what Welch assumed them to be) offered a glint of hope amid the gloom. In 1953 Welch published another book, *The Life of John Birch*, with the resounding subtitle "In the Story of One American Boy, the Ordeal of His Age." The young man, Welch said, had not just been murdered. His death went unpublicized because, he wrote, the Truman administration was bent on a Communist victory in China.

Birch and the alleged crimes against him became Welch's obsession, and in 1958 he gathered a group of like-minded businessmen as the founding board of the John Birch Society (among them was Fred Koch, the father of Charles and David). Overnight it became the refuge for many of the most die-hard partisans of the Red Scare, and within five years claimed between 60,000 and 100,000 members. For decades to come it stood synonymous with the right-wing fringe in American politics; it was also an incubator for its next generation of anti-Communist, anti-government radicals.

Alfred Kohlberg joined the Birch board a year later. By the late 1950s he too had soured on the Republican Party. He believed that despite all the effort that men like Welch and McCarthy had put into fighting the left-wing conspiracy, the Communists had won. Eisenhower had accepted the New Deal. He had placed Warren on the Supreme Court. John Foster Dulles had allegedly failed to clean house at the State Department, and his brother, Allen, had likewise provided a haven for Communists at the Central Intelligence Agency, where he was director. The Communists had taken over—they just hadn't announced themselves. Generations later, the heirs to Welch and Kohlberg would call it the deep state. The government itself was now the enemy.

Welch focused much of his early fire on the chief justice, who by 1958 was an object of extreme, violent derision on the right. Soon after founding the John Birch Society, Welch announced his Movement to Impeach Earl Warren. His animus derived not simply from Warren's "Red Monday" decisions; just as much, if not more, came from the chief justice's lead role in the 1954 *Brown v. Board of Education* decision outlawing school segregation. In the minds of people like Welch, the two went together: It was the Communists who were driving anti-segregation efforts. Over the next decade Welch turned out thousands of roadside billboards, pamphlets, and flyers. Other, like-minded groups quickly followed suit. One such organization, the American Nationalist, based in Inglewood, California, printed a flyer rendered like a Wanted poster with a frontal and sideways shot of Warren. "Warren has been accused of giving aid and comfort to the Communist Party on frequent occasions," it read. "He has illegally transformed the Supreme Court into a Soviet-type Politburo with power over the Congress and over the various state governments."

Welch long remained on the outskirts of conservative politics, shunned by the establishment and even many of those keen to push the movement to the right—most famously the young journalist William F. Buckley Jr., who embraced, then publicly denounced him. But there was a limit to such criticism; Buckley was careful to keep his attack to the man and not the Bircher rank and file. The same went for Senator Barry Goldwater, and later Ronald Reagan, during their runs for the presidency. Both distanced themselves from the group but were careful not to shun it completely. "Every other person in Phoenix is a member of the John Birch Society," Goldwater reportedly told Buckley in 1964. "I'm not talking about commie-haunted apple pickers or cactus drunks. I'm talking about the highest caste of men of affairs." That might be an exaggeration, but the underlying sentiment was correct: The furies of the Red Scare had subsided, but they had not been extinguished; like a coal-seam fire, they continued to burn underground, even if they were unseen from above.

The Red Scare had inflamed a passionate core of hard-right conservatives, who were prepared to believe the worst about the government and liberals, and to act on it. The era left a permanent scar on the left, one measured not only in lives and livelihoods lost, but in the deepened and lasting divide between moderates and progressives. But it transformed the right to a much greater extent. The Republican Party had accepted the hard right into its ranks after it refused to deploy anti-Communism in the 1948 presidential election. Eisenhower and his allies managed to push it back out, but they had shown the possibility of capturing the party, even if doing so might take decades.

For the countless diehards who had boycotted films and libraries and followed McCarthy to the end, the closing of the Red Scare era seemed like a defeat. They had been told Communists ran the government, and that there would be some great apocalyptic reckoning, when McCarthy—or someone of his kind—would cleanse the temple of the snakes. But it had never happened; instead, McCarthy was the one cast out. To the true believers, the snakes still occupied the temple. Men like Kohlberg had organized them, and McCarthy had shown how they could be organized into a potent voting bloc. It was left to future generations of Republican politicians to decide whether to keep such sentiments on the fringe, or to invite them into the center of the party.

EPILOGUE

Helen Reid Bryan, the executive secretary of the Joint Anti-Fascist Refugee Committee, walked out of the women's prison camp in Alderson, West Virginia, in February 1951. The last five years had been a terrifying blur. After she refused to hand over her group's records to HUAC, back in 1946, the House of Representatives had voted her in contempt, then referred her case to the Department of Justice. No one expected the government, especially under a Democratic president, to prosecute. "If we had any premonition that imprisonment would result from this, no one of us would have allowed Helen Bryan to take the fall," wrote Howard Fast, a member of the committee's board. But it did: Her conviction came quickly, though she fought it, all the way to the Supreme Court—which ruled against her on May 9, 1950. She entered Alderson in November.

Back in New York City, she tried to put her life back together. So much had changed since the heady days of the 1930s, when her progressive politics were on the march. Now those same politics were getting people like her sent to jail. Even as she had appealed her conviction, she kept working for the refugee committee, but she was sailing a sinking ship. She organized rallies, though increasingly they were focused on saving the organization, not refugees. A group of left-leaning writers, led by Lillian Hellman and Dashiell Hammett, organized the Citizens to Safeguard the JAFRC. But then the attorney general added the refugee aid group to his list of subversive organizations, without a hearing, without even explaining why it belonged there. Treasury agents rifled through its files, and in February 1948 the IRS canceled its tax-exempt status. It became hard for Bryan to find venues willing to rent space for events. Forget Madison Square Garden, where it had once held boisterous rallies. Third-tier country clubs wouldn't have them, and even liberal organizations like the

Boston City Club canceled contracts. Five board members resigned, and Bryan found it impossible to locate people willing to replace them. The organization simply collapsed.

Bryan worked, for a while, for the American Labor Party. She wrote a book about her experience at Alderson, entitled *Inside: The Story of One Prisoner and One Prisoner's Friends in the Federal Penitentiary for Women*. It sold well, mostly because people wanted to hear the story of this woman's stand against HUAC. But the book said little about her pre-imprisonment life. Her time at Alderson had convinced her that dramatic reform of American's penal system was necessary, a message that few people wanted to hear in the early 1950s, when exaggerated fears of organized crime and juvenile delinquency dominated the media almost as much as exaggerated fears of Communism.

One person who did pay attention to Bryan's message was a prison reformer in Massachusetts named Miriam Van Waters, who ran the Massachusetts Reformatory for Women in Framingham, outside of Boston. She drew inspiration from the Social Gospel movement and urban reformers like Jane Addams, infusing their legacy with a brave, strident feminism wholly out of sync with the traditional mores of the 1950s. She lauded *Inside* in a review for *The Nation*, and finally met Bryan through a friend in 1953.

It was a hard time for both women. Bryan had recently undergone brain surgery. Van Waters's daughter had died in a car accident. The two women struck up a correspondence, and Van Waters invited Bryan to speak at the prison. Soon Bryan was coming to visit Framingham regularly, dining with Van Waters, going with her to church, diving into conversations about prison reform and politics and feminism, finding long-sought solace in each other. They peppered their letters with phrases like "love of my life," "sweet, my dear," and other terms of endearment. "To tell you that you have lived your life gloriously during this past year," Bryan wrote to Van Waters, "to tell you that you have transmuted the pain of her leaving into a greater love for those around you—to tell you that you have transformed losing her into helping others to find life—is, I know, not what will comfort—not what will still the agony that is yours."

Van Waters hired Bryan as an assistant at Framingham in June 1953.

Estelle Freedman, Van Waters's biographer, wrote that she might have even been considering Bryan as her successor, a position she had once hoped her daughter would fill. Bryan had reason to hope that, finally, her old life was behind her, and that a new one was beginning. But within days, the past caught up with her. Although Bryan had served her sentence and was no longer working with the Joint Anti-Fascist Refugee Committee, the FBI had continued to keep tabs on her, and it seems likely that the bureau tipped off anti-Communist politicians in the Massachusetts legislature about a convicted subversive working in the state prison system. Governor Christian Herter, a moderate Republican who had once criticized HUAC as a member of Congress, expressed his support for Van Waters but called Bryan's hiring "unfortunate." Anti-Communist legislators opened a probe of Framingham and the state's prison system. Its commissioner suggested to Van Waters that for everyone's sake, Bryan should resign, citing health reasons. She quit on July 1, 1953, less than a month after she began. "You know that I have never in my life been a member of the Communist Party," she wrote to Van Waters.

Bryan returned to New York City. Once more she struggled to find work. Her claim about her health was no mere excuse. The rehabilitation following her brain surgery and a weakened heart left her lethargic. She volunteered for the Salvation Army, collecting clothes for prisoners. She tried to find work but was everywhere rejected; she suspected, not without reason, that federal agents were behind her employment difficulties. She began spending extended periods at her family's house in Vermont. She remained close to Van Waters, who came to visit her frequently. In between they traded letters daily using an anonymous mailbox in downtown Framingham. The FBI, still watching Bryan closely, kept meticulous notes filled with intrusive opinions about the two women's friendship.

By the late 1950s Helen Bryan was spending most of her time in Dorset, Vermont, about as out of the way as one could get and still be within a day's drive of friends and family in New York and around New England. Dorset is a speck on all but the most local maps, but it is near the summer vacation spot of Manchester, which gave Bryan access to enough folks coming out from Boston and New York to keep her life interesting. Her house, just east of the town center, had been in the Bryan family for decades and had long been a waystation for passing progressives. She had hosted the Black intellectual W. E. B. Du Bois there in 1932, and soon after the Black poet and civil rights figure James Weldon Johnson. Bryan sold the house in 1955, had a new one built nearby, and settled in Dorset permanently in early 1958.

The FBI continued to monitor Bryan, but there was not much to see. She embedded herself in Dorset's intellectual life, organizing study groups and carrying on long, deep conversations about religion and politics over dinner at the Pelican, a nearby restaurant. She entertained visitors, including Van Waters. She found a job as treasurer of the town's Congregationalist Church. FBI agents canvassed the area around Dorset, and in their reports noted that no one had ever "noted anything about Miss Bryan's demeanor or speech with would cast the slightest suspicion on her loyalty." In 1955 the Justice Department canceled her entry in its security index, which among other things had marked her for summary detention in the case of a national emergency.

The bureau paid her one final visit. On May 22, 1958, two agents drove seventy miles from the FBI field office in Albany, New York, to Dorset. Bryan's new house was just north of the town center, across from the Dorset Field Club golf course. It was a modest one-story ranch, set back two hundred feet from the road. It was painted white, with black shutters. They knocked on her front door, and Bryan welcomed them in. She offered them water, but otherwise kept her hospitality to the minimum required in a situation like this.

The two men asked her about the Joint Anti-Fascist Refugee Committee. Yes, she said, she had been a part of it. No, it had not been Communist-dominated. No, none of its staff had been party members. Maybe, she conceded, some of the board members had Communist leanings, but she ran the organization, set its agenda, and hired its staff. "She stated that inasmuch as there was no Communist direction of her activities it followed that there could be no Communist direction of the activities of the Committee," the agents wrote in their report.

They pressed on. Did the party fund the refugee committee? No, she said, but sometimes it sent checks. Did she know Earl Browder, onetime head of the Communist Party? Yes, she said, she knew Earl Browder. In fact she admired him greatly, and thought he was a good man. But he had never tried to influence the committee, nor would she have allowed him to if he had.

Why were these men here? she wondered. After all the fights, the pain that HUAC and the FBI and the Department of Justice had caused her, after they had conceded, in 1955, that she wasn't a suspect after all, why now were these men here? She had done all she could to leave that world, that part of her life, behind.

Abruptly, she cut them off. No more questions. She showed them to the door, politely but curtly. As the two wrote, "She did not think she wanted to talk to Special Agents of the FBI any more."

ACKNOWLEDGMENTS

I began this book in the fall of 2019, which means that for a good bit of the time I would have normally spent deep in the archives, I was locked out of libraries by the pandemic. Fortunately, I was aided immensely by librarians, archivists, and students who helped me get much of what I needed. They include Michael Koncewicz and Cole Stallone at New York University, Colton Babbitt at the University of Misssippi, Caroline Qi-Ao Chen at Stanford, Sarah Hutcheon at the Harvard Schlesinger Library, and Rebecca Goldman at Wellesley. Thanks to you all. In many cases before and after pandemic restrictions, I was able to visit archives personally and fruitfully, thanks to the assistance of people like Jean McElwee Cannon at the Hoover Institution, Sarah Waitz and the National Archives, Eric Dillalogue at the University of Pennsylvania, and Kathleen Monahan at the Boston Public Library.

In the meantime I was able to carry out significant research on my own online, thanks to a visiting fellowship in American studies at Columbia University, made possible by Andrew Delbanco. Thank you, Andy. Many thanks as well to my dear friend Kate Singer, who helped me immensely with additional research opportunities.

I would not have made it through this project without the support of my writers group, who read early chapter drafts and in general gave me a standard of excellence in scholarship and prose to reach for: Matthew Connelly, Jim Goodman, David Greenberg, Jim Ledbetter, Natalia Mehlman Petrzela, Michael Massing, Claire Potter, Jim Traub, Ted Widmer, and Brenda Wineapple.

I am heavily indebted to the family of Helen Reid Bryan, including Anna Carlson Gannett, Alison Carlson, and their mother, Helen Garland, who was Bryan's niece and namesake. I had the pleasure of speaking with

Mrs. Garland at her home in Gloucester, Massachusetts, shortly before her death in 2022.

My editor at *The New York Times*, Bill McDonald, graciously gave me four months of leave to write my initial draft, and then was kind enough to welcome me back. Writing obituaries has been great training for writing history, as well as an immensely fulfilling job, and I appreciate Bill for giving me the opportunity.

This is the fourth book I've written with the guidance of my agent, Heather Schroder. I trust her immensely and without reservation. This book would not exist without her. The same can be said for my editor, Kathy Belden, who took a scruffy, confused first draft and turned it into something I am proud to see published.

And finally, Joanna, Talia, and Elliot—I love you, and your patience with me along this journey shows how much you love me in return.

SOURCE NOTES

Prologue

1 *She was in a hearing chamber:* New York Times, January 25, 1946.

1 *An FBI report:* Re: Helen Reid Bryan, September 14, 1944, 1498516-0-Section 1, FBI FOIA (Helen Reid Bryan).

1 *Another report:* Re: Helen Reid Bryan, May 16, 1945, 1498516-0-Section 2, FBI FOIA (Helen Reid Bryan).

1 *In December 1945:* Helen Reid Bryan Prepared Statement to HUAC, January 24, 1946, TAM.070 Box 2, Joint Anti-Fascist Refugee Committee (JAFRC) Papers, Tamiment Library, New York University.

1 *A month later:* Report from Helen Reid Bryan, N.D., TAM.070 Box 2, JAFRC Papers, Tamiment Library.

2 *they, nor her lawyer:* Untitled memoir of Helen Garland, September 6, 1984, Family Papers of Helen Reid Bryan; Deery, *Red Apple*, p. 17.

2 *No one who knew her:* Re: Helen Reid Bryan, May 16, 1945, FBI FOIA; Untitled Memoir of Helen Garland, Family Papers of Helen Reid Bryan.

2 *She corresponded with:* Letter from Helen R. Bryan to W. E. B. Du Bois, October 18, 1935, W. E. B. Du Bois Papers (MS 312), Special Collections and University Archives, University of Massachusetts Amherst Libraries; *The Swarthmorean*, July 6, 1934, p. 1; Fundraising letter, April 1942, Box 584, JAFRC, RG 233, NARA.

2 *After some formalities:* Testimony of Helen Reid Bryan, House Committee on Un-American Activities, 79th Cong., 2nd Session, January 24, 1946.

4 *"Miss Bryan has not":* Washington Post, February 5, 1946.

5 *Between 1929:* "Managing the Crisis: The FDIC and RTC Experience—Chronological Overview," https://www.fdic.gov/bank/historical/managing/chronological/pre-fdic.html, accessed April 2, 2024; James Lee and Filippo Mezzanotti, "Bank Distress and Manufacturing: Evidence from the Great Depression," August 2017, https://www.kellogg.northwestern.edu/faculty/mezzanotti/documents/lee_mezzanotti_greatdepression.pdf, accessed April 2, 2024; "How Bad Was the Great Depression? Gauging the Economic Impact," Federal Reserve Bank of St. Louis, https://www.stlouisfed.org/the-great

-depression/curriculum/economic-episodes-in-american-history-part-3, accessed April 2, 2024.

5 *"No man was an island"*: Kempton, *Part of Our Time*, p. 1.

6 *"A large segment"*: Trilling, *The Middle of the Journey*, p. xxviii.

6 *"Communism"*: Isserman, *Which Side Were You On?*, p. 9.

6 *"really the only"*: Lyons, *The Red Decade*, p. 173.

6 *"You were a Communist"*: Gornick, *The Romance of American Communism*, pp. 113–14.

7 *In 1932, 49 percent*: Robert Cohen, *When the Old Left Was Young*, p. xiv.

7 *"I was in the grips"*: Walter Bernstein, *Inside Out*, p. 53.

7 *"Across the land"*: Schlesinger, *The Crisis of the Old Order*, p. 2.

8 *In the mid-1930s*: Wolfskill, *The Revolt of the Conservatives*, p. 61.

8 *The 1937 Conservative Manifesto*: "The Conservative Manifesto," The North Carolina History Project, https://northcarolinahistory.org/encyclopedia/the -conservative-manifesto/, accessed April 2, 2024.

9 *"red revolutionaries"*: Erickson, " 'I Have Not Had One Fact Disproven.' "

10 *One Republican*: Katznelson, *When Affirmative Action Was White*, p. 236.

10 *In 1934 Hamilton Fish*: Hamby, *Man of Destiny*, p. 218.

11 *In 1916, before the United States*: "Black Tom 1916 Bombing," https://www .fbi.gov/history/famous-cases/black-tom-1916-bombing, accessed April 2, 2024.

12 *In March 1946*: "Iron Curtain Speech," National Archives, https://www .nationalarchives.gov.uk/education/resources/cold-war-on-file/iron-curtain -speech/, accessed April 2, 2024.

13 *In 1947 Truman instituted*: Goldstein, "Prelude to McCarthyism."

13 *more than two dozen organizations*: *New York Times*, December 5, 1947, p. 18.

14 *During his 1946*: Oshinsky, *A Conspiracy So Immense*, p. 52.

14 *By 1953*: *Chicago Tribune*, August 25, 1953, p. 1.

15 *Public support*: "Harry S. Truman Public Approval," The American Presidency Project, https://www.presidency.ucsb.edu/statistics/data/harry-s-truman -public-approval, accessed April 2, 2024.

15 *More than five million*: "Truman's Loyalty Program," Harry S. Truman Library and Museum, https://www.trumanlibrary.gov/education/presidential -inquiries/trumans-loyalty-program, accessed April 3, 2024.

16 *In 1953*: "Minute Women of the U.S.A.," Texas State Historical Association, https://www.tshaonline.org/handbook/entries/minute-women-of-the-usa, accessed April 3, 2024.

16 *"The American Communist Party"*: United States v. Dennis et al., 183 F.2d 201 (2d Cir. 1950), https://law.justia.com/cases/federal/appellate-courts/F2/183 /201/266559/, accessed April 19, 2023.

16 *Dalton Trumbo:* Letter from Dalton Trumbo to Eleanor Barr Wheeler, May 18, 1956, in Trumbo, Manfull, ed., *Additional Dialogue*, p. 336.

17 *"He believes himself":* "The Pseudo-Conservative Revolt," in Hofstadter, *The Paranoid Style in American Politics*, p. 47.

18 *"It is the purpose":* "Statement Issued by the Honorable John S. Wood of Georgia, Chairman, House Committee on Un-American Activities," January 24, 1946, Box 1, JAFRC Papers, Tamiment Library.

18 *Helen Gaghan Douglas: Congressional Record*, April 16, 1946, p. 3768.

18 *"I shall vote":* Ibid., p. 3769.

18 *Of the 430:* Ibid., pp. 3772–73.

19 *A few days later:* Untitled memoir of Helen Garland, September 6, 1984, Family Papers of Helen Reid Bryan. In 2006, Graydon Carter, then the editor of *Vanity Fair*, and several partners bought the restaurant and reopened it as the Waverly Inn.

Chapter 1: A Blue Envelope

23 *Dean Acheson:* Acheson, *Present at the Creation*, p. 217.

23 *In a profile: Manchester Guardian*, January 10, 1949.

24 *Acheson's visitor:* Ibid.

24 *not going to stop them:* Acheson, *Present at the Creation*, p. 217.

25 *But now it seemed:* Ibid., pp. 196–98.

26 *Salka Viertel:* Viertel, *The Kindness of Strangers*, p. 276.

26 *Lyudmila Pavilichenko:* Isserman, *Which Side Were You On?*, p. 128.

26 *In 1944 the War Shipping: San Bernardino Sun*, February 27, 1944.

26 *He picked a fight:* Acheson, *Present at the Creation*, pp. 195–96.

27 *That point:* 861.00/2 - 2246: Telegram, https://nsarchive2.gwu.edu/coldwar/documents/episode-1/kennan.htm, accessed April 3, 2024.

27 *In a subsequent article:* X (George F. Kennan), "The Sources of Soviet Conduct," *Foreign Affairs* (July 1947): 566–82.

27 *"Greece was in":* Acheson, *Present at the Creation*, p. 221.

27 *Britain was having: The Guardian*, February 7, 2018.

28 *And yet:* Acheson, *Present at the Creation*, pp. 215–18.

28 *"Under the circumstances":* Ibid., p. 218.

29 *The following Monday:* Ibid., p. 219.

29 *led to the war in Vietnam:* Ibid.

29 *Arthur Vandenberg: New York Times*, June 6, 1972.

29 *Truman did just that:* Truman Doctrine (1947), https://www.archives.gov/milestone-documents/truman-doctrine, accessed April 3, 2024; Acheson, *Present at the Creation*, p. 222.

30 *The only member: New York Times*, March 13, 1947.

30 *The left-leaning journalist:* I. F. Stone, *The Truman Era*, p. xxi.

31 *"A curious uneasiness"*: *The Progressive*, October 22, 1945.

31 *"He could, and did"*: Acheson, *Present at the* Creation, p. 730.

31 *When Truman*: Ibid., p. 104.

32 *The agriculture economist*: Haynes and Klehr, *Venona*, pp. 62–63.

32 *Victor Perlo*: Ibid.

32 *Perhaps the most incendiary*: Chambers, *Witness*, pp. 399–401.

33 *He told Phil Graham*: Aldous, *Schlesinger*, pp. 147–48.

33 *With so much chatter*: Haynes and Klehr, *Venona*, p. 332.

33 *Arthur Adams*: Ibid., pp. 173–75.

33 *At the end of 1944*: Gage, *G-Man*, p. 325.

34 *In January*: Klehr and Radosh, *The Amerasia Spy Case*, passim.

34 *Then, in September 1945*: Knight, *How the Cold War Began*, passim.

34 *Even more significant*: Olmsted, *Red Spy Queen*, passim.

34 *in mid-1945*: Elizabeth Bentley, *Out of Bondage*, p. 286.

34 *In November 1945*: Memo to J. Edgar Hoover, November 16, 1945, Silver-master 65-56402-1. All 162 volumes of the FBI's Silvermaster files, which cover most aspects of the bureau's counterespionage efforts of the late 1940s, can be found at https://archive.org/details/FBISilvermasterFile/FBI%20File %20Silvermaster%20Part%201%20November%201945/ (accessed August 1, 2024).

35 *mentioned someone*: Olmsted, *Red Spy Queen*, pp. 56, 200.

35 *Hoover immediately*: J. Edgar Hoover to Brigadier General Harry Hawkins Vaughan, November 8, 1945, Silvermaster 65-56402-403; Gage, *G-Man*, p. 328.

35 *At one point*: J. Edgar Hoover to Attorney General, November 17, 1945, Sil-vermaster 65-56402-403-581x; Gage, *G-Man*, p. 329.

35 *He was*: Gage, *G-Man*, pp. 12–14.

35 *Hoover graduated*: Ibid., pp. 43–48; Tally Edmondson, "The Campus Con-federate Legacy We're Not Talking About," *The Chronicle of Higher Education*, July 8, 2020, https://www.chronicle.com/article/the-racist-fraternity-that -tried-to-shut-me-up?sra=true, accessed April 5, 2024.

36 *As Hoover's biographer*: Gage, *G-Man*, p. 30.

36 *On July 1, 1919*: "The Palmer Raids," https://www.fbi.gov/history/famous -cases/palmer-raids, accessed April 5, 2024.

36 *The campaign culminated*: Adam Hochschild, "When America Tried to De-port Its Radicals," *The New Yorker*, November 14, 2019.

37 *As 1920 progressed*: Ibid.

37 *Hoover had lost a bid*: Gage, *G-Man*, p. 206.

37 *Roosevelt, worried*: "World War, Cold War, 1939–1953," https://www.fbi.gov /history/brief-history/world-war-cold-war; Theoharis and Cox, *The Boss*, p. 157.

37 *Even before:* Gage, *G-Man,* p. 216.

38 *During the war:* Theoharis, "The FBI and the American Legion Contact Program, 1940–1966."

38 *if an apartment-dweller:* My grandfather carried out such investigations during wartime Chicago. He said most of them went like this: A Mr. Goldberg would call the office and say, "You all need to check out my neighbor, Mr. Schmidt. He's a Nazi." My grandfather would interview Mr. Schmidt, who would offer compelling evidence that he was not, in fact, a Nazi. But he would also add, "You should check out Mr. Goldberg; he's a Communist." My grandfather would then go interview Mr. Goldberg, who would give similarly compelling evidence of his non-communist bona fides. Finally, my grandfather would interview a third neighbor, to see what was going on. "Oh, Mr. Goldberg and Mr. Schmidt are just fine," the neighbor would say. "But ever since Goldberg's tree fell into Schmidt's yard, they have hated each other!"

38 *Truman, in private:* McCullough, *Truman,* p. 550.

38 *On February 1, 1946:* Memo, Harry S. Truman to Fred M. Vinson, With Attachment, February 6, 1946, The Truman Administration's Loyalty Program, President's Secretary's Files, Harry S. Truman Library and Museum.

39 *On November 25:* Lewy, *Federal Loyalty-Security Program,* p. 3.

39 *The resulting:* Executive Order 9835, Library Collections, Truman Library, https://www.trumanlibrary.gov/library/executive-orders/9835/executive-order-9835, accessed March 23, 2023.

40 *The flaws: New York Times,* April 13, 1947.

40 *"the government is entitled":* Cited in Durr, "The Loyalty Order's Challenge to the Constitution," p. 303.

40 *A few months:* "A Legless Veteran's Struggle," *Against the Current,* No. 184, September/October 2016. https://againstthecurrent.org/atc184/p4762/, accessed March 23, 2023.

41 *Even more worrisome:* Walter White to Harry S. Truman, November 26, 1948, The Truman Administration's Loyalty Program, Official File, Truman Library, https://www.trumanlibrary.gov/library/research-files/walter-white-harry-s-truman, accessed March 23, 2023.

41 *During its five:* Lewy, *Federal Loyalty-Security Program,* p. 4.

41 *"This is not":* Truman, *Memoirs by Harry S. Truman: Years of Trial and Hope: 1946–1952,* pp. 280–81.

42 *"Yes, it was terrible":* McCullough, *Truman,* p. 553.

Chapter 2: Swimming-Pool Communists

43 *A red-faced pug of a man: New York Times,* November 20, 1970.

43 *"practically every":* Gladchuck, *Hollywood and Anticommunism,* p. 114.

44 *During the:* U.S. Congress, House, Special Committee on Un-American Ac-

tivities, Investigation of Un-American Propaganda Activities in the U.S., Vol. 4, 75th Cong., 2nd Sess., 1938, p. 2857.

44 *"It is a menace"*: J. Parnell Thomas to Harry S. Truman, March 31, 1947, The Truman Administration's Loyalty Program, Official File, Harry S. Truman Library and Museum, https://www.trumanlibrary.gov/library/research-files/correspondence-between-j-parnell-thomas-and-harry-s-truman, accessed March 16, 2023.

45 *John Thomas Taylor:* U.S. Congress, House, Committee on Un-American Activities, Investigation of Un-American Propaganda Activities in the U.S., 80th Cong., 1st Sess., 1947, p. 6.

45 *May Talmadge:* Ibid., p. 272.

45 *"The FBI and HUAC":* Ibid., Part 2, p. 33.

46 *"We don't know":* Goodman, *The Committee*, p. 172.

47 *In her memoir:* Viertel, *The Kindness of Strangers*, p. 215.

47 *"The communists had led":* Walter Bernstein, *Inside Out*, p. 134.

48 *At the top:* Many thanks to Maurice Isserman for explaining the party structure around this time to me.

48 *"I knew that":* Walter Bernstein, *Inside Out*, pp. 11–12; Kempton, *Part of Our Time*, p. 191.

49 *There was a:* Critchlow, *When Hollywood Was Right*, p. 35.

49 *In 1934:* Mitchell, *The Campaign of the Century*, p. xiii.

49 *Up until:* "When Hitler's Henchman Called the Shots in Hollywood," *The Daily Beast*, December 2, 2017.

50 *In April 1933:* "The Screen Writers' Guild: An Early History of the Writers Guild of America," https://www.wgfoundation.org/screenwritersguild-history, accessed April 6, 2024.

50 *In early 1945:* The Hollywood Reporter, September 28, 2021.

51 *On October 5:* Los Angeles Times, October 6, 1945

51 *"sympathetic":* Cogley, *Report on Blacklisting I*, pp. 63–64.

51 *In Los Angeles:* The Hollywood Reporter, November 30, 2012; Wilkerson, *Hollywood Godfather*, p. 218.

52 *Wilkerson's column:* The Hollywood Reporter, July 29, 1946; Wilkerson, *Hollywood Godfather*, p. 219.

52 *"a near-hopeless":* Reagan, *Where's the Rest of Me?*, p. 126.

52 *"Most of us":* Ibid., p. 128.

52 *"pronounced":* Ibid., p. 150.

52 *Soon he:* Brands, *Reagan*, p. 97.

52 *to J. Edgar Hoover:* Reagan, *Where's the Rest of Me?*, pp. 128, 150–53.

53 *They even had:* Ceplair and Englund, *The Inquisition in Hollywood*, pp. 210–11; Friedrich, *City of Nets*, p. 168; Cogley, *Report on Blacklisting I*, p. 11.

53 *"The influence of Communists":* Rand, *Screen Guide for Americans*, https://

archive.lib.msu.edu/DMC/AmRad/screenguideamericans.pdf, accessed March 15, 2023.

54 *"This is the raw"*: The New Yorker, February 14, 1948.

54 *in May 1947*: Ceplair and Englund, *The Inquisition in Hollywood*, pp. 258–59.

54 *"Nobody can"*: Ibid., p. 259.

55 *He also confirmed*: U.S. Congress, House, Committee on Un-American Activities, Communist Infiltration of Hollywood Motion-Picture Industry, 80th Cong., 1st Sess., 1947, pp. 351–52, 355.

55 *infiltration in Hollywood*: Bob Thomas, *The Clown Prince of Hollywood*, p. 146.

Chapter 3: We'll All Go to Jail

56 *The screenwriter*: Interview with Christopher Trumbo, *Trumbo* (documentary), 2007.

56 *"a resolute"*: James Lardner, "The Dalton Trumbo I Knew," *The New Republic*, February 24, 2016.

56 *Trumbo attributed*: Letter to Maud Trumbo, November 1, 1949, in Trumbo, Manfull, ed., *Additional Dialogue*, pp. 132–33.

57 *He'd always been*: Cook, *Dalton Trumbo*, p. 46.

57 *Trumbo spent*: Ibid., pp. 52, 59–60.

57 *During that time*: Ibid., p. 56.

57 *He dabbled*: Ibid., pp. 61, 63.

57 *He found*: Ibid., pp. 78–88.

57 *By then*: *Trumbo* (documentary).

57 *the median screenwriter*: Ceplair and Englund, *The Inquisition in Hollywood*, p. 3.

58 *in 1940 he wrote*: "Harry Bridges: A Discussion of the Latest Effort to Deport Civil Liberties and the Rights of American Labor."

58 *In 1943*: Cook, *Dalton Trumbo*, p. 148.

58 *"Rankin is one"*: Ibid., p. 171.

58 *had singled out*: The Hollywood Reporter, November 30, 2012.

58 *Forty-two*: New York Times, October 26, 1947.

59 *Guy Endore*: Ibid.

59 *One left-leaning director*: Dmytryk, *It's a Hell of a Life but Not a Bad Living*, p. 95.

59 *A dozen*: Gordon Kahn, *Hollywood on Trial*, p. 135.

59 *Another writer*: New York Times, November 2, 2000.

59 *"Only two of them have talent"*: Quoted in Friedrich, *City of Nets*, 304.

60 *The writer and director*: Dmytryk, *It's a Hell of a Life but Not a Bad Living*, p. 304.

60 *The Supreme Court*: Ring Lardner Jr., *The Lardners*, p. 320.

60 *A few days:* Bessie, *Inquisition in Eden*, p. 186.

61 *The hearings: Time*, November 3, 1947.

61 *Two days:* Friedrich, *City of Nets*, p. 311.

61 *In Los Angeles:* Bessie, *Inquisition in Eden*, p. 190.

61 *Then they boarded:* Kanfer, *A Journal of the Plague Years*, p. 59.

62 *Trumbo and the ten:* Dmytryk, *Odd Man Out*, pp. 50–51.

62 *One of them:* Dmytryk, *It's a Hell of a Life but Not a Bad Living*, p. 98.

62 *The night before:* Gordon Kahn, *Hollywood on Trial*, p. 5.

62 *Chairman Thomas: New York Times*, October 26, 1947.

63 *The* Los Angeles Times: *Los Angeles Times*, October 21, 1947; *New York Times*, October 26, 1947.

63 *Jack Warner:* U.S. Congress, House, Committee on Un-American Activities, Hearings Regarding the Communist Infiltration of the Motion Picture Industry, 80th Cong., 1st Sess., 1947, p. 10.

64 *Louis B. Mayer:* Ibid., p. 70.

64 *Sam Wood:* Ibid., p. 54.

64 *"Under certain":* Ibid., p. 94.

64 *"If you mention":* Ibid, p. 66.

64 *The actor Gary Cooper:* Ibid., p. 221.

64 *One discordant note: Los Angeles Times*, October 22, 1947; *Washington Post*, October 22, 1947.

65 *Warner even:* Hearings Regarding the Communist Infiltration of the Motion Picture Industry, p. 33.

65 *"You paint":* Ibid., p. 90.

65 *"If outlawing":* Ibid., p. 170.

65 *When Taylor finished: Atlanta Constitution*, October 23, 1947; *New York Times*, October 23, 1947.

66 *Rather, he insisted:* Hearings Regarding the Communist Infiltration of the Motion Picture Industry, p. 215.

66 *It was, he said:* Ibid., p. 330.

68 *The chairman continued: Time*, November 10, 1947.

68 *Like many: New York Times*, October 3, 2008.

68 *"I have written":* Hearings Regarding the Communist Infiltration of the Motion Picture Industry, p. 494.

69 *He settled: New York Times*, August 16, 1956.

69 *A rally:* Bessie, *Inquisition in Eden*, p. 219.

69 *"We're not through": New York Times*, December 7, 1947.

69 *On November 24: Washington Post*, November 25, 1947.

69 *Less than: New York Times*, December 6, 1947.

69 *The real shock: New York Times*, November 25, 1947; Cogley, *Report on Blacklisting I*, pp. 21–23.

70 *Eric Johnston:* Mann, *Kate,* p. 360.

70 *"Our ticket buyers":* The Hollywood Reporter, November 19, 2012.

70 *There must be a blacklist:* Ceplair and Englund, *The Inquisition in Hollywood,* p. 329; *The Hollywood Reporter,* November 5, 1947.

70 *"probably the most":* The Nation, May 4, 1957.

70 *The actions:* New York Times, November 26, 1947.

71 *he was announcing exactly that:* Trumbo, *The Nation,* May 4, 1957, pp. 383–87; Cogley, *Report on Blacklisting I,* pp. 21–23; Dmytryk, *Odd Man Out,* p. 91.

71 *"It should be fully realized":* New York Times, December 7, 1947.

71 *Dmytryk and Scott:* Dmytryk, *Odd Man Out,* p. 90.

71 *Zanuck couldn't stomach:* Ceplair and Englund, *The Inquisition in Hollywood,* p. 331.

71 *Bogart called:* Bogart, Humphrey. "I'm No Communist," *Photoplay,* May 1948.

71 *Eventually even stalwarts:* Friedrich, *City of Nets,* p. 326.

72 *The ten faced:* Kanfer, *A Journal of the Plague Years,* pp. 77–78; Cook, *Dalton Trumbo,* p. 190.

Chapter 4: A Civil War on the Left

73 *Truman's approval numbers:* "Harry S. Truman Public Approval," The American Presidency Project, https://www.presidency.ucsb.edu/statistics/data/harry -s-truman-public-approval, accessed April 7, 2024.

74 *He was born:* New York Times, November 19, 1965.

74 *He once gave:* Hellman, *Scoundrel Time,* p. 126.

74 *"You feel that he":* New York Times, February 8, 1948.

75 *Arthur Schlesinger Jr.:* Los Angeles Times, March 12, 2000.

75 *In September 1946:* Washington Post, September 13, 1947.

75 *But Byrnes:* New York Times, September 19, 1946.

75 *In his diary:* Cited in Hamby, *Beyond the New Deal,* p. 133.

76 *In January 1947:* New York Times, January 11, 1947.

76 *In March 1947:* New York Times, April 1, 1947.

76 *But a month later:* New York Times, April 18, 1947.

77 *Bruce Bliven:* Devine, *Henry Wallace's 1948 Presidential Campaign and the Future of Postwar Liberalism,* p. 36.

77 *"Wallace had rather":* Ibid.

77 *"I knew from":* Devine, *Henry Wallace's 1948 Presidential Campaign and the Future of Postwar Liberalism,* p. 36.

77 *he was expected:* Osler L. Peterson, "Henry Wallace: A Divided Mind," *The Atlantic,* August 1948.

78 *His adviser Clark Clifford:* Memo, Clark Clifford to Harry S. Truman, No-

vember 19, 1947, The 1948 Election Campaign; Political File, Harry S. Truman Library and Museum, https://www.trumanlibrary.gov/library/research
-files/memo-clark-clifford-harry-s-truman?documentid=NA&pagenumber
=1, accessed March 29, 2023.

78 *At a speech:* New York Times, March 18, 1948.

78 *Speaking at Gilmore Stadium:* New York Times, September 24, 1948.

78 *"Communists perform":* New York Times, December 19, 1947.

78 *"the one movement":* New York Times, January 15, 1948.

78 *In April 1948:* New York Times, April 12, 1948.

78 *A month later:* New York Times, May 30, 1948.

79 *At a press conference:* Cited in Devine, *Henry Wallace's 1948 Presidential Campaign and the Future of Postwar Liberalism,* p. 126; New York Times, July 24, 1948.

79 *When a* New York Times: *New York Times,* February 8, 1948.

79 *William Leuchtenburg:* Cited in Devine, *Henry Wallace's 1948 Presidential Campaign and the Future of Postwar Liberalism,* p. 190.

80 *In January 1947: New York Times,* January 5, 1947.

81 *In September 1948:* Telegram, Leon Henderson to Harry S. Truman, September 27, 1948, The Truman Administration's Loyalty Program, Official File; Truman Library, https://www.trumanlibrary.gov/library/research-files/telegram
-leon-henderson-harry-s-truman?documentid=NA&pagenumber=3, accessed March 30, 2023.

81 *When the group's:* International Herald Tribune, November 2, 1947; Summary Report, May 1, 1948, J. B. Matthews Papers, Box 39, Folder 3, Duke University Libraries; New York Times, November 11, 1947.

81 *When Wallace: Chicago Tribune,* April 1, 1948.

81 *The Pittsburgh Press: Pittsburgh Press,* May 1, 1948, clipping in Box 39, Folder 3, Matthews Papers.

Chapter 5: Un-American Activities

84 *Without solid evidence:* Memo from J. Edgar Hoover, April 1, 1948, Silvermaster 65-56402-3177.

84 *"We would like":* New York Daily Mirror, May 14, 1948

84 *Although more than:* New York Journal-American, April 2, 1948.

84 *HUAC ordered:* Belknap, *American Political Trials,* p. 210.

85 *But, Quinn and Donegan said:* Olmsted, *Red Spy Queen,* pp. 121–22.

85 *The act barred:* U.S. Code › Title 8 › Chapter 10 › § 451.

85 *And the Supreme Court: Bridges v. Wixon,* 326 U.S. 135 (1945).

86 *When Donegan and Quinn:* Olmsted, *Red Spy Queen,* pp. 121–22.

86 *"I told Mr. Quinn":* Memo from J. Edgar Hoover, April 1, 1948, Silvermaster 65-56402-3177.

86 *In late June:* Martelle, *The Fear Within*, p. 29.

87 *Finally, on July 20:* Washington Post, July 21, 1948; *New York Times*, July 21, 1948.

87 *Before the men:* New York Times, July 21, 1948.

87 *They were:* New York Times, July 22, 1948.

87 *Foster was visibly ailing:* Ibid.

88 *She had already:* Memo from H. B. Fletcher to D. M. Ladd, April 3, 1948, Silvermaster 65-56402-3185.

88 *her version of the story:* Silvermaster 65-56402-407.

88 *The morning after:* New York World-Telegram, July 21, 1948.

89 *Condon was:* New York Times, March 27, 1974,

89 *In March 1948:* Washington Post, March 2, 1948.

90 *Thomas then demanded:* New York Times, March 5, 1948.

90 *He claimed:* New York Times, March 2, 1948.

90 *Marquis Childs:Washington Post*, March 3, 1948.

90 *Thomas Mattingly:* Washington Post, March 12, 1948.

90 *Condon got:* The New Republic, March 15, 1948.

90 *"the country can feel absolutely safe":* Washington Post, March 2, 12, 13, 1948; The New Republic, March 15, 1948.

90 *"does have considerable information":* New York Times, July 28, 1948; Olmsted, *Red Spy Queen*, p. 128; Memo from L. B. Nichols to Clyde Tolson, July 26, 1948, Silvermaster 65-56402-3293.

91 *in 1928:* Wall Street Journal, January 21, 2022.

91 *"When the mouth opened":* Lionel Trilling, foreword to *The Middle of the Journey*, pp. xxii–xxiii.

91 *"Chambers exulted":* Tanenhaus, *Whittaker Chambers*, p. 87.

92 *"Faith is the central":* Chambers, *Witness*, p. xlvi.

92 *Ignatz Reiss:* Ibid., p. 36.

92 *Juliet Poyntz:* Ibid.

92 *twenty-one different addresses:* Tanenhaus, *Whittaker Chambers*, p. 154.

92 *He was baptized Episcopalian:* Chambers, *Witness*, p. 483.

92 *He got a job:* Ibid., pp. 64–65.

93 *Eventually he was moved:* Ibid., p. 478.

93 *three hundred acres:* Tanenhaus, *Whittaker Chambers*, p. 170.

93 *The FBI interviewed:* Ibid., pp. 206–7.

93 *in July 1948:* Ibid., p. 210.

93 *William Remington:* Time, May 15, 1950.

94 *She told them:* U.S. Congress, Senate, Testimony of Elizabeth Bentley Before the Senate Permanent Subcommittee on Investigations, 80th Cong., 2nd Sess., July 30, 1948, pp. 1854–64.

94 *When Stripling:* U.S. Congress, House, Committee on Un-American Activi-

ties, Hearings Regarding Communist Espionage in the United States Government, 80th Cong., 2nd Sess., July 31, 1948, pp. 503–62.

95 *Stripling had first:* Stripling, *The Red Plot Against America*, p. 104.

95 *Chambers traveled:* Chambers, *Witness*, pp. 531–32.

95 *"There is one man":* Ibid.

96 *to the top of Duke Law School:* He graduated third in his class. *New York Times*, May 6, 1994.

97 *he threw himself:* U.S. Congress, House, Committee on Un-American Activities, Hearings Regarding the Communist Infiltration of the Motion Picture Industry, 80th Cong., 1st Sess., 1947, pp. 20–21.

97 *"It is essential":* Nixon, *RN*, pp. 45–46.

97 *Meanwhile he:* New York Times, June 5, 1948.

97 *Nixon did not think:* Nixon, *RN*, p. 52.

98 *"Let 'em read something!":* Chambers, *Witness*, pp. 464–65.

98 *"It was three pages":* Stripling, *The Red Plot Against America*, p. 97.

98 *"shabby gentility":* Kempton, *Part of Our Time*, p. 33.

99 *Nixon had met:* Tanenhaus, *Whittaker Chambers*, p. 231.

99 *He had already:* Stripling, *The Red Plot Against America*, p. 100; Tanenhaus, *Whittaker Chambers*, p. 219.

99 *"a buzzing surge":* Chambers, *Witness*, p. 466.

99 *Chambers understood:* Ibid., p. 539.

100 *"I regarded my action":* U.S. Congress, House, Committee on Un-American Activities, Hearings Regarding Communist Espionage in the U.S. Government, 80th Cong., 1st Sess., 1948, p. 564.

100 *"The purpose of this group":* Ibid., p. 565.

100 *that Communism was:* Ibid.

100 *"at what I considered":* Ibid., p. 572.

101 *"It took me":* Chambers, *Witness*, p. 474.

101 *"The Thomas committee":* New York Times, August 4, 1948.

102 *"So far as I know":* New York Times, August 4, 1948; Weinstein, *Perjury*, p. 18.

Chapter 6: One of You Is Lying

106 *"I remember":* Kempton, *A Part of Our Time*, p. 20.

106 *"I am not":* U.S. Congress, House, Committee on Un-American Activities, Hearings Regarding Communist Espionage in the U.S. Government, 80th Cong., 1st Sess., 1948, p. 643.

107 *Jerome Frank:* Ibid., p. 644.

107 *When Karl Mundt:* Ibid., p. 647.

108 *From then on:* Interview with Allen Weinstein, cited in Tanenhaus, *Whittaker Chambers*, p. 234.

108 *Nixon suggested:* Hearings Regarding Communist Espionage in the U.S. Government, p. 651.

108 *And as much as:* Nixon, *Six Crises,* p. 2.

108 *"absolutely took over":* Interview with Allen Weinstein, cited in Tanenhaus, *Whittaker Chambers,* p. 227; Nixon, *Six Crises,* p. 5.

108 *Hiss's performance:* Nixon, *Six Crises,* p. 6.

109 *The Washington Post: Washington Post,* August 6, 1948.

109 *"I don't want":* Nixon, *Six Crises,* p. 11.

109 *A few hours later:* The President's News Conference, August 5, 1948, Harry S. Truman Library and Museum, https://www.trumanlibrary.gov/library/public-papers/170/presidents-news-conference, accessed April 12, 2023.

109 *"in a state":* Nixon, *Six Crises,* p. 10.

110 *"I was opposing":* Ibid., pp. 10–11.

110 *Just two days:* Hearings Regarding Communist Espionage in the U.S. Government, p. 666.

111 *"not so much":* Nixon, *Six Crises,* p. 21.

111 *Nixon and Chambers:* Nixon, *RN,* p. 57.

111 *Nixon went:* Nixon, *Six Crises,* p. 23.

112 *"The principles":* Hearings Regarding Communist Espionage in the U.S. Government, p. 879.

112 *"For a person":* Ibid., p. 881.

112 *Three days later: New York Times,* August 18, 1948.

112 *"I certainly knew":* I. F. Stone, *The Truman Era,* p. 48.

112 *Michael Straight: The New Republic,* August 16, 1948.

113 *"I do not recall":* Hearings Regarding Communist Espionage in the U.S. Government, p. 938.

113 *"The face has a":* Ibid., p. 940.

113 *At one point:* Ibid., p. 951.

113 *Hiss said that:* Ibid., p. 963.

113 *"Tennis and":* Ibid., p. 961.

114 *Chambers was first:* Chambers, *Witness,* p. 601.

114 *Hiss arrived:* Hearings Regarding Communist Espionage in the U.S. Government, p. 975.

114 *"edgy, delaying":* Nixon, *Six Crises,* p. 31; *Time,* August 30, 1948.

114 *"That is a good idea":* Hearings Regarding Communist Espionage in the U.S. Government, p. 978.

115 *"I don't need to ask":* Ibid., p. 986.

115 *"It is quite significant": New York Herald Tribune,* August 19, 1948.

116 *the first congressional hearing: New York Times,* May 6, 1984.

116 *Though only about 350,000 households:* Ponce de Leon, *That's the Way It Is,* p. 6.

116 *"Confrontation Day"*: For a thorough examination of that day, see Tanenhaus, *Whittaker* Chambers, pp. 265–75.

116 *It was hot: Washington Post*, August 25, 1948.

116 *"one of these"*: Hearings Regarding Communist Espionage in the U.S. Government, p. 1076.

117 *exactly 198 times: Time*, September 6, 1948.

117 *"a self-confessed liar"*: Hearings Regarding Communist Espionage in the U.S. Government, p. 1162.

117 *he described Hiss:* Ibid., p. 1183.

117 *"The story has spread"*: Ibid., p. 1191.

118 *A reporter in Baltimore: Los Angeles Times*, August 28, 1948.

118 *Finally, on August 27, 1948: New York Times*, September 28, 1948.

118 *John Foster Dulles:* Library of Congress Interview with Mr. Thomas L. Hughes.

118 *despite assurances:* Brinkley, *The Publisher*, p. 358.

118 *"somewhat queer"*: Tanenhaus, *Whittaker Chambers*, p. 271.

118 *"No American"*: Ibid., p. 279.

119 *"You feel"*: Chambers, *Witness*, p. 642.

Chapter 7: Foley Square

120 *He captured:* "1948 Electoral College Results," National Archives, https://www.archives.gov/electoral-college/1948, accessed April 9, 2024.

120 *"has done more": New York Times*, October 27, 1948.

120 *Early on the morning: New York Times*, November 3, 1948.

121 *"He thought it"*: Quoted in Lichtman, *The Supreme Court and McCarthy-Era Repression*, p. 17.

121 *Other rumors got around:* Nixon, *Six Crises*, p. 46.

121 *He and Nixon:* Tanenhaus, *Whittaker Chambers*, p. 299.

121 *"I don't think"*: Ibid.

122 *"every Communist"*: U.S. Congress, House, Committee on Un-American Activities, Hearings Regarding Communist Espionage in the U.S. Government, 80th Cong., 1st Sess., 1948, p. 1204.

122 *"The simple fact"*: Chambers, *Witness*, p. 653.

123 *In the early evening: Time*, December 13, 1948.

123 *"pure dynamite": Time*, December 13, 1948; Nixon, *Six Crises*, p. 49.

123 *calling Chambers:* Nixon, *Six Crises*, pp. 52–53.

124 *After a heated argument:* Ibid., p. 57.

124 *for example, that the typeface:* The dispute over the Hiss typewriter continued to be a major point in the debate over his guilt for decades to come, e.g.: https://algerhiss.com/history/the-hiss-case-the-1940s/the-typewriter/what-the-fbi-knew-and-hid/, accessed April 9, 2024.

124 *But after an expert: Washington Post*, December 16, 1948.

125 *Laurence Duggan:* Washington Post, December 21, 1948.

125 *"We will give":* Washington Post, December 27, 1948.

125 *"consult their actions":* CBS News Radio, December 21, 1948.

125 *Archibald MacLeish:* MacLeish, *Collected Poems (1917–1952).*

125 *Duggan was:* Vassiliev and Weinstein, *The Haunted Wood,* pp. 3–21.

126 *After graduating from Barnard:* New York Times, March 1, 2011.

127 *The Foreign Agents Registration:* Lamphere and Shachtman, *The FBI-KGB War,* pp. 100–103.

127 *"a serious person":* Haynes and Klehr, *Venona,* p. 157.

127 *"Sima is without doubt":* Hoover to SAC, Washington Field Office, December 31, 1948, Silvermaster 65-58365-3.

128 *and created a task force:* Lamphere and Shachtman, *The FBI-KGB War,* p. 110; *United States v. Coplon,* 84 F. Supp. 472 (S.D.N.Y. 1949).

128 *It took the agents:* Lamphere and Shachtman, *The FBI-KGB War,* pp. 110–11; Memorandum from D. M. Ladd to Mr. Fletcher, March 4, 1949, Silvermaster 65-58365-177.

128 *Gubitchev had an envelope:* Memorandum for the Attorney General, December 31, 1948, Silvermaster 65-58365-8; Field Report, January 15, 1949, Silvermaster 65-58365-24; Memo from H. B. Fletcher to D. H. Hall, January 27, 1949, Silvermaster 65-58365-46; Lamphere and Shachtman, *The FBI-KGB War,* pp. 110–12; *New York Times,* March 2, 2011.

128 *The Department of Justice:* New York Times, March 2, 2011.

129 *"She seemed":* New York Times, March 4, 2011.

129 *"In my opinion":* Washington Post, March 6, 1949.

129 *The first trial:* Washington Post, April 25, 1948.

129 *Prosecutors fought:* Washington Post, May 13, 1949.

129 *The jury took twenty-seven hours:* New York Times, July 1, 1949.

129 *The judge rejected:* New York Times, July 2, 1949.

130 *the thirty-seven-story building:* Today it is called the Thurgood Marshall United States Courthouse.

130 *the architecture critic:* New York Times, May 7, 2006.

131 *Harold Medina:* Time, October 24, 1949; *New York Times,* March 7, 1949.

131 *"I think the case":* Martelle, *The Fear Within,* p. 57.

132 *The trial began:* New York Times. January 17, 1949.

132 *Courtroom 110:* Time, April 4, 1949.

132 *"It was planned":* John F. X. McGohey, Opening Statement on Behalf of the Government, March 21, 1949, https://historymatters.gmu.edu/d/6446, accessed April 9, 2024.

133 *"The revolutionary doctrines":* Ibid.

133 *Louis Budenz:* New York Times, April 2, 1949; Joseph Alsop, "The Strange Case of Louis Budenz," *The Atlantic,* April 1952.

133 *Herbert Philbrick: New York Times*, April 7, 1949.

134 *"Our comrades"*: Quoted in Belknap, *American Political Trials*, p. 217.

134 *"solely for the purpose"*: Cited in Martelle, *The Fear Within*, pp. 78–79.

134 *"Your honor will"*: *Sacher v. United States*, 343 U.S. 1 (1952).

134 *"I'm through"*: *Time*, March 7, 1949.

135 *just two floors: New York Times*, June 25, 1949.

135 *"You would have ran"*: Cited in Tanenhaus, *Whittaker Chambers*, p. 388.

135 *Stryker intoned: Time*, June 13, 1949.

136 *"In the tropics"*: *Life*, July 18, 1949.

136 *"It is a fact"*: Cited in Tanenhaus, *Whittaker Chambers*, p. 359.

136 *July 8: New York Times*, July 9, 1949.

Chapter 8: Peekskill USA

137 *People's Artists, Inc.:* Fariello, *Red Scare*, p. 76.

138 *55,000:* Paul Leroy Robeson, National College Football Hall of Fame, https://www.cfbhall.com/inductees/paul-robeson-1995, accessed April 10, 2024.

138 *"He is the most"*: Duberman, *Paul Robeson*, p. 14.

138 *Robeson's political convictions:* Ibid., pp. 70–71.

138 *In 1937:* "Council on African Affairs," African Activist Archive, https://africanactivist.msu.edu/organization/210-813-673, accessed April 10, 2024.

139 *He stumped: Baltimore Afro-American*, April 22, May 15, and June 3, 1944; *Boston Globe*, May 15, 1944.

139 *In April 1947: Chicago Tribune*, April 18, 1947.

139 *the New York State Assembly: New York Herald Tribune*, May 7, 1947.

139 *"There is no such thing"*: *Time*, May 19, 1947.

139 *"I want to use"*: *Boston Globe*, April 20, 1947.

139 *Liberals tried:* Hamby, *Beyond the New Deal*, p. 495.

139 *HUAC called:* U.S. Congress, House, Committee on Un-American Activities, Control of Subversive Activities, 80th Cong., 2nd Sess., 1948, p. 10.

139 *Even the NAACP:* News Release, Council on African Affairs, May 11, 1949, reprinted in *Robeson Speaks*, pp. 197–98.

140 *Why? he asked:* Fast, *Peekskill USA*, p. 5.

140 *"racial disturbances"*: *Washington Post*, February 24, 2020.

140 *"If someone insists"*: Whitfield, *The Culture of the Cold War*, p. 21.

140 *A group of organizers:* Fast, *Peekskill USA*, p. 18.

141 *"inspire illegal"*: *New York Times*, August 27, 1949.

141 *"It was such a soft"*: Fast, *Peekskill USA*, p. 5.

141 *"As we appeared"*: Ibid., p. 7.

141 *One man:* Ibid., p. 22.

141 *someone set fire:* Ibid., p. 23.

142 *"Lynch Robeson!"*: Ibid., p. 29.

142 *First a trio:* Ibid., pp. 46–48.

142 *350 people: New York Times*, August 29, 1949.

142 *"Our objective": New York Times* August 30, 1949.

143 *"These boys": New York Times*, August 29, 1949.

143 *The next day: New York Times*, August 30, 1949.

143 *The only such organization: New York Times*, August 31, 1949.

144 *rally in the city: New York Times*, September 2, 1949.

144 *men, women, even children: New York Times*, September 5, 1949.

144 *Robeson went on:* Walter Bernstein, *Inside Out*, p. 147; *New York Times*, September 5 and September 6, 1949.

145 *The drivers: The New York Times*, September 5, 1949.

145 *"There was no safety":* Walter Bernstein, *Inside Out*, pp. 147–50.

145 *A bus carrying:* Fariello, *Red Scare*, p. 79.

145 *they stuck Robeson:* Ibid., pp. 77–78.

146 *About 145: New York Times*, September 5, 1949.

146 *Irving Potash:* Martelle, *The Fear Within*, p. 204.

146 *"We will continue to demonstrate": New York Times*, September 6, 1949.

146 *The Westchester: New York Times*, September 11 and September 21, 1949.

146 *"What happened": New York Times*, September 6, 1949.

Chapter 9: A Clear and Present Danger

147 *The greatest shock:* "Soviet Breakthrough: 'Joe I' Soviet Nuclear Test," https://www.atomicarchive.com/history/hydrogen-bomb/page-9.html, accessed April 10, 2024.

148 *When J. Robert Oppenheimer:* Davis, *Lawrence and Oppenheimer*, p. 294, cited in Halberstam, *The Fifties*, p. 26; U.S. Congress, Joint Committee on Atomic Energy, Executive Session of September 23, 1949, 81st Cong., 1st Sess., 1949.

148 *The country: New York Times*, March 4, 1950.

148 *Her lawyer: New York Times*, January 18 and February 3, 1949.

148 *Finally the judge: New York Times*, March 10, 1949.

149 *Hoover insisted:* Washington *Evening Star*, June 27, 1949; Correspondence Between Harry S. Truman and Clifford J. Durr, June 20, 1949, The Truman Administration's Loyalty Program, Official File, Harry S. Truman Library and Museum, https://www.trumanlibrary.gov/library/research-files/correspondence-between-harry-s-truman-and-clifford-j-durr?documentid=NA&pagenumber=2, accessed April 17, 2023.

149 *"I think it":* Memo from Edward Scheidt, December 8, 1950, Silvermaster 65-14932-1027.

149 *He came to court: Time*, February 13, 1950.

150 *"I am confident":* Ibid.

150 *"Whatever the outcome":* New York Times, January 26, 1950.

150 *"prouder than ever":* Tanenhaus, *Whittaker Chambers,* p. 436.

150 *"disgusting":* McCullough, *Truman,* p. 760.

150 *James Davis: Time,* February 6, 1950.

150 *"has upon his conscience":* Acheson, *Present at the Creation,* pp. 359–60.

151 *Such a requirement:* Martelle, *The Fear Within,* p. 169.

152 *"It got so": Time,* September 15, 1952.

152 *He was melodramatically: Time,* October 24, 1949.

152 *Born and raised: Time,* July 18, 1949.

152 *By the time: Time,* October 24, 1949.

153 *"Words may be":* New York Times, October 14, 1949.

153 *seven hours: New York Times,* October 16, 1949.

153 *Medina ordered: New York Times,* October 12, 1949.

153 *A week later: New York Times,* October 22, 1949.

153 *"witch hunters":* Geoffrey Stone, *Perilous Times,* p. 399.

154 *"The American Communist Party": United States v. Dennis* et al., 183 F.2d 201 (2d Cir. 1950), https://law.justia.com/cases/federal/appellate-courts/F2/183 /201/266559/, accessed April 19, 2023.

154 The New York Times: *New York Times,* August 3, 1950.

Chapter 10: The Ballad of Harry Bridges

155 *As a boy: New York Times,* March 31, 1990.

155 *When he was fifteen:* Cherny, "The Making of a Labor Radical," *Pacific Historical Review,* Vol. 64, No. 3 (August 1995): pp. 365–70.

156 *Bridges was there:* "Worker Unrest: The 1917 General Strike and 1919 Seamen's Strike," Australia National University, https://archives.anu.edu.au /exhibitions/struggle-solidarity-and-unity-150-years-maritime-unions -australia/worker-unrest-1917, accessed April 10, 2024.

156 *He passed through:* Cherny, "The Making of a Labor Radical," p. 373.

156 *He walked off:* Ibid.

156 *After his stepson:* Ibid., p. 380.

157 *The writer Louis Adamic: The Nation,* May 6, 1936.

157 *when he helped: San Francisco Chronicle,* July 5, 2014.

157 *In 1937:* "The ILWU Story," https://www.ilwu.org/history/the-ilwu-story/, accessed April 10, 2024.

157 Time *magazine: Time,* July 19, 1937.

158 *The CIO and its founder:* Kennedy, *Freedom from Fear,* p. 315.

158 *During a wave:* "Analysis of Strikes in 1937," The U.S. Department of Labor.

158 *workers and police: New York Times,* January 12, 1937.

159 *"Our report confirms":* Cherny, *Harry Bridges,* p. 185.

159 *"I've seen so": The New Yorker,* October 11, 1941.

159 *"By God":* Gage, *G-Man*, 243–44.

159 *One case against: Bridges v. Wixon*, 326 U.S. 135 (1945).

159 *Five days after: Boston Globe*, August 9, 1945.

160 *The Citizens Committee for Harry Bridges:* Cherny, *Harry Bridges*, p. 190; Lyrics at http://www.protestsonglyrics.net/Labor_Union_Songs/Song-for -Bridges.phtml, accessed June 7, 2023; Dalton Trumbo, *Harry Bridges*.

160 *"To Communists": New York Times*, May 11, 1947.

160 *Joe Curran:* Ibid.

160 *Nearly 13 million:* Leo Troy, "Trade Union Membership, 1897–1962," National Bureau of Economic Research, 1965, p. 1.

161 *The Communists and their allies:* Filippelli and McColloch, *Cold War in the Working Class*, p. 2.

161 *Nearly 400,000 workers:* "Work Stoppages Caused by Labor Management Disputes, 1945," Bulletin No. 878 of the United States Bureau of Labor Statistics, p. 3.

161 *Some 4.6 million workers:* "Work Stoppages Caused by Labor-Management Disputes in 1946," Bulletin No. 918 of the United States Bureau of Labor Statistics, p. 3.

161 *A Gallup poll: Washington Post*, July 5, 1946.

161 *"Reuther decides":* Fones-Wolf, *Selling Free Enterprise*, p. 21.

161 *In September 1946:* U.S. Chamber of Commerce, "Communist Infiltration in the United States: Its Nature and How to Combat It," p. 22.

162 *at one point in 1946:* "Work Stoppages," Ibid.

162 *When A. F. Whitney:* "Radio Address to the American People on the Railroad Strike Emergency," May 24, 1946, Harry S. Truman Library and Museum, https://www.trumanlibrary.gov/library/public-papers/124/radio-address -american-people-railroad-strike-emergency, accessed April 11, 2024.

162 *Representative Fred Hartley Jr.:* Cited in Filippelli and McColloch, *Cold War in the Working Class*, p. 1.

162 *The bill sailed:* "1947 Taft-Hartley Passage and NLRB Structural Changes," National Labor Relations Board, https://www.nlrb.gov/about-nlrb/who-we -are/our-history/1947-taft-hartley-passage-and-nlrb-structural-changes, accessed April 11, 2024.

162 *"more rights": New York Times*, May 6, 1947.

163 *"If I had my way": New York Times*, February 29, 1944.

163 *"He looked more like":* Boyle, *The UAW and the Heyday of American Liberalism*, p. 34.

163 *"Communism is in":* Ibid., p. 32.

164 *"If you carry through":* Cited in Lichtenstein, *Walter Reuther*, pp. 124–25.

164 *He took control: Baltimore Sun*, March 28, 1946; *Chicago Trubine*, March 31, 1946.

164 *During his first year: Boston Globe*, November 1, 1947; *Washington Post*, October 23, 1949.

164 *"The Communist program": Time*, November 7, 1949.

164 *"We have come":* Filippelli and McColloch, *Cold War in the Working Class*, p. 138.

165 *He found the CIO boss: Time*, November 7, 1949.

165 *He held: Time*, November 14, 1949.

165 *At war's end:* Cherny, *Harry Bridges*, p. 210.

166 *It accused: Los Angeles Times*, May 26, 1949.

166 *Still, he was shocked: Los Angeles Times*, April 5, 1950.

166 *On August 30: Los Angeles Times*, August 30, 1950.

166 *the CIO had cut: Time*, September 11, 1950.

166 *"That will save us":* Cited in Lichtenstein, *Walter Reuther*, p. 269.

167 *After a pair of strikes:* Cherny, *Harry Bridges*, p. 236.

167 *"He wants American": Fortune*, February 1945.

167 *The director of one: New York Times*, January 26, 1950.

Chapter 11: I Have in My Hand a List

168 *afterward he intended:* Tye, *Demagogue*, p. 120.

168 *had recently hired:* Oshinsky, *A Conspiracy So Immense*, p. 108.

168 *"any man":* Ibid., p. 82.

169 *Father Edmund Walsh:* Ibid., p. 107.

169 *Still, a reporter:* "Excerpts from McCarthy's Speech to the Ohio County Republican Women's Club," Ohio County Public Library, https://www.ohiocountylibrary.org/wheeling-history/5655#speach, accessed April 12, 2024.

169 *James Byrnes:* Richard Rovere, "Communists in a Free Society," *Partisan Review*, Vol. 19, No. 3 (1952): 341.

169 *Nor did he much care:* Oshinsky, *A Conspiracy So Immense*, p. 110.

170 *trounced McMurray:* "Statistics of the Congressional Election of 1946," Clerk of the House of Representatives, 1947.

170 *John Peurifoy: New York Times*, February 14, 1950.

170 *"Sewer Politics": Washington Post*, February 14, 1950.

170 *"When called upon": Chicago Tribune*, February 13, 1950.

171 *The Democrats: Washington Post*, February 21, 1950.

171 *Harry Bridges: Congressional Record*, February 20, 1950, p. 1960.

171 *"a well-known general":* Ibid., p. 1959.

171 *"I do not believe":* Ibid.

171 *"Will the senator tell us":* Ibid.

171 *"The senator can come":* Ibid.

172 *"McCarthy was a dream story":* Oshinsky, *A Conspiracy So Immense*, p. 118.

172 *"Americanism with":* Tye, *Demagogue*, p. 160.

173 *"I look at that fellow"*: McCullough, *Truman*, pp. 760–61.

174 *"My own attitude"*: Letter from Sokolsky to Brewer, October 9, 1954, Box 29, George Sokolsky Papers, Hoover Institution Archives.

174 *"I, who believe"*: Letter from Sokolsky to Brewer, October 26, 1954, Box 29, Sokolsky Papers.

175 *offering McCarthy*: Gage, *G-Man*, pp. 384–89.

175 *A woman named*: U.S. Congress, Senate, Committee on Foreign Relations, State Department Employee Loyalty Investigation, 81st Cong., 1st Sess., 1950, p. 18.

176 *"Senator McCarthy"*: *New York Times*, March 9, 1950.

176 *"A Poor Beginning"*: Ibid.

176 *So did Dean Acheson*: Acheson, *Present at the Creation*, p. 363.

Chapter 12: A Government Within the Government

177 *"Is the senator aware"*: *Congressional Record*, April 25, 1950, p. 5703.

177 *"It is my belief"*: Ibid., p. 5712.

178 *"a national coming-out"*: Cited in "LGBTQ Histories from the WWII Home Front," National Park Service, https://www.nps.gov/rori/learn/historyculture /lgbtq-histories-from-the-wwii-home-front.htm, accessed April 12, 2024.

179 *"government within the government"*: U.S. Congress, Senate, Subcommittee on Investigations, Committee on Expenditures in Executive Departments, Homosexuality in Government and Risk to National Security, 81st Cong., 2nd Sess., 1950, p. 2099.

179 *"sexual perverts who have infiltrated"*: *New York Times*, April 19, 1950.

179 *David K. Johnson*: Johnson, *The Lavender Scare*, pp. 166–67.

179 *James Kirchick*: Kirchick, *Secret City*, p. 184.

179 *Offie was born*: https://www.findagrave.com/memorial/44383396/carmel -offie, accessed April 12, 2024; Morgan, *A Covert Life*, p. 209.

179 *In October*: Hersh, *The Old Boys*, p. 44.

179 *When John F. Kennedy*: Bullitt, *For the President, Personal and Secret*, p. 272.

180 *For that he blamed*: Brownell and Billings, *So Close to Greatness*, p. 190.

180 *Bullitt got ahold*: Hersh, *The Old Boys*, p. 150.

180 *Offie was himself*: Memo to J. Edgar Hoover, September 9, 1943, Carmel Offie FBI File (FOIA).

180 *Fortunately for him*: Morgan, *A Covert Life*, p. 211.

180 *"I made more new"*: Loughery, *The Other Side of Silence*, p. 151

180 *Offie went to work*: Hersh, *The Old Boys*, pp. 153–54. The Medal of Merit, though impressive, is not to be confused with the Presidential Medal of Merit, created by John F. Kennedy in 1961. The latter is the highest award available to civilians from the federal government.

181 *Offie went back*: Gerolymatos, *Castles Made of Sand*, p. 130.

181 *He would rub:* Hersh, *The Old Boys*, p. 253.

181 *In 1946 the Washington:* Beemyn, *A Queer Capital*, p. 138.

182 *"homosexual proclivities":* Gage, *G-Man*, p. 279.

182 *The FBI had opened:* Ibid., p. 405.

182 *A rider attached:* Johnson, *The Lavender Scare*, p. 21.

182 *"sisterhood in our":* Ibid., p. 70.

182 *In October 1949:* Morgan, *A Covert Life*, p. 212.

182 *February 1950:* U.S. Congress, Senate, Committee on Appropriations. Departments of State, Justice, Commerce and the Judiciary Appropriations for 1951, 81st Cong., 2nd Sess., 1950, p. 603.

183 *Tydings implored: Congressional Record*, April 25, 1950, p. 1950.

184 *Senator Wherry:* Baxter, "Homo Hunting in the Early Cold War," pp. 119–21.

184 *"Only the most naïve":* Kenneth Wherry, Report of the Investigations of the Junior Senator of Nebraska on the Infiltration of Subversives and Moral Perverts into the Executive Branch of the U.S. Government, Subcommittee on District of Columbia, Committee on Appropriations, Senate, May 1, 1950, p. 10.

184 *Lieutenant Roy Blick: Chicago Tribune*, May 21, 1950. Playing on the sudden national interest in the lurid side of Washington, in 1951 two journalists, Jack Lait and Lee Mortimer published *Washington Confidential*, the latest in a series of "confidential" books that promised to peel back the pleasant surface of places like New York (and later Martha's Vineyard) to expose the criminal and perverse layers below. Though the book also covered subjects like corruption and adultery by high-ranking public officials, its overwhelming focus was on the city's homosexual demimonde. The pair estimated that there were seven thousand gay men and lesbians in Washington, who flock to "orgies beyond description and imagination. Every invention of Sacher-Masoch and the marquis de Sade has been added to and improved upon, and is in daily use."

184 *Harry B. Mitchell:* Johnson, *The Lavender Scare*, pp. 80–81.

184 *forwarded the names:* These reports can be found in Boxes 40-20 and 40-22, Record Group 46, National Archives.

184 *the FBI:* Charles, *Hoover's War on Gays*, p. 36.

184 *Meanwhile, a seminar:* Johnson, *The Lavender Scare*, p. 106.

185 *Two staff members:* Ibid., pp. 73–75.

185 *In June: New York Times*, June 7, 1950.

185 *Eight months later: Washington Post*, February 7, 1951.

185 *in October 1951: Chicago Tribune*, October 5, 1951.

185 *By 1953:* Letter from Carlisle H. Humelsine to James Webb, undated 1950, https://catalog.archives.gov/id/54962916?objectPage=4, accessed June 16, 2023.

185 *Andrew Ference:* Johnson, *The Lavender Scare*, p. 159.

185 *Peter Szluk:* Cited in Fariello, *Red Scare*, p. 124.

186 *Among them was Charlotte Tuttle:* Storrs, *The Second Red Scare and the Unmaking of the New Deal Left*, p. 19.

186 *11 percent of the lawyers:* Ibid, p. 22.

186 *"Our capital is a femmocracy":* Lait and Mortimer, *Washington Confidential*, p. 74.

187 *"sex-starved government gals":* Ibid., p. 101.

187 *"women employees":* The New Yorker, April 22, 1950.

187 *He tried to keep:* Kirchick, *Secret City*, p. 141.

187 *The officer:* U.S. Congress, Senate, Subcommittee on Investigations, Committee on Expenditures in Executive Departments, Homosexuality in Government and Risk to National Security, 81st Cong., 2nd Sess., 1950, p. 2090.

188 *Hillenkoetter then offered:* Ibid., p. 2103.

188 *"Since it is possible":* Adkins, "These People Are Frightened to Death," Prologue, Summer 2016, https://www.archives.gov/publications/prologue/2016/summer/lavender.html, accessed April 12, 2024.

188 *Dr. Leonard Scheele:* Ibid.

188 *Hoey, in his:* U.S. Congress, Senate, Committee on Expenditures in Executive Departments, Employment of Homosexuals and Other Sex Perverts in Government, 81st Cong., 2nd Sess., 1950, p. 4.

188 *Senator Jenner said: Congressional Record,* July 21, 1950, p. 10792.

188 *"colonies of such persons":* Washington Post, March 17, 1950. Paradoxically, a few months later, in specific reference to anti-Communist hearings, the same editorial board wrote that "witch-hunting will drive out of government the very brains which alone can give us victory in the cold war," *Washington Post*, May 21, 1950.

189 *"Although the matter":* Johnson, *The Lavender Scare*, p. 28.

Chapter 13: The China Lobby

190 *"I am willing":* Time, April 3, 1950.

190 *"the top Russian espionage agent":* Ibid.

191 *"It is up to the president":* Ibid.

192 *"warmthless smile,":* The Reporter, April 29, 1952.

192 *The New York Times called him:* Letter to John Foster Dulles, June 7, 1955, Box 617, Alfred Kohlberg Papers, Hoover Institution Archives.

192 *He called himself:* New York Times, April 8, 1960.

192 *By the late 1930s:* Leahy, "Alfred J. Kohlberg and the Chaoshan Embroidered Handkerchief Industry, 1922–1957."

192 *Senator Knowland:* Blackwell, "'The China Lobby': Influences on U.S.-China Foreign Policy in the Post War Period, 1949–1954."

193 *"I believe very strongly"*: Quoted in Halberstam, *The Coldest Winter*, p. 247.

193 *Over a two-hour*: Keely, *China Lobby Man*, p. 3.

193 *The money represented*: "United States Relations with China, with Special Reference to the Period 1944–1949," Department of State Publication, 1949, p. xv.

194 *"None seem"*: Cited in E. J. Kahn, *The China Hands*, p. 125.

194 *empty-handed*: Letter to John Foster Dulles, June 7, 1955, Box 617, Kohlberg Papers.

195 *General Albert Wedemeyer: Time*, December 29, 1947.

195 *"The real"*: Cited in Blackwell, "'The China Lobby': Influences on U.S.-China Foreign Policy in the Post War Period, 1949–1954."

195 *In a 1947 letter*: Letter to Styles Bridges, January 14, 1947, Box 19, Kohlberg Papers.

196 *"Rather than acknowledging"*: Davies, *China Hand*, p. 291.

196 *"I soon saw"*: *The Reporter*, April 29, 1952.

196 *"You have allowed"*: Kohlberg to the IPR trustees, August 31, 1945, Box 16, J. B. Matthews Papers, Duke University Libraries.

196 *"I tried to clean"*: *The Reporter*, April 29, 1952.

197 *In 1946 he gathered: New York Times*, May 15, 1946.

197 *"I myself count"*: Mao, *Asia First*, p. 71.

198 *"done deliberately"*: Kohlberg to Members of Congress, March 24, 1949, Box 616, Kohlberg Papers; *Plain Talk*, December 1948.

198 *"Although I know"*: Alfred Kohlberg to Joeseph McCarthy, June 6, 1950, Box 616, Kohlberg Papers.

198 *"with guts enough"*: *Washington Post*, January 25, 1978.

198 *"McCarthy is a great guy"*: *The Reporter*, April 29, 1952.

198 *The news from Korea*: McCullough, *Truman*, p. 928.

199 *"made it clear"*: Ibid., p. 775.

199 *"McCarthyism will have"*: *The Nation*, July 8, 1950.

199 *In Congress, Senator Knowland*: Acheson, *Present at the Creation*, pp. 357–58.

200 *"American boys"*: *Baltimore Sun*, July 3, 1950.

200 *the Department of Justice: New York Times*, August 8, 1950.

200 *"Will we continue appeasement?"*: *Congressional Record*, June 26, 1950, p. 9154.

201 *"The Hiss survivors"*: *Congressional Record*, September 21, 1950, p. 15412.

Chapter 14: The Russians Are Coming!

202 *Before the sun: Boston Globe*, May 8, 1950.

202 *"elevate the debate": New York Times*, May 2, 1950; *The New Republic*, October 22, 2020.

203 *"The townspeople": Boston Globe*, May 8, 1950.

203 *the day before: Baltimore Sun*, May 1, 1950.

203 *In June: The New Republic*, October 22, 2020; *Chicago Tribune*, June 15, 1950.

204 *"before the New Deal"*: Halberstam, *The Fifties*, p. 5.

204 *He ordered:* Ibid., p. 217.

205 *church membership:* Fried, *The Russians Are Coming! The Russians Are Coming!*, p. ix.

205 *By the start of the war:* Elaine Tyler May, *Homeward Bound*, pp. 51, 59.

206 *motherhood and the nuclear family:* Ibid., p. 18.

206 *in 1947: New York Times*, August 20, 1947.

206 *It was especially close:* Gage, *G-Man*, p. 395.

207 *Founded in the early 1920s:* Jeff Stoffer, "The Definition of Americanism," January 22, 2019, https://www.legion.org/magazine/244581/definition -americanism, accessed May 8, 2023.

207 *At the other: New York Times*, May 4, 1954.

207 *it ran:* Arthur Miller, *The New Yorker*, October 13, 1996.

207 *a group of women: Los Angeles Times*, June 22, 1952

207 *When organizers: Chicago Tribune*, November 18 and December 6, 1951.

207 *In September 1949:* "Minute Women of the U.S.A.," Texas State Historical Association, https://www.tshaonline.org/handbook/entries/minute-women-of -the-usa, accessed May 10, 2023; Carleton, "McCarthyism Was More Than McCarthy."

207 *she boasted of 500,000 members: Chicago Tribune*, May 15, 1952.

207 *She called herself:* Carleton, "McCarthyism Was More Than McCarthy."

208 *And while Stevenson herself:* "Minute Women of the U.S.A."

208 *She had them:* Carleton, p. 115; *Time*, November 2, 1953.

208 *subversive books: Washington Post*, October 31, 1954.

208 *the Houston chapter: The Daily Cougar*, March 2, 2000, http://archive.thedaily cougar.com/vol65/107/opinion/oped-index.html, accessed May 10, 2023; *Time*, November 2, 1953.

209 *In October 1950: New York Times*, November 24, 1950.

209 *A year later the board: New York Times*, December 7, 1951.

209 *And in 1951:* Ibid.

209 *In July 1950: Chicago Tribune*, July 19, 1950.

209 *Governments as large: New York Times*, August 4, 1950.

209 *It was even in bubble gum:* These items are held at The Gilder-Lehrman Institute of American History in New York City.

209 *The book sold: Time*, August 17, 1953.

210 *Ayn Rand:* "Ayn Rand Speaks Up for Mickey Spillane (Part 1)," https://new ideal.aynrand.org/ayn-rand-speaks-up-for-mickey-spillane-part-1/, accessed April 13, 2024.

210 *"I killed more people":* Spillane, *One Lonely Night* in *The Mickey Spillane Collection*, p. 169.

210 *At the end of the decade:* Whitfield, *The Culture of the Cold War*, p. 34.

210 *In July 1950: Time,* July 30, 1950.

210 *Around the same time:* Ibid.

210 *a fellow prisoner: New York Times,* October 24, 1953.

211 *A year later: New York Times,* November 24, 1954.

Chapter 15: The Pink Lady

212 *"raped and rifled":* Cited in Rovere, *Senator Joe McCarthy,* p. 150.

213 *"inconclusive": New York Times,* July 23, 1950.

213 *On June 1, 1950: Congressional Record,* June 1, 1950, pp. 7894–95.

213 *Republicans signed on:* They were Charles Tobey of New Hampshire, George Aiken of Vermont, Wayne Morse of Oregon, Irving Ives of New York, Edward Thye of Minnesota, and Robert Hendrickson of New Jersey.

214 *In September: New York Times,* September 25, 1950.

214 *in fifteen states: Boston Globe,* November 22, 1950.

214 *he appeared:* Deason, "Scott Lucas, Everett Dirksen, and the 1950 Senate Election in Illinois," p. 34.

214 *Through a thinly: New York Times,* November 12, 1950.

215 *"ten of the twelve":* Scobie, *Center Stage,* p. 24.

215 *Helen joined:* Helen Gahagan Douglas, *A Full Life,* p. 150.

215 *"I felt that":* Nixon, *RN,* p. 75.

215 *Nixon's campaign strategist:* Farrell, *Nixon,* p. 145.

216 *"a fight basically": New York Times,* May 29, 1946.

216 *Florida Democratic primary:* Pepper, *Eyewitness to a Century,* pp. 204–5.

216 *"dirtiest in the history of American politics": The Orlando Sentinel,* September 16, 2012.

216 *"If Helen":* Farrell, *Richard Nixon,* p. 146.

216 *Nixon promised:* Ibid., pp. 150–51.

217 *Chotiner first:* Ibid., p. 150.

217 *Nixon hired:* Ibid.

217 *That clever turn of phrase:* Ibid., p. 146.

217 *Melvyn Douglas:* Helen Gahagan Douglas, *A Full Life,* pp. 317, 324.

217 *"Mrs. Douglas":* Farrell, *Richard Nixon,* p. 153.

218 *defeating Douglas: Boston Globe,* November 22, 1950.

218 *"McCarthyism": New York Times,* January 7, 1951.

Chapter 16: Running with the Hounds

219 *"What would you say":* Radosh and Milton, *The Rosenberg File,* p. 90.

219 *On the street:* Ibid.

221 *Rosenberg's network collected:* Usdin, "Tracking Julius Rosenberg's Lesser Known Associates," *Studies in Intelligence,* Vol. 49, No. 3 (2005), https://www.cia.gov/resources/csi/static/Rosenberg_2.pdf, accessed April 13, 2024.

222 *Morton Sobell told:* New York Times, September 11, 2008.

222 *"Soviet archival":* The Weekly Standard, October 17, 2014.

222 *After confessing:* Sam Roberts, The Brother, p. 491.

222 *"There is no question":* Radosh and Milton, The Rosenberg File, p. 90.

223 *During a closed:* Ibid., p. 146.

223 *March 6, 1951:* Gage, G-Man, p. 377.

223 *Irving Saypol:* New York Times, July 7, 1977.

223 *He said the Rosenbergs:* United States of America v. Julius Rosenberg et al., trial transcript, p. 180.

224 *"the court":* Ibid., p. 703.

224 *"Despite the fact":* Ibid., p 705.

224 *"My opinion is":* Ibid, p. 2390.

224 *He held a number:* Ibid., p. 277.

225 *"Citizens of this country":* Ibid., p. 2449.

225 *"It is not in my power":* Ibid., p. 2454.

226 *Morton Sobell:* New York Times, March 20, 2011.

227 *"The government framed":* Roberts, The Brother, p. 509.

227 *Frankfurter's Happy Hot Dogs:* Washington Post, July 9, 1988.

228 *"basis of national security":* Minersville School District v. Gobitis, 310 U.S. 586 (1940).

228 *"My position":* Memo from Felix Frankfurter to Stanley Reed, March 12, 1951, and memo from Stanley Reed to Felix Frankfurter, March 13, 1951, both in Felix Frankfurter Papers, Harvard Law School Archives.

229 *"If the government":* Dennis v. United States, 341 U.S. 494 (1951), https://supreme.justia.com/cases/federal/us/341/494/#tab-opinion-1940191, accessed April 20, 2023.

229 *"We need not":* Ibid.

229 *"depends not on":* Ibid.

230 *"Never, never":* William O. Douglas, The Court Years, p. 103.

230 *"running with the hounds":* Ibid., p. 96.

230 *Less than a month later:* Geoffrey Stone, Perilous Times, p. 412.

230 *In* Garner v. Los Angeles Board of Public Works: *Garner v. Los Angeles Board of Public Works, 341 U.S. 716 (1951).*

231 *Another 1952 case:* Geoffrey Stone, Perilous Times, p. 412.

231 *Dorothy Bailey:* New York Herald Tribune, October 13, 1950; Storrs, "Attacking the Washington 'Femmocracy.' "

Chapter 17: Naming Names

233 *"You might say":* The New Yorker, February 14, 1948.

233 *As early as 1946:* Los Angeles Times, October 11, 1946.

233 *and in 1950:* Los Angeles Times, October 13, 1950; Time, July 30, 1950.

234 *In 1953 the guild:* Navasky, *Naming Names*, p. 184.

234 *they had surrendered:* New York Times, December 11, 1947.

234 *convicted in April:* Los Angeles Times, April 20, 1948.

234 *speaking tour:* Bessie, *Inquisition in Eden*, p 227; JAFRC Flyer, Box 2, Joint Anti-Fascist Refugee Committe Papers, Tamiment Library, NYU.

234 *In June 1949:* Lawson v. United States, 176 F.2d 49 (D.C. Cir. 1949).

235 *A thousand people:* Letter from Dalton to Cleo Trumbo, June 11, 1950, in Trumbo, Manfull, ed., *Additional Dialogue*, p. 151.

235 *Ring Lardner Jr.:* New York Times, November 1, 2000.

235 *Lester Cole:* Ceplair and Englund, *The Inquisition in Hollywood*, p. 357.

235 *Another, Herbert Biberman:* Ibid.

235 *Between November 1948:* Bessie, *Inquisition in Eden*, p. 231.

236 *"At First":* Cogley, *Report on Backlisting I*, p. 127.

236 *out one day:* Walter Bernstein, *Inside Out*, p. 24.

236 *Bernard Gordon:* Gordon, *Hollywood Exile*, p. 43.

237 *Walter Bernstein:* Walter Bernstein, *Inside Out*, p. 166.

237 *The Hollywood Legionnaire:* The Hollywood Legionnaire, January 1952, Box 26, George Sokolsky Papers, Hoover Institution Archives.

237 *"We've worked":* The New Yorker, February 14, 1948.

238 *"Gold, Mister":* Ibid.

238 *The sci-fi hit:* Report on *The Day the Earth Stood Still*, Box 26, Sokolsky Papers.

238 *Bosley Crowther:* New York Times, April 9, 1952.

239 *American Business Consultants:* Bernhard, *U.S. Television News and Cold War Propaganda, 1947–1960*, p. 56.

239 *It amassed:* See the American Business Consultants, Inc. *Counterattack*: Research Files, Tamiment Library, NYU.

239 *The superintendent:* Washington Post, September 13, 1950.

239 *After Bernstein and several other writers:* Walter Bernstein, *Inside Out*, p. 152.

240 *the Wage Earners Committee:* Robbins, "Fighting McCarthyism Through Film," p. 291.

240 *Myron Fagan:* "Documentation of the Red Stars in Hollywood," Box 1, Francis Walter Files, RG 233, National Archives.

240 *Theodore Kirkpatrick:* New York Times, September 8, 1950.

241 *The entry:* Red Channels, pp. 40–41.

241 *But she had also:* New York Times: August 29, 1950; Red Channels, p. 113; United Press International, January 14, 1981.

241 *Gypsy Rose Lee:* New York Times, September 13, 1950.

241 *in January 1951:* New York Times, January 1, 1951.

241 *one actor friend:* Walter Bernstein, *Inside Out*, p. 175.

242 *In the years between:* Letter from Trumbo to Nelson Algren, June 15, 1951, in Trumbo, Manfull, ed., *Additional Dialogue*, p. 213.

242 *"I did not know"*: Walter Bernstein, *Inside Out*, pp. 240, 256.

242 *In 1954*: Fariello, *Red Scare*, pp. 280–84.

242 *"Surprisingly, we laughed"*: Walter Bernstein, *Inside Out*, p. 173.

243 *"I think Miss Muir's"*: New York Times, August 30, 1950.

243 *"We cannot take"*: Walter Bernstein, *Inside Out*, p. 25.

243 *"It all had"*: Ibid., p. 26.

243 *"The onus is on"*: Vincent Hartnett to Roy Brewer, October 13, 1953, Box 29, Sokolsky Papers.

244 *The Black singer*: Lena Horne to Roy Brewer, June 28, 1953; Roy Brewer to James O'Neil, November 13, 1952, Box 29, Sokolsky Papers.

244 *In a November 1952*: Roy Brewer to James O'Neil, November 11, 1952, Box 29, Sokolsky Papers.

244 *In March 1948*: New York Times, March 17, 1948, and December 23, 1949.

245 *"In so doing"*: Letter from John Huston to Ralph Brandon, January 29, 1953, Box 29, Sokolsky Papers.

245 *"Somebody had to go"*: Cogley, *Report on Blacklisting I*, p. 88.

245 *by twenty-two*: Hayden, *Wanderer*, p. 209.

245 *"The Most Beautiful Man in the Movies"*: New York Times, May 24, 1986.

246 *Coincidentally*: Walter Bernstein, *Inside Out*, p. 100.

246 *In 1947*: Bessie, *Inquisition in Eden*, p. 195.

246 *Hayden rang up*: Hayden, *Wanderer*, p. 371.

246 *He and Gang*: Ibid., p. 375.

247 *Edward G. Robinson*: New York Times, November 1, 1950; *Red Channels*, p. 133.

247 *In January 1951*: Los Angeles Times, February 10 and February 17, 1951.

247 *Fourteen more*: New York Times, February 21, 1951.

248 *As Chairman Wood*: Goodman, *The Committee*, p. 298.

248 *The playwright*: Hellman, *Scoundrel Time*, p. 93.

249 *Larry Parks*: Chicago Tribune, May 8, 1951; *New York Times*, April 15, 1975.

249 *"I don't think"*: U.S. Congress, House, Committee on Un-American Activities, Communist Infiltration of Hollywood Motion-Picture Industry, 81st Cong., 1st Sess., 1950, p. 107.

249 *Gale Sondergaard*: Los Angeles Times, March 23, 1951; Sondergaard to Screen Actors Guild, March 13, 1951, Box 652, J. B. Matthews Papers, Duke University Libraries.

249 *"A whole galaxy"*: Los Angeles Times, March 23, 1951.

249 *Roy Brewer*: New York Herald Tribune, May 8, 1951.

250 *The* Chicago Tribune: *Chicago Tribune*, April 16, 1951.

250 *Out of the 110*: Ceplair and Englund, *The Inquisition in Hollywood*, p. 371.

250 *"It was the stupidest"*: Communist Infiltration of Hollywood Motion-Picture Industry, p. 144.

250 *"I swung"*: Hayden, *Wanderer*, p. 25.

250 *"I don't think"*: Ibid., p. 378.

251 *Dashiell Hammett*: *Los Angeles Times*, July 10, 1951.

251 *"If any actor"*: Cited in Ceplair and Englund, *The Inquisition in Hollywood*, p. 368.

251 *He got out*: Dmytryk, *Odd Man Out*, p. 153.

251 *The Saturday Evening Post*: *The Saturday Evening Post*, May 17, 1951.

252 *He was still working*: Schickel, *Elia Kazan*, p. 254.

253 *The liberal producer*: Ibid.

253 *"A film director"*: Kazan, *A Life*, p. 455.

253 *"I have come"*: U.S. Congress, House, Committee on Un-American Activities, Communist Infiltration of Hollywood Motion-Picture Industry, 81st Cong., 2nd Sess., 1952, p. 2408.

253 *Lucille Ball hemmed and hawed*: Ball had already answered questions about her registration in a closed session before HUAC, saying that she had done so to please her grandfather. She never joined the party. She was nevertheless smeared as a party member by Walter Winchell and other columnists, leading to a flurry of hate mail (though not a decline in ratings for her TV show). Thank you to Todd Purdum for his insight on her case.

254 *"taste of the police state"*: *New York Times*, April 13, 1952.

254 *Kazan invited Miller*: Miller, *Timebends*, pp. 332–33.

254 *At the 1999 Oscars*: *New York Times*, March 22, 1999.

Chapter 18: The China Hands

256 *"My staff tells me"*: Acheson, *Present at the Creation*, p. 424.

256 *"blighted the name"*: Ibid., p 127.

257 *"my loveable fascist"*: Cited in Halberstam, *The Coldest Winter*, p. 377.

257 *"American Communist brains"*: Ibid.

257 *In Japan in the late 1940s*: *The Reporter*, August 19, 1952, pp. 25–30; Halberstam, *The Coldest Winter*, p. 377.

257 *Willoughby was later*: *The Reporter*, August 19, 1952, pp. 25–30.

257 *After retiring from the Army*: Ibid.

258 *"To give up any part"*: Cited in Halberstam, *The Coldest Winter*, p. 386.

258 *"I was ready"*: Truman, *Memoirs by Harry S. Truman: Years of Trial and Hope: 1946–1952*, p. 559.

258 *"I deeply regret"*: Statement and Order by the President on Relieving General MacArthur of His Commands, April 11, 1951, The American Presidency Project, https://www.presidency.ucsb.edu/documents/statement-and-order -the-president-relieving-general-macarthur-his-commands, accessed May 19, 2024.

258 *"I fired him"*: Truman reportedly said this in the early 1960s, though it was not quoted in print until it appeared in *Time* on December 3, 1973.

258 *"I charge that this country"*: New York Times, March 11, 1985.

258 *"who for varying reasons"*: Transcript of General Douglas MacArthur's Address to Congress, April 19, 1951, Harry S. Truman Library and Museum, https://www.trumanlibrary.gov/library/research-files/transcript-general -douglas-macarthurs-address-congress?documentid=NA&pagenumber=7, accessed May 3, 2023.

258 *He threw out*: Brands, *The General vs. the President*, p. 373.

258 *it was among*: Stars and Stripes, April 20, 1951.

259 *"It is not from"*: Brands, *The General vs. the President*, p. 374.

259 *already abysmally low*: "Harry S. Truman Public Approval," The American Presidency Project, https://www.presidency.ucsb.edu/statistics/data/harry-s -truman-public-approval, accessed April 14, 2024.

259 *In June 1951*: Oshinsky, *A Conspiracy So Immense*, p. 197.

260 *Hubert Humphrey*: Traub, *True Believer*, p. 136.

260 *"I realize full well"*: Congressional Record, June 14, 1951, pp. 6556–6604.

262 *"a known associate"*: New York Times, February 4, 1999.

262 *"reasonable doubt as to his loyalty"*: Service v. Dulles, 354 U.S. 363 (1957).

262 *"reasonable doubt as to Vincent's loyalty"*: New York Times, December 5, 1972. Fittingly, his *Times* obituary was written by Alden Whitman, himself a victim of the *Times*'s own anti-Communist purges.

263 *"We should not now"*: Memorandum by the Second Secretary of Embassy in China (Davies), November 15, 1944, 893.00/1–1049, https://history.state .gov/historicaldocuments/frus1944v06/d499, accessed April 15, 2024.

263 *At one point in 1943*: New York Times, December 24, 1999.

263 *In fact he was known*: Ibid.

263 *"Throughout the fateful years"*: The Saturday Evening Post, January 7, 1950.

Chapter 19: Terror by Index Cards

265 *"promoted"*: New York Times, January 27, 1951.

265 *"You get to the point"*: Time, October 22, 1951.

266 *"Let a Quaker"*: Time, December 25, 1950.

266 *"If you will"*: Rovere, *Senator Joe McCarthy*, p. 49.

266 *"I am afraid"*: New York Times, June 17, 1951.

267 *On August 8, 1951*: Washington Post, August 9, 1951.

267 *In September 1951*: New York Times, September 20, 1951.

267 *"pathological"*: New York Times, February 1, 1952.

267 *"It would be a waste"*: Meet the Press, June 3, 1951.

267 *"The louder they scream"*: Washington Post, February 2, 1952.

267 *"mental midget"*: Time, April 21, 1952.

268 *investigating McCarthy's*: New York Times, August 9, 1951.

268 *In January 1952: New York Times,* January 1, 1952.

268 *"There are certain points":* Oshinsky, *A Conspiracy So Immense,* p. 199.

268 *"fully justified": New York Times,* January 22, 1952.

268 *"If one case":* Oshinsky, *A Conspiracy So Immense,* p. 133.

269 *He claimed: Washington Post,* August 15, 1952.

269 *Stevenson supported: New York Times,* October 6, 1952.

269 *"I was privileged":* https://www.eisenhowerlibrary.gov/sites/default/files /research/online-documents/mccarthyism/1952-10-03-sixth-draft.pdf, accessed May 21, 2023.

270 *"I've been booed":* Adams, *First-Hand Report,* p. 31.

270 *"The differences": New York Times,* October 4, 1952.

270 *"It is this paper's hope": Washington Post,* March 24, 1952.

271 *"We have a new president": Washington Daily News,* November 8, 1952.

272 *"None of these persons":* Gage, *G-Man,* pp. 231–32, 242.

272 *in Indiana:* Nozette, "Constitutional Law-First Amendment-Loyalty Oaths-Vagueness Standard Relaxed for Affirmative Oaths."

272 *In New York State: New York Times,* May 7, 1957.

273 *In Chicago: Chicago Housing Auth. v. Blackman,* 4 Ill. 2d 319, 122 N.E.2d 522 (Ill. 1954).

273 *"It was a time":* Clark, oral history, October 17, 1972, and February 8, 1973, Harry S. Truman Library and Museum, https://www.trumanlibrary.gov /library/oral-histories/clarktc, accessed April 15, 2024.

273 *American military intelligence:* Press release, U.S. Army, "Ralph Van Deman Becomes Father of Modern American Military Intelligence," April 10, 2017, https://www.army.mil/article/185798/ralph_van_deman_becomes_father _of_modern_american_military_intelligence, accessed May 5, 2023.

274 *"Working feverishly":* Pittman, "Lifting the Veil: Public-Private Surveillance Networks."

274 *he witnessed:* Dawson, "From Fellow Traveler to Anticommunist."

275 *Matthews had hoped:* Ibid.; Matthews, *Odyssey of a Fellow Traveler,* p. 60.

275 *"bourgeois democracy is":* Kempton, *Part of Our Time,* pp. 159–60.

275 *"J.B. Matthews would always":* Ibid.

275 *"regarded himself": Time,* August 10, 1953.

276 *He had voted:* Kempton, *Part of Our Time,* p. 168.

276 *Matthews counted:* Lichtman, "J. B. Matthews and the 'Counter-subversives.'"

276 *"probably the largest": Time,* July 13, 1953.

277 *"There is something":* Letter from J. B. Matthews, December 1948, Folder 3, Box 39, J. B. Matthews Papers, Duke University Libraries.

277 *A December 1951: American Legion,* December 1951.

277 *"He is not":* Powers, *Not Without Honor,* p 233.

278 *McCarthy was:* Logevall, *JFK,* p. 476.

Chapter 20: Positive Loyalty

283 *"Now it will be unnecessary"*: Rovere, *Senator Joe McCarthy*, p. 187.

283 *"By their act"*: Statement by the president, February 11, 1953, Box 26, NSC Staff Papers, PSB Central Files, Dwight D. Eisenhower Presidential Library & Museum.

284 *In his inaugural address*: *New York Times*, May 25, 1959.

284 *crafted their executive order*: The original draft, written by Attorney General Brownell, did not include homosexuality among its list of security risks, alongside "any criminal, infamous, dishonest, immoral, or notoriously disgraceful conduct, habitual use of intoxicants to excess," and "drug addiction." But Eisenhower's national security adviser, Robert Cutler, recommended a different version, with, among other changes, "sexual perversion" added to its list of red flags. Eisenhower agreed, and signed Executive Order 10450 on April 27. Decades later, Cutler's great-nephew, Peter Shinkle, discovered his diary, which revealed that he was gay. Shinkle, *Ike's Mystery Man*, p. 116.

284 *"an almost perfect"*: Purdum, "The Politics of Security," p. 13; *Time*, March 30, 1953.

284 *When asked*: Purdum, "The Politics of Security," p. 41.

284 *including twenty-four*: *Time*, March 30, 1953.

284 *"McLeod's was a name"*: *The Reporter*, May 5, 1955.

284 *"McCarthy Poses"*: *New York Times*, February 22, 1953.

285 *Bohlen and his wife*: Gerolymatos, *Castles Made of Sand*, p. 126; Hersh, *The Old Boys*, pp. 444–45.

286 *"The campaign"*: *Los Angeles Times*, April 13, 1953.

286 *"was too important"*: Bohlen, *Witness to History*, p. 323.

286 *the committee approved*: *Time*, March 30, 1953.

287 *"acid test"*: Ibid.

287 *McCarthy tried*: Purdum, "The Politics of Security," p. 24; *Time*, March 30, 1953.

287 *Dulles arranged*: Bohlen, *Witness to History*, pp. 328–29.

287 *A few weeks*: Ibid., pp. 334–35.

287 *Eleven of the*: *New York Times*, March 28, 1953.

288 *George Sokolsky*: Oshinsky, *A Conspiracy So Immense*, p. 267.

288 *The Voice of America*: *Time*, March 9, 1953.

288 *Secretaery Dulles*: *Chicago Tribune*, May 7, 1953.

289 *After they flew*: *Time*, March 22, 1954.

289 *"junketeering gumshoes"*: Ibid.

289 *"we don't work"*: Oshinsky, *A Conspiracy So Immense*, p. 279.

289 *During fifteen sessions*: Hearings, Permanent Subcommittee on Investigations, Committee on Government Operations. Senate, State Department Information Program—Information Centers, Part 2, March 27, pp. 132–35.

290 *"run down the purchase orders"*: New York Times, April 8, 1953.

290 *"If Eisenhower"*: Adams, First-Hand Report, p. 135.

290 *"In the early part"*: Rovere, Senator Joe McCarthy, p. 17.

290 *"I will not"*: White House meeting notes for December 3, 1953, Box 68, C. D. Jackson Papers, Eisenhower Library.

290 *"My good friends"*: Chicago Tribune, August 29, 1953.

291 *"The Soviet International"*: New York Times, August 24, 1953.

291 *"a greater menace"*: Los Angeles Times, September 1, 1953.

291 *In New York*: New York Times, November 11, 1954.

291 *The Democratic governor*: New York Times, May 19, 1954.

291 *Legislatures*: Chicago Tribune, November 167, 1951; New York Herald Tribune, December 11, 1951; Chicago Tribune, December 13, 1952; New York Herald Tribune, October 19, 1950.

291 *The New York City*: New York Times, August 28, 1951.

291 *And in Baltimore*: Washington Post, July 4, 1953.

292 *"The American Communist Party"*: Gornick, The Romance of American Communism, p. 170.

292 *"I have come"*: Albert Maltz, "What Shall We Ask of Writers?," New Masses, February 12, 1946.

292 *"They were walking"*: Kempton, Part of Our Time, p. 202.

292 *"American Communist Party"*: New York Times, July 1, 1951.

Chapter 21: How Red Are the Schools?

293 *Hlavaty was born in Piestany*: Time, March 23, 1953; interview with Arthur Hlavaty, May 28, 2023.

293 *Hlavaty was registered*: U.S. Congress, Senate, Committee on Government Operations, State Department Information Program—Voice of America: Hearings Before the Subcommittee on Investigations, 105th Cong., 1st Sess., 1953, p. 676.

294 *"I may say"*: Ibid., p. 709.

294 *"No matter what"*: Ibid., p. 714.

295 *Three weeks later*: New York Times, April 10, 1953.

295 *A week after that*: New York Times, April 18, 1953.

295 *One witness told*: Chicago Tribune, April 25, 1953.

296 *"No one indoctrinates"*: Time, March 16, 1953.

296 *"Propaganda for New Deal"*: New York Times, August 1, 1951.

296 *"The public schools"*: Los Angeles Times, July 11, 1951.

296 *A 1953 Gallup poll*: Washington Post, April 17, 1953.

297 *its 1949 convention*: Foster, "Red Alert!," p. 8; Boston Globe, July 8, 1950.

297 *The organization built ties*: Foster, "Red Alert!," p. 7.

297 *At its 1952 meeting: Baltimore Sun,* August 9, 1952.

298 *The Board of Education:* Smith, "The Dress Rehearsal for McCarthyism." Ironically, Yergan later renounced Communism to become an outspoken anti-Communist. He denounced former friends like Paul Robeson and Helen Reid Bryan—to whom he had been engaged—and eventually grew so extreme in his views that he supported right-wing guerrillas and white supremacist militias in Southern Africa, on the premise that their opposition to left-wing groups like the African National Congress outweighed their other sins.

298 *In 1949: Time,* April 11, 1949.

298 *"Is there evidence":* I. F. Stone, *The Truman Era,* p. 202.

298 *Another teacher: Adler v. Board of Education of City of New York,* 342 U.S. 485 (1952).

299 *In Scarsdale: Time,* March 16, 1953; "Scarsdale H.S. Career Conference Infiltrated," pamphlet, Box 28, Church League of America Papers, Tamiment Library, NYU.

300 *Four principals: New York Times,* April 4, April 11, and May 7, 1952.

300 *National Council for American Education: Time,* July 16, 1951; *The Harvard Crimson,* December 20, 1951.

301 *An attempt: New York Times,* September 17, 1954.

301 *After a 1952: New York Times,* May 25, 1952.

301 *In 1951 a conservative: Commentary,* May 25, 1952.

301 *The board of education: Washington Post,* January 28, 1951.

301 *The school board: The Amsterdam News,* April 26, 1952.

301 *In California: Los Angeles Times,* April 4, 1951.

302 *School districts also:* Gage, *G-Man,* p. 393.

302 *"The law inevitably": Adler v. Board of Education,* 342 U.S. 485 (1952).

302 *In a poll:* Foster, "Red Alert!," p. 4.

302 *A 1953 survey: New York Times,* June 9, 1953.

302 *"Far more to be feared": New York Times,* June 29, 1953.

302 *Already in 1948:* Schrecker, *No Ivory Tower,* pp. 94–96.

303 *but in 1950:* Gardner, *The California Oath Controversy,* p. 217.

303 *"America's colleges":* Schrecker, *No Ivory Tower,* p. 218.

303 *Harvard:* https://www.thecrimson.com/article/1965/6/17/the-university-in-the-mccarthy-era/, accessed May 20, 2024.

304 *His sole book: New York Times,* June 29, 1953.

305 *The use of: New York Times,* June 26, 1953.

305 *A worldwide survey: New York Times,* June 11, 1953.

305 *In June 1953:* https://www.presidency.ucsb.edu/documents/remarks-the-dartmouth-college-commencement-exercises-hanover-new-hampshire, accessed May 20, 2024.

Chapter 22: A Race for Death

307 "*Among the grown-ups*": Roberts, *New York Times*, June 6, 2008.

307 *In a widely read: The National Guardian*, August 1951.

307 *Grassroots groups like:* Radosh and Milton, *The Rosenberg File*, p. 322.

308 "*She called*": *New York Times*, August 10, 2015.

308 *That fall translated:* Glynn, "L'Affaire Rosenberg in France," p. 501; Memorandum, Kirk to Smith re: foreign response to Rosenberg case, January 16, 1953, Box 26, NSC Staff Papers, PSB Central Files Series, Dwight D. Eisenhower Presidential Library & Museum.

309 *The philosopher:* Glynn, "L'Affaire Rosenberg in France," p. 501.

309 *Jacques Duclos:* Ibid., p. 509.

309 *By late spring 1953:* Ibid., p. 515.

309 *In a call with:* Notes from call with Brownell, June 12, 1953, Box 1, Telephone Conversation Series, John Foster Dulles Papers, Eisenhower Library.

310 *On May 15:* Telegram, Ambassador Douglas Dillon regarding foreign response to Rosenberg case (and reply), May 20, 1953, Box 32, Administration Series, Presidential Papers, Eisenhower Library.

310 "*The actions*": President Eisenhower's response to Clyde Miller, June 10, 1953, Box 32, Administration Series, President Papers, Eisenhower Library.

311 *Three days:* William O. Douglas, *The Court Years*, pp. 80–81; Lichtman, *The Supreme Court and McCarthy-Era Repression*, pp. 60–61.

311 *Frankfurter, never a fan:* Simon, *The Antagonists*, p. 188.

311 *The Rosenbergs had been:* William O. Douglas, *The Court Years*, pp. 80–81; Lichtman, *The Supreme Court and McCarthy-Era Repression*, pp. 60–61.

312 "*The question*": William O. Douglas, *The Court Years*, pp. 80–81.

312 *Douglas made it:* Ibid.

312 *hurried back to Washington:* According to Ronald Radosh and Joyce Milton, Vinson claimed that he had in fact tried to contact Douglas—but also that he had already decided to call the special session in the event of a stay the night before Douglas left.

312 "*This is a race*": William O. Douglas, *The Court Years*, p. 82.

312 *Clerks several offices:* Snyder, *Democratic Justice*, p. 566.

313 "*The Rosenbergs were*": William O. Douglas, *The Court Years*, p. 82.

313 *The court announced:* Radosh and Milton, *The Rosenberg File*, p. 415; Newman, *Hugo Black*, p. 424.

313 *Their executions:* United Press International, June 19, 1953.

313 *Julius went first: New York Times*, June 20, 1953.

313 *One person was shot:* United Press International, June 19, 1953; *New York Times*, June 19, 1953; *Chicago Tribune*, June 20, 1953.

314 *Hecklers surrounded:* Gordon, *Hollywood Exile*, p. 69.

314 *"the most anguishing"*: Snyder, *Democratic Justice*, p. 561.

314 *"perfection may not"*: *Rosenberg v. United States*, 346 U.S. 273 (1953).

314 *"I know of"*: William O. Douglas, *The Court Years*, p. 84. Italics in original.

Chapter 23: A Dry Crucifixion

315 *Some 130,000 people*: Halberstam, *The Fifties*, p. 30.

315 *For their inaugural issue*: *Physics Today*, May 1948.

316 *"a destroyer of worlds"*: Oppenheimer's translation is a bit off; a more precise rendering is: "I am all-powerful Time which destroys all things."

316 *Victor Weisskopf*: Halberstam, *The Fifties*, p. 332.

316 *That began to change*: Bird and Sherwin, *American Prometheus*, pp. 106, 124.

317 *Later scholarship*: See, for example, John Earl Haynes and Harvey Klehr, "J. Robert Oppenheimer: A Spy? No. But a Communist Once? Yes."; Herken, *Brotherhood of the Bomb*; John Earl Haynes, Harvey Klehr, and Alexander Vassiliev, *Spies: The Rise and Fall of the KGB in America*. For a careful summary of the debate over Oppenheimer's possible membership in the party, see *The New York Times*, Oct. 8, 2024.

317 *At Berkeley*: Ibid., pp. 104–5.

317 *the FBI had opened*: Hoover to Tolson et al., November 15, 1945, Silvermaster file 65-56402-403.

317 *even though HUAC*: Bird and Sherwin, *American Prometheus*, p. 400.

317 *The politics of atomic warfare*: Schlesinger, *The Atlantic*, October 1954.

319 *"more elbows than an octopus"*: *New York Times*, January 22, 1974.

319 *"If you disagree"*: Joseph and Stewart Alsop, *We Accuse!*, p 31.

319 *William Borden*: Halberstam, *The Fifties*, pp. 332–33.

320 *"It seems reasonable"*: *In the Matter of J. Robert Oppenheimer*, pp. 837–38.

320 *The senator was already interested*: Bird and Sherwin, *American Prometheus*, pp. 478–79.

321 *He allowed Oppenheimer*: Halberstam, *The Fifties*, p. 350.

321 *"If it is a question"*: Schlesinger, *The Atlantic*, October 1954.

321 *"They cleared him"*: Associated Press, June 2, 1954.

321 *Gordon Gray*: Ibid.

322 *"When the winning side"*: Schlesinger, *The Atlantic*, October 1954.

322 *in the few years*: *The News of St. John*, July 24, 2023.

322 *"You know"*: Bird and Sherwin, *American Prometheus*, p. 552.

Chapter 24: The Tonangeber

325 *unfit for the high court*: *The Atlantic*, June 1976.

325 *Speculation had it*: Newton, *Justice for All*, pp. 3–5.

326 *Now, Warren pressed his case*: Ibid., p. 9.

326 *"He's a Democrat"*: Schwartz, *Super Chief*, p. 262.

327 *Early on, he led:* Kamisar, "How Earl Warren's Twenty-Two Years in Law Enforcement Affected His Work as Chief Justice," p. 11; Newton, *And Justice for All*, pp. 47–48.

328 *One such organization:* "Why the West Coast Opposes the Japanese," pamphlet, Native Sons of the Golden West Collection, University of California, Berkeley, https://digitalassets.lib.berkeley.edu/jarda/ucb/text/cubanc6714 _b274t01_0072.pdf, accessed May 5, 2024; Newton, *And Justice for All*, p. 75.

328 *"The Japanese situation":* Newton, *And Justice for All*, p. 128.

328 *"We believe that":* U.S. Congress, House, Select Committee to Investigate National Defense, National Defense Migration, 77th Cong., 2nd Sess., 1942, p. 11015.

329 *Warren's support:* Schwartz, *Super Chief*, p. 14.

329 *He knew enough:* Simon, *The Antagonists*, p. 222.

330 *He blanketed Warren's desk:* Schwartz, *Super Chief*, p. 149.

330 *heard the case: Irvine v. California*, 347 U.S. 128 (1954); Newton, *And Justice for All*, p. 338.

331 *In one of his first: Barsky v. Board of Regents*, 347 U.S. 442 (1954).

Chapter 25: Who Promoted Peress?

332 *"This means eight more years":* Hofstadter, *The Paranoid Style in American Politics*, p. 45.

332 *Privately, Eisenhower thought:* Letter to Milton Eisenhower, October 9, 1953, Box 12, Name Series, Presidential Papers, Dwight D. Eisenhower Presidential Library & Museum.

332 *In April 1953, he had played: New York Times*, April 20, 1953.

333 *Matthews published: Time*, August 10, 1953; Matthews, "Reds in Our Churches," *The American Mercury*, July 1953.

333 *He had Vice President Nixon:* Staff Notes on Senator Joseph McCarthy, July 29, 1953, Box 25, Administrative Series, Presidential Papers, Eisenhower Library; Brownell, *Advising Ike*, p. 256.

334 *But the rumors:* Tye, *Demagogue*, p. 385.

334 *in early October: Chicago Tribune*, October 10, 1953.

334 *for several weeks: New York Herald Tribune*, October 13, 1953.

334 *"If this develops": New York Times*, October 23, 1953.

335 *"McCarthy Charges": New York Times*, October 23, 1953.

335 *just days ahead: New York Times*, November 6, 1953.

335 *A White House aide: New York Times*, November 7, 1953.

335 *Representative Harold Velde: New York Times*, November 13, 1953.

335 *a televised address denouncing: New York Times*, November 17, 1953.

336 *The next day Hoover appeared: New York Times*, November 18, 1953; *Boston Globe*, November 18, 1953.

336 *"this whole thing"*: The President's News Conference, November 18, 1953, https://www.presidency.ucsb.edu/documents/the-presidents-news-conference-490, accessed May 5, 2024.

336 *"infinitely better than"*: Adams, *First-Hand Report*, p. 139; Recording, WNYC, November 25, 1953, https://www.wnyc.org/story/joseph-r-mccarthy-a-speech-against-harry-s-truman/, accessed May 22, 2023.

336 *"declared war on Eisenhower"*: Meeting notes November 27 and November 30, 1953, Box 68, C. D. Jackson Papers, Eisenhower Library.

337 *"fair, thorough"*: The President's News Conference, December 3, 1953, https://www.presidency.ucsb.edu/documents/the-presidents-news-conference-475, accessed May 5, 2024.

337 *That same month*: Brownell, *Advising Ike*, p. 256.

337 *Eisenhower also ordered Nixon*: Hitchcock, *The Age of Eisenhower*, p. 136.

337 *As part of the hunt: New York Times*, November 7, 1953.

337 *Brownell arranged a meeting*: Brownell, *Advising Ike*, p. 257.

338 *Adams dropped a bomb*: Ibid., pp. 257–58.

338 *After finding him*: Adams, *First-Hand Report*, p. 145.

338 *Brownell and Sherman Adams*: Ibid.

338 *dentist named Irving Peress*: Notes from conversation with Lt. Col. Edward H. Kurth, undated, Joseph N. Welch Papers, Boston Public Library.

339 *McCarthy launched: Time*, March 1, 1954.

339 *Robert Stevens: New York Times*, February 21, 1954.

339 *The meeting took place*: Tye, *Demagogue*, p. 397.

340 *Nixon called the meal*: Nixon, *RN*, p. 142.

340 *"Senator McCarthy achieved today"*: Cited in Rovere, *Senator Joe McCarthy*, p. 31.

340 *"We just can't work"*: Hitchcock, *The Age of Eisenhower*, p. 138.

340 *"We must be"*: The President's News Conference, March 3, 1954, https://www.presidency.ucsb.edu/documents/the-presidents-news-conference-348, accessed May 22, 2023.

340 *"If a stupid": Time*, March 14, 1953.

340 *"Ike really made up"*: Minutes, March 8, 1954, Box 1, James Hagerty Papers, Eisenhower Library.

340 *On March 8: New York Herald Tribune*, March 14, 1954.

341 *"brief talk"*: Flanders speech transcript, https://archive.vpr.org/vpr-news/senator-flanders-speech-to-the-senate-march-9-1954/, accessed May 23, 2023.

341 *He and his producer*: Oshinsky, *A Conspiracy So Immense*, p. 398.

342 *"His primary achievement"*: *See It Now*, March 9, 1954, https://www.youtube
.com/watch?v=dMgoi9pBRwg, accessed May 23, 2023.

342 *But it was overwhelmed*: Tye, *Demagogue*, p. 402.

342 *On the morning*: Notes from conference with Mr. Lee Berry, Joseph N. Welch
Papers, Boston Public Library.

342 *Stuart Symington: Time*, March 29, 1954.

343 *So too was news: New York Times*, March 11 and March 12, 1954.

343 *Saltonstall demurred: Time*, March 29, 1954.

343 *Surprisingly, McCarthy agreed*: Adams, *First-Hand Report*, p. 149.

343 *At the suggestion*: Brownell, *Advising Ike*, p. 260; *Newsweek*, June 7, 1954;
"Welch, Joseph Nye," *Dictionary of American Biography*.

344 *Karl Mundt took one: New York Times*, April 22, 1954.

344 *As Welch paused: Life*, July 26, 1954.

345 *"On the way"*: Ibid.

345 *calling "point of order": Time*, May 10, 1954.

345 *when on April 27*: Ibid.

345 *"A pixie?"*: U.S. Congress, Senate, Committee on Government Operations,
Special Senate Investigation on Charges and Countercharges Involving: Sec-
retary of the Army Robert T. Stevens, John G. Adams, H. Struve Hensel, and
Senator Joe McCarthy, Roy Cohn and Francis P. Carr before the Permanent
Subcommittee on Investigations, Part 14, 83rd Cong., 2nd Sess., 1954, p. 543.

346 *"individuals who have placed": New York Times*, May 28, 1954.

346 *Finally, on May 17*: Eisenhower to the Secretary of Defense, May 17, 1954,
Box 25, Administrative Series, Presidential Papers, Eisenhower Library.

346 *"Here is the thing"*: Transcript, June 8, 1954, Executive Sessions of the Senate
Permanent Subcommittee on Investigations of the Committee on Government Operations, Vol. 5, p. 276.

346 *At their first meeting*: Memo from Joseph N. Welch, April 5, 1954, Joseph N.
Welch Papers, Boston Public Library.

347 The New York Times *reported it: New York Times*, April 16, 1954.

347 *So, early in the negotiations*: Tye, *Demagogue*, p. 438.

347 *"Mr. Cohn, tell me"*: Special Senate Investigation on Charges and Countercharges, Part 59, pp. 2426–30.

349 *one witness, a gleam: The New Yorker*, July 22, 2020.

Chapter 26: McCarthywasm

350 *The hearings plodded along: Time*, June 28, 1954.

350 *Welch was right*: He was wrong, though, about something else. He told reporters at the end of the hearings that he would now fade from memory. Instead, he was the subject of glowing magazine profiles and celebrity hounds
for months. He extended his fame further by dabbling in acting: In 1959 he

played a judge in Otto Preminger's *Anatomy of a Murder*—a performance good enough to garner a Golden Globe nomination.

350 *The Gallup poll:* "Public Opinion on the '4s' Through Recent History," Gallup.com, June 6, 2014, https://news.gallup.com/opinion/polling-matters /176441/public-opinion-recent-history.aspx, accessed May 23, 2024.

351 *"tends to bring":* The New Yorker, September 18, 1954.

351 *"Regardless of what":* Chicago Tribune, November 14, 1954.

351 *In March 1954 McCarthy barnstormed: Chicago Tribune,* June 24, 1954.

351 *the* Chicago Tribune *sent a reporter:* Ibid.

352 *the* Los Angeles Times *found similar results: Los Angeles Times,* June 28, 1954.

352 *In November 1954: Time,* November 29, 1954.

352 *One of its leaders:* Oshinsky, *A Conspiracy So Immense,* p. 486.

352 *"Dear Commie Senator":* Ibid., p. 487.

352 *On December 2, 1954: New York Times,* December 2, 1954

353 *"shrinking show of weakness": Time,* December 20, 1954.

353 *"It's no longer McCarthyism":* Notes from June 21, 1955, meeting, Box 1, White House Office of the Staff Secretary, Arthur Minnich Series, Dwight D. Eisenhower Presidential Library & Museum. What was McCarthyism? Some historians, like Ellen Schrecker, argue that it is synonymous with the entire Red Scare era—that the same tactics used by the Wisconsin senator can be found in the actions of HUAC, presidential loyalty boards, and local red squads throughout the country. But that seems to be asking too much of a single word. The Red Scare era encompassed an array of strategies, attitudes, organizations, and goals, only a few of which come close to resembling McCarthy's. Plus, labeling the entire era as "McCarthyist" overlooks some of the very legitimate concerns raised over the very real, if limited, problem of Communists in government and labor unions. And, at least in popular usage, calling the entire era McCarthyist limits the timespan involved, giving the impression that the Red Scare began in January 1950 in Wheeling, West Virginia, and ended in December 1954 on the floor of the Senate. Better, then, to limit the term to a very specific meaning, namely the use of innuendo, guilt by association, and outright lies to smear a political enemy. McCarthy was not the first person to use those tactics during the Red Scare, nor would he be the last. But McCarthyism, defined that way, only covers some of what made the Red Scare so terrible—and, in fact, McCarthy's years in the spotlight obscured the steady work of political repression going on in the shadows behind him, work that began long before he emerged and continued long after he receded.

354 *In a June 1954 speech he touted:* Statement by the President on the Record of the Department of Justice in Dealing with Subversive Activities, June 2, 1954,

https://www.presidency.ucsb.edu/documents/statement-the-president-the-rec ord-the-department-justice-dealing-with-subversive, accessed May 6, 2024.

354 *He also encouraged:* McAuliffe, "Liberals and the Communist Control Act of 1954," p. 361.

355 *commending it as a weapon:* Remarks on the Communist Control Act of 1954, August 24, 1954, https://www.presidency.ucsb.edu/documents/remarks -the-communist-control-act-1954, accessed May 24, 2023.

356 *"Protecting America includes":* "Address at the Columbia University National Bicentennial Dinner, New York City, May 31, 1954," The American Presidency Project, https://www.presidency.ucsb.edu/documents/address -the-columbia-university-national-bicentennial-dinner-new-york-city, accessed May 27, 2024.

356 *In January 1956: New York Times,* January 19, 1956.

356 *In 1955 New York: Newsday,* October 20, 1955; *New York Times,* May 7, 1957.

356 *On May 1, 1956: New York Herald Tribune,* May 2, 1956.

357 *"self-defense organization":* Mitford, *A Fine Old Conflict,* p. 79.

357 *Howard Fast: New York Times,* February 1, 1957.

357 *The Daily Worker:* Fast, *Being Red,* p. 354.

358 *best story Oscar: The Brave One* was, in fact, the last film to win this particular award, which went to the best treatment and was distinguished from the best screenplay. The category was abolished the following year.

358 *In a June 1960 interview: Variety,* June 1960.

358 *In April 1960: New York Times,* April 9, 1960.

358 *The director Sidney Lumet:* Walter Bernstein, *Inside Out,* p. 262.

358 *A few desultory picketers: New York Times,* February 4, 1961; American Legion News Service, June 3, 1960, https://archive.legion.org/_flysystem/fedora /2022-06/aa002470.pdf, accessed May 6, 2024.

359 *In 1956 it found: New York Herald Tribune,* May 20, 1956.

359 *The subcommittee claimed:* U.S. Congress, Senate, Committee on Un-American Activities, Investigation of the Unauthorized Use of U.S. Passports, 84th Cong., 2nd Sess., 1956.

Chapter 27: Red Monday

362 *On October 19, 1956:* Schwartz, *Super Chief,* p. 226; *Jencks v. United States,* 353 U.S. 657 (1957); Dickson, *The Supreme Court in Conference, 1940–1985,* p. 555.

363 *The judge had told them:* Caballero, *McCarthyism vs. Clinton Jencks,* pp. 158–60.

363 *"treason's biggest victory":* U.S. News & World Report, June 28, 1957.

363 *After a report:* Warren, *The Memoirs of Chief Justice Earl Warren,* p. 323.

363 *in protest:* The *Jencks* ruling had an unintended consequence. J. Edgar

Hoover was frantic over the possibility that prosecutors who relied on his vast and secret files would be forced to make them public, or else not use them at all. He had already been preparing for such an eventuality for at least two years, building the innocuously named Counterintelligence Program, or COINTELPRO, which involved a series of secret and often illegal projects to disrupt the Communist Party through dirty tricks. Hoover was so pleased with COINTELPRO that he would use it over and over during the next fifteen years, against civil rights groups, antiwar protesters, and anyone else he deemed a threat to his conservative vision of America.

364 *The legal scholar Geoffrey Stone:* Geoffrey Stone, *Perilous Times*, p. 413.

364 *"There is no power":* Schwartz, *Super Chief*, pp. 236–37; Simon, *The Antagonists*, p. 237.

364 *Warren was equally exercised: Sweezy v. New Hampshire*, 354 U.S. 234 (1957).

364 *Warren felt: Service v. Dulles*, 354 U.S. 363 (1957).

365 *The trial judge:* Sabin, *In Calmer Times*, pp. 161–63.

365 *Harlan, finally:* Geoffrey Stone, *Perilous Times*, p. 413; Newton, *Justice for All*, pp. 353–54; *Yates v. United States*, 354 U.S. 298 (1957).

366 *Scores of people protested: San Francisco Chronicle*, February 3, 2017.

366 *At the hearing:* Swerdlow, *Women Strike for Peace*, pp. 110-13.

366 *"By now":* Goodman, *The Committee*, p. 410.

366 *in 1966, Jerry Rubin: Time*, September 9, 1966.

Chapter 28: The Coal-Seam Fire

368 *Joe McCarthy checked into: New York Times*, May 2, 1957.

368 *He talked to friends: Time*, May 13, 1957.

368 *"Mortuis nihil nisi bonum":* Acheson, *Present at the Creation*, p. 362.

368 *J. Robert Oppenheimer:* Schweber, *Oppenheimer and Einstein*, p. 225.

368 *"Senator McCarthy was hounded":* Sokolsky, syndicated column, June 5, 1957.

369 *In Washington: New York Times*, May 7, 1957.

369 *"The stinking hypocrite":* New Hampshire *Union Leader*, May 8, 1957.

370 *He had brought him:* Program, Hotel Astor, July 28, 1954, Box 35, Alfred Kohlberg Papers, Hoover Institution Archives.

370 *"the dirtiest deal":* Matthew Dallek, *Birchers*, pp. 24–25.

371 *"It is my utterly sincere belief":* Welch, *May God Forgive Us*, p. 76.

371 *The tome: New York Times*, November 16, 1952; Mao, *Asia First*, pp. 106-8.

371 *It was Knowland:* Dallek, *Birchers*, p. 26.

371 *In 1953 Welch:* Ibid., pp. 26–27.

371 *and in 1958:* John Birch Society Records, Brown University, https://www.riamco.org/render?eadid=US-RPB-ms2013.003&view=biography, accessed May 7, 2024.

371 *within five years claimed:* Ibid.

371 *Alfred Kohlberg:* Letter from Alfred Kohlberg to Robert Welch, Box 17, Alfred Kohlberg Papers, Hoover Institution Archives.

372 *One such organization:* The poster can be found at https://dlc.library.columbia.edu/catalog/cul:95x69p8fb8, accessed May 7, 2024.

372 *"Every other person":* Washington Post, January 15, 2021.

373 *But it transformed the right:* Politico, March 31, 2023. Alfred Kohlberg would not be there to watch. He had suffered a series of heart attacks in the mid-1950s that left him increasingly debilitated. Even his correspondence slowed, save for a few select friends like Welch. He died on April 7, 1960, in New York City.

Epilogue

375 *"If we had any premonition":* Fast, Being Red, p. 151. Thirty years later, Fast would draw on Bryan's life in creating Barbara Lavette, the lead character in a six-part series of novels about the many generations of a progressive family.

375 *ruled against her:* New York Times, May 9, 1950.

375 *led by Lillian Hellman:* Flyer for "Deadline for Freedom" rally, n.d., Box 2, Joint Anti-Fascist Refugee Committee Papers, Tamiment Library, NYU.

375 *Treasury agents:* Helen Reid Bryan letter to supporters, February 3, 1948, Box 2, JAFRC Papers, Tamiment Library.

376 *Boston City Club:* Helen Reid Bryan Letter to Executive Board, February 4, 1948, Box 2, JAFRC Papers, Tamiment Library.

376 *willing to replace them:* Letter from Edward Barsky, February 6, 1948, Box 2; Minutes of the JAFRC Executive Board, September 15, 1947, Box 2, JAFRC Papers, Tamiment Library.

376 *She lauded* Inside: The Nation, May 2, 1953.

376 *finally met Bryan:* Freedman, Maternal Justice, p. 324.

376 *"love of my life":* Ibid.

377 *Bryan as her successor:* Ibid., p. 325.

377 *"You know that":* Ibid., p. 326.

377 *volunteered for the Salvation Army:* Memo from SAC New York to FBI Director, July 16, 1954, 1498516-0-Section 3, FBI FOIA (Helen Reid Bryan).

377 *The FBI, still watching:* Freedman, Maternal Justice, p. 327.

378 *Bryan sold the house:* Interview with Alison Carlson.

378 *She found a job:* Report form, March 31, 1958, 1498516-0-Section 3, FBI FOIA (Helen Reid Bryan).

378 *"noted anything":* Ibid.

378 *security index:* Memo to Assistant Attorney General William Tompkins, October 17, 1955, 1498516-0-Section 3, FBI FOIA (Helen Reid Bryan).

378 *On May 22, 1958:* Report form, May 29, 1958, 1498516-0-Section 3, FBI FOIA (Helen Reid Bryan).

BIBLIOGRAPHY

Archives

Andover-Harvard Theological Library
    Unitarian Service Committee Records
Boston Public Library
    Joseph N. Welch Papers
Family Papers of Helen Reid Bryan
Duke University Libraries
    J. B. Matthews Papers
Dwight D. Eisenhower Presidential Library & Museum
    Herbert Brownell Papers
    John Foster Dulles Papers
    Dwight D. Eisenhower Presidential Papers
    C. D. Jackson Papers
Harvard Law School Archives
    Zechariah Chafee Papers
    Felix Frankfurter Papers
Hoover Institution Archives
    Alfred Kohlberg Papers
    George Sokolsky Papers
Library of Congress
    NAACP Papers
National Archives
    House Committee on Un-American Activities Papers
New York Public Library
    Arthur M. Schlesinger Jr. Papers
Princeton University Archives
    Harold Medina Papers
Schlesinger Library, Radcliffe Institute
    Ava Bohlen Papers
    Miriam Van Waters Papers

Southern Illinois University
  John Howard Lawson Papers
Tamiment Library and Robert F. Wagner Labor Archives at New York University
  Church League of America Papers
  Edward Barsky Papers
  Joint Anti-Fascist Refugee Committee Papers
  Charlotte Stern Papers
Harry S. Truman Library and Museum
  Harry S. Truman Presidential Papers
University of California, Los Angeles
  Dalton Trumbo Papers
University of Mississippi
  John Rankin Papers
Wellesley College
  Helen Reid Bryan Papers

Books and Theses

Acheson, Dean. *Present at the Creation: My Years in the State Department.* New York: W. W. Norton, 1969.

Adams, Sherman. *First-Hand Report: The Story of the Eisenhower Administration.* New York: Harper & Brothers, 1961.

Afrasiabi, Peter. *Burning Bridges: America's 20-Year Crusade to Deport Labor Leader Harry Bridges.* Culver City: Thirlmere Books, 2017.

Aldous, Richard. *Schlesinger: The Imperial Historian.* New York: W. W. Norton, 2017.

Alsop, Joseph, and Stewart Alsop. *We Accuse! The Story of the Miscarriage of American Justice in the Case of J. Robert Oppenheimer.* New York: Simon & Schuster, 1954.

Anthony, David Henry, III. *Max Yergan: Race Man, Internationalist, Cold Warrior.* New York: New York University Press, 2006.

Beemyn, Genny. *A Queer Capital: A History of Gay Life in Washington, D.C.* New York: Routledge, 2014.

Beisner, Robert L. *Dean Acheson: A Life in the Cold War.* New York: Oxford University Press, 2006.

Belfrage, Cedric. *The American Inquisition, 1945–1960.* Indianapolis: Bobbs-Merrill, 1973.

Belknap, Michael R. *American Political Trials.* Westport: Praeger, 1994.

Bentley, Elizabeth. *Out of Bondage: The Elizabeth Bentley Story.* New York: Devin-Adair, 1951.

Bentley, Eric, ed. *Thirty Years of Treason: Excerpts from Hearings Before the House Committee on Un-American Activities, 1938–1968.* New York: Nation Books, 2001.

Bernhard, Nancy E. *U.S. Television News and Cold War Propaganda, 1947–1960.* Cambridge: Cambridge University Press, 2003.

Bernstein, Carl. *Loyalties: A Son's Memoirs.* New York: Touchstone, 1990.

Bernstein, Irving. *The Turbulent Years: A History of the American Worker, 1933–1940.* Chicago: Haymarket Books, 2010.

Bernstein, Walter. *Inside Out: A Memoir of the Blacklist.* New York: Da Capo, 2000.

Bessie, Alvah. *Inquisition in Eden.* New York: Macmillan, 1965.

Bird, Kai, and Martin Sherwin. *American Prometheus: The Triumph and Tragedy of J. Robert Oppenheimer.* New York: Alfred A. Knopf, 2005.

Bohlen, Charles E. *Witness to History, 1929–1969.* New York: W. W. Norton, 1973.

Boyle, Kevin. *The UAW and the Heyday of American Liberalism, 1945–1968.* Ithaca: Cornell University Press, 1995.

Brands, H. W. *The General vs. the President: MacArthur and Truman at the Brink of Nuclear War.* New York: Doubleday, 2016.

———. *Reagan: The Life.* New York: Doubleday, 2015.

Brinkley, Alan. *Liberalism and Its Discontents.* Cambridge: Harvard University Press, 1998.

———. *The Publisher: Henry Luce and His American Century.* New York: Alfred A. Knopf, 2010.

Brownell, Herbert. *Advising Ike: The Memoirs of Attorney General Herbert Brownell.* Lawrence: University Press of Kansas, 1993.

Brownell, Will, and Richard Billings. *So Close to Greatness: The Biography of William C. Bullitt.* New York: Macmillan, 1993.

Bryan, Helen Reid. *Inside: The Story of One Prisoner and One Prisoner's Friends in the Federal Penitentiary for Women.* Boston: Houghton Mifflin, 1953.

Bullitt, William C. *For the President Personal & Secret: Correspondence Between Franklin D. Roosevelt and William C. Bullitt.* New York: Houghton Mifflin, 1972.

Caballero, Raymond. *McCarthyism vs. Clinton Jencks.* Norman: University of Oklahoma Press, 2019.

Caro, Robert. *The Years of Lyndon Johnson: Master of the Senate.* New York: Alfred A. Knopf, 2002.

Caute, David. *The Fellow-Travelers: Intellectual Friends of Communism.* New Haven: Yale University Press, 1988.

———. *The Great Fear: The Anti-Communist Purge Under Truman and Eisenhower.* New York: Simon & Schuster, 1978.

Ceplair, Larry, and Steven Englund. *The Inquisition in Hollywood: Politics in the Film Community, 1930–1960.* New York: Anchor, 1980.

Chambers, Whittaker. *Witness: A True Story of Soviet Spies in America and the Trial That Captivated the Nation.* New York: Regnery, 1952.

Chaplin, Charlie. *My Autobiography*. New York: Simon & Schuster, 1964.

Charles, Douglas M. *Hoover's War on Gays: Exposing the FBI's "Sex Deviates" Program*. Lawrence: University Press of Kansas, 2015.

Cherny, Robert W. *American Labor and the Cold War: Grassroots Politics and Postwar Political Culture*. New Brunswick: Rutgers University Press, 2004.

———. *Harry Bridges: Labor Radical, Labor Legend*. Champaign: University of Illinois Press, 2023.

Cochran, Bert. *Labor and Communism: The Conflict That Shaped American Unions*. Princeton: Princeton University Press, 1978.

Cogley, John. *Report on Blacklisting I: Movies*. New York: Fund for the Republic, 1956.

———. *Report on Blacklisting II: Radio-Television*. New York: Fund for the Republic, 1956.

Cohen, Lizabeth. *Making a New Deal: Industrial Workers in Chicago, 1919–1939*. Cambridge: Cambridge University Press, 1991.

Cohen, Robert. *When the Old Left Was Young: Student Radicals and America's First Mass Student Movement, 1929–1941*. Oxford: Oxford University Press, 1997.

Cook, Bruce. *Dalton Trumbo: A Biography of the Oscar-Winning Screenwriter Who Broke the Blacklist*. New York: Scribner, 1977.

Cooke, Alistair. *A Generation on Trial: U.S.A. v. Alger Hiss*. New York: Alfred A. Knopf, 1952.

Critchlow, Donald T. *When Hollywood Was Right: How Movie Stars, Studio Moguls, and Big Business Remade American Politics*. Cambridge: Cambridge University Press, 2013.

Dallek, Matthew. *Birchers: How the John Birch Society Radicalized the American Right*. New York: Basic Books, 2023.

Dallek, Robert. *An Unfinished Life: John F. Kennedy, 1917–1963*. New York: Little, Brown, 2003.

Davies, John Paton, Jr. *China Hand: An Autobiography*. Philadelphia: University of Pennsylvania Press, 2012.

Davis, Nuel Pharr. *Lawrence and Oppenheimer*. New York: Simon & Schuster, 1968.

Dean, Robert D. *Imperial Brotherhood: Gender and the Making of Cold War Foreign Policy*. Amherst: University of Massachusetts Press, 2001.

Deery, Philip. *Red Apple: Communism and McCarthyism in Cold War New York*. New York: Fordham University Press, 2014.

Denning, Michael. *The Cultural Front: The Laboring of American Culture in the Twentieth Century*. New Haven: Yale University Press, 1996.

Devine, Thomas W. *Henry Wallace's 1948 Campaign and the Future of Postwar Liberalism*. Chapel Hill: University of North Carolina Press, 2013.

Dick, Bernard F. *Radical Innocence: A Critical Study of the Hollywood Ten.* Lexington: University of Kentucky Press, 1989.

Dickson, Del, ed. *The Supreme Court in Conference, 1940–1985.* Oxford: Oxford University Press, 2001.

Dmytryk, Edward. *It's a Hell of a Life but Not a Bad Living: A Hollywood Memoir.* New York: Times Books, 1978.

———. *Odd Man Out: A Memoir of the Hollywood Ten.* Carbondale: Southern Illinois University Press, 1996.

Donner. Frank J. *The Un-Americans.* New York: Ballantine, 1961.

Dos Passos, John. *The Best Times: An Informal Memoir.* New York: New American Library, 1966.

Douglas, Helen Gahagan. *A Full Life.* New York: Doubleday, 1982.

Douglas, William O. *The Court Years: 1939–1975.* New York: Random House, 1980.

Duberman, Martin. *Paul Robeson: A Life.* New York: New Press, 1995.

Fariello, Griffin. *Red Scare: Memories of the American Inquisition.* New York: W. W. Norton, 1995.

Farrell, John A. *Richard Nixon: The Life.* New York: Doubleday, 2017.

Fast, Howard. *Being Red: A Memoir.* Armonk: M. E. Sharpe. 1990.

———. *Peekskill USA: Inside the Infamous 1949 Riots.* Mineola: Dover, 1951.

Filippelli, Ronald L., and Mark D. McColloch. *Cold War in the Working Class: The Rise and Decline of the United Electrical Workers.* Albany: SUNY Press, 1994.

Fischer, Nick. *Spider Web: The Birth of American Communism.* Champaign: University of Illinois Press, 2016.

Fones-Wolf, Elizabeth A. *Selling Free Enterprise: The Business Assault on Labor and Liberalism, 1945–60.* Champaign: University of Illinois Press, 1995.

Freedman, Estelle B. *Maternal Justice: Miriam Van Waters and the Female Reform Tradition.* Chicago: University of Chicago Press, 1996.

Freeland, Richard M. *The Truman Doctrine and the Origins of McCarthyism: Foreign Policy, Domestic Policy, and Internal Security, 1946–48.* New York: New York University Press, 1985.

Fried, Richard M. *Nightmare in Red: The McCarthy Era in Perspective.* Oxford: Oxford University Press, 1990.

———. *The Russians Are Coming! The Russians Are Coming!: Pageantry and Patriotism in Cold-War America.* Oxford: Oxford University Press, 1998.

Friedrich, Otto. *City of Nets: A Portrait of Hollywood in the 1940s.* Berkeley: University of California Press, 1997.

Gaddis, John Lewis. *The Cold War: A New History.* New York: Penguin, 2006.

Gage, Beverly. *G-Man: J. Edgar Hoover and the Making of the American Century.* New York: Penguin, 2022.

Gardner, David P. *The California Oath Controversy.* Berkeley: University of California Press, 1967.

Gerolymatos, Andre: *Castles Made of Sand: A Century of Anglo-American Espionage and Intervention in the Middle East.* New York: Thomas Dunne Books, 2010.

Gilmore, Glenda Elizabeth. *Defying Dixie: The Radical Roots of Civil Rights, 1919–1950.* New York: W. W. Norton, 2008.

Gladchuk, John J. *Hollywood and Anticommunism: HUAC and the Evolution of the Red Menace, 1935–1950.* London: Routledge, 2007.

Goodman, Walter. *The Committee: The Extraordinary Career of the House Committee on Un-American Activities.* New York: Farrar, Straus & Giroux, 1968.

Gordon, Bernard. *Hollywood Exile: or How I Learned to Love the Blacklist.* Austin: University of Texas Press, 1999.

Gornick, Vivian. *The Romance of American Communism.* New York: Basic Books, 1977.

Halberstam, David. *The Coldest Winter: America and the Korean War.* New York: Hachette, 2007.

———. *The Fifties.* New York: Ballantine, 1994.

Hamby, Alonzo L. *Beyond the New Deal: Harry S. Truman and American Liberalism.* New York: Columbia University Press, 1976.

———. *Man of Destiny: FDR and the Making of the American Century.* New York: Basic Books, 2015.

Hamilton, Nigel. *JFK: Reckless Youth.* New York: Random House, 1992.

Hayden, Sterling. *Wanderer.* New York: Random House, 1963.

Haynes, John Earl. *Communism and Anti-Communism in the United States, an Annotated Guide to Historical Writings.* Oxford: Oxford University Press, 1987.

———. *Red Scare or Red Menace? American Communism and Anticommunism.* Chicago: Ivan R. Dee, 1996.

Haynes, John Earl, and Harvey Klehr. *The American Communist Movement: Storming Heaven Itself.* Woodbridge: Twayne, 1992.

———. *In Denial: Historians, Communism and Espionage.* New York: Encounter Books, 2003.

———. *Venona: Decoding Soviet Espionage in America.* New Haven: Yale University Press, 2000.

Haynes, John Earl, Harvey Klehr, and Alexander Vassiliev, *Spies: The Rise and Fall of the KGB in America.* New Haven: Yale University Press, 2012.

Hellman, Lillian. *Scoundrel Time.* New York: Little, Brown, 1976.

Herken, Gregg. *Brotherhood of the Bomb: The Tangled Lives and Loyalties of Robert Oppenheimer, Ernest Lawrence, and Edward Teller.* New York; Henry Holt & Co., 2002.

———. *The Georgetown Set: Friends and Rivals in Cold War Washington.* New York: Alfred A. Knopf, 2014.

Hersh, Burton. *The Old Boys: The American Elite and the Origins of the C.I.A.* New York: Scribner, 1992.

Hitchcock, William. *The Age of Eisenhower: America and the World in the 1950s.* New York: Simon & Schuster, 2018.

Hofstadter, Richard. *The Paranoid Style in American Politics.* New York: Vintage, 2008.

Horne, Gerald. *The Final Victim of the Blacklist: John Howard Lawson, Dean of the Hollywood Ten.* Berkeley: University of California Press, 2006.

Isserman, Maurice. *Which Side Were You On? The American Communist Party During the Second World War.* Middletown: Wesleyan University Press, 1982.

Johnson, David K. *The Lavender Scare: The Cold War Persecution of Gays and Lesbians in the Federal Government.* Chicago: University of Chicago Press, 2003.

Kahn, E. J. *The China Hands: America's Foreign Service Officers and What Befell Them.* New York: Viking, 1975.

Kahn, Gordon. *Hollywood on Trial: The Story of the 10 Who Were Indicted.* New York: Boni & Gaer, 1948.

Kaiser, Charles. *The Gay Metropolis: The Landmark History of Gay Life in America.* New York: Grove, 2007.

Kanfer, Stefan. *A Journal of the Plague Years: A Devastating Chronicle of the Era of the Blacklist.* New York: Athenaeum, 1973.

Katznelson, Ira. *Fear Itself: The New Deal and the Origins of Our Time.* New York: Liveright, 2013.

———. *When Affirmative Action Was White: An Untold History of Racial Inequality in Twentieth-Century America.* New York, Liveright, 2005.

Kazan, Elia. *Elia Kazan: A Life.* New York: Da Capo, 1997.

Keely, Joseph. *China Lobby Man: The Story of Alfred Kohlberg.* New Rochelle: Arlington House, 1969.

Kelley, Robin D. G. *Hammer and Hoe: Alabama Communists During the Great Depression.* Chapel Hill: University of North Carolina Press, 2015.

Kempton, Murray. *Part of Our Time: Some Ruins and Monuments of the Thirties.* New York: Simon & Schuster, 1955.

Kennedy, David M. *Freedom from Fear: The American People in Depression and War, 1929–1945.* Oxford: Oxford University Press, 2001.

Kirchick, James. *Secret City: The Hidden History of Gay Washington.* New York: Henry Holt, 2022.

Klehr, Harvey. *The Heyday of American Communism: The Depression Decade.* New York: Basic Books, 1984.

Klehr, Harvey and Ronald Radosh. *The Amerasia Spy Case: Prelude to McCarthyism.* Chapel Hill: University of North Carolina Press, 1996.

Knight, Amy. *How the Cold War Began: The Igor Gouzenko Affair and the Hunt for Soviet Spies.* Toronto: McClelland & Stewart, 2005.

Koen, Ross Y. *The China Lobby in American Politics.* London: Octagon, 1974.

Kurtz-Phelan, Daniel. *The China Mission: George Marshall's Unfinished War, 1945–1947*. New York: W. W. Norton, 2018.

Lait, Jack, and Lee Mortimer, *Washington Confidential*. New York: Dell, 1952.

Lamphere, Robert J., and Tom Schachtman. *The F.B.I.-K.G.B. War: A Special Agent's Story*. London: W. H. Allen, 1987.

Lardner, Ring, Jr. *The Lardners: My Family Remembered*. New York: Harper & Row, 1976.

Latham, Earl. *The Communist Controversy in Washington: From the New Deal to McCarthy*. Cambridge: Harvard University Press, 1966.

Leuchtenburg, William E. *Franklin D. Roosevelt and the New Deal: 1932–1940*. New York: Harper & Row, 1963.

Lewy, Guenter. *Federal Loyalty-Security Program: The Need for Reform*. Washington: American Enterprise Institute Press, 1983.

Lichtenstein, Nelson. *Walter Reuther: The Most Dangerous Man in Detroit*. New York: Basic Books, 1995.

Lichtman, Robert M. *The Supreme Court and McCarthy-Era Repression: One Hundred Decisions*. Champaign: University of Illinois Press, 2015.

Lipsitz, George. *Class and Culture in Cold War America: "A Rainbow at Midnight."* Westport: Praeger, 1981.

Logevall, Fredrik. *JFK: Coming of Age in the American Century, 1917–1956*. New York: Random House, 2020.

Loughery, John. *The Other Side of Silence: Men's Lives & Gay Identities—A Twentieth-Century History*. New York: Henry Holt, 1998.

Lyons, Eugene. *The Red Decade: The Classic Work on Communism in America During the Thirties*. New York: Simon & Schuster, 1970.

MacLeish, Archibald. *Collected Poems (1917–1952)*. New York: Houghton Mifflin, 1952.

Mann, William J. *Kate: The Woman Who Was Hepburn*. New York: Henry Holt, 2006.

Mao, Joyce. *Asia First: China and the Making of Modern American Conservatism*. Chicago: University of Chicago Press, 2015.

Maraniss, David. *A Good American Family: The Red Scare and My Father*. New York: Simon & Schuster, 2019.

Martelle, Scott. *The Fear Within: Spies, Commies, and American Democracy on Trial*. New Brunswick: Rutgers University Press, 2011.

Marton, Kati. *True Believer: Stalin's Last American Spy*. New York: Simon & Schuster, 2016.

Matthews, J. B. *Odyssey of a Fellow Traveler*. Mount Vernon: Mount Vernon Publishers, 1938.

May, Elaine Tyler. *Homeward Bound: American Families in the Cold War Era*. New York: Basic Books, 1988.

May, Gary. *China Scapegoat: The Diplomatic Ordeal of John Carter Vincent*. New York: New Republic Books, 1979.

———. *Un-American Activities: The Trials of William Remington*. Oxford: Oxford University Press, 1994.

McCullough, David. *Truman*. New York: Simon & Schuster, 1992.

Miller, Arthur. *Timebends: A Life*. New York: Grove, 1987.

Mitchell, Greg. *The Campaign of the Century: Upton Sinclair's Race for Governor of California and the Birth of Media Politics*. New York: Random House, 1991.

Mitford, Jessica. *A Fine Old Conflict*. New York: M. Joseph, 1978.

Morgan, Ted. *A Covert Life: Jay Lovestone: Communist, Anti-Communist, and Spymaster*. New York: Random House, 1999.

———. *Reds: McCarthyism in Twentieth-Century America*. New York: Random House, 2003.

Nash, George H. *The Conservative Intellectual Movement in America Since 1945*. New York: Basic Books, 1976.

Navasky, Victor. *Naming Names*. New York: Viking, 1980.

Newman, Roger K. *Hugo Black: A Biography*. New York: Fordham University Press, 1997.

Newton, Jim. *Justice for All: Earl Warren and the Nation He Made*. New York: Riverhead Books, 2007.

Nixon, Richard M. *RN: The Memoirs of Richard Nixon*. New York: Simon & Schuster, 1978.

———. *Six Crises*. New York: Doubleday, 1962.

Ogden, August Raymond. *The Dies Committee: A Study of the Special House Committee, 1938–1944*. Washington, D.C.: Catholic University of America Press, 1945.

Olmsted, Kathryn S. *Red Spy Queen: A Biography of Elizabeth Bentley*. Chapel Hill: University of North Carolina Press, 2002.

Oshinsky, David. *A Conspiracy So Immense: The World of Joe McCarthy*. New York: Simon & Schuster, 1983.

Patterson, James. *Mr. Republican: A Biography of Robert A. Taft*. New York: Houghton Mifflin, 1972.

Pepper, Claude. *Eyewitness to a Century*. New York: Harcourt, 1987.

Ponce de Leon, Charles. *That's the Way It Is: A History of Television News in America*. Chicago: University of Chicago Press, 2022.

Powers, Richard Gid. *Not Without Honor: The History of American Anticommunism*. New York: Free Press, 1995.

Purdum, Todd S. "The Politics of Security: The Eisenhower State Department and Scott McLeod." Senior thesis, Princeton University, 1982.

Radosh, Ronald, and Joyce Milton. *The Rosenberg File: A Search for the Truth*. New York: Holt, Rinehart & Winston, 1983.

Reagan, Ronald. *Where's the Rest of Me? The Autobiography of Ronald Reagan.* New York: Duell, Sloan & Pearce, 1965.

Record, Wilson. *The Negro and the Communist Party.* Chapel Hill: University of North Carolina Press, 1951.

Robeson, Paul, (Philip Foner, ed.). Paul Robeson Speaks: Writings, Speeches, Interviews, 1918-1974. Levittown: Brunner/Mazel, 1978.

Robeson, Paul, Jr. *The Undiscovered Paul Robeson: An Artist's Journey, 1898–1939.* Hoboken: Wiley, 2001.

Rovere, Richard. *Senator Joe McCarthy.* New York: Harper & Row, 1959.

Ryan, James G. *Earl Browder: The Failure of American Communism.* Tuscaloosa: University of Alabama Press, 1997.

Sabin, Arthur J. *In Calmer Times: The Supreme Court and Red Monday.* Philadelphia: University of Pennsylvania Press, 1999.

Schickel, Richard. *Elia Kazan: A Biography.* New York: Harper, 2006.

Schlesinger Jr., Arthur. *The Crisis of the Old Order.* Boston: Houghton Mifflin Company, 1957.

———. *The Coming of the New Deal.* Boston: Houghton Mifflin, 1958.

———. *The Vital Center: The Politics of Freedom.* Boston: Houghton Mifflin, 1949.

Schrecker, Ellen. *The Age of McCarthyism: A Brief History with Documents.* New York: St. Martin's Press, 1994.

———. *Many Are the Crimes: McCarthyism in America.* Princeton: Princeton University Press, 1998.

———. *No Ivory Tower: McCarthyism and the Universities.* Oxford: Oxford University Press, 1986.

Schwartz, Bernard. *Super Chief: Earl Warren and His Supreme Court, A Judicial Biography.* New York: New York University Press, 1983.

Schweber, Silvan S. *Oppenheimer and Einstein.* Cambridge: Harvard University Press, 2008.

Scobie, Ingrid Winther. *Center Stage: Helen Gahagan Douglas, a Life.* Oxford: Oxford University Press, 1992.

Shinkle, Peter. *Ike's Mystery Man: The Secret Lives of Robert Cutler.* Lebanon: Steerforth Press, 2018.

Simon, James F. *The Antagonists: Hugo Black, Felix Frankfurter, and Civil Liberties in Modern America.* New York: Simon & Schuster, 1989.

Smith, Richard Norton. *The Colonel: The Life and Legend of Robert R. McCormick, 1880–1955.* New York: Houghton Mifflin, 1989.

Snyder, Brad. *Democratic Justice: Felix Frankfurter, the Supreme Court, and the Making of the Liberal Establishment.* New York: W. W. Norton, 2022.

Starobin, Paul. *American Communism in Crisis, 1943–1957.* Berkeley: University of California Press, 1975.

Stern, Seth, and Stephen Wermiel. *Justice Brennan: Liberal Champion*. New York: Houghton Mifflin Harcourt, 2010.

Stone, Geoffrey. Perilous Times: *Free Speech in Wartime, From the Sedition Act of 1798 to the War on Terrorism*. New York: W. W. Norton, 2004.

Stone, I. F. *The Haunted Fifties, 1953–1963*. New York: Little, Brown, 1989.

———. *The Truman Era, 1945–1952*. New York: Little, Brown, 1988.

———. *The War Years: 1939–1945*. New York: Little, Brown, 1988.

Storrs, Landon R. Y. *The Second Red Scare and the Unmaking of the New Deal Left*. Princeton: Princeton University Press, 2013.

Stripling, Robert E. *The Red Plot Against America*. Drexel Hill: Bell Publishing, 1949.

Swerdlow, Amy. *Women Strike for Peace: Traditional Motherhood and Radical Politics in the 1960s*. Chicago: University of Chicago Press, 1993.

Tanenhaus, Sam. *Whittaker Chambers: A Biography*. New York: Random House, 1997.

Taylor, Clarence. *Reds at the Blackboard: Communism, Civil Rights, and the New York City Teachers Union*. New York: Columbia University Press, 2013.

Tenney, Jack. *The Tenney Committee: The American Record*. Tujunga: Standard Publications, 1952.

Theoharis, Athan and John Stuart Cox. *The Boss: J. Edgar Hoover and the Great American Inquisition*. Philadelphia: Temple University Press, 1988.

Thomas, Bob. *The Clown Prince of Hollywood: The Antic Life and Times of Jack L. Warner*. New York: McGraw Hill, 1990.

Thomas, Evan. *The Very Best Men: The Daring Early Years of the C.I.A.* New York: Simon & Schuster, 2006.

Traub, James. *True Believer: Hubert Humphrey's Quest for a More Just America*. New York: Basic Books, 2024.

Trento, Joseph J. *The Secret History of the C.I.A.* New York: Basic Books, 2005.

Trilling, Lionel. *The Middle of the Journey*. New York: Viking, 1947; republished 2002 by The New York Review of Books.

Truman, Harry S. *Memoirs by Harry S. Truman: Years of Trial and Hope: 1946–1952*. New York: Doubleday, 1946.

Trumbo, Dalton (Helen Manfull, ed.). *Additional Dialogue: Letters of Dalton Trumbo, 1942–1962*. New York: M. Evans, 1970.

———. *Harry Bridges: A Discussion of the Latest Effort to Deport Civil Liberties and the Rights of American Labor*. New York: League of American Writers, 1941.

———. *The Time of the Toad: A Study of Inquisition in America*. New York: Harper, 1972.

Tye, Larry. *Demagogue: The Life and Long Shadow of Senator Joe McCarthy*. New York: Houghton Mifflin Harcourt, 2020.

Vickers, Kenneth W. "John Rankin: Democrat and Demagogue." Master's thesis, Mississippi State University, 1993.

Viertel, Salka. *The Kindness of Strangers*. New York: New York Review of Books Classics, 2019.

Von Hoffman, Nicholas. *Citizen Cohn: The Life and Times of Roy Cohn*. New York: Doubleday, 1988.

Warren, Earl. *The Memoirs of Chief Justice Earl Warren*. New York: Doubleday, 1977.

Weinstein, Allen. *Perjury: The Hiss-Chambers Case*. New York: Alfred A. Knopf, 1978.

Weinstein, Allen, and Alexander Vassilev. *The Haunted Wood: Soviet Espionage in America—The Stalin Era*. New York: Random House, 1997.

Welch Jr., Robert H.W. *May God Forgive Us*. Chicago: Henry Regnery, 1952.

Wheatley, Christopher J., ed. *20th-Century American Dramatists*. Detroit: Cengage Gale, 2000.

Whitfield, Stephen J. *The Culture of the Cold War*. Baltimore: Johns Hopkins University Press, 1996.

Wilkerson, W. R., III. *Hollywood Godfather: The Life and Crimes of Billy Wilkerson*. Chicago: Chicago Review Press, 2018.

Wolfskill, Gregory. *The Revolt of the Conservatives: A History of the American Liberty League, 1934–1940*. Boston: Houghton Mifflin, 1962.

Woods, Jeff. R. *Black Struggle Red Scare: Segregation and Anti-Communism in the South, 1948–1968*. Baton Rouge: Louisiana State University, 2003.

Journal and Magazine Articles

Adkins, Joyce. " 'These People Are Frightened to Death': Congressional Investigations and the Lavender Scare." *Prologue*, Vol. 48, No. 2 (Summer 2016). https://www.archives.gov/publications/prologue/2016/summer/lavender.html.

Alsop, Joseph. "The Strange Case of Louis Budenz," *The Atlantic*, April 1952.

Baxter, Randolph W. "Homo-Hunting in the Early Cold War: Senator Kenneth Wherry and the Homophobic Side of McCarthyism." *Nebraska History* (Fall 2003): 118–32.

Blackwell, Jeff. " 'The China Lobby': Influences on U.S.-China Foreign Policy in the Post War Period, 1949–1954." *The Forum: Journal of History*, Vol. 2, No. 1 (2010): 43–58.

Carleton, Don E. "McCarthyism Was More Than McCarthy: Documenting the Red Scare at the State and Local Level." *The Midwestern Archivist*, Vol. 12, No. 1 (1987): 13–19.

Chern, Kenneth. "Politics of American China Policy, 1945: Roots of the Cold War in Asia." *Political Science Quarterly*, Vol. 91, No. 4 (Winter 1976–1977): 631–47.

Cherny, Robert W. "The Making of a Labor Radical: Harry Bridges, 1901–1934." *Pacific Historical Review*, Vol. 64, No. 3 (August 1995): 363–88.

Cohen, Warren. "Who's Afraid of Alfred Kohlberg?" *Reviews in American History*, Vol. 3, No. 1 (March 1975): 118–23.

Dawson, Nelson. "From Fellow Traveler to Anticommunist: The Odyssey of J. B. Matthews." *The Register of the Kentucky Historical Society*, Vol. 84, No. 3 (Summer 1986): 280–306.

Deason, Brian. "Scott Lucas, Everett Dirksen, and the 1950 Senate Election in Illinois." *Journal of the Illinois State Historical Society*, Vol. 95, No. 1 (Spring, 2002): 33–51.

Devinatz, Victor G. "Red Unionism During the Depression and Under McCarthyism: Reflections on Mine-Mill, the Workers Unity League, and the Minneapolis Teamsters." *American Communist History*, Vol. 13, Nos. 2–3 (2014): 189–98.

Durr, Clifford J. "The Loyalty Order's Challenge to the Constitution." *University of Chicago Law Review*, Vol. 16, No. 2 (1948): 298–306.

Erickson, Christine K. " 'I Have Not Had One Fact Disproven': Elizabeth Dilling's Crusade Against Communism in the 1930s." *Journal of American Studies*, Vol. 36, No. 3 (December 2002): 473–89.

Fine, Gary, and Bin Xu. "Honest Brokers: The Politics of Expertise in the 'Who Lost China?' Debate." *Social Problems*, Vol. 58, No. 4 (November 2011): 593–614.

Foster, Stuart J. "Red Alert!: The National Education Association Confronts the 'Red Scare' in American Public Schools, 1947–1954." *Education and Culture*, Vol. 14, No. 2 (Fall 1997): 1–16.

Friedman, Andrea. "The Smearing of Joe McCarthy: The Lavender Scare, Gossip, and Cold War Politics." *American Quarterly*, Vol. 57, No. 4 (December 2005): 1105–29.

Glynn, Robert B. "L'Affaire Rosenberg in France." *Political Science Quarterly*, Vol. 70, No. 4 (December 1955): 498–521.

Goldstein, Robert Justin. "Prelude to McCarthyism: The Making of a Blacklist," *Prologue*, Vol. 38, No. 3 (Fall 2006). https://www.archives.gov/publications/prologue/2006/fall/agloso.html.

Haynes, John Earl, and Harvey Klehr. "J. Robert Oppenheimer: A Spy? No. But a Communist Once? Yes." *Washington Decoded*, Feb. 11, 2012. https://www.washingtondecoded.com/site/2012/02/jro.html, accessed Oct. 10, 224.

Hochschild, Adam. "When America Tried to Deport Its Radicals," *The New Yorker*, November 14, 2019.

Hunt, Jonathan. "Communists and the Classroom: Radicals in U.S. Education, 1930–1960." *Composition Studies*, Vol. 43, No. 2 (Fall 2015): 22–42.

Johns, Michael. "Winning for Losing: A New Look at Harry Bridges and the 'Big Strike' of 1934." *American Communist History*, Vol. 13, No. 1 (2014): 1–24.

Kamisar, Yale. "How Earl Warren's Twenty-Two Years in Law Enforcement Affected His Work as Chief Justice." *Ohio State Journal of Criminal Law*, Vol. 3, No. 11 (2005–2006): 11–32.

Kennan, George (writing as "X"). "The Sources of Soviet Conduct," Foreign Affairs, (July 1947): 566–82.

Lardner, James. "The Dalton Trumbo I Knew," *The New Republic*, February 24, 2016.

Larrowe, C. P. "Did the Old Left Get Due Process? The Case of Harry Bridges." *California Law Review*, Vol. 60, No. 1 (January 1972): 39–83.

Leahy, Stephen M. "Alfred J. Kohlberg and the Chaoshan Embroidered Handkerchief Industry, 1922–1957." *Social Transformations in Chinese Societies*, Vol. 14, No. 2 (2018): 45–59.

Lecklider, Aaron. "Two Witch-hunts: On (Not) Seeing Red in LGBT History." *American Communist History*, Vol. 14, No. 3 (2015): 241–47.

Lichtman, Robert. "J. B. Matthews and the 'Counter-subversives.'" *American Communist History*, Vol. 5, No. 1 (2006): 1–36.

Maltz, Albert. "What Shall We Ask of Writers?," New Masses, February 12, 1946.

Matthews, J.B. "Reds in Our Churches," *The American Mercury*, July 1953.

McAuliffe, Mary S. "Liberals and the Communist Control Act of 1954," *Journal of American History*, Vol. 63, No. 2 (September 1976): 351–67.

Nozette, Mark D. "Constitutional Law-First Amendment-Loyalty Oaths-Vagueness Standard Relaxed for Affirmative Oaths." *Cornell Law Review*, Vol. 58, No. 2 (January 1973): 383–98.

Peterson, Osler L. "Henry Wallace: A Divided Mind," *The Atlantic*, August 1948.

Pittman, Scott. "Lifting the Veil: Public-Private Surveillance Networks." *California History*, Vol. 91, No. 4 (Winter 2014): 43–55.

Pozniakov, Vladimir. "A NKVD/NKGB Report to Stalin: A Glimpse into Soviet Intelligence in the United States in the 1940s." *Cold War International History Project Bulletin*, Vol. 10 (March 1998): 220–22.

Robbins, Louise. "Fighting McCarthyism Through Film: A Library Censorship Case Becomes a 'Storm Center.'" *Journal of Education for Library and Information Science*, Vol. 39, No. 4 (Fall 1998): 291–311.

Rovere, Richard. "Communists in a Free Society," *Partisan Review*, Vol. 19, No. 3 (1952): 339–46.

Smith, Carol. "The Dress Rehearsal for McCarthyism." *Academe*, July–August 2011. https://www.aaup.org/article/dress-rehearsal-mccarthyism.

Storrs, Landon R.Y. "Attacking the Washington 'Femmocracy': Antifeminism in the Cold War Campaign against Communists in Government." *Feminist Studies*, Vol. 33, No. 1 (2007): 118–52.

Theoharis, Athan. "The FBI and the American Legion Contact Program, 1940–1966." *Political Science Quarterly*, Vol. 100, No. 2 (Summer 1985): 271–86.

INDEX

ABOUT THE AUTHOR

Clay Risen is a reporter at *The New York Times*, a member of the Society of American Historians, and a fellow at the Perry World House at the University of Pennsylvania. He is the author of several previous books on American history, including *The Crowded Hour: Theodore Roosevelt, the Rough Riders, and the Dawn of the American Century*, a *New York Times* Notable Book of 2019; *The Bill of the Century: The Epic Battle for the Civil Rights Act*; and *A Nation on Fire: America in the Wake of the King Assassination*. He lives in Brooklyn.